HOW ART CAN BE **THOUGHT**

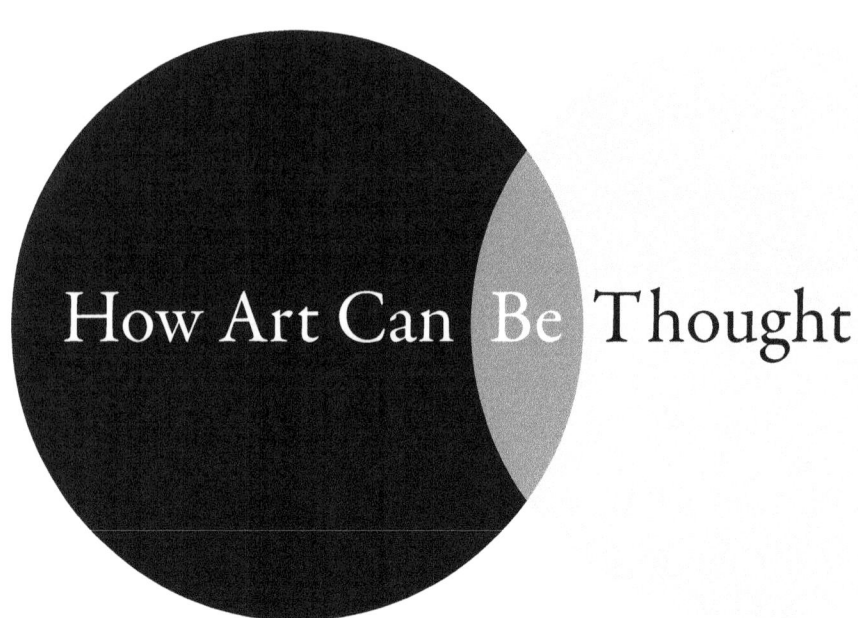

How Art Can Be Thought

A HANDBOOK FOR CHANGE

Allan deSouza

DUKE UNIVERSITY PRESS · DURHAM AND LONDON · 2018

Designed by Heather Hensley
Typeset in Garamond Premiere Pro by Westchester Publishing Services

Library of Congress Cataloging-in-Publication Data
Names: DeSouza, Allan, [date] author.
Title: How art can be thought : a handbook for change / Allan deSouza.
Description: Durham : Duke University Press, 2018. | Includes
    bibliographical references and index.
Identifiers: LCCN 2018008220 (print) | LCCN 2018009565 (ebook)
ISBN 9781478002185 (ebook)
ISBN 9781478000365 (hardcover)
ISBN 9781478000471 (pbk.)
Subjects: LCSH: Art. | Art—Study and teaching. | Art—Terminology. |
    Art appreciation.
Classification: LCC N7425 (ebook) | LCC N7425.D459 2018 (print) |
    DDC 701/.18—dc23
LC record available at https://lccn.loc.gov/2018008220

Cover art: Allan deSouza, *Polar Sky (fghtbtwntgrndbffl)*, from the
Redactions series, 2011. Digital painting, 60 × 40 in. Courtesy of the artist
and Talwar Gallery, New York and New Delhi.

Contents

Image Notes

With the exception of works by Daniel Joseph Martinez and Susan Silton (both of whom have been colleagues of mine at different schools), and Aaron Hughes, the images in this book are the works of my former students. I hope the reader perceives this not as nepotism but as a deliberate choice closely entwined with the book's arguments on pedagogy, historiography, and the development of artistic ideas and practices. The artworks I discuss in the book are mostly well-known, even canonical, modernist works by the likes of Henri Matisse and Pablo Picasso. My intention is to propose continuities and interruptions between these works that are discussed and the works that are depicted, and regardless of the intentions of the former students. In the case of Shari Paladino and Paige Davis, selected because of the general trajectory of their work, I asked them if they would "respond" to the works by Marcel Duchamp and Édouard Manet, respectively. Davis made a "blind" contour drawing from Manet's painting *A Bar at the Folies-Bergère* (1882), and describes it as "a drawing done by looking only at/into the woman's eyes, using my peripheral vision to fill in the rest of the image." Readers can tease out relations between her method and the various discussions in the text around the gaze and visuality, and employ similar modes of interplay with the other images.

The selection of other former students' works was made directly by me. Their inclusion is not to single them out as that of the "best" students but because of the coincidence of their works to the artists I have discussed.

However, I have to admit how proud I am—though I take no credit—that as artists in the early stages of their careers, they are each deeply engaged in the development of their work and in how it will function in the world.

Last, though first encountered, the cover image is from one of my own works, connecting my writing (and pedagogy) with what might be considered a more conventional studio practice. In this case, the image is from my *Redactions* series, in which paintings by Paul Gauguin and here, Henri Rousseau, are "redacted" by overlaying a single color, chosen from the horizon in the original painting, onto the rest of the painting surface. The *Redactions* have been written about elsewhere, so I will mention here only that their process overlaps with the investigations and intentions in this book, of decolonizing Euro American modernism by restaging or perhaps translating its aesthetic and affective possibilities.

·●

Acknowledgments

To my students, teachers, and editors, future, present, and past.

Like any writing, and despite the many hours spent alone, this book has been a collective endeavor. I would not have been able to work on or complete it without the support of my family, my partner Zeina Barakeh, and numerous friends, fellow artists, and academic colleagues. The many faculty, staff, and students at different schools have been instrumental in the book's conception and material. Particular thanks to the students, faculty, and staff at the Vermont College of Fine Arts, Low Residency MFA program, the Performance department at the Art Institute of Chicago, the Photography department at Bard College MFA Program, and to the New Genres department at the San Francisco Art Institute—the MFA students in my Critique Seminars were the first to receive the "*Lexicon of Contested Terms*," which morphed into the present chapter 5. Thank you to my Art Practice colleagues at UC Berkeley for helping me be a better Chair even while I was working on this book, and to my graduate students who have been test subjects, as readers and critters. A number of these, alumni of both SFAI and UC Berkeley have contributed the majority of images in the book.

The book began to take shape following two jointly written essays, one with Allyson Purpura, published as "Undsciplined Knowledge" in *African Art, Interviews, Narratives: Bodies of Knowledge at Work,* edited by Joanna Grabski and Carol Magee, the other with Jeannene Pryzblyski, published as "ArtSchooling" in *Shifter*, no. 20, 2013, edited by Rit Premnath and Matthew Metzger. Part of the entry, [#Time] in chapter 5, was published as "What It Is, Now," in the issue of *Representations* journal, *Time Zones: Durational Art and Its Contexts*, edited by Julia Bryan-Wilson and Shannon Jackson, Vol. 136, No. 1, Fall 2016.

Thank you to the readers of different sections of the manuscript, including Karen Fiss, Jackie Francis, and Allyson Purpura. My studio assistants, Shari Paladino and Alexandra Nicole Solis-Sison, contributed invaluable help.

I want to thank the UC Berkeley Townsend Center for funding a faculty manuscript review workshop. Workshop participants, and cherished friends, to whom I am deeply grateful for their close readings and many questions, were Michelle Dizon, Sonia Katyal, Leigh Raiford, Jeffrey Skoller, and Anne Walsh.

A big thank you to Deepak Talwar, my gallerist, who has been my enabler in the best sense possible.

And finally, my two anonymous readers, the production team and my editors at Duke, Ken Wissoker (who seems to have worked on a substantial number of books in my library), Elizabeth Ault, and Sara Leone for their encouragement, diligence, and guidance.

My heartfelt thanks to each of you.

Thought in reality spaces itself out into the world. It informs the imaginary of peoples, their varied poetics, which it then transforms, meaning, in them its risk becomes realized.

———————————

ÉDOUARD GLISSANT, *Poetics of Relation*, 1

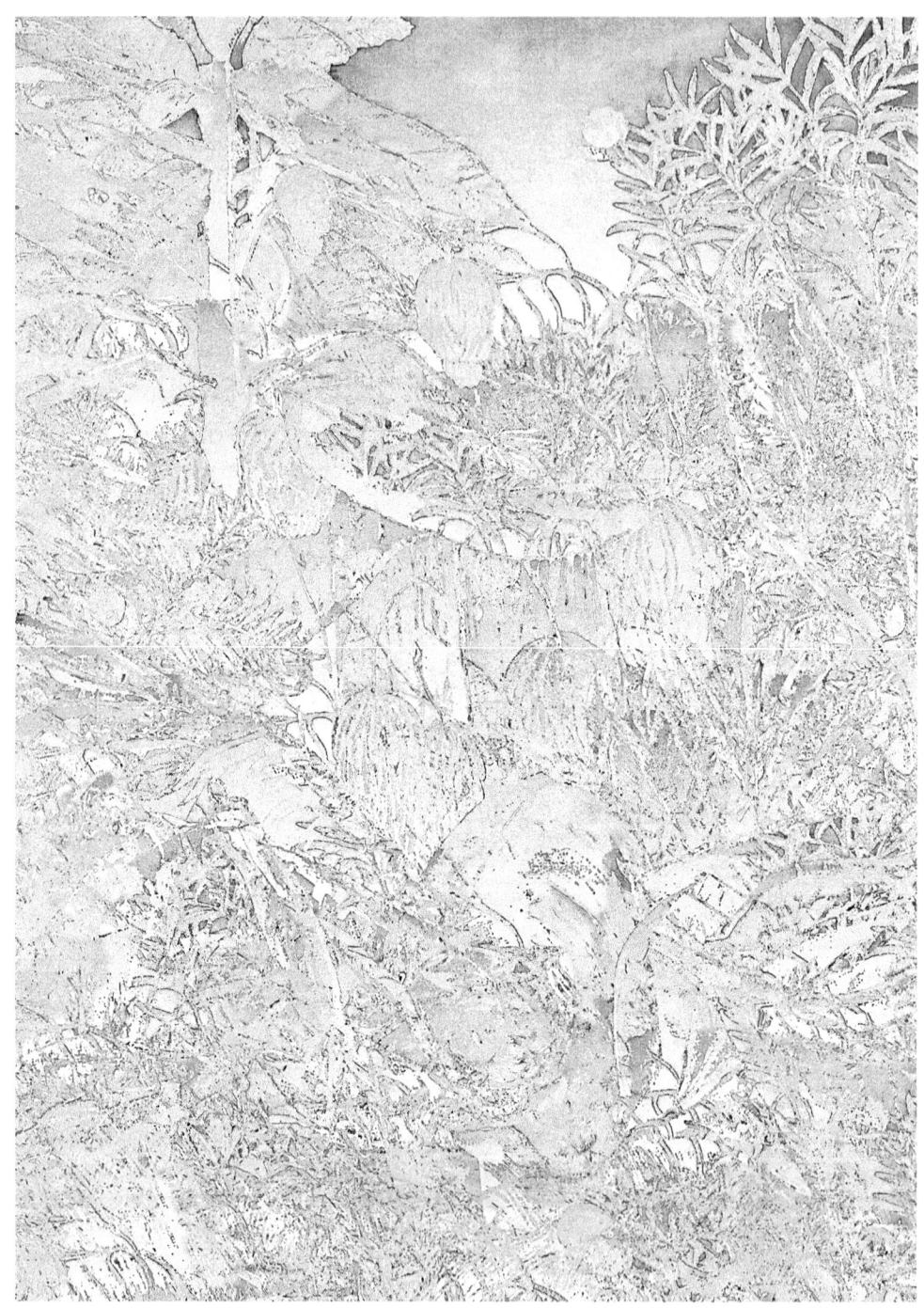

Fig. Frontis.1 • Allan deSouza, *Polar Sky (fghtbtwntgrndbffl)*, from the *Redactions* series, 2011. Digital painting, 60 × 40 in. Courtesy of the artist and Talwar Gallery, New York and New Delhi.

Although I have offered a childhood story to begin
this preface, it is a fable irreducible to fact.

JUDITH BUTLER, *GENDER TROUBLE*

A FOOT IN THE DOOR

VeXing

I began writing a straightforward biography of where I had studied and had taught, thinking it would help students to know about my personal experience of becoming an artist. My ambivalence was that, as an artist (of color), I am often required to authenticate myself, with my work too often read primarily or only in terms of autobiography, as though I can only speak from within some anthropological containment field. Rather than a personal biography, then, I hope to mark pathways through the maze of contradictory and often routinely discriminatory practices within art institutions.[1] I'm not offering myself as a victim, nor do I warrant commendation for endurance. My intention is to situate my experience in broader historical and institutional frameworks.

I have taught at numerous schools, but my full-time, long-term teaching has been primarily at the San Francisco Art Institute, a small private art school, and at UC Berkeley, a large public university. I have taught painting, photography, performance, writing, "new genres," theory, and critical studies. I have assumed administrative positions (I use this phrasing to suggest self-punishment) of chair and director of different programs. It's fair to say that as a student, educator, and administrator, I have covered a fair amount of experiential, geographic, temporal, disciplinary, and conceptual ground. Let me trace some of these routes.

A possible beginning moment might have been in 1976, in high school in London, when I announced to my art teacher that I had been accepted into the Foundation Art course at Goldsmiths College. I remember his disbelief, and his demand to see the proof. It was something that neither of us could have put into words at the time, but I understood even then that there was no trajectory for someone like me to be an artist. "Someone like me," meaning an "East African Asian"—to use the nomenclature of the time—one of the first generation to be primarily educated in an England that had yet to come to terms with immigration from its former colonies. People like me did not become artists.

After the foundation year, I applied three years running to bachelor of fine arts programs.[2] Applicants were required to send a physical portfolio of work to their first choice of three schools. If the school was interested in the work, they called you in for an interview. If not, you were passed on to the next-choice school, and so on, until you ended up in a pool of applicants waiting for any remaining places. For three years, I was interviewed at every school I had listed. Each time I walked in the door, I registered the surprise on the faces of the interviewing faculty. There was nothing in my name and, in the cases of telephone preinterviews, nothing in my accent to let them know that I was not white.[3] Each time, at the end of consistently awkward interviews, I would be told that they liked my work, but that they "didn't think I would fit in to their school." The decision, I knew, had been made the moment I walked in the door.

After twelve interviews, and in my fourth year of applying, I was accepted to Bath Academy of Art in the painting department, possibly because a number of their faculty—including the just-retired Howard Hodgkin—were Indophile painters. However, when I arrived for my first semester, I felt they were disappointed that I wasn't Indian *enough*, and unlike some of the faculty who made regular trips to India, I had never been there. Despite encouragement about the "wonderful opportunity," I also declined to be Hodgkin's gardener. It wasn't the last time I'd be told how ungrateful I was.

Not being Indian enough was probably getting under my skin, so to speak, and so, during my first year, I went to India. With the brashness of youth, I simply showed up at art schools, looking for artists. With unbounded generosity, I was welcomed and introduced to artists and critics such as Vivan Sundaram and Geeta Kapur in Delhi, Nalini Malani in Bombay (now Mumbai), Bhupen Khakhar, Ghulam Mohammed Sheikh, and Nasreen Mohamedi, and then students Rekha Rodwittiya and Ajay Desai in Baroda. These artists were establishing international careers, prompted in no small part by the incisive writings of Geeta Kapur.

After my BFA, and back in London, the idea of a career for an "Indian-ish" artist, with now Indianish work, seemed too distant. I was repeatedly told that I was too tainted by the West. This was an obvious catch-22, an effective lockout. Whenever I would walk through any door, I was too westernized, but not Western enough—"white, but not quite," in Homi Bhabha's inimitable phrase—or I would be required to perform an orientalist Indianness. If I were an actor, I would have gotten auditions only for roles with bad accents.

While at Bath, I *had* become involved with theater, and together with a number of peers had formed a theater group. We had petitioned the school to have our performance work reviewed as part of our degree but were refused on the grounds that it wasn't "art." I had also studied the dancelike form of expressive mime, and was influenced, or perhaps smitten, by having seen years earlier a live performance of *Flowers* by the Lindsay Kemp company. Now back in London, I wanted a similarly immediate interaction between performer and audience. I also wanted something more collaborative, and more directly political, than the isolated studio that art school had tried to prepare me for.

I was squatting in South London at the time, part of an organized response to homelessness and the government policies that excluded the young from already limited stocks of affordable housing. The network of squatters formed my primary collaborators and audience. Our collective artistic outlets were at weekly meetings, producing newsletters, stickers, and posters for different campaigns and political organizations. I was also part of a street theater group that produced events during demonstrations and pickets, such as the Campaign for Nuclear Disarmament, or Stop the City mass demonstrations that prefigured the Occupy movement. Larger buildings were mass squatted and turned into public "peace centers" that included living spaces; cafés; and music, performance and art spaces, and provided legal and squatting advice. The centers tended to be short lived, since they attracted the immediate attention of the police and fascist gangs, and needed constant defending, often physically.[4] My first exhibitions were in such spaces, although I considered myself a "cultural agent" intimately connected to my living surroundings, rather than an "artist," which is what I then thought of as someone aloof from the rigors of everyday life.

Financially buoyed by the "dole," as were all art workers that I knew, I also had a succession of part-time jobs, from messengering to kitchen worker to road sweeper. These were invariably short-term, and mind-numbingly repetitive.

I alleviated the boredom with "art interventions," thinking to stimulate my mostly bemused fellow workers.[5] As a messenger, for example, I added my own mail for office workers, with instructions to make drawings and leave them in the outgoing mail for pick up. I installed guerilla exhibitions of these in office elevators. The drawings tended to be revealingly depressing, of coffins, withering cacti, locked cubicles, and the like. By the end of the day, if any drawings remained in the elevators, they would invariably be covered with racist, misogynist scrawls and anticommunist rants, as though any interruption of normal routine could only have been conducted by infiltrating communists.

During those years, it was almost normal to be constantly confronted by racism, from the "polite" remarks of how well one spoke English to the violence of street confrontations. I was drawn to the artistic and/or political organizations set up in response, and which strove to represent "British Asian" experiences. I joined theater companies: Tara Arts, and Hounslow Arts Collective (HAC), and its offshoot, the Hounslow Asian Visual Artists Collective (HAVAC), a group of South Asian artists in west London. Hardial Rai, the theater director of HAC, remembers that such groups grew out of a DIY punk ethic that prioritized political commitment over formal training.[6] In a HAVAC group art exhibition, one of my artworks about immigration and police brutality, and depicting a Union Jack flag, was removed, as its "political nature might cause offense to the *indigenous* community" (emphasis added).[7] This was another instance of being made to feel like an interloper who should have been grateful for any opportunities but was instead biting the feeding hand.

During this time, I also joined a socialist, anarchist-leaning (though *not* communist) artist collective called Community Copyart. In the years before Kinko's, Copyart provided cheap and creative photocopying for a broad clientele, including community and youth groups, individual artists, and activist organizations. The collective had begun providing mobile workshops with a single photocopier and a van. It eventually squatted in a large building in London's Kings Cross, equipped with a number of different photocopiers. This new space was the site for ongoing exhibitions, sometimes in partnership with other groups, for example hosting the Festival of Plagiarism.[8]

After three years with Copyart, I cofounded Panchayat, an arts and education database and training facility whose emphasis was to provide documentation on "Third World, First Nation" artists.[9] This was partly in response to the then common refrain from grade school teachers that they couldn't teach a multicultural curriculum because they didn't have the materials or training. Panchayat ran teacher-training workshops in conjunction with local councils and teacher centers, and trained artists to work in schools.

I was hired as an artist-in-residence at various schools around the country. The most challenging was in 1986 at an East London all-boys high school. The students were split into two rival factions of Bangladeshi and white youth, with some of the latter being self-described fascist skinheads. All the students were working class, but the two groups were disenfranchised in different ways. The skinheads used preexisting, conveniently redirected racist discourses of immigration, employment, and eugenics to blame their disenfranchisement on the Bangladeshi students. They had been conducting a regime of attacks against the local Bangladeshi population, attacks violent enough to make national news. The older Bangladeshi students formed self-defense groups to protect younger students, but as the attacks diminished, the Bangladeshi students, unwilling to give up their newfound street presence, were themselves beginning to reformulate into gangs. Although I was hired as an artist, it was quite clear that I (as a brown-skinned role model) was expected to differently empower the Bangladeshi students and to help diffuse the situation by also working with the white youths (by somehow transcending my brown skin). Critique methods, inadequately used by me at that time, would have been useful to address the overtly racist imagery being produced by some of the white students in the same art classes as the Bangladeshi students it was directed against (with teachers either ignoring or condoning the imagery as "self-expression" and as "English culture"). Teachers in other departments were campaigning against racist attacks, but there were no procedures or language in place in the art department for examining the (displaced) anxieties of white, working-class students, nor any artistic means to undo the intimidation and physical violence experienced by the Bangladeshi students and to redirect *their* anger and fear.

This experience educated me profoundly in the broader workings of British racial politics. I might have always been dealing with race, but not in such a protective role on behalf of others, nor in such volatile circumstances. Throughout my own formal education in England, I was invariably the only person of color in a classroom, in a department, or at a school. During my four years as an art student, I had not had a single faculty of color, and there had been one black student, one semester.[10] At Goldsmiths, I had compensated by socializing with the large international student body in other departments. While at Bath, I had become aware of students "like" me in other schools, and had begun to read about and attend their exhibitions on trips to London. Many of these, such as Keith Piper, Chila Burman, Said Adrus, Eddie Chambers, and Marlene Smith, would later become my professional peers. After graduating, the squatters and punks I was living and working with were again mostly white. My diasporic experience, and the very labeling of being "East African Asian," meant that I had grown up with a fractured sense of location and the necessity of performing multiple positions. I inhabited many worlds: queer, trans, and straight; black, South Asian, and white; and all kinds of assimilating, oppositional, alternative, and "marginalized" groups.[11] This was "normal." Less understandable to me was how others remained within their one group, or identified as only one subject position.

My first gallery participation in what became known as the Black Arts Movement (BAM), was through an invitation by Lubaina Himid to exhibit at her new gallery space, The Elbow Room. Indebted to the groundwork of an older generation of artists, such as David Medalla, as well as the pivotal Rasheed Araeen, the founder of the journals *Black Phoenix* and *Third Text*, BAM developed from the first generation of the "colonized within," who saw Britain as their rightful base, even if they hadn't experienced it in any way as homely. This was the first generation of students to enter British art schools, students who were either born (like myself) in the former colonies in Africa, the Caribbean, and South Asia, and primarily raised in England, or the first generation born in England to immigrant parents from those former colonies. Having grown up within a virulent period of British racism and the beginnings of Thatcherism, they, we, were aligned with activism around immigration and antideportation, racial equality, housing, workers' rights, and the cultural movements around carnival, reggae, punk, and bhangra. BAM was modeled as an anticolonial cultural movement, extending those activisms to deterritorialize the otherwise exclusive and segregated art institutions. This extensive network, including the likes of Stuart Hall, Sonia Boyce, Zarina Bhimji, Isaac Julien, Yinke Shonibare, Mona Hatoum, and Kobena Mercer—to name only a few of the more well known—is what enabled me to rethink the term "artist" and feel that this designation had a role to play in the world. It also felt like a world-making responsibility.

The Elbow Room exhibition received a lot of press coverage, what artists think of as their "break." It did lead to other exhibitions, but for the most part, these were initiated and curated by other artists of color. Institutions might organize a large group show, but then feel that they had fulfilled their "ethnic" quota for the decade, leaving their other programing intact. Very few artists of color had solo exhibitions in galleries that were not run by their peers.[12]

In 1989, I participated in the 3rd Havana Biennial, as part of a small delegation of "Black British" artists.[13] Along with Carlos Villa, from San Francisco, we were the first artists based in the global north to be included. This had been my first professional visit outside Britain, and it opened my eyes to an internationalism beyond England's island mentality, and outside my supposed ethnic connection to Indian contemporary art.

In 1991, I was included in the exhibition *Interrogating Identities*, curated by Kellie Jones and Thomas Sokolowski, opening at the Grey Art Gallery in New York, and traveling to numerous other venues around the United States. The exhibition examined the term black, as it was differently applied in the United Kingdom, the United States, and Canada. America's specific history of slavery overwhelmed the then British use of Black to signify a political coalition along anticolonial lines rather than as a description of race or skin color.

In the United States, it made no sense for me to claim the term black, or it was understood only as that I was mixed-race. However, when I said that I was Indian, I was once asked, in all seriousness, "What tribe?"

After moving to New York in 1992, I became involved with Asian American art, and in particular with the artists' network Godzilla.[14] Godzilla's focus, and the coalitional possibility that attracted me, was the space *between* Asia and America as a space of multiplicity, connection, and possibility rather than how the "hyphenated identities" are framed as sites of isolation, segregation, and limitation. An instance of this "multiplicity, connection, and possibility" as artistic practice was a video I made with Yong Soon Min, my then partner, for Shu Lea Chang's multiartist, multichannel video installation *Those Fluttering Objects of Desire* for the infamous Whitney Biennial in 1993.

I mention these groups and movements in passing—and with numerous gaps and omissions—though they each require their own histories, alongside the histories of their constituent individuals—all of whom are necessary to any broader grasp of art histories.[15] I would also point to them as precursors for what would later become known as "social practice."

In New York, I attended the critical studies component of the Whitney Independent Studies Program, while enrolled in the Bronx Museum's Artist in the Marketplace program. I taught art workshops at the Bronx, as well as in the AIDS center and at the secure prisoners' unit at Saint Vincent's Midtown Hospital. I also taught a contemporary art seminar at the College of New Rochelle, my first college-level teaching job in the United States.[16] In England, I had been a visiting or guest lecturer at numerous colleges and art schools but had never held a regular position.

The Whitney was my first structured introduction to theory. Like many art students, I was initially resistant. In my case, I imagined my street knowledge to have qualified me as better informed. However, theory and the rigorous seminars provided me with language tools to better examine, think through, and bring together the "different worlds" that had made up my life. The broad range of visiting faculty also made it seem like we were engaged *with* the world, rather than isolated from it. Theory for me became a means for inquiry. It also provided me with ammunition against those who wielded it as authority.

After the Whitney, I moved to Los Angeles, and nineteen years after entering Goldsmiths, I began an MFA in photography at UCLA. It was difficult being a student again, given my experience and what by now could be termed a "career." However, I wanted to teach, and needed an MFA. While I was highly attracted to a university environment, and the opportunity to take classes in other disciplines, the UCLA art department had gained a reputation of laying a glittering pathway to commercial galleries for its students. Once again I entered a school with no faculty of color, and with a largely market-driven focus on what it meant to be an artist—though the prevailing rhetoric was of individual, "posteverything" freedoms. In my first year, the only female faculty were married to male faculty (this had also been the case at Bath Academy of Art). This is not to question the female faculty's capabilities but to criticize the department's limited hiring practices. At the end of my first year, when the school hired Mary Kelly as incoming chair, the mood was that it marked the end of the department's heyday. For some, it was the end of the party.[17] With continuing new hires, the department continues to remain highly ranked, and has lost its previous "bad (white) boys' club" mentality.

I was never an exemplary student, and seemed to consistently generate low or no expectations from faculty. At worst, faculty's sweeping pronouncements about art and society were rarely sweeping enough to encompass my experience. Not only did it make *them* seem limited, it placed me outside of their knowledge, as though there was no place and no language for my own. Even as I was molded through these institutions and their behaviors, I reacted against much of what they thought they were imparting to me. However, I am entirely in their debt, and in the case of the US institutions, I mean this literally.

My teaching experiences have been mostly rewarding, and occasionally inspiring, but have also included the idiotic, the antagonistic, and the shameful (and shaming). I have personally encountered numerous incidents of ignorant and overt discrimination by which students and faculty are ostracized. While these can sometimes be addressed as they occur, there are also more insidious, pervasive, difficult-to-identify patterns of discouragement and exclusion whose *deliberate* and *practiced* invisibility is what allows them to continue (while it is connected, I am not referring to the chronic sexual harassment and violence on campuses that is only now being exposed). I knew that if I were to teach, I would want to work against institutional, procedural, and curricular limitations. Those were the more important questions, yet the everyday, casual dismissals that I had faced or saw around me are the ones that remain most immediately in memory: being told that I was in the West now, I didn't need to make work that looked Indian (though white students around me were incorporating Hindu gods and henna into their work); after "getting emotional" because of something offensive that was said to me, being told by my faculty advisor that I should be in a "secure" institution, not an art institution; female students being "encouraged" that getting naked would lead to artistic liberation; overhearing faculty discussing how it was hardly worth teaching female students since, upon leaving school, they were more likely to make babies than art; a black student being told that no one wants to see paintings of black people; an Iranian student being told that her country was bigoted and repressive and that the faculty member didn't see any reason why he should look at her work; faculty ridiculing transgender students behind their backs; a review committee telling a student that they're not interested in work about motherhood (I would now advise that student to respond that, psychoanalytically, *all* artwork is about motherhood; what makes her work necessary to an *adult* conversation is that it's from the experience and perspective *of* a mother); students being told that work about identity is so "over"; students of color having their work talked about only in terms of and being dismissed as restricted to their identity even when *they* never use the term and describe their work only in formal terms. There were also (only slightly) more coded dismissals of work being "too pretty," "not muscular enough," "too Third World," "not universal," "for the wrong audience," or "not having an audience." I've had a student snap, "I don't know where you're from, but that's not how we do things in *this* country." A white faculty member welcomed me to a new school, saying that we are the same because she has a Native American grandmother, with the insinuation that this ancestral legacy made her, and hence the department, *already* "diverse." In faculty meetings, a faculty member made cracks about Africans and coconuts, and after waiting for white faculty to respond, I eventually stopped the proceedings to be told that "it's only jokes" and that "not everything's racist." Basically, I'm told to "lighten up." The still ongoing, six years later, trolling emails and Facebook posts from that former disgruntled, *entrumpled*, colleague after I was a witness at arbitration proceedings about his supposed jokes. The time when a senior faculty of another school said he would "blacklist" me from ever teaching in Southern California because I asked why I was the only writer of color in a book he was editing on contemporary art and black humor, and if I could include his racist emails to me in my essay (I was "withdrawn" from the publication, and told that it was now *my* fault that there were no writers of color included). The constant presumptions that I am a student, since I don't (nor do I "imagine ever wanting to") fit the template of an art professor, let alone of a chair or director—a presumption faced particularly by female faculty of color.

These individual encounters reflect the ignorance and prejudices of the aggressors but, more importantly, they act in concert to bring unruly subjects to heel. To make them conform, or to isolate, ostracize, and silence them. Their *intent* is to cause female faculty and faculty of color to fail, then drive them out, thus reinforcing the intimidators' own "success." A demographically homogenous faculty group can easily function under the delusion that they have attained their positions because they are the best ones *for* and *in* those positions, rather than considering that they have attained those positions because others have been systemically eliminated *before* they could be contenders. When better to start? As early as possible, when they are still students.

Whoever criticizes these behaviors risks ostracism and loss of opportunities, not only from the institution—with its disciplinary consequences of failure to be rehired, denial of tenure, and so on—but also social ostracism by colleagues for not being "able to take a joke," for being "noncollegial" and disruptive. The shrill woman, the dragon lady, the newly minted nasty woman, the uppity person of color, the angry black man, the troublemaker, the chip-on-the-shoulder, the narcissist, the egotist, the nut job, the whiner, the victim, and the holier-than-thou are stereotypes commonly deployed against those who dissent.

The self-perpetuating cultures of discrimination, the sad but vicious behaviors of those holding on to meager power, are often normalized to the extent that there is no language to address them. They retreat to an imagined past of when art schools were "great" (with only white art students and white male faculty, and white European art history). Their demands for assimilation ("*lighten up*") over other models of coexistence amount to playground bullying conducted on institutional, systemic levels.

There might be little or nothing within the curricula or other forms of speech that offer any counter or that inform and empower students (and faculty) to speak back against the provincialism that determines what success would be and who would achieve it. While these attitudes and circumstances are unfortunately not as rare as one might hope, my interest is to examine their effect on what and how art histories are discussed, what (low) expectations are placed upon artworks and students, and what terms are used to discuss and reinforce them. This provincialism and its operative methodologies necessarily (should) become subject to historical, aesthetic, political, and conceptual inquiry within art pedagogy.

Despite the repertoire of exclusion described above, I have also found enormous support, and any success or longevity (or endurance) I have gained as an artist or as an educator is wholly attributable to these many peers and colleagues. While my critique is of the various forms of white suprematism (I am deliberately conflating terms to suggest a racialized art movement), many of my closest allies (and best friends!) are white.

Needless to say, my pedagogy is focused against discriminatory practices. Speaking back not just to those experiences so as not to give them more substance than they deserve, but also speaking back to their enabling cultures remains central for me—whether as a teacher, administrator, or artist. This then leads to other questions of the most effective means, forms, and language—including this book—through which to speak back. And to speak forward, as it were.

•

Questions of who succeeds, on whose terms, and what constitutes success form the macro and daily politics of academia, and also of art. These mirror artistic questions about art's function in and with the world (I am using Paulo Freire's phrasing of "in" and "with" to emphasize being as relational).[18] What does art do? Should art respond to the present? Is art's purpose—as one is often taught in art schools—to take the longer view; to not be swayed by ever-changing current circumstances, petty politics, and crises; to not be caught in the short term of only ever reacting? Should art have a conscience, or is it meant to be above that? When does being "above" conscience mean avoiding one? Perhaps we now expect art *to* respond, and various forms of social practice and "artivism" do just that, prioritizing the response above other criteria.

At various schools where I teach and visit, these are not isolated questions: students are frustrated with the lack of political engagement; they demand increased diversity of faculty and presumably of opinion. They want their work to mean something in/with the world. Balancing this, they are painfully aware of the long-term financial burden of art education, and want reassurance that they've made the right decision to pursue art.

There are no reassurances, and art does not supply easy answers, ways forward, or a viable career—paid or otherwise. Nor does education. Both can be fully coopted to become means of containment and pacification, while supplying promise, entertainment, and escape. And yet I pursue both art and teaching, believing that they play crucial roles in how we are and act in/with the world.

ForeWords

If it were possible to produce a full account of how art is taught it might be *a boring, irrelevant, pernicious document, something that should be locked away.*
—James Elkins, *Why Art Cannot Be Taught*

The fictive narratives and accepted truths of the languages through which art is discussed, defined, controlled, circulated, and valued; the different desires of artists; and the ways in which art is learned and taught—what constitutes "art speech" and the discursive mechanisms of the "art world"—are this book's broader playing field. Within that, my primal scene of scrutiny is the preparatory training that artists undergo in the art school critique.

The book, aspiring to be pernicious, is divided into seven main sections. This introduction, "A Foot in the Door," lays out some broad pedagogical groundwork, including the role of the pedagogue within decolonizing processes. In the first section, "How *Art* Can Be Thought," the primary questions I pursue, as per the book title, are how we think and speak about art, and what the material, aesthetic, and political consequences might be. The second section, "Entry Points," returns to fundamental questions of art and pedagogy, particularly around quality, equality, and diversity. The third and fourth sections, "How Art Can Be Taught" and "Critique as Radical Prototype," focus on how these questions are put into practice within the art school, particularly in MFA programs, and their primary pedagogical form of the critique.

A clear model for the fifth section, "How Art Can Be Spoken: A Glossary of Contested Terms," is Raymond Williams's *Keywords: A Vocabulary of Culture and Society*.[19] Williams's methodology, as elucidated in his introduction, is what I aspire to. This is not to claim any parallel insight or equivalent research on my part but to acknowledge Williams's influence on the field of critical studies and its intersections with art practices.

In the last section, "Afterwords: *How, Now*, Rothko?" I return to some of the book's arguments through looking at Mark Rothko's paintings. I reconsider learned viewing habits and propose ways to move forward, as artist, educator, and art viewer.

Throughout the book, I will persist with questions of decolonization, of why it arises as a necessary project within art and pedagogy, how it can be pursued, and what outcomes might be expected. A major aspect of this project is that thinking and speaking about art are proposed as active processes that lay the discursive foundations from which art is generated.

Like an exhibition, a book does not mark the end of a project but its entry into public dialogue. The impetus is always to what comes next. In this, I draw support from the current resurgence of discourses and activism that seek to dismantle discriminatory practices, particularly around race, sex, and trans/gender. While education and pedagogy are certainly implicated, art may be seen to be less so in its material effects and consequences on *which* lives and *how* lives matter. For educators, the lives of each student have to matter equally, but to arrive at that equality requires institutional and societal overhaul—with policies of inclusion as only a first step. To maintain, in the present moment, that all lives matter equally, ignores the sometimes blatant effects of how policies and policing treat different people differently. Pedagogy can be utopian in its ambition but is a necessary *practice* toward the possibility that all lives might matter equally (notice to what extent this claim is qualified).

While my interest here is to develop decolonizing languages *within* what might otherwise be the colonizing language of art industries, this can lead me toward the polemical. I am conflicted about this, partly because I feel called upon to write for a fictional general reader, and partly because I feel that I am not being polemical enough to address the high stakes of what roles culture can play in what feels like a time of constant crisis.

In contrast to my wish to be polemical as response to the present is an equal pull as an educator to stand back and to measure my words. I am constantly called upon to engage only on artistic terms. Is my teaching role to remain above both conscience and the fray? To keep my political (what detractors might call my "race-based") views to myself, and address only the artistic issues of students' work—if such separations can indeed be made?[20] These are delicate plays, and extend to how one engages with artwork, allowing for its affect without rushing to judgment. This is tactical, patient, and deferring, rather than neutral. A central role of pedagogy is to expand students' critical facilities, whereas to be neutral is to align with keeping things as they are, as a holding operation *against* student development. This book is intended as a handbook for change, which means that there will be no neutral reader.

My apologies, then, for being too polemical and for not being polemical enough.

Pedagogy and Embodied Subjects

Pedagogy, broadly speaking, is the theory and practice of education. In ancient Greece, a pedagogue was not a teacher but a slave who accompanied children to school—where a teacher would take over. The teacher would provide a more formal education (didactics), whereas the pedagogue would assist in social education and the general welfare of the child. In both cases, the meaning of pedagogy remains—to lead a child—though the pedagogue's role of accompanying and "being with" is more nuanced, not least because of the pedagogue's ambiguous status of being entrusted while being enslaved. Pedagogues are compelled to assist in producing the next generation of masters, which is to assist in perpetuating their own subjugation. What do they teach the young masters? To be more human, and therefore to elevate the humanity of others? To challenge the hierarchy that empowers them to subjugate others?

Closer to the present, in the American South, and in South Africa, generations of white boys have been raised and taught by black women (other countries and cultures practice similar class- and caste-based servitude). These boys might have "loved" the individual black women who were forced to abandon their own children to raise them. They might have had their first sexual desires for these women. But as a political, privileged class, they grew up—too easily— to overlook the humanity of these women, and continued—too easily—to treat them as less than human.

The pedagogue's only hope was to humanize those in their care. Their own lives were too perilous to act otherwise. And yet, theirs is a profound generosity and forgiveness, refraining from enacting revenge upon the child for the actions of their parents, their class, their privilege, their wielded power, their violence, and their political system. Or perhaps, generosity, forgiveness, and humanity were the only viable, enduring revenge. In the overthrow of South African apartheid, one can witness this profound generosity in the Truth and Reconciliation Commission (TRC) of 1994—however one may see it as weighted toward the perpetrators and a political mistake for not bringing those responsible to account.[21]

In present-day art schools, teachers may feel their roles are wrenched between leading, accompanying, and serving, and buffeted by national curricula, constrained academic freedoms, administrative expectations/exploitations, and student demands. The status and economic viability of teachers has been continually plummeting as they are made into scapegoats for high costs and lowered resources. Teaching status can range from the precarity of adjunct teaching to "art star" professors (though these elevated positions remain subject to administrations). Teachers might see the prime purpose of pedagogy as ranging from having students assist them in their own quest for mastery status to assisting students toward becoming independent, critical thinkers and artists—in whatever form that takes, and through whatever form of art that takes.

This expansiveness of "whatever form" is art pedagogy's limitation and its greatest potential. The "form" can prioritize a single medium or technique (the primacy of realist painting, for example, in some art "academies"). It can entail rote copying of the instructor's technique, sometimes using the language of acquiring mastery. It can be "poststudio," where the student is inculcated into a conceptual vocabulary but appears to learn no practical skills. It can be something in between, where skills are taught as necessary to make ideas manifest. It can lead to artists as object manufacturers, or emphasize art as intervention, with the artist as "aesthetic activist" intervening into or interrupting existing social relations. These few possibilities (and all are being taught now, somewhere, in art schools) are political and economic decisions, and responsive to the perceived needs and pressures of the times.

●

My focus is on what might be seen as conventional, even traditional media, such as painting, photography, and sculpture, rather than digital media and social practice. Not because I have less interest in these "new" forms but because I want to attend to what are popularly held to be the core conventions of art. Similarly, many of my references are to the artistic canon of popularly known, established artists. As an educator, I am acutely invested in the directions taken by art schools. I want to maintain the different disciplines on offer, seeing them—much as I would written or spoken languages—as worldviews that provide singular, though relational, engagements with the world, and whose loss we could not begin to fathom. I want students to learn any and all of the available histories and languages (disciplines), and adapt them to their present lives, remaking those disciplines in the process.

My emphasis will be less on the formal instruction of didactics, of dispensing skills and information, and more on "being with" students as fully embodied subjects in their quests as critical thinkers and makers. In service to this, I am proposing pedagogies gleaned from decolonial models, from those artists, theorists, and activists who have worked *against* the myriad forms that enslavement takes, and *toward* fuller, humane potentials.

While the terms "colonialism," "decolonizing," "decolonial" might cause some readers to feel that I am addressing a "minority," I am using those terms to refer to all subjected peoples, that is, to everyone. We are each subjected in different ways and to different extents—no matter to what degree we might benefit from our participation in subjection. For example, those who—however unknowingly—benefit from hierarchies that are identified by terms such as "white privilege" or "patriarchy" might nevertheless *feel* their hierarchical position not as a privilege but as an economic, social, and bodily constraint, alongside with *feeling* their own bodies threatened, producing both an envy of othered bodies, and an anxiety and competitive resentment of "them." To live with this anxiety, just one of the effects of the constant jockeying to maintain or raise one's hierarchical position, is a form of constraint, no matter to what extent it is displaced onto others, no matter the extent to which one benefits from it, and no matter how self-manufactured it is to appease one's conscience and mask one's elevated position within the hierarchy.

I am not drawing any equivalence between forms of subjection, nor implying that colonizers, colonized, and their descendants are subjected to equal forms of violence and constraint. We each participate in multiple ways and from multiple positions within hierarchies of power, even to the extent that those in positions of power might see themselves as being victimized by the powerless or the less powerful. The bottom line that informs my arguments is that there can be no liberation for only a few, nor for only specific groups. Having said this, I have to admit that I am less motivated by the "suffering" of the privileged.

While these are implicit and explicit questions of how we function as societies, I will concentrate my arguments on how they play out within art and pedagogical practices.[22] The practices I am most focused on here appear neither discriminatory nor overtly violent. They are so normalized and everyday that they form the fabric of our most intimate and social selves, but whose very normalization is cumulatively discriminatory and enacts a slow violence. In the particular scenario of the art critique, I mean "decolonizing" in a broad sense, as a weaning from, a counter to, a reconception and implementation of strategies by subjected, hierarchized individuals against that subjection and hierarchization by disciplining power. This power is identified in the various means through which it multiply manifests and acts to limit bodily experience, whether these manifestations are articulated and *organized* through racial, gender, class, and/or sexual constraints—the "isms" that delimit what experience can be, who/what can have them, and *how* those experiences can be felt, shared, and understood. Privileges, whatever they might be, are maintained at the expense of siding against—and, if required, *acting* against—those without the same privileges.

Two aspects of colonization that I will continually reference are its control over history (time and memory) and its exertions upon the body (affect and mobility). Colonization aspires to determine history, controlling how time and the past are narrated in order to produce future narratives. It does so in part by creating a rupture from the past as well as within the present, a cut from any sense of historical continuity. Its capacity to wield these cuts is not only as an outside force but also one that is fully embodied, psychically and physically acting upon and from within the body, forming how each one of us is organized, how and what we know, how we feel, think, and act in/with the world; that is, intimately producing any sense of "who we are" in relation to "our" history and to the bodies and histories of others.

Intrinsic to "who we are" are practices of both remembering and forgetting. Writing about the closed Plantation system of the Americas, Édouard Glissant outlines how two cultures develop that are integral to modernism: one is a culture of actively forgetting, the other is one of remembering actively— I am deliberately linking this to activism.[23] This remembering is undertaken at great risk, against the strictures, impediments, and punishments imposed on remembering one's languages, one's histories, one's humanity, and the violence that has been perpetrated against those. Forgetting is also not a simple or lightly undertaken erasure, since it too is activist in its demands for returns to imagined pasts. Not only brutal in its eradications, forgetting can entertain, or rather, infotain, eventually producing, for example, the plantation as heritage tourist destination through the industry jargon of "authentic recreations" of willing participation, of happy, cared-for slaves singing in the fields.[24]

Glissant reminds us that landscape, a supposedly neutral genre of nature observation, is highly implicated in this practice of forgetting, emphasizing the "conventional splendor" of the Caribbean landscape over the lives and death grounds of slaves—an eviscerated landscaping that is integral to how contemporary tourists imagine themselves in that landscape (and how the imagining is enacted for them). In this resort equivalent of terra nullius, the only natives are there to provide "luxe, calme, et volupté."[25]

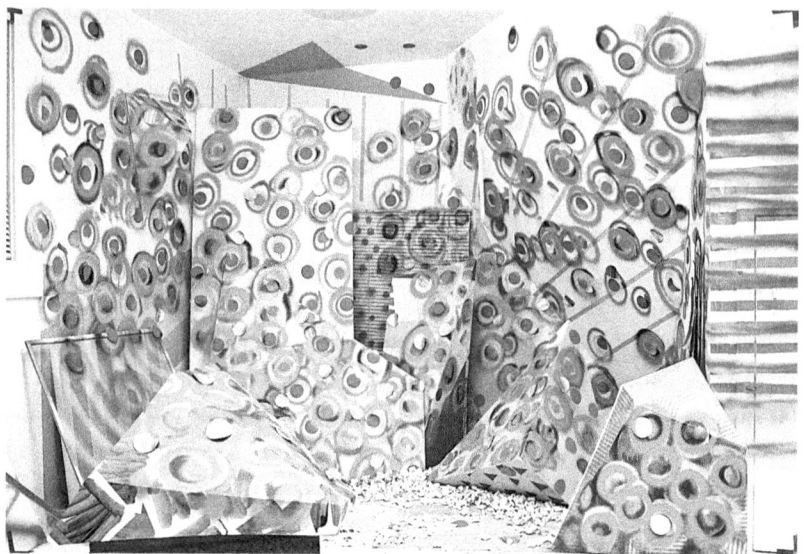

Fig. I.1 • Sofie Ramos, *decorate/defecate*, 2015. Multimedia installation, variable dimensions. Courtesy of the artist.

The will to forget and the will to remember. How and what does one remember, if a (pre)dominant modernism produces a culture of forgetting? How does art function as island of forgetting within seas of turmoil, as "comfortable armchair"—to keep Henri Matisse in mind—in the rooms of the living and the caverns of the dying?[26] While Matisse himself was almost obsessively driven, and hardly the epitome of an "armchair painter," I dredge him up since his work has come to stand for not quite an escape, but a point of view, and an experience that "rises above" the troubles of the world, a rising that marks a central aspiration for Western modernism. The critic Peter Schjeldahl epitomizes this aspiration at exactly the moment of crisis, as a salve to the mowing down of revelers along the Nice waterfront in July 2016: "To share in the delicate truth [that rigorous art can be at one with routinely melting pleasures], you look at, show, or send a picture by Matisse. People have been doing that often, these awful recent days."[27]

Similarly, in a review of a Matisse exhibition in 1992 Hilton Kramer writes, "It has the effect of making one feel a lot better about the century in which we live—a terrible century in so many ways, yet one in which we can nonetheless feel an immense sense of pride if, beside its unremitting record of suffering, bloodshed, and tragedy, it can also boast of an achievement as sublime as

Matisse's." Curiously, this rebalancing of the scales of beauty leaves Kramer mourning Matisse, though his mourning is symptomatic of a more generalized melancholia for a world that never was. He concludes, "When we exit this exhibition and return to the sordid cultural landscape of this last decade of the century, it is hard to believe that we shall ever again witness anything like it, now or in the foreseeable future."[28]

In these examples, forgetting—closeting melancholy—is purposeful and elevating, with beauty as the engine whisking us away from the tragedies of the world. The will to forget and escape are understandable, but we might also measure privilege by the degree to which we *can* forget, ignore, or be whisked away from the tragedies of others (including the privilege of being able to think of them *as* other).

Artists such as Glenn Ligon, Carrie Mae Weems, Betye Saar, and Kara Walker (to name only a few of the more well known) might be considered as doing the work of remembering (of slavery and the plantation system).[29] A different tactic of remembering is pursued by the artist Simone Leigh. As well as creating counterrepresentations, Leigh works directly with and upon the body of the viewer, transforming galleries and museums into healing spaces for the traumatic memories that have been generationally inscribed onto black and brown bodies, and that are reexperienced in the onslaught of ongoing racism and sexism. Leigh turns the gallery into a site of (self and communal) actualization, to activate viewers to new forms of representation.

A more demanding, destabilizing way to think of these artists is that they play resounding roles in repurposing (post)modernist forms and languages against the (modernist) project of forgetting. Rather than framing such artists as addenda to a central narrative, how might we rethink that central narrative of modernism when we replace what has been purposefully removed and forgotten? And rather than policing the political effectiveness of black artists in / accepted by white institutions, we might—to use the vernacular of the plantation—consider that the work of remembering and replacement needs to be done as much in the big house as in the slaves' quarters, at least until the institutional architectures and locations of memory work have been rebuilt.

The other main considerations I will consider through colonization will be on control over mobility and access, of how emotions, languages, and ideas circulate, of which bodies have mobility and institutional access, including to ideas, and through which artistic practices and vocabularies these are extended and simultaneously withheld.

Throughout the book I will return to these questions, of memory and forgetting, of language, mobility, and access, and what implications they have for looking at and understanding art, for pedagogy, and for social relations (and disconnections) developed around art.

In doing this, I am not prescribing what a decolonizing culture and its forms can or will be, since any such prescriptions should be suspect as returns to and applications of colonizing authority. My aim, then, is not to prescribe what art can *be* but to work toward language to describe what it *does* and *does not do*, how it does that, and what it *can* do—language being the prime means to articulate what those possibilities might be.

Decolonizing culture, and the modes of art-political inquiry that I am proposing, cannot exist in isolation or with any claim to autonomy. They are entwined with and can only be experienced, understood, and enacted *as* decolonizing through art's institutions, practices, discourses, and participants. Like any other object or event, art/political work becomes politicized through the culture, agents, institutions, and systems that (re)produce it, through which it operates, and which it in turn produces.

By turning to the political (and I concede that what the "political" means and how it functions are always contested and temporal), and in pulling from different sources, my interest is in placing a spectrum of ideas and practices in service of the idealism that many art students have and continue to have (in more subdued form) as artists. It's an idealism that desires more from art than being a commodity, that grounds art politically and socially while repurposing aesthetic and formal invention, that pursues art as complex intersections between individual and collective interests. It is an idealism that continues to inspire (me), yet it is an idealism that currently lacks an adequate language to articulate, investigate, and interrogate its interests, desires, demands, methods, and outcomes.

CHAPTER 1

HOW *ART* CAN BE THOUGHT

While the rest of the glossary follows later, in alphabetical order, it seems only fitting to acknowledge and examine early the elephant on the page:

A typical popular definition of "art" may read something like this:

Something that is created with imagination and skill and that is beautiful or that expresses important ideas or feelings.[1]

The definition leaves too many questions unanswered, not to mention that it doesn't apply to much of contemporary art.

To break it down into its component parts:

Something

[Anything? Does it have to be a *thing*, that is, be an object with material form? This would exclude performance, conceptual, or digital work. If it is a video or film, clearly the "art" is more than the materiality of the videotape or the film reel, which is the apparatus for the art, and which can be accessed only through other viewing devices such as projectors—and I am not dismissing experimental film and video that emphasize the material properties of the medium.]

that is created

[What does it mean to create? Presumably it means more than "fabricate" or "build," since these can be performed by assistants, including highly skilled ones.]

with imagination

[In "created with imagination" is the object the manifestation of, a product of, or a translation from imagination? How do viewers measure the degree of imagination? How much is imagination tied to ideas of "newness," of conceiving something that didn't preexist? Is artwork necessarily linked to the new? How do we evaluate parody, appropriation, collage, assemblage, the readymade, the restaging, and the critical, which are not dependent on newness or even on imagination in any conventional sense? Imagination suggests an interior source, whereas art might proceed from external, mechanical, mathematical, linguistic, social, or interactive processes.]

and skill

[If the work is *skillfully* made by an assistant, do we still attribute skill to the artist? Does the application of skill elevate the artisan to the artist? If the work is a readymade, is skill attributed to the manufacturer? Is skill simply a learned and well-practiced method? Is skill defined only as physical rather than mental abilities? Is "badly made" work not art? Does intervention performance require skills?]

and that is beautiful

[Who decides what's beautiful, with what criteria and measures? Is beauty absolute, or relative? Is there a spectrum from beauty to ugliness, and is the ugly no longer art? Are some artworks more beautiful than others?]

or that expresses

[What does it mean to express? Presumably not like breast milk?[2] Or perhaps that is exactly the meaning we want, a bodily *humor* that leaks out into the world?]

important

[Who judges, and what is or isn't important? According to what criteria and what timeline? Does importance change over time?]

ideas

[*Any* ideas? Are some better than others? How do we track what the ideas are when we look at an object or event?]

or

[Why not *and* rather than *or*, ideas *and* feelings? Is there a hierarchy between the two?]

feelings

[Were these experienced by the artist before or while making the work? Are these to be experienced by the viewer? How do we know if these same feelings are experienced by different viewers? How do feelings change over time or after repeated viewing? How do feelings change according to the setting and conditions in which the work is experienced? Is there a required intensity of feeling? Does it matter if the feeling is fleeting or enduring? Do *any* feelings count? Rage, hatred, anger, disgust . . . ? If work appeals only to the intellect, with no apparent response of feelings, does it make it not-art?].

●

One could continue, ad nauseam, with such questions. The point is that for the most part we don't really know what we're talking about *because* such definitions of art produce so many variables and unanswered questions. If discussions of art proceed from only these kinds of definitions, we would operate only on the *presumption* that we know what we are experiencing, what we are talking about, and the *presumption* that others have the same incommunicable experiences and understandings.

For a moment, let's consider other attempted definitions:

- Art is nature as seen through a temperament.—Camille Corot
- Art is either plagiarism or revolution.—Paul Gauguin
- Art does not reproduce what is visible; it makes things visible.—Paul Klee
- Art is vice. You don't marry it legitimately. You rape it.—Edgar Degas
- [Art is] . . . a man's timid attempt to repeat the miracle that the simplest peasant girl is capable of at any time, that of magically producing life out of nothing.—Oskar Kokoschka
- It is self-evident that nothing concerning art is self-evident.—Theodore Adorno
- You cannot define electricity. The same can be said of art. It is a kind of inner current in a human being, or something which needs no definition.—Marcel Duchamp
- Art is probably the only thing that doesn't need a reason to exist.—Lawrence Weiner

- To see something as art requires something the eye cannot decry [*sic*]—an atmosphere of artistic theory, a knowledge of [the] history of art: an artworld.—Arthur C. Danto
- A work of art in the classificatory sense is (1) an artifact (2) a set of the aspects of which has had conferred upon it the status of candidate for appreciation by some person or persons acting on behalf of a certain social institution (the artworld).—George Dickie
- The point of art is not the exposure of the truth but the creation of public situations for reimagining reality.—Nikos Papastergiadis
- The role of artworks is no longer to form imaginary and utopian realities, but to actually be ways of living and models of action within the existing real, whatever the scale chosen by the artist.—Nicholas Bourriaud
- Once we accept the simple fact that the work of art is produced by a human being who has been socialized by family, school, religion, and the media, then it can take its place in the larger range of human production and be seen as a reciprocating device in the social mechanism, caught up and determining the dynamics of change itself.—Albert Boime[3]

In these desperately inadequate attempts (all written by men, mostly Euro American), some common themes emerge:

1. Art as indefinable
2. Art as mediated nature
3. Art as unmediated expression of the (male) artist's interiority, a process sometimes equated to a woman giving birth (not far behind this is the conviction that since women can/should give birth, they can't/shouldn't make art)
4. Art as masculine enterprise and conquest
5. Art as cultural, social practice.

The first theme maintains that art is perennially mysterious and enigmatic, that its affects cannot be quantified or put into words. This mystery is a necessary prerequisite for (en)forcing the separation of art from the realms of political, social, and cultural practices. Art's ostensible separation from economics is paradoxically what gives it economic value. Thus removed, and made autonomous, art is conceived as the product of isolation, genius, even divinity.

The second and third themes are archaic but still operative in less gendered form, and will be addressed throughout the book.

The fourth theme (overlapping with those previous), that art is a masculine enterprise (with craft as its feminine counterpart), remains both overtly and covertly resilient. This is comparable to the similarly resilient proposition of art as a racialized *European* enterprise, with everything else as artifacts of ritual or of the "natural." Degas's jarring quote to the effect that art is rape is hardly an isolated example, and speaks to art as a dominating practice. Art history is lousy with artworks and careers built on (sometimes highly aestheticized) violence depicted or enacted upon the female body as metaphor for the (male) artist's interiority, and his musings on religion, politics, and the nation. Beyond muse, the female body may be the *instrument* of production (see, for example, the "living brushes" of Yves Klein's *Anthropometries* of 1960).

One of the problems any potential discussion of art faces is when participants hold to only the four first themes, or in holding to them to some degree, find themselves conflicted in how or even *whether* to discuss art.

It is the fifth theme, art as a cultural, social practice, that enables art to be brought into language and to be investigated and discussed. This forms the core of this book, that art comprises forms of knowledge of being *in/with* the world, which I distinguish from knowledge *about* the world. I'm not trying to make a case for art as objectively verifiable *information* about the world; for that we might better look to the sciences, although it is worth recalling Aimé Cesaire: "Poetic knowledge is born in the great silence of scientific knowledge."[4] While Cesaire is speaking to the disciplinary project of European rationalization, aka the enlightenment, I'm pointing more narrowly to art providing different kinds of knowledge, *within* science's gaps of how to be *in* and *with* the world. My use is similar to how Kobena Mercer references art as manifestations of "aesthetic intelligence embodied in actual works of art as objects of experience."[5]

While art is coded knowledge, generated and interpreted through learned and historicized disciplines and media, an artwork is a manifested "object of experience," of being in/with the world from the very particular perspective of an artist's historicized, embodied, located, enculturated subjectivity. Viewers engage this complex of perspectives with their own similarly complex subjectivities. [#Authenticity]

•

Contemporary art is expansive enough that artists can work across m/any disciplines, including law, anthropology, dance, tourism, cartography, nanotechnology, bioengineering, and so on. Not only do artists play out the assertion that anyone can be an artist, but they put into practice that artists can be anyone. An important consideration across any medium and discipline is how art "comes into being." This can occur through a multiplicity of manifestations, practices, and functions: individuals and groups constantly amass data through multiple means, including experience, surveillance, research, investigation, imagination, and memory. We store, decipher, categorize, translate, reconfigure, speculate, forecast, endure, replay, act upon, and are acted upon by these through complex bodily, emotional, intellectual, material, social, political, technological, and virtual systems. Any of these activities, in any combination, and the gestures and forms they produce might be what we inadequately call "art."

This is another way to say that art is anything and everything. This provides rich potential, but it doesn't really help as a definition. Slightly less expansive (and without judging which are "better"), are a number of working possibilities: artworks are design elements and spatial enhancements, affective encounters, sensory and ethical triggers that can be both activating and placating, transformation devices, identity and communal markers, cultural values and ritual practices, archives of the contemporary and of the historical, provisional meaning systems and social interventions, entertainment and touristic attractions, luxury goods and status markers, stock options and liquid assets, tax breaks and trade goods, and histories of imagination, thinking and making; objects and acts that help us create and allot meaning, that define us to ourselves, that define us in opposition to others; vessels and conveyances that paradoxically direct us toward the uncontained and uncontainable; and practices that we believe (and hope) can aid us toward understanding and insight, that connect us to each other, to transcendent experiences, and to "higher powers."

Only some of these possibilities might be widely considered as art, and others are popularly rejected. They are all social practices, with political and material consequences, processes that are always in flux, impermanent functions even as they are invested with the semblance of permanence, always being tested and adjusted, always responsive to codependent factors and forces. The designation "art" itself is a political naming, with choices made by artists, galleries, and viewers (or producers, distributors, and consumers) based on vested interests. Those interests need investigation for us to understand why and how certain forms of art are recognized and valued over others.

These beginning considerations of what art does are still too expansive for everyday use, but they begin to allow for a discussion of what specifics we may mean when we talk about "art."

Here is one commonly encountered response, especially from students: "Art is whatever I say it is." Invoking professorial authority, I could counter, "No, whatever *I* say it is." This idea of "whatever" is alluring precisely because it mirrors the claim to autonomy that is one of modernism's foundational mythologies. Autonomy of the artist, autonomy of art, the artist as originator, as (de)terminator—Austrian accent optional. This individual "right" to self-definition and self-determination is a defining, almost national characteristic of America, and of the global capitalist economy. However, while the artist can make a case for why it is art, it is accepted *as* art only when there is a collective agreement that it is. To begin to think through the individualist stance, we can take another starting point for defining art:

Proposal and/or action and/or object, plus discourse.

"Proposal and/or action and/or object" refers to the prior "whatever I say it is." But it is the more collective and historicized "discourse" (with marketing as an increasingly prevalent component) that determines whether it becomes art or not.

Art is identified and defined through discursive and theoretical models, and not by simply encountering it. For example, if a dominant theoretical model defines art as primarily a mimetic practice, then abstraction will be considered only as inept (childish and/or primitive and/or the result of insanity), or as a hoax. A theoretical understanding of art has to (and did) shift from art imitating reality to art creating its own reality through new forms and new ways of looking. [#Theory] We can trace similar shifts:

- Art depicting realities beyond the tangible and reason-regulated (Surrealism)
- Art depicting interior realities (Expressionism)
- Art creating new realities through already existing forms (collage and readymades)
- Subsequent shifts have brought into question our grasp of and access to reality through questions of mediation and collective participation (institutional critique and social practices)
- Other shifts (postmodernist, feminist, postcolonial, queer) have brought into question those subjectivities (whether of artists, critics, patrons, or viewers) that have historically laid claim to describing and projecting their particular experienced reality as universal truth.

In other words, theory as a tool for examining and imagining our experience in/with the world needs to continuously adapt as the world itself changes and is changed. This is not to suggest a causal relationship that theory leads the way and that art follows. Art itself functions theoretically (through and beyond its own materiality), and has theoretical and material effects on other art, with further effects through its interpretation and translation into verbal language (much of what we identify as art industries is formed around these functions).

"Whatever I say it is," then, is paradoxically a stance that is itself collectively enabled.

●

Returning to the earlier equation about what art is, or does (*proposal and/ or action and/or object, plus discourse*), we would need to account for a priori experience and information, the grounding discourses from which the artistic proposal or action derives, and the discourses and practices that direct the viewer and viewing. Thus:

Discourse, proposal and/or action and/or object, plus discourse.

We can push further this temporality by suggesting that an artwork is in process of becoming (and I include gesture within this). In the equation, replacing "proposal" with "process" removes the narrative sequence between "proposal" and "action" and suggests that the process constitutes the work rather than it being only a consequence of a preceding thought or action. Process locates the work as performance by an embodied subject or a group of subjects, regardless of medium. Process emphasizes "becoming," and the potential for ongoing meaning-in-the-making; therefore:

Discourse, plus process and/or object, plus discourse.

While it sounds obvious, it's important to keep in mind that art is not a "natural" phenomenon but is produced by socialized individuals who are located through histories and cultural geographies—one might say that art is produced *through* socialized individuals. Art is activated by similarly socialized viewers and participants. The viewer is a vital agent in the work's becoming, since the viewer produces meaning from myriad sources *before*, *during*, and *after* their encounter with the work. The work never arrives at nor is delivered a final meaning but is always in this process of (potential) becoming, in similar ways that the viewer herself is. How each viewer participates in this process of becoming is subject to a complex of discourses, but it is also an opportunity for activating the viewer's own criticality and agency; hence:

Discourse, process and/or object, plus discourse, *plus viewer*.

Since discourse, object, and viewer are already part of the process of the art-work's becoming, we might "simplify" art to:

Process.

This simplification, by itself and without its components, won't be of much use in casual conversation, but it will help to address many of the mythologies surrounding art. The complex of relations within process enable us to think about what constitutes art and—perhaps a more useful set of questions—about how art comes into being and how it functions. It might be necessary to refrain from fully encompassing definitions (but not from discussions), since art—by definition—might be that which resists definition. At least in contemporary terms, art is the experience yet to come, the meaning yet unformed, the activity always in process.

•

The shifts from what artworks *are* to what artworks *do*, and how they come into being (doing), have major repercussions on how contemporary viewers—or rather, interactors or enactors—engage with, assess, and continue to think and act upon these works.

Where and how we encounter artworks are crucial to how they are activated. The studio, the exhibition space, and the accompanying catalogue (and the museum and the monograph) become archives of artworks whose contextualized and context-specific displays profoundly affect and inf(l)ect how we engage with individual works and their interrelations, aesthetically, temporally, materially, and socially. However, we are just as if not more likely to encounter artworks online, where the work might be removed from any initial artistic or curatorial framing, or be entirely recontextualized and dehistoricized.

Some "context-based" or "social practice" works can only be evaluated through the "effectiveness" of their social engagement. For critical purposes, evaluative criteria applied to these works can be applied to works that are "object-based," and vice versa. Similarly, we might apply criteria of "time-based" works to "still" works, and vice versa. Through such demands placed upon criticism by expanded criteria and different sets of questions, we are able to assess the continuing roles, relevancies, and effects of any evaluative criteria, of artworks and art practices. Can we track genealogies of different operative criteria? Which ones are shared between current participants or viewers? In what circumstances do criteria and their hierarchy change? Are there some criteria that we are more willing to change or be flexible about than others? What are the consequences of the criteria that we use? The viewer, an *active* factor in this equation of where and how meaning is produced, is simultaneously brought under critical interrogation.

•

Some questions about what art does can be approached through semiotics or linguistics—that is, as systems of signifiers and practices with some similarities to language, even though artworks might never fully resolve into signification. That in/ability to fully cohere into what we may think of as linguistic systems where meaning can be identified and communicated is what might be art's defining characteristic, an inability that can be a refusal, a rejection, as well as an *a*bility. Art's particular trait might be the excess that cannot be brought entirely into meaning, whose functions and affects cannot be fully quantified or qualified, that function beyond translation into speech. Indeed, when we *can* qualify and quantify art, when we think we can fully account for it through speech, our tendency is to dismiss it as propaganda, as didactic, as information, as not-art. However, not attempting to examine, question, account for, celebrate, and extend the possibilities of art through speech is to remain in the realm of the authoritative, the conventional, and the superficial.

Art's excessiveness encroaches upon our bodies and experience, and can lead into and away from ourselves and to other experiences. While that excess cannot be fully accounted for by linguistic theory, linguistics nevertheless offers one of the most (currently) useful tools to pry open and articulate what happens in the encounter between art and viewer. We may, for example, apply lessons from the equation that Ferdinand de Saussure makes between *langue* and *parole*.[6] Briefly, *langue* refers to the written form of any given language, its history, its grammatical structure . . . the collective history, form, and culture that the speaker of that language inherits, acquires, and is taught, and through which that speaker is formed. *Parole* refers more to individual speech, and to the particular lived and present forms that speaker gives (crafts) to that language (*langue*), through intonation, inflection, context, and so on, and through which language (*langue*) is furthered.

This model applied to art and artists allows that artists are trained and otherwise acquire various artistic histories, socializations, and practices—the history and culture through which their work and they themselves are formed (*langue*). Artists will inflect and apply those histories and cultures in particular and individualized ways to remake them in the present, which extends and redirects those histories and cultures toward other future forms (*parole*).

•

What constitutes art and how we define, or at least account for, it has important cultural, economic, civilizational, and identitarian consequences. Authoritarian regimes understand and fully implement this, commissioning works to the glory of the state and the figurehead of the dictator, as well as eliminating—as political subversion—artistic freedoms and dissent (which come to represent both individual and collective rights).

Less dramatic, though played out over a longer time scale that is no less restrictive, is the global hegemony of Euro American art, with other art forms seen as lesser, imitative, or designated as not-art. One sees this almost casually schematized in art survey books or in art museums that have implemented categories of contemporary, modernist, and primitive or tribal art. In New York's Metropolitan Museum of Art, for example, one encounters artworks within the Oceania section by contemporary, named individuals (e.g., Wanyi Abwiyeti, a member of the Mariwai Village Artists Workshop). These contemporary works are displayed under the guise of "tribal" art and amid other artworks from earlier time periods. Here, work from the present era is displayed as not having progressed from the collective and ritualistically functional premodern and is therefore considered as Not-Art in the Western sense. Even a simplified idea of the contemporary, as that which exists and functions in the period in which "we" *now* live, is not an idea that is universally applied. It is tied instead to the notions of "developed" and "developing" that are applied to nations and to artists from those nations: some have "arrived," and others have yet to arrive. Those who are "still arriving" are therefore not ascribed with the *individual* imagination, intelligence, visualization, feelings, skills, enterprise, and agency otherwise attributed to Euro American artists.

While exhibitions and museums continue to make these kinds of separations, efforts to "integrate" artworks are equally fraught, as evidenced by the continuing controversies over exhibitions such as the New York MoMA exhibition *"Primitivism" in Twentieth-Century Art: Affinity of the Tribal and the*

Modern (1984) or the Pompidou Center's *Magiciens de la terre* (1989).[7] The curatorial ploy of staging "affinities" risks dehistoricizing works by removing them from their formative particularities in order to assimilate them into "universalist" discourses. This assimilation through discourses of affect and transcendence not only rewrites the artworks but also reinscribes the viewer as an ahistorical, culturally unbound, colonizing, and cannibalizing subject for whom the "global" exhibition constitutes a tasting menu. A more recent example is the Menil Collection's exhibition *Affecting Presence and the Pursuit of Delicious Experiences* (2015). I will quote its exhibition intention at some length, since it elaborates two common contemporary methods of engaging with art—first, prioritizing the agency of the viewer, and second, that of the artwork:

> *Affecting Presence* gathers a diverse selection of objects . . . to experiment with two complementary ways of understanding experiences of art. One stresses the primacy of the viewer; the other the commanding agency of the work of art. The works on view range from ancient sculptures and functional objects from Europe, Africa, North America, and the Pacific to Euro-American paintings and works on paper from the recent past—all of which exemplify the reduction of form or the absence of representation.
>
> The exhibition highlights abstraction as an artistic means used across time, place, and culture to make present the ineffable forces that shape human experiences. 20th-century abstractions . . . are presented alongside a variety of abstract forms from earlier eras, showcasing the rich history of this aesthetic practice. The exhibition explores the convergence of a viewer's individual pursuit of transcendent experiences in art with each object's power and "affecting presence."[8]

The exhibition seeks to offer only the "neutrality" of authentic, transcendent experience, which operates across "time, place and culture." It appeals to viewers' freedoms and the artworks' aesthetic agency—both untainted by intellectual, critical, or historicizing interference. These underlying fantasies of unconstrained mobility for some and tightly regimented constraint for others are hallmarks of empire, in both its earlier colonial and current capitalist forms. [#Movement; #Universal/ism]

Rather than accepting the above, operations of viewing and the viewer herself are necessarily subject to examination. The linguistic models of *langue* and *parole* can apply to the histories, cultures, and individualized inflections (through personal experience, including the intellectual and emotional) of each viewer and their complex act of viewing. How we experience the artwork, what it (potentially) means to us, and how it comes into meaning occur through negotiations of these complex *intersections* that call for equally complex articulations rather than the self-comforting variations of transcendence and "I know what I like." I emphasize intersections so as not to prioritize any particular aspects of this engagement of viewing art, whether the bodily or emotional (how it makes me feel), the intellectual (over any physical response), the individual (over the historical, cultural), or the historical and cultural (over the individual).

The provisional accounting above is only the beginning of any discussion of *how* art is, and *how* it does what it does. More complex questions about time, duration, location, site, mobility, language, curatorial framing, and so on are still unaccounted for. Necessarily incomplete, we at least have some points from which to proceed.

CHAPTER 2

ENTRY POINTS

Good Schools, Good Artists

What is art? What is "good" art? Who is a "good" artist? These questions form a highly politicized battleground. The "common sense," seeming neutrality, and inarguable benevolence of "goodness" (Q: *What right-thinking person could possibly be against goodness, quality, and universality?* A: *A left-thinking person*) are already political in how well they mask what is in question, what is at stake, and what roles education plays in them.

Art schools depend on producing artists, or at least on cultivating them.[1] Every school claims to produce good artists. Other than through the successes of its students' future employment, exhibitions, prizes, and so on, how can schools identify and track what makes a good artist, and their role in producing one?

Rather than the commonly perceived artistic attributes of talent, quality, greatness, and genius, a host of other circumstances and abilities come into play. Luck is often identified as a prime factor, but this can also be broken down into more mundane factors, such as the confidence and opportunities to know where to be, who to speak to, who to be friends with, where to show, or how to capitalize on opportunities, what in other fields constitutes career planning and social networking, including when others—such as teachers or galleries—do it for you. Advertising, as in any saturated market, is of increasing importance for visibility, infiltrating all levels of artists' interactions. On social media, for example, artists employ the false modesty of being "humbled, thrilled, honored" to be in shows, receive grants, and meet famous people, as though this does not constitute advertising.

Tenacity and endurance might be the most important factors, and these are greatly enabled if one has moral, emotional, social, labor, and financial support, including from parents and partners—which tend to favor male artists, with women tending to provide the support. As supporters (enablers), rather than supported (enabled), women already face an unequal working field. Tenacity can also be generated by a complex of psychically manifested but arguably socially produced factors, including alpha displays of unabashed ego, self-confidence, and a rejection of others' opinions, as well as fear of failure and shame (in the face of other shaming encounters—not fitting in, not being good at anything else—art may often be the only activity that provides a sense of worth, even if only to oneself).

And let's not forget the daily privileges and constraints of class, race, gender, sexuality, wealth, and previous education (including having parents who are artists).[2] All of these factors may contribute to producing a successful artist, if we define success in terms of quantifiable production and recognition for it—which usually means sales and visibility.[3] But this is still not equivalent to being a "good" artist, and we have yet to arrive at a measure of that.

⚫

The art critic Deborah Solomon offered a two-for-one, typical criticism of the art school: "In the visual arts, at least, the MFA boom has not been accompanied by a growth in the amount of first-rate art being created in this country. In fact many critics feel that art schools are directly responsible for a decline in the quality of art. 'When I go to the New York galleries, all I see is art-school art,' says Barbara Rose, the art historian. 'The art is either feminist or deconstructionist, and basically it looks like homework, because what is homework but learning how to follow the teacher's rules?'"[4]

In 2011, Jane Chafin of Off-Ramp Gallery conducted research into the career value of MFA programs. Her conclusions: "An MFA doesn't give you an advantage in getting into commercial galleries or museums, making a living as an artist or getting grants. It's very expensive and saddles you with student debt that you have very little chance of paying off by working in your chosen field. Save your money, live your life, read, travel, pay attention, learn to think for yourself. Work hard, look inside yourself and make yourself the best artist you can be."[5] When considering work for her gallery, Chafin says, "A degree is not something I look for when selecting artists. . . . The bottom line is always the work. I look for work that's honest, creative, original, skillfully executed and intensely visual. It's supposed to be VISUAL art after all."

The critic Jerry Saltz describes the art he sees at the Venice Biennale of 2011 as "some mannered International School of Silly Art," and surmises that "art schools are partly the villain here."[6] I will concede, however, that these critics might be referring predominantly to art schools in New York and Los Angeles, both being major art markets that attract students who seek a direct line *to* the market. While other regional schools may not provide the market entry that some students crave, they can offer other possibilities, such as faculty attention (rather than the art stars present in name only), financial support, enhanced facilities, and opportunities for less competitive, more supportive development. There are two larger points here, however. First, art schools are already an integral function of art industries, and while they do require scrutiny and criticism, it is disingenuous to isolate them from broader criticisms of the same industry that includes art critics and historians, dealers and galleries. Art students in fact may be more influenced by what is showing in galleries than their faculty, and adapt their work accordingly, and in that rapid adaptation see themselves as *more* contemporary than their faculty. This "now-ness" is exactly what galleries might be scouting for. The art school and faculty may instead offer a temporary, protective levee and possible alternatives against market forces. Second, a subtext is that education is elitist and for the already privileged. This is only so when education is a for-profit industry. We might consider the role of education very differently if it were accepted as free, a societal necessity, and a universal right. It is more productive for these kinds of possibilities to be investigated by those same critics who otherwise rail against the market takeover of art.

If art education is valued *only* according to its career prospects, as it tends to be by parents who will pay for it, then it won't seem to be worth pursuing. But this is like valuing art *only* according to its market value, and unexamined terms such as "honesty," "creativity," "originality," and "skillful execution and intense visuality" or Chafin's self-help clichés of "learn to think for yourself," "work hard," and "look inside yourself and make yourself the best artist you can be" *are* part of art's marketable value, and as such, remain *intentionally* unexamined.

Solomon's (and Rose's) comments—"many critics feel . . ."—invoke the kind of self-evident, commonsense, public opinion that I have referred to earlier, and

Chafin and Saltz, too, invoke an appealingly no-nonsense, commonsense attitude that is the vernacular of political populism.

While I don't mean to cull these particular observers from the herd of "many critics" who routinely declare what is good and what is bad (nor do I devalue their many other contributions to how we may think through art), I will return later and throughout the book to their feast of assumptions (and famine of examination) about artistic quality, the role of the art school, and the place of theory.

Though I might contest the premises on which "many critics" base their observations, I can't rightly say that they are wrong (except when they propose that galleries are excluding "regular" artists, or have at any point been overflowing with "feminist" or "deconstructionist" or "minority" or "multicultural" art). If anything, such critics reveal both a preemptive mourning for the perceived passing of modernism (i.e., for the repeated *spectacle* of the reassuring and normative) and an inflated anxiety posed by the threat of supposed minorities and contrary voices, neither of which is borne out statistically by what is actually on display in galleries.[7] This is similar to the art faculty who bemoan being overrun by female and minority faculty (even when those bemoaners are themselves female and/or minority). What are primarily being mourned are not modernist artworks themselves—the critics mentioned are broadly eclectic in their tastes—but the dethroning of comfortable, self-affirming authority; a single, self-apparent, and universally shared experience of quality; the vacuum and vacuity of autonomous art; the belief in a singular measure of progress and betterment; and the insistence that we all believe and want the same (as long as we have critics to tell us what that is). These, in themselves, might seem to be laudable pursuits toward human commonality, except that they are also the histories and practices of cultural dominance.[8]

Although *many critics*—and art faculty—speak from their particular positions that are informed by their histories and sociality, by invoking an imagined, like-minded collective they produce an authoritative (and colonial) class. This (racialized, gendered) class almost never reveals what its criteria are for artistic quality or what relationships art schools and theory might have to those criteria (except by what are gleaned from their nostalgic mourning, and their negative reactions to even the mention of theory—despite or *because* of their clinging to outmoded theory that is no longer adequate to address the contemporary world). If anything, their commonly espoused prime determinant of artistic quality is "mystery," which is located beyond language and examination. Therefore, we can't begin to have a conversation about quality but resort instead to a silencing mysteriousness. And it is partially through this lack of examination of its operating terms that this class derives its authority—an authority that deliberately shrouds itself under a populism that "tells it like it is."

•

In posing the question "What makes a good artist?" we could follow Linda Nochlin's example of questioning the question itself. In her groundbreaking essay "Why Have There Been No Great Women Artists?" (1971), she advises against answering the question "as it is put" by, for example, researching and creating new art histories, or by postulating that women artists require different criteria for evaluating their "greatness."[9] She continues (and it is worth quoting her at length),

> But in actuality, as we all know, things as they are and as they have been, in the arts as in a hundred other areas, are stultifying, oppressive, and discouraging to all those, women among them, who did not have the good fortune to be born white, preferably middle class and, above all, male. The fault lies not in our stars, our hormones, our menstrual cycles, or our empty internal spaces, but in our institutions and our education—education understood to include everything that happens to us from the moment we enter this world of meaningful symbols, signs, and signals. The miracle is, in fact, that given the overwhelming odds against women, or blacks, that so many of both have managed to achieve so much sheer excellence, in those bailiwicks of white masculine prerogative like science, politics, or the arts.[10]

As Nochlin points out, this is not a numbers game, or not one of statistics: "The question 'Why have there been no great women artists?' is simply the top tenth of an iceberg of misinterpretation and misconception; beneath lies a vast dark bulk of shaky *idées reçues* about the nature of art and its situational concomitants, about the nature of human abilities in general and of human excellence in particular, and the role that the social order plays in all of this."[11]

The questions of what art is and through what means, discourses, and practices it is constituted are not answered by increasing the percentage of representative "other" faces and bodies, even though their presence in all tiers of art industries are necessary to implement different possibilities of what art could be. Art histories that address questions of power and difference would provoke more complex, intersecting art practices than the still-dominant version of a single Euro American lineage subsequently emulated by "peripheral" regions of the globe. Simply put, a homogenous art world and homogenous art practices ultimately limit *everyone's* horizons.[12]

e/Quality

A current institutional mode of addressing these questions, when addressed at all, is through the necessary but limited terminologies of diversity and cultural pluralism. Art schools, often because of funding pressures, pay at least lip service in their mission statements and stated policies to diversity and pluralism as "celebrations of difference." These are enacted within an expansive field of differences being *already* commodified through the myriad forces of global capitalism, of which art industries and the art school are important sites of cultural production and regulation. The celebration of difference, then, can make good market sense, since it creates new consumers and new products. Diversity, when conceived of *only* as celebratory, is merely tacked on to what's already in place. It does not interrogate dominant histories, does not necessarily entail policy (re)making and implementation of counterpolicy, and might only arise as an issue when difference becomes a "problem" (for example, a wheelchair user suing a school because of lack of physical access). Similarly, one might argue that pluralism, within the US context, has formed from segregationist policies and practices of coexistence as separate but grudgingly and neglectfully equal.[13] This mode of coexistence, celebrated as tolerance, is tolerated only when everyone keeps to their place, hence the emphasis on authenticating oneself through origin narratives of place and history.

One might recall Homi Bhabha's insistence that "the representation of difference must not be hastily read as the reflection of pregiven ethnic or cultural traits set in the fixed tablet of tradition. The social articulation of difference, from the minority perspective, is a complex, ongoing negotiation that seeks to authorize cultural hybridities that emerge in moments of historical transformation."[14] Difference, then, as historically produced, is already hybrid and dynamic, is ongoing social negotiation. If diversity is reconceived as relations of egalitarianism across difference, and as negotiated processes of intersocial reinvention, what would its policies entail if implemented across all physical, social, and discursive levels? How would one teach art and art histories if shifted from a singular narrative of Euro American modernist progress(ion), if one attempts to overcome languages of hierarchy, of omission, of sometimes inadvertent and sometimes deliberate discrimination? How would one uncloak the invisible and sometimes overt operations of exclusion and separation? How would one support social reinvention that differs from and perhaps destabilizes one's own preconceptions? And, more to the point, why would one do so?

Diversity can instead be remade into a holding operation, a technology to keep things as they are by allocating spaces (in the "soft" academic departments such as art) in which difference can visibly operate, using the models of both the reservation and the touristic display. Similarly, those who are designated *as* diverse might be allocated the job of *doing* diversity work, allowing the rest of the institution to remain unchanged and celebrate that diversity is being done in its name (the museum equivalent is to have a "multicultural" exhibition every ten years, or to organize multicultural family days).[15]

It would be a mistake to assume that there is widespread desire for actual egalitarianism, let alone consensus on what that would entail. Much of the art and education industries, trumpeting their only interest being quality, routinely practice exclusivity and exceptionalism, and consider issues of difference and equality as not only artistically irrelevant but artistically limiting.

Raising the issue of egalitarianism or taking steps toward it inevitably meets fierce opposition from some quarters decrying the loss of quality. Moves toward redress, such as the various "affirmative action" policies, are attacked as "reverse discrimination," as institutional interference, and as counter to the freedoms of market competition.[16] If excellence is viewed as being produced through enterprise and competition (and justified by the pseudobiological argument of "survival of the fittest"), equalizing policies are denounced as unnatural interference producing only mediocrity [#Mediocre]. Within the culture of competitive individualism, "assistive" programs (seen to promote a mediocracy) engender resentment against those "assisted," as though this were an unfair advantage rather than an attempted lessening of disadvantage. Those who feel that they are the rightful inheritors of the nation and its territories, and whom the government is supposed to serve, do not take lightly the redistribution of "their" resources to "others."[17]

Individualism is promoted as a kind of "top-down" ethics by which the actions of "outstanding" individuals benefit and elevate culture, and society at large. This ideology (and it is ideology) fails to recognize or value the collective labor and knowledge *already* expended to produce any given individual and which forms the history behind what that individual produces (I include unpaid as well as paid labor—parents, teachers, informal advisors, friends and lovers, colleagues, peers, previous employers, the multitude who clean up after, etc.). In this regard, *every* artist and artwork has a collective lineage.

Also seen to be under attack would be the art historical canon, presuming that the history of (straight) white males would be knocked off the pedestal of centrality or with current living ones feeling directly discriminated against (as, for example, by "political correctness"). [#Politically (In)Correct] A ramp toward equality would be attacked as the promotion of interest groups rather than seen as enacting the already-claimed ideals of universality. Some would decry the promotion of "victim art" that is measured not by its artistry but by its perceived wallowing in what the art critic Robert Hughes termed the "culture of complaint."[18] [#Victim] The critic Dave Hickey, perhaps the fastest gun of the antiacademic, cowboy criticism, escalates this outcry against whining by casting what he terms "regular" artists as the true victims of this supposed culture: "If you're just a regular artist, whose work doesn't come with a social excuse, or a letter from a doctor, you're kinda fucked."[19] This bemoaning of special interests is cast as the downfall of true art by the introduction of politics, not least of which is this perceived politics of victimhood and envy.

Essentially, these examples of political conservatism—of returning to how things *used to be*—function on the call for quality *against* equality. Earlier, I listed a swamp of discriminatory experiences. [#VeXing] In each case, the people conducting the discrimination would insist that their only criterion was quality and that there was no discrimination involved. They would insist that the person in question (often me) was just not very good.

The integral problem of quality is its inseparableness from discriminatory practices. How can a student of color, say, separate critique from discrimination? How can they evaluate their own work if the "double consciousness" of seeing through another's eyes is possibly a discriminatory vision that seeks not to evaluate their work but to exclude *them*?

Quality, *Idealized*

Quality as a commonly shared and instantaneously understood *value* is rendered problematic, if not irrelevant, when one considers competing and overlapping interests. Value is an imagined unity, following Judith Butler's observation, "It is not that there was once a unity that subsequently has come apart, only that there was once an idealization, indeed, a nationalism, that is no longer credible, and ought not to be."[20]

In Butler's sense, quality is an idealization, a desire—and not an irrelevant one—for a commonality of what *should* be. Quality, thus, is group identification, a measure by which a group marks its place and values, and represents those to itself.[21] Quality is one of the traits through which the collective "we" is produced, with individuals seemingly exercising their independence from the group while claiming their place within its ranks. Quality is necessarily exclusive, dismissive of that which doesn't meet its standards, with this dismissal, or *discrimination*, being its practice of judgment. [#Us]

In order to mark one's social place, it is not necessary to *produce* quality—that would be the role of the artist. It is enough to be associated with quality, to be able to recognize and sell it (the role of the curator, gallerist, and dealer), to contextualize and historicize it (the role of the curator and scholar), to appreciate it (the connoisseur), or to own it (the collector and museum). All these associations, the ability to discern, work, and live with quality, are considered practices of skilled discrimination but are more usefully understood as exercises of power and belonging.

As a value based on exclusivity, quality is used to police the boundary of what may enter its sanctum. This is similar to how it is employed within art schools by both faculty and students to maintain "standards," with these standards employed to select who else may join the school/club.

What is required instead of these impositions of universalized values are examinations of how artworks come into being, and how they activate and are activated by people with different interests, both historically and in the present. We need to examine how artworks intersect with, are produced by, and produce other works and discourses; what frames of reference the viewer brings to their viewing (and to any evaluation they may make—including of quality). We need to examine the desires produced by artworks in viewers, and what and whose purposes those desires serve. It's the stakes, then, of what art is, what it could be, what it does, what it means, how it is valued, who it represents, who it serves, and what kind of world/view it reflects back to differing imaginations and ambitions—it is these questions that passionately seethe behind the seemingly neutral and dispassionate mask of quality.

On Different Artists

These stakes are the provocations posed by difference, and by a world in which "those who are different" are better able to speak and act in their own interests. A recognition of difference cannot presume that others have the same views, especially given differing histories, circumstances, and social positions, *not even if we think we are the same*; nor can one presume that the views that any one of us has are *applicable* to differing histories, circumstances, and social positions. The only possibilities toward common grounds are through intersections between differences. The master's tools of common sense, quality, and individual genius impose unquestioned and unquestionable rules that flatten out the 3-D possibilities: difference, dissent, and dialogue.[22]

The art school that depends to some extent on public funding cannot financially afford to promote views based *only* on those master tools without some kind of nod toward the 3-Ds, and toward a more leveled if not equal opportunity. Even as the school might lean toward rhetoric of equality, it might in practice operate toward homogeneity, competition, and bulwarks of quality (this is a common enough scenario, of the school publicly advocating one set of views and operating on another).

The views we each hold about diversity, let alone on their implementation, are highly mediated by economics, including that of cultural capital. Artists and artist-teachers, the majority of whom are financially poor but culturally wealthy, and schooled in competition and exclusivity, are therefore (predis)-positioned to accept that diversity and equality are artistically irrelevant and limiting. However, many faculty, and schools, will resist that predisposition and actively work against it being implemented. The point, though, is that policies toward diversity and equality as *foundations* for artistic freedoms should be the norm within education, rather than lines of resistance, or, as bell hooks, invoking Paulo Freire, puts it, "the difference between education as the practice of freedom and education that merely strives to reinforce domination."[23] *What* those policies are and how they might be implemented over time requires further questions dependent on the changing conditions of each locality (with the production of locality understood in relation to the global). How might a faculty approach these questions if they imagined themselves as an artist collective, with the institution and pedagogy as their social practice projects?

It is useful to consider diversity in terms of subjectivities competing for the same territories. Instead of the more common scenario, in which there is an assumed stable center to which are added so many markers of difference to produce the celebratory tapestry of colors, the language of competing subjectivities recognizes that what is being fought over is the power to determine who gets to make art, who gets to determine what art is, who teaches it, what it should look like, how it is spoken and written about, how it is disseminated, exhibited, sold, and who gets paid for all those functions. Diversity's goal is not a more colorful roster enacting the same policies but is instead about who gets to determine what the school/gallery is and does, and how that is disseminated through wider culture. The diversity industry and the subjects produced through its institutional restraints are also to be brought under scrutiny.

When the language of art accounts for competing subjectivities, it destabilizes the fiction of universalism, becomes grounded in everyday (and not so everyday) experience, becomes more relevant to and more engaged with wider, multilocal constituents, and in turn produces more engaged, invested, translocal *participants*.

Can We Just Get Along?

Implicit to these questions of difference, diversity, and quality within the art school are considerations of who are the "we" that do the thinking, teaching, learning, and making of art. How is learning imparted to and within these different constituents, and how inclusive is what is taught and learned? Are certain values—whose values, and to what ends?—being imposed without the counteraction of opposing values?

Without some degree of transparency and clarification of pedagogical methods that are specific to the art school, the alternatives may too often devolve to the classroom equivalent of hanging out in a bar. Anyone with experience at an art school knows that this is, in fact, a celebrated teaching "method." John Baldessari, in conversation with Michael Craig-Martin—both are artists who are celebrated as teachers—offers this example: "The only way I got Sol LeWitt to teach was he wouldn't go on campus—you'd meet off campus. We just hung out in a bar, and that worked. You know, it's like all the planets surrounding you have to line up in the right way: the right students, the right time, the right faculty, the right city. Everything just aligns for a few moments."[24]

Cosmic design fueled by alcohol might sound like an apt description of the art world, and one is reminded of Tom Marioni's ongoing artwork and possible worldview *The Act of Drinking Beer with Friends is the Highest Form of Art*.[25] The unexamined gendered, hierarchical undertows of his artwork are revealed by Marioni himself: "Many of my installations also contain three symbolic elements: bottles for male, refrigerator for female (nourishment, womb), and yellow light for spirit."[26]

Convivial (and anachronistic) as these examples are, what is being celebrated, including under the guise of community, is what Baldessari considers to be the "right" elements: homogeneity, student artists molded in the image of their master, the romanticized figure of the artist-provocateur—a figure that is almost exclusively male, white, and (I'm presuming) heterosexual.[27] Such figures—one can add Lazlo Moholy-Nagy, Joseph Albers, Joseph Beuys, and Michael Asher, to name a few artists celebrated as educators—have clearly had an enormously valuable impact on art education and upon generations of artists (including myself, having "studied" with Craig-Martin at Goldsmiths and with Baldessari at UCLA).[28] However, this conviviality, the huddle over beers, is too narrow a culture, a fraternizing that all too quickly invokes its allied associations, the ritualized inclusions and exclusions of fraternities, not to mention the sexualized double standards (and potentially violent consequences) inflicted on those women who do and those who don't (drink). Alcohol can usefully loosen the formality of the institution. However, it is fully complicit with the institution when it reinforces normative hierarchical behavior.[29] While belonging to a group can feel wonderfully comforting, not examining the terms of that belonging risks that comfort being predicated on excluding the "wrong" people and ideas.

·•

Collegiality is the institutionalized form of education-related conviviality. It too sounds innocuous and only benevolent, a pursuit of collective and common interests; but it can also be used to enforce conformity and compliance, especially to administrative policies and unwritten social rules. The person who disagrees or who behaves differently may thus be isolated as "noncollegial."

The term "civility" has similarly been brandished to curtail dissident opinions. A case in point is the "dehiring" of Steven Salaita from a tenured position at the University of Illinois at Urbana-Champaign. Chancellor Phyllis M. Wise, in her open letter to the campus, insisted that Salaita's hiring was blocked not because of his political views or his criticism of Israel's bombing of Gaza in 2014 but because of the "uncivil" nature of his criticism on social media, a forum that was unconnected to campus discourse.[30]

While civility would suggest that we would achieve accord if only we were to conduct civil discussions—and the reference to being "civilized" is deliberate—it presumes a level playing field, or masks that one side can marshal greater force(s) to affirm its opinion, such as the power of the institution, public opinion (through greater access to media outlets and cultural capital); to hiring policies and other punitive employment/salary measures; and to more aggressive forms of coercion and intimidation if it chooses (such as the police, the National Guard, the military—as have been experienced too often on university campuses).

Civility, in cases of uncivil "civil unrest," may thus take the form of calls for "keeping the peace," "maintaining order," or "abiding by the law," *before* the causes of that unrest may be addressed. This is revealingly similar to the parental admonition, "If you will just calm down / If you will just behave yourself / If you will just stop what you're doing . . . we can talk about it." Civility, then, can be a form of restoring order in favor of the status quo, and in favor of those imposing order. Yet civil unrest usually occurs when the state/institution breaks the terms of its agreement with its citizens/participants to have their civil rights met in return for behaving according to commonly agreed civil expectations. In such cases, the only recourse citizens/participants may feel they have is to *withdraw* their civil behavior.

●

The art world's language for difference is couched within that of individualism, with every true artist being a unique individual (genius being an enhanced form of individualism). The rest presumably have not "got in touch" with their own difference but merely follow in the wakes of others. This individualism is related to capitalism's promise of unlimited choice, with each artist being one more brand on a palette of the perpetually new or the comfortably familiar. Individualism is also pitted against collective difference, as when an artist may identify through group affiliation (Blackness, queerness, etc.). As a gallerist once disapprovingly said to me, "Why would any artist want to call themselves a 'black artist'?" In other words, why would one give up the expansive scope of individuality to function within a social and artistic ghetto? The insinuation is that one is simply not a "good" enough artist to function individually without the crutch of identification with a particular group (feminist, Black, queer, etc.). What this insinuation fails to grasp is that a group affiliation located around "difference" may also stem from a rejection or *refusal* of assimilation, rather than a *failure* to assimilate (I will address this more below). Assimilation demands that one "adjust" to the reality produced by an already established complex of practices and social relationships *without* the "critical capacity to make choices and to transform that reality."[31] To paraphrase Freire, the degree of "adjustment" is symptomatic of one's dehumanization.

Assimilation presumes that the dominant race (gender, class, etc.) is the best one possible and what everyone else aspires to be, and if they can't be that, it's what they envy (Freudian allusion intended). The marginal shifts from assimilationist toward diversity models are at least a beginning acknowledgment that assimilation is a hierarchical, coercive practice and sometimes a practice

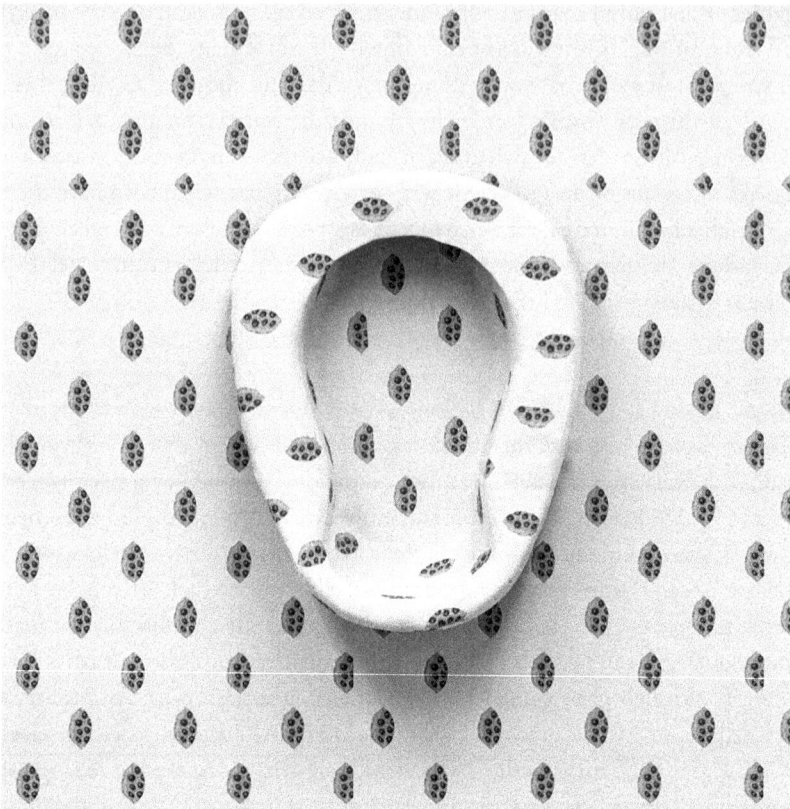

Fig. 2.1 • Shari Paladino, *The Urinas* (detail of *Habitas*), 2017. Printed polyester, plastic, variable dimensions. Courtesy of the artist.

of bureaucratized violence, with education having historically been a central component of that violence. A widespread question of the contemporary world, and one debated within many nations, is how to manage (and contain) what is seen as the refusal to assimilate.

Refusing the establishment (the establishing, policing forces of dominant practices and social relationships) should be no surprise to the establishment, since these have been founding moments of modernism. Following their rejection from the official Paris Salon of 1863, artists including Gustave Courbet, Édouard Manet, Camille Pissaro, and Paul Cézanne exhibited in the Salon des Refusés to overflow crowds. Similarly, we might remember the rejection of Marcel Duchamp's *Fountain* from the Society of Independent Artists in New York in 1917.[32] Even though these artists have since become pillars of institutionally validated art history, their initial rejection by the "establishment" has been a radical badge of honor.

Refusalon

What if one used thinking and language tools (theory), without, in the artist Daniel J. Martinez's terms, imagining wanting to be white? Can these tools be wielded only in the master's interests? Or can we reconfigure Audre Lorde's insistence that "the master's tools will never dismantle the master's house"? What if the use of language tools entailed a different kind of imagining and rising up?

Martinez at the Whitney Biennial of 1993 was the upstart doorman. His work consisted of a tag viewers were given on paying admission to the museum. Each tag was a word or phrase from the sentence, "I can't imagine ever wanting to be white." Visitors couldn't enter the museum without participating in his artwork, each one becoming a tagged performer. Martinez was in the master's house, but he made it clear that he, and others like him, the so-called multicultural angry artist, didn't want to be—not be *like*, but not *be*—the master even though he was clearly reveling in the possibility of kicking the master out. "How could you *not* want to be white?" seemed to be the most unsettling question for some museum visitors. Especially if, within the popular imagination, to be cultured or artistic means to be white and of a certain class. And if one is irreparably "colored," shouldn't one automatically desire assimilation, with the added bonus of serving up a little local color?[33]

Paul Gilroy describes the "postmodern predicament" as that which can be "approached through the translocal impact of political ideologies, social relations, and technological changes that have fostered a novel sense of interdependence, simultaneity and mutuality in which the strategic and economic choices made by one group on our planet may be connected in a complex manner with the lives, hopes, and choices of others who may be far away."[34] And, I would add, with those who have moved in next door, and are now within the same building. As the artist Ernesto Pujol succinctly states, "Globalism is a network of intimacies."[35]

In Martinez's piece—though careful, even tentative in its wording of refusal: "I can't imagine ever wanting . . ."—those questions of location, proximity, and intersection come into play, albeit within the museum's sheltered space, and with subsequently limited material and psychic consequences.

This tentativeness (if I may for the moment refer to it as that) in Martinez's piece—though the reception to it was outright hostility and outrage from

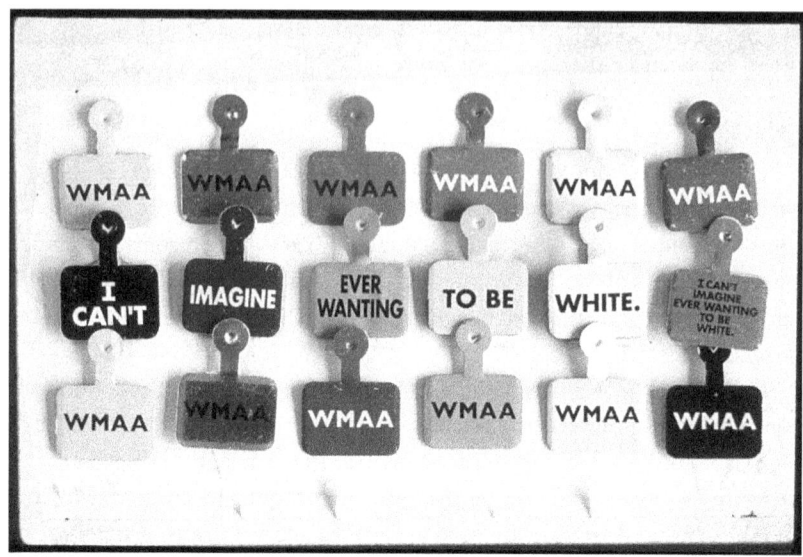

Fig. 2.2 • Daniel Joseph Martinez, *Museum Tags: Second Movement (Overture); or, Overture con Claque (Overture with Hired Audience Members)*, 1993. Metal and enamel paint, 12 × 15 in. Whitney Biennial, Whitney Museum of American Art. Collection of Michael Brenson, New York. Courtesy of the Artist and Roberts & Tilton gallery, Los Angeles.

many quarters—is an indication of the limits of the art institution, and that those artists and art students who succeed within and through them have also been disciplined by and through the same institutions. Refusals enacted within institutions, therefore, have already been tempered and tampered by those institutions. I include myself as appropriately "disciplined," the perceived but questionable trade-off being that as an "insider," one has a platform from which to speak and act. Martinez participates in order to speak from within, from the visibility/speech that the institution confers, but muses on the ambivalence of what is offered and taken away, with the musing itself as a rejection of assimilation. [#Mainstream]

This position of the infiltrator who gains access in order to have a voice is similar to the subaltern whom Gayatri Spivak, drawing upon Antonio Gramsci, proposes as a subject or class without agency under colonialism and without access to the colonial powers. As all other forms of knowledge are eradicated or subsumed within colonial knowledge systems, the colonized (subaltern), in order to gain a voice and to be heard, have to adopt the colonizers' means of knowing, reason, language and manners, and institutions.

Spivak is careful about agency as institutionally validated action and therefore restricted in its scope.[36] However, the romanticized position of "infiltrating outsider" is endemic to art industries. Artists, curators, academics, and museum and gallery professionals don't consider themselves to be fat-cat insiders feeding off the labor of others. Everyone, it seems, no matter their position within the status and economic hierarchy, considers themselves as radical infiltrators subverting and shaking up the system from within. [#Outsider]

Art history provides many examples of artists (as per the Paris Salons already mentioned) beginning from a position of willing participation, following through with negotiations as problems arise, and finally enacting their refusal and withdrawal if the institution is not forthcoming in its negotiation.

While accepting the necessity of withdrawal and refusal, I want to consider here possibilities of negotiation and engagement without advocating for ranked strategies. The situation in which I conduct my own social practice, a university art department, is a typically "layered" site, ensconced firmly within a bureaucratic hierarchy. Such hierarchies, like those of government, corporations, military, and social hierarchies in general, systematize individual ascent, stagnation, and descent but impede more collective mobility—especially those that might lead to more horizontal methods of organization. Within such limitations and obstacles, I want to consider avenues for negotiation, partly because these are the most common systems in which teaching artists will operate, even as these negotiations lack the glamour of radical refusal and autonomy. Refusals to participate may feel righteous, ennobling, and principled, and may often be absolutely necessary. But in some circumstances, refusals to participate may not necessarily be radical in their consequences and may in fact lead to further impositions. What tends to happen in practice is the formation of breakaway vanguard groups that seek to create change from the outside of institutions. While these groups perform vital functions, my interest as a teacher is on how to act from within institutions, with the perspective that institutions are a primary mode for organizing people, whether through disciplinary means or by providing the means and tools to organize.

Within ranked systems, one may use one's rank to advocate for those "below" as much as one can, up to the point of one's own refusal to participate. This infiltration is a common position one finds within the art and academic worlds. An immediate question is at what point does negotiation become collaboration? But the position I'm proceeding from is that we all collaborate. If we didn't, we would not (be able to) participate in/through institutions at all. This "turning away" is a constant issue for artists, and I will return to it later.

I imagine infiltration or negotiated engagement as somewhere between Roland Barthes's theorizing of the opposition between "to destroy" and "to decompose."[37] Destruction presupposes a position external to any situation or institution and from a site of speech "whose one characteristic would be exteriority: exterior and motionless: in other words, dogmatic language. . . . Whereas by decomposing, I agree to accompany such decomposition, to decompose myself as well, in the process."[38]

Barthes offers another image of the infiltrator: "That we deliberately pretend to remain within this [bourgeois] consciousness and that we will proceed to dismantle it, to weaken it, to break it down on the spot, as we would do with a lump of sugar by steeping it in water."[39]

The position of outside is often an enabling site from which to act, similar to "insideness," with both outside and inside being the temporarily shared collective identifications that Gayatri Spivak has referred to as "strategic essentialism." But note that Barthes situates such identifications as a "deliberate pretense," a performance, a fiction, a counter-lie. Spivak's own warning and subsequent disclaimer of essentialism as a viable strategy is that the lie too easily takes hold, the fiction believed.

Barthes's use of "decomposing" has other potential. Like the dispersion of sweetness, the transubstantiation of sugar into water, creativity—the supposed wellspring of artistic genius—can be seen as a transmigration from one state into another, from a granular accumulation into a less differentiated, more fluid condition. Creativity as a response, as a manifestation or enactment of sentience, and, most usefully, as translation, not from one truth to another, but as intersecting, workable fictions.

Given this mobile, trackless state, this state of infinite difference, dispersion, and cross-translation, how can we track anything (histories, geographies, subjectivities, meanings)? Barthes again: "Difference is the very movement of dispersion, of friability, a shimmer; what matters is not the discovery, in a reading of the world and of the self, of certain oppositions but of encroachments, overflows, leaks, skids, shifts, slips."[40]

In the contemporary world's volatile state of proliferating and adaptive difference, meaning cannot be isolated, determined, or fixed (which is why fundamentalisms of any stripe can only ever be at war with the world, since their certainties are perennially threatened by the uncertainties of actual existence), but meanings—as the fictions that they are—can only be temporal and temporarily agreed upon, and more often than not, fought over. Meanings, like artworks, can be narrated (as the fictions that they are) only through their excesses, their encroachments, overflows, leaks, skids, shifts, and slips.

Glossophobia to Glossolalia

Art industries, including art schools, are ambivalent about artists' use of written or spoken language. It is still common to encounter artists and students who cling to and even celebrate their inarticulateness, whether it is about their work or their ideas. Some fear that articulating their work might deplete their creative energy. Others think that oververbalizing (equated with overthinking) their work will rob it of its pleasure. While some of these—to me—arcane attitudes are still prevalent in art industries, artists are also increasingly expected to participate on panels, lectures, conferences, and so on, much in the role of public intellectual.

Artists might be expected to be dumb (in both senses of that word), and celebrated for it, with their "autonomous" artworks speaking for themselves *and* for the artist. In most commercial galleries, the lack of wall text points to the desire for artworks to be physically encountered without interruption by external information (this is less the case in museums, which perform more contextualizing, historicizing, and pedagogical roles). Other kinds of infiltration, of gaining a voice other than the one of the ventriloquized and ventriloquizing artwork, has been and continues to be a necessary consideration for many artists. The more forceful speech, such as the Dadaist call for the destruction of all art institutions (sMash the sTate!) or rejecting any contact with them, still provides a romantic allure, but even these acts of rebellion have been defanged and now suckle upon the museum (MoM-A?), which promotes its own narratives of rebellion.

A supposed signature of the art school is its "academic" and "theory-laden" language, pitted against the "plain-speaking" language of the real world, and, better yet, the no language at all of true art, which apparently speaks for itself. A secular parallel to religious-speak, plain-speak is the purposeful language of advertising and commerce. It is the language of conviction, repurposed to convince the viewer to invest themselves in art, whether ideologically or financially. In its conviction, plain-speak is a forked tongue, a doublespeak of non sequiturs made meaningful by repetition.

This is a problem for theory, a set of tools to reconfigure previous tools that have become fossilized in their conversion into the common sense of the everyday. Theory sounds difficult, it sounds convoluted, it sounds boring. And it's no match for the populist allure of plain-speak, of *telling it like it is*.

Plain-speak is a numbing, dumbing, colonizing language. It reduces possibilities for—and I will refer here to myself—addressing the nuances of what my senses are experiencing, that can help me sort through the connections my brain is making, that helps me ask questions, that can help me situate the art I encounter into the world in which I, we all, live.

My emphasis on language as integral to this decolonizing process of *who we are*, and more accurately to who we *become*, is due to language's necessity to articulate what happens in our encounters in/with the world (and with art), and how we make sense of those experiences to ourselves and to others. Language predirects our most intimate experiences (partly by narrating prior experience). If we enter into subjectivity through language (discourse), language also allows us to examine and critique the formation of that subjectivity. If our encounters with art are prescribed and disciplined by Euro American art histories and their hierarchies of value, we risk remaining subject to their colonizing affects unless we can also begin to counter those affects through language. While this is a highly politicized project, at its least it is an attempt to move past outdated artistic and pedagogical formations that no longer or refuse to account for the decolonial work already performed by artists and scholars, and which produces new possibilities in the contemporary world.

Even within the sheltered, privileged spaces of the museum and the art school, how do we upgrade language (and other practices), and decompose dogmatic languages (and other dogma) from their tarnished, varnished fantasies of how they want the world to be, to address the world as it actually is (in its messy, dangerous excesses, encroachments, overflows, leaks, skids, shifts, and slips), and to the experiences of diverse peoples with conflicting interests rather than continuing to serve only the interests of the dominating and power-seeking castes? I am hardly alone in proposing such questions. They have in fact been sufficiently theorized and implemented as fields of study to have already entered academia. Even within these sheltered spaces, how do we bring into language the complexities and nuances of conflicting experience and difference, and employ language and other practices to articulate the diversity of approaches and engagements, as well as refusals?

There is no consensus that language *does* need upgrading. One is just as likely to encounter strong reactions against what might be seen as impositions of politically correct speech. A case in point, and one that is exemplary of the conflict over these questions, is around the use of gendered pronouns. A trans- or a-gender person might prefer or insist on being referred to using only gender-neutral pronouns; for example, instead of "she" or "he," the singular "they."

Typically, this poses a spectrum of difficulties (and opportunities) for faculty, staff, and students. Some adapt, seeming to easily incorporate the new language within their flow of speech. Others struggle, and occasionally stumble, correcting their own initial use of gendered pronouns. Others continue, almost adamantly, in their persistence with gendered terms, while others listen uncomfortably. Occasionally, there will be a gentle corrective inserted into the conversation.

There is a hyperawareness and discomfort for some on degendering language, and even whether or how to raise it as a question for discussion. In the absence of people who are transgender, would these questions arise? Would we in fact be politically correct in adopting the "proper" speech patterns only when under scrutiny or in the presence of those who might "take offense?"[41] Rather than this political convenience, there is a genuine politics of liberation at play here, to transcend the constraints of gender, and to verbally recognize those who are already resisting its constraints. This is liberation for all, rather than that of a supposed minority. Faculty always demand of students, and of themselves as artists, that they think outside the box or that they think and act creatively. What could be more boxed in and uncreative than these most ingrained gender values that infect our every speech?

These patterns of speech and behavior replicate earlier scenarios of racialized or sexed language, which now might be received as variously offensive, archaic, and anomalous, with others responding to correct, criticize, ignore, agree, or remain silently embarrassed. One still hears the term "oriental," for example, including from Asians. That term, while offensive in recalling and reimplanting stereotypes, seems archaic, out of step with the current world (in which Asia is central). There are those, however, who continue to use such terms as deliberate defiance of what they see as a liberal agenda to undermine traditional, even sacred, values and to restrict free speech. This is the case with the use of gender-neutral pronouns. Gender is, in fact, one of our most deeply held, deeply ingrained value systems, so enmeshed with our values of biology that those thinking across gender are accused of acting against nature.

In other scenarios, particularly that of technology, students (more so than faculty) might be supremely eager to adopt new terminologies, with every new product and app seeming to create its own new vocabulary, with acronyms and emoticons virally entering everyday speech. The willingness to adapt to technology's new languages is through the "benefits" and currency they accrue, while adapting to rethinking gender might feel like an imposed demand, and loss of a previous stability.[42]

How do we upgrade language to help imagine and make the world for the future, without its dogmatic impositions? The question is itself upgraded from that old truism of artists wanting to change the world, an ambition that now sounds charmingly naive when an MFA student has the hubris to actually voice it. Yet somehow the same claim seems plausible, or at least unashamed, when now made by MBA programs. It would be heartening if artists could reclaim this ambition to "change the world" and make it seem even remotely convincing. However, it is a mark of the corporatization of art industries—and art schools—that it is now only the "business arts," with a straight face and despite using language learned from the "fine arts," that lay claim to be changing the world.[43]

Gayatri Spivak offers another perspective, that of affirmative sabotage: "I used the term sabotage because it referred to the deliberate ruining of the master's machine from the inside. The idea is of entering the discourse that you are criticizing fully, so that you can turn it around from inside because the only way you can sabotage something is when you are working intimately with it."[44]

CHAPTER 3

HOW ART CAN BE TAUGHT

MFA: What Is It Good For?

What uses an MFA serves is under particular scrutiny when studio programs are questioned as to their economic value. Students, understandably, don't want to be saddled with massive debt and few prospects of employment. Administrations are drawn to the coupling of art with design, subsuming fine art into more fundable, financially lucrative, practical, and quantifiably productive functions. Both students and administration might find themselves using similar languages of innovation, human enrichment, and social concern to justify usefulness and financial viability.

In a society in which everything is delegated a purpose and valued according to its economic use (even if its use value is largely symbolic), art and the MFA serve counterfunctions in not being reduced to professional, political, ideological, social, or financial purposes or placed in service to set beliefs and established practices. Art and the MFA may and do necessarily perform all of these functions, but they even more necessarily resist being *reduced* to those functions. Without abandoning all else that they can achieve and produce, art and the MFA should also strive to be *for* absolutely nothing, the nothing that is resistant to being instrumentalized for other purposes, and that allows for other, as yet unconstrained possibilities.[1] This is not the same as the modernist, still-lingering call for artistic autonomy but an inquiry into what else art can do beyond the economic demands placed upon it.

As an example of conflicting desires between administrations and students, at the end of their semester in spring 2015, the entire cohort of seven MFA students "resigned" their studentships at the University of Southern California (USC) Roski School of Art and Design (already renamed from the school formerly known as Roski School of Fine Arts).[2] The students' main grievances were the broken promises made by the administration against a background of the university opening a new, heavily funded "academy" bearing its donor names, the USC Jimmy Iovine and Andre Young Academy for Arts, Technology, and the Business of Innovation. In Iovine's words, "We wanted to build a school that we feel is what the entertainment industry needs right now. . . . The kid who's going to have an advantage in the entertainment industry today is the kid who speaks both languages: technology and liberal arts. That's what this school is about." Iovine further clarifies: "We want kids who can work at Beats or at Apple."[3]

While USC has since rebuilt the collapsed MFA program with an influx of new faculty, the academy's "Arts, Technology, and the Business of Innovation" functions as industry feeder, a "creative" version of trade schools that, despite its rhetoric of "disruptive innovation," is based less on ideals of liberatory education, and more on education as incorporation.[4]

There are important lessons to be learned in preparing students for the world, but design and business innovation schools that are *led* by outside industries threaten the demise of public art education represented by the arts and humanities, including BFA and MFA studio art programs—a demise that has already been impending due to high tuition rates. An ideal of learning and critical engagement as fulfilling, valuable experience in itself, rather than as a means toward future employment, begins to seem *too* idealistic—almost a wasteful indulgence—when measured against market pressures and real-world crises. While we cannot and might not wish to return to the permissive high point of art schools of the 1960s through the early 1980s, this "wasteful indulgence" is also a prevalent attitude toward art generally, especially when permissiveness now means free-trade enterprise. In this fully enterprised period, BFA and MFA programs are required to justify what exactly they mean by "studio arts" at the particular moment when the very notion of art has become so expansive as to evade identification. In order to consider their value, we need to examine what art schools do, and ultimately what art does.

Art schools might be understood as preparing students for being contemporary, professional artists—though there is a broad spectrum of what this might mean in practice. While there might be an obligation to prepare students for making a living as artists, including through the most celebrated route of commercial galleries, art fairs, and museum and biennial exhibitions, this route is one of many and should be a choice rather than the only means through which an artist's work is valued. I am also ambivalent about prioritizing this model, since the current cultural and economic climate conceives of the successful artist within the primarily *business* models of entrepreneurship and the entertainment and service industries. While there are practicalities that artists need to learn and acquire from these models, I am wary of how they may curtail and redirect artistic ambitions, and am more drawn to consider artists as similar to how Edward Said, for example, describes the intellectual: as "endowed with a faculty for representing, embodying, articulating a message, a view, an attitude, philosophy or opinion to, as well as for, a public."[5] Said goes on to explain, "One task of the intellectual is the effort to break down the stereotypes and reductive categories that are so limiting to human thought and communication."[6]

Though art is considerably more nuanced and complex than messages and views, there is much of use here in the ambition and, yes, idealism, of these *functions* of representation, embodiment, and articulation, with these being directed toward and for a public. One might even use this as a definition of the political in relation to art. Let me add Roland Barthes's clarification of *functions*: "to inform, to represent, to surprise, to cause to signify, to provoke desire."[7] I should further add that I'm not suggesting that there exist ready-made publics for art, but that art's functions include participation within and production of the public sphere, creating new audiences alongside the artworks.

While some may consider that to suggest any purpose for art is to be reductive and to constrain art's possibilities, I'm not proposing any conformity for art. My interest is in expanding the critical tools to bring more artistic possibilities into play. To conflate, paraphrase, and reiterate Barthes and Said, their points form a clear directive for the expansive possibilities of an MFA program, and point toward ambitions for art itself: a facility and a faculty to break down the stereotypes and reductive categories that are so limiting to human thought and communication, and to inform, to represent, to surprise, to cause to signify, to provoke desire, and to embody and articulate consent and dissent through a plethora of views, attitudes, philosophies, forms, representations and actions to generate a public through those practices.

Degrees of Coercion

Students enter MFA programs having varying degrees of motivation, professional desires, and ambitions about being an artist, and what kind of artist that might be. Ideally, faculty work *with* students to identify these. In practice, faculty juggle their own ambitions and ambivalences, and those of the administration, and will cultivate some student ambitions and discourage others. They do so through personal contact as well as through the institutional structures of grading, reviews, merit scholarships, and so on.

Despite the (self-)celebrated individualism of some faculty, teaching is a necessarily collective endeavor, structured through the mission of the department and the wider school, with methods and ideas reinforced, implemented, or challenged between one course and another, with the intention of preparing every student with the confidence, skills, and critical abilities to function in the contemporary and future world. Each medium and form, whether painting, printmaking, performance, sculpture, video, photography, or any of their combinations and offshoots, can be a vital part of this present and future, as ways to develop, maintain, and broaden visual and other literacies.

Art schools, at least those that are accredited and offer degrees, necessarily involve aspects of coercion, which are balanced by their more public claims to radical innovation and artistic freedoms. I'm drawing upon Gayatri Spivak's proposition that education (the humanities specifically) function as an "uncoercive rearrangement of desires."[8] The school, at its most basic, balances the sometimes overlapping, sometimes conflicting desires of its various constituents—students, faculty, staff, administration, trustees—and promotes some vision of a consolidated desire to its outlying constituents, such as its immediate locality, potential applicants, alumni, competing schools, art viewers, funders, and general public. These desires can range from the mundane, such as keeping running costs down or buying new equipment, to the more ideological, such as what kind of art the school promotes. Not all its constituents will feel the same, and the school, through its hierarchical structures and according to economic pressures, will prioritize which desires will be pursued and met, which deferred, and which will be coerced into existence and which out.

Admission and selection processes, scholarships, reviews, grades, and graduation are all rites and structures of passage and therefore of incentivization, coercion, and discipline. Similar processes, such as tenure systems, committees, administrative procedures, and attendant positions operate across the school and apply similarly to faculty and staff, but my focus here is on those procedures that operate most directly upon students. Even without these overt disciplinary structures in place, the hidden, regulatory forces of competition, peer pressure, favoritism, cronyism, and exclusion still operate if left unacknowledged (and, as mentioned previously, the easy conviviality of hanging out in bars is precisely where and when these hidden forces are particularly operative).

Mediating the polarities of discipline and freedom are the school's assessment procedures. Though decried as bureaucratic interference, and while they can and are used as disciplinary measures, assessments can be a way to track a number of questions: What are students learning? How are they learning it? At what rate are they learning? Are there ways to optimize learning? Which students are not learning? Why are they not learning? What pedagogical methods are appropriate to the present student body?

These are highly contested questions for any subject but particularly in relation to art, since what is taught and learned cannot be measured through the typical educational methods of testing, nor through the corporatized demand for efficiency or preparation for the job market.

Artists who teach often have an antagonistic relationship to these policies and find different ways to circumvent them. Joseph Beuys, probably the best-known example, was famously fired in 1972 from his professorship at the Dusseldorf Art Academy for opening his classes to students who had failed the entrance exams. But Beuys was also notoriously authoritarian in the classroom even as he zealously espoused antiauthoritarian politics.[9] Beuys (successfully rehabilitated as a political artist after volunteering for the Hitler Youth and Luftwaffe) continues to resonate with students and faculty in today's art schools, but figures like him, no matter how "charismatic," might also seem like holdovers from a previous era.

Since we live in multiply and complexly coercive societies that have nevertheless benefited from and adapted in various degrees to and against movements for social justice, the school bears some responsibility to prepare students to function (and thrive) within—and to resist—the coercive, competitive, contemporary world. This needs to be done alongside developing uncoercive alternatives or counterpractices, partly to maintain, defend, continue, and extend those egalitarian movements (it might seem that schools have no obligation to perform these latter roles, even when students demand such obligations from the school; this, however, is one place for carefully drafted policies that require schools to prevent the discrimination that occurs under the guise of healthy competition or that attributed to the charm of individual faculty). In order to perform these multiple tasks, the school needs to recognize, articulate, and align its own disciplinary and counterdisciplinary practices, and to do so on every level of its functioning, beyond its marketing rhetoric of artistic freedoms.

Reskilling

Art schools, particularly within undergraduate programs, might be expected to educate students across a six-track program:

1. To acquire and develop practical production skills across different disciplines, e.g., digital media, painting, photography, sculpture, video, and so on
2. To gain knowledge of art histories and how art discourses and practices have morphed into current understandings and forms
3. To gain conceptual and associative skills in the generation and evaluation of artistic work
4. To learn (to apply) theory and analytic (art critical) skills, including in speech and writing
5. To develop the above skills as part of or within social and ethical practices
6. To translate all the above toward professional and career development.

Teaching art is most commonly approached through techniques of making. Students are taught various technical skills, which might be accompanied by histories of making. Knowledge of *who, what, where,* and *when* are certainly necessary for any artist to understand the sources for "their" ideas. But these can mislead and misinform—in that they invariably consider only Europe and North America, almost exclusively white Euro American and predominantly male artists. Art history books, for example, might try to compensate by having a concluding chapter on "identity" in which women and nonwhite artists are grouped; art schools may also provide an addendum in the form of a "global perspectives" course. Both strategies leave the canon uncontested, intact, and centralized, and suggest that identity is the concern of only women and nonwhite artists (and that identity is their *only* concern). [#Identity]

Even within the restricted geoculture of the canon, attention is further limited to just Paris and New York if the time period being taught is within the last one hundred and fifty years. What tends to be neglected within these scenarios—and there now are numerous contestations of their centrality—is the how and the why, including *why* so much of the globe and its populations are omitted from the when, where, and who.

I'm not proposing that the canon should no longer be taught, or should simply be replaced by a "more colorful" roster. Any work needs to be historicized in its own time, in relation to other works, ideas, movements, and practices that both support and counter it. Students cannot be taught to think critically if they are provided only with singular narratives. Nor am I suggesting that one can adequately teach any kind of global scope within the limited frames of art school classes. No curriculum can cover everything, but nor should anything (art history, a skill, a mode of thinking) be taught as though it were the *only* knowledge or the only method. If technical skills, language, and information are tools of instruction, three of the means through which art can be taught, those tools not only need to be placed and nurtured in the hands and minds of students, but the skills, language, information, and tools to *examine* skills, language, information, and tools are a crucial part of that teaching to better enable students to advance and invent new means rather than replicating only what they have been taught.

Skills, language, information, and tools have value, and these values also need to be taught—not simply so they can in turn be valued, but to understand *why* they are valued, *by whom*, how that value changes according to different circumstances, and what purposes that value *serves*. The *how*, the *why*, the *with what, for what*, and *why* again are crucial in the teaching of art, even though the narrowed *what*, *who*, *where* and *when* are easier and more likely to be taught, and with that narrow focus—essentially a parochial identitarian view—consequently standing in for the global and the universal.

These limitations of what gets taught are also a question of habit—to be generous—and intent—to be less so. Art schools generally want their faculty to appear to be at the forefront of whatever's considered important within art—to attract and keep students—and so they have a vested interest in teaching the kind of work, ideologies, and histories that reflect their own faculties and that make their faculties look attractive to prospective and ongoing students. As older faculty fade off into their more or less in/glorious sunsets, their students—taught in the same kinds of work, ideologies and histories—will replace them to perpetuate the same parochialism. While this "Great Chain of Being" is still common, thankfully it is becoming increasingly unlinked.

•

The above are questions of what is practically taught—questions that schools can fairly easily decide. But core conceptual and political questions that determine the practical include: How does one teach or learn art? And can art be taught or learned? These are questions that the art school tends to avoid, even as many of its faculty may answer in the negative. A previous touchstone for my perusal of these questions is James Elkins's book *Why Art Cannot Be Taught*.[10] I recognize the polemical impetus behind Elkins's title, and have opted for a similar titling. Embedded in *my* title are other meanings of how we think through art, and how art making itself can be a form of thinking.

Despite the homonym of my title, I don't think "Can art be taught?" is the right question. If we could say exactly what art is and what it is not, then we could teach it. But that would be to teach what is already known and what has been done. Students are taught the tools and skills of a discipline, within the greater or lesser confines of what is understood, advocated, and practiced by the instructor. When art, or art making, is being taught, it might often be art like that of the instructor or art as understood by the instructor, and what gets made in the guise of art might tend toward a continuation of that instructor's work and ideas. This is a fully normalized mode of teaching within most academic disciplines, with faculty generally teaching their research areas, or with graduate students assisting and participating in their professors' research. Unlike art pedagogy, where assumptions are that information and technique are highly subjective, the assumption in most other disciplines is that one is imparting objective information and dispassionate technique. That mode of teaching one's immediate artistic discipline and methodology *is* a large practical part and common aspect of art teaching, but it shouldn't be its primary *intent*. Students are taught a discipline (including its histories and ideologies) with the *intent* that they can apply themselves to further that discipline. How they might further it is, by definition, not yet known. This is true of any discipline, whether literature, physics, engineering, or law, though each discipline will invest different weight in "tradition."

I want to expand on this by reemphasizing the "how" and the "different ways." Two examples might suffice for now. In the first example, while teaching technical skills, it is important to teach students how to recognize productive accidents. When something might appear to be wrong or to have turned out different from expectations, a skill is knowing to identify and act upon what possibilities might be opened up by the accident. An accident, what Glissant calls "the joy of poetics," is when something fails to follow the rules, which is different from actually failing, since it may now operate along different lines (that have not yet become rules).[11] Crucial aspects of an artist's training are learning what those rules are and how to activate their fissures. If a teacher's method is to tell the student what is good and bad, the student is being instructed on *what* to think and to act "correctly" within the rules (along the same patterns as the instructor), but not how to make such evaluations for herself based on different sets of criteria for different circumstances and different kinds of work—all of which come into play when accidents happen.[12]

In the second example, not all students will go on to pursue research, in the same way that not all artists will produce as yet unknown forms of art. Most will continue to work within the realm of the familiar. We couldn't function as a society in the same ways if this were not the case: artistic labor takes many forms in maintaining the familiar within different industries and services, including making or keeping our private and public spaces habitable, pleasurable, and even meaningful (which might be another way to think of what is often disparaged as design and decoration).[13] The research that *some* students will pursue will uncover new material, new insights, and new techniques, but also reuses, revisions, and reconfigurations of the old and already existing. The former teachers of these students will not have known any of these future discoveries or revisions, so it's technically accurate to say that they wouldn't have taught them.

Yet *some* things have been taught, and I would say that prime among these are ways to implement one's own learning in growing independence from one's teachers. Closely linked to this is how to direct one's focus.[14] One might also word it this way: Teaching provides students with different ways to think (at least within and through the disciplines being taught). Art, then, strictly speaking, *isn't* taught. What are taught instead are *technical, conceptual, and critical methods to pursue art*. In being taught how to pursue art, the student is better prepared to develop her *own* work. Being taught art, and subsequently being a working artist, is implemented in ways similar to what Edward Said writes of, in relation to the intellectual, "not as a fixed task to be learned once and for all from a how-to-do-it manual but as a concrete experience constantly threatened by modern life itself."[15] If the teaching of art is traditionally held as the teaching of the known, that is, of the past, the challenge is to teach art in ways for students to implement the known of the past in order to envisage futures and to adapt to continuous, threatening presents.

CHAPTER 4

CRITIQUE AS RADICAL PROTOTYPE

Genealogies

In an era of rapid technological and social changes—progressive *and* retrogressive—that cause disruptive social anxiety and upheaval, what does it mean to espouse the radical?[1] In relation to critique, we may well ask what is its radical potential, and what is it to be radical? For what radical possibilities is critique a prototype? First, critique seeks to actively dismantle the building bricks of what may lead to the totalitarianisms of both mundane and "radical" fundamentalisms. Second, it is not a call for newness, which is a typical demand of the radical. If anything, critique examines and readdresses what is already in place (or imagined to have been in place—a familiar imagining by fundamentalisms). Following Foucault, "The most radical discontinuities are the breaks effected by a work of theoretical transformation 'which establishes a science by detaching it from the ideology of its past and by revealing this past as ideological.'"[2] Critique's partial aim, through discontinuities, insubordinations, and interruptions, is to reveal the ideological patterns through which art (in this case) is experienced, to detach and transform it from its foundations, and to make it differently operational in the present/future—these various moves tracked as genealogies.

While critique is a primary mode of art pedagogy, it can be situated more broadly in relation to performance and as an art practice in itself, closely related to social practice. It can be considered as rehearsal, staging, or prototype for social behavior, following Allan Kaprow's "Happenings" alongside radical theater practices, such as those of Augusto Boal and Jerzy Grotowski, with their respective proposals of theater of the oppressed and poor theater. I cite these with caution regarding their calls toward authentic experience as precursors to liberation (Grotowski: "Art is a ripening, an evolution, an uplifting which enables us to emerge from darkness into a blaze of light. We fight then to discover, to experience the truth about ourselves; to tear away the masks behind which we hide daily."). More immediate references for what it means *to* critique are drawn from theorists Michel Foucault and Judith Butler.

Drawing upon its genealogies, critique is a participatory event and an adaptive system that requires participation in order to *be* adaptive and critical. The critique is also the strategy, labor, and *practice* of thinking together. To paraphrase Édouard Glissant, critique is a *criticality in relation*, "in which each and every identity is extended through a relationship with the Other."[3] This is principally how critique differs from what Grotowski is suggesting above. The critique is not in search of uncovering truths but in developing different relations, or rather, relations across difference, founded in mutual inquiry.

These functions of critique take on increased urgency in how individuals and collectives act in/with the world, and in how art becomes a site and discourse of experience, consent, dissent, and interrogation of historicized contemporaneity.

Methodologies

While critique needs to be continually adaptive, these are some of its most common forms:

1. The student introduces their work:
   a. The student initiates discussion with a short presentation on their work, perhaps from a written statement. The class enters into discussion and asks questions of the student, to which the student may reply. The limitation here is that the statement and the student's intentions might inflect how the class responds to the work, to the extent where the class might be responding as much as or more to the statement than to the work itself. The student's intention can be given varying importance: from none at all to determining the viewers' understanding of the meaning of the work.
   b. Each student in the class writes down their individual responses; the responses are collected and major points are discussed without

reference to who wrote them. This has the benefit of enabling quieter students to have a greater input. Students whose first language is not English might also find this method easier.

2. The instructor initiates discussion with a series of questions, which includes the student being critiqued.

3. The student may initiate discussion with a series of questions or directions on what they would like to be addressed within the critique. This is particularly useful for a second or third critique of the student's work, so as not to replicate previous discussions. It should not be used, however, to preclude other discussions that have not been directed by the student.

4. Anyone can begin the discussion with any thought that arises; the student being critiqued joins in the discussion, explaining or defending her work as necessary.

5. The student whose work is being discussed may only provide a title for the work, and beyond that does not speak (or may provide only a short, uninterrupted response at the end of the class discussion).

I favor the last model, and explain that preference by suggesting an analogy with the gallery space in which the viewer encounters the work without description from the artist, while the presenting student is also freed from having to defend or explain the work. This method shifts the emphasis to the viewers, and to how meaning is constructed through engagement with the work. This is also where discussion can clarify the prior knowledges, and the critical and theoretical approaches that might be available to viewers to understand and interpret their viewing.

The critique takes account of the work, the viewer, and the encounter between them, including a bodily engagement in relation to senses and affect, the physical form/space of the work, and the form/space in which the work is encountered. The critique is the site or event—the happening—for the production of knowledge that is localized and contextualized through the art object/site/event, but also an examination of that knowledge and its processes of coming into being. If meaning is accumulated and constructed through the viewers' (note the plural) sensory encounters with the art object/event, the role of the critique is to examine those encounters and the processes through which meaning is constructed, individually and collectively. Since encounters occur within a system of discourses, those discourses through which meaning is produced also need to be examined.

In its necessary shift toward the interdisciplinary, the critique is loosened from defined structures to uncover and/or produce different meanings and potentially new structures. It can be understood as crossing disciplines to generate new connections, but also as knowledge that is akin to art making itself, as a process of bringing into being that which might not have previously existed. It is a method that links learning to discovery and invention, where participants are not taught what to think but practice the tools through which they become independent thinkers.

The critique models that I outlined are informed by poststructuralist literary criticism and rhetorical analysis. These engage the artwork as a text, with all that "reading" entails, less to be interpreted as to *what* the artwork means, and more to investigate how the artwork *is brought into* meaning by its readers within and beyond the particular dynamics of the critique.

Regarding structure, consistency, and content, the critique benefits when there is a process/methodology that is understood by its participants. As facilitator, the faculty member (usually) is required to pose questions, to listen to and correlate (the perhaps fragmentary) responses from the group, and to interpret them toward a coherent argument or toward further questions; to maintain the desired dynamics of the group ensuring each person is enabled to contribute, that no one person dominates, to maintain "constructive" criticism, to acknowledge but curtail "unproductive" criticism, and to ensure that no one is bullied—an outsider might be shocked at the level this can occur within critiques; and to enable a momentum of discussion, to maintain a level of equanimity by returning to the subject under discussion. It is these processes as *intentional practices* that form the pedagogical model, that make intent visible, that generate consistency and content.

To use the metaphor of the "field" of study: any given field, even an "expanded" one, is defined by its boundaries.[4] An expandable field necessitates a mobile boundary. The critique networks those boundaries that separate and connect, and that are also spaces unto themselves. Imagine then, a network of these "boundaries" as connective tissue that allows movement between fields, that allows (re)linking them in ways that respond to continually changing conditions.

The critique requires these different, mobile fields of knowledge. Some approaches involve, obviously, knowledge of art history and of contemporary art. Other interpretive tools include criticism developed through feminism, postcolonial studies, queer theory, psychoanalysis, and so on. I emphasize these tools for the critique as a bodily encounter—one that is sensory, spatial, experienced—primarily because these are "embodied theories," in that they speak to, and from, specifically located bodily encounters of being in/with the world. While the critique might not provide the time to expound on theory, it is the place where participants can experience theory's application. Discussions might proceed from seemingly obvious questions: How do we know or interpret what we (or our senses) experience? And how do we share that experience through language? These investigations may also attempt to address the ambivalence, contradiction, and multiplicity of experience.

Rather than favor one method exclusively over another, each might allow particular insights, and their cross-referencing and testing in relation to the artwork being critiqued allows us to develop expanded models of interpretation that might otherwise not be available.

The critique is ostensibly for the benefit of the student showing their work, and there is a required act of generosity on the part of the other participants to engage with that student's work, even though they expect generosity to be reciprocated when it is their turns. It's a mutual generosity, but it is also a trade. The critique benefits all participants in that they learn and practice how to track and articulate their responses to another's work, and to artwork in general, and—most importantly for them as artists—this practice enables them to apply the same process to their own work. They learn, in effect, how to become their own critical audience.

Critique participants comprise a selective group, and a group that over a semester becomes more familiar with each other and their different works. In this case, the critique is cumulative, with each student's work critiqued twice or perhaps three times over the semester, and with each member learning about and from each other, with the development also of different affiliations and antagonisms. This accumulated experience and knowledge is a necessary one for any engagement with art, and is a further counter to the otherwise celebrated attitude I have already mentioned of equating an open mind with a blank mind.

Critter Training

For a first critique with any group, it is sometimes useful to slow down the process and track how individuals access information about the artwork before they begin processing and making sense of it. We can begin from the entrance of the room, *as* we enter. What are the first things we see (hear, smell, touch, physically register)? It's surprising how quickly most of us speed past this stage to try and narrate the work before tracking what our senses have registered. Looking, listening, smelling, touching (if the work requires it) and a sense of scale (how much space and how the work occupies space in relation to our own bodies and to the architecture of the space in which we encounter the work)— all of these complex and vast amounts of information are swiftly registered without conscious thought, what is referred to as "sensory memory." And yet this is the data that is processed and from which meaning is first generated. After that come all the associations, our own memories and experiences ("it makes me think of . . ."), emotions ("it makes me feel . . ."), art historical associations, theoretical insights and questions, political issues, and so on.

The critique can delay all these connections until further discussion of sensory input, which may also be approached as formal concerns of color, size, shape, line, gesture, and duration. From there the critique can investigate the associations and sources for the work's formal and material aspects, and from *there* continue with each participant's other free-associated responses, while bringing the discussion always back to the work itself.

The venue where the critique takes place is a prime factor in determining its processes and possible outcomes. Generally the critique will take place in the artist's studio, with the work to be addressed surrounded by the paraphernalia of the artist's other projects, raw and research materials, and sketches. Typically, the artist will have already made a selection of what is to be addressed, of what is the work and what isn't. This selection can itself be brought into question in the critique, which may reidentify what and where the work is, since the space in which the work is encountered constitutes the experiential field. Treating the entire space as installation, and as discursive field, may lead to connections that the artist might not have made between objects (some of which might not yet be identified as works), with the possible result of redirecting the work.

The structure above is more of a suggestion for viewer training as an *active* process, and isn't how the critique itself will actually work. In practice, it will flit in and out of any of these observations and connections, as participants will want to voice whatever thoughts arise, when they arise. This looseness is also necessary, since most of us can't suppress our own eager thoughts *and* simultaneously follow someone else's convoluted and often partially articulated comments.

But this is what is required of the faculty: to keep track of everyone's contributions, acknowledge each one, sometimes rearticulate and translate, but maintain the flow and direction of the larger discussion and return to other points when the opportunity arises or when they are relevant to the discussion. The faculty also needs to make sure no one person (including themselves!) is dominating the discussion, that whoever wants to speak is given a chance, and those who don't seem to want to speak should also be coaxed, perhaps with direct questions. While all this is going on, and since this is a school and likely a class, the faculty has to maintain a sense of each person's engagement and participation (two different things, since engagement is not necessarily verbal), and make their own evaluation of the work for whatever requirement the class and school puts on grading.

Critical Language

Any critique method requires language that is purposeful and directed toward enabling and clarifying meaning—despite how obfuscating, nonsensical, and even pretentious the critique might appear to visitors or to those new to it. If we don't examine the critique, we maintain the actual obfuscations, non-sense, pretentions, and narrowed perspectives that too often constitute discussions of art.

I'm not proposing that clarity and transparency of language, or an insistence on rationality, can be blanket substitutes for other practices such as empathy and listening for what isn't said, or that speech can always account for and translate sensory experience. The critique implements an aspiration *toward* articulation. It necessitates simultaneously tracking the unspoken in order to bring into language what might otherwise be unspeakable. This is particularly the case since participants are attempting to articulate their own sensory responses through the psychic narratives they have formed (and that have formed them).

Precision of language is not an end in itself but a tool to describe the conjunctions and consequences of these multiple experiences, locations, subjectivities, and encounters. One consequence is that, through these repositions of the work and the viewer, both are decentered from their previously held authority, or, more accurately, from their unchallenged insularity and silences, and are variously reconnected to the positions of others. This is not a process without conflict, especially considering that the critique may challenge participants' most deeply held views.

Clarity and flexibility of language are essential to the critique. By "flexibility" I mean being able to adapt language from different sources, including various theoretical models, popular culture, and art history, toward analyzing the artwork and translating its affect. Clarity is not to be confused with simplistic language, with plain-speak, or with euphemistic language that hides meaning. It is not meant to make theory "accessible." It is not meant to spare us from the *labor* of thinking. It strives for language that is nimble, expansive, precise, and adequate to the multiform tasks of describing and identifying what happens in the encounter with art. It requires locating each person's responses in dialogue with the responses of others.

Yet the critique is where individuals with different language skills together attempt to put into words emotions, partial thoughts, fleeting impressions, and associations that many might not yet have vocabularies for. This is difficult enough without throwing into the mix introverts and extroverts, friendships, antagonisms, ambitions, shyness, egos, garrulousness, showboating, and a whole slew of other social strategies, skills, and dysfunctions.

Conflict Irresolution

The critique is not intended toward avoiding or pacifying conflict but toward identifying and articulating the motivating desires, anxieties, and investments that, when left unaddressed, underlie and produce conflict. Nor is the critique intended to produce resolution or even arbitration. The critique's role is to "bring forth" different and sometimes conflicting identifications, meanings, understandings, and possibilities, which, in turn, is not to suggest that all positions carry equal weight or are equally valid. Everyone might be entitled to an opinion, but there is no entitlement to have one's opinion given equal weight as others. The critique tracks histories of any position and view in order to examine their formations and consequences.

Rather than promoting a rosy vision of the critique as an idealistic event where we can "all just get along" and convivially uncover art's meanings, the critique is inevitably a place of irresolution, where one's identifications, positions, and assertions are recognized as only *some* among others.[5] Failing to acknowledge and address these irresolutions can escalate conflict, even when discernible conflict is suppressed and rendered mute. As I have already stated, the critique's role is not to solve or pacify these conflicts but to produce a different model whereby conflicting opinions can coexist, without resort to more aggressive forms of antagonism. Allowing for the coexistence of conflicting opinions also means that one's own opinions are always provisional.

Like any social gathering, there are too many hierarchies, emotions, vested interests, competitive egos, and conflicting opinions, with all manner of incentives and disincentives to participate. Many students will feel reticent to speak forthrightly, to say what they "really" think. Others will feel it their moral imperative to speak without filters. The more there is at stake, the more participants might hold back on expressing their opinions in order to avoid conflict or to avoid exposing vulnerabilities.

Critique participants might be offended or angered by certain works, with offense experienced as bodily hurt. Offense might also be caused but not voiced. Defending creative works as protected by free speech does not address that offense or anger. An underlying reason for being offended by artworks is that we still tend to believe that art should be uplifting and somehow good for us. We can instead address one function of art as testing limits, even if it is only aesthetic limits. We can consider that art necessarily produces levels of comfort and discomfort. We might still not want to look at an artwork, but we are less offended if our attention is directed toward what produces discomfort, why it is produced, and how it is experienced. When offense is caused (voiced or not), whether by a work or by something said, it remains important to develop modes of address without dismissal, where what is causing offense, why offense was taken, and the precursors and consequences of the offense—cause and effect—can be acknowledged and examined. This cannot always be addressed in the heat of the moment when offense is caused, since it will invariably lead the discussion away from the artwork, and with the student being critted resenting that their crit "has been hijacked by someone else's feelings" (as it is commonly voiced). The faculty may need to acknowledge the offense, and return to it later as a specific discussion, and without putting the onus of explanation on the person who is offended. A person of color, for example, shouldn't have to perform the labor of explaining why a work or comment is racially offensive; this kind of labor should be undertaken by the whole group.

●

The critique proceeds from the processing of sensory data to examine the means, tools, and language through which meaning is generated. The production and *ownership* of meaning always carries with it threatening aspects, since it raises the likely prospects of disagreement, misunderstanding, nonunderstanding, incommensurability, and open conflict, particularly given that the critique group will consist of individuals already selected for their ambition and self-interest.[6] It is a mix that can expose or produce responses of withdrawal, isolation, shame and shaming, fear, anxiety, anger, and chronic hurt, as well as the more intended responses of insight, knowledge, fulfillment, pleasure, validation, criticality, and intersectional thinking.

The critique differs from so-called real-life outside art school in its agreement of mutual recognition of intersecting selves.[7] Without that ideal—and it is an ideal that is often not practiced—there is no investment in listening to and incorporating different, let alone opposing, opinions. If the critique cannot face and address these within its managed, slightly protected space, it can't begin to address questions of difference, the negotiation of which in the contemporary world forms the basis for our sociability or lack of it.[8] In the real world, difference of opinion and position might be escalated by political divisions, as well as locked into bodily difference—and *those* differences are variously punished by a catalogue of exclusion and violence.[9] The critique aims to track and unpack such cataloguing, in order to further unpack constructions of difference. This is not to separate difference into identifiable and hierarchical categories but to proceed from the understanding that any sense of self is constructed through difference, and is therefore to further understand individual investments in both isolating and incorporating difference.

While the critique is an event in which actual social relations are enacted with the artwork as one intermediary, the critique might also be considered a rehearsal or trial space where ideas and social interaction are tested within the relative safety of limited consequences. Despite occasional provocations by faculty and students, and claims to artistic license and academic freedoms, critiques are nevertheless controlled zones subject to the school's chain of authority. The critique is a sheltered, directed space rather than a safe space. Students *will* be challenged and destabilized, but the critique can at least offer the possibility of not humiliating anyone for their views, opinions, or comments, even as those are interrogated and tested against others. Discriminatory views do get voiced, and they need to be attended to. But it is also a pretense to imagine that we are free from such views, that if they are not voiced that they are not held, or that when they are voiced we can surmount them by shouting them down. If the critique is to uncoercively rearrange desires (and anxieties), they have to be aired and attended to, as they occur, or they may be acknowledged and returned to later. And like the critique's attitudes toward other forms of judgment, judgment here should also be deferred.

An imperative within the critique is not the banal celebration of difference that some dismiss as the diluted hallmarks of both multiculturalism and postmodernism but to address the multiple positionings from which different subjectivities experience the artwork (and, through multiple extensions, the world beyond). One can also approach this from the imagined perspective of the artwork: how would the artwork function in different locations and with different viewers? This is a useful exercise, though it has to be remembered that it is a fictional undertaking and runs the risk of speaking for others.

Even as I haltingly distinguish the critique from real life, I am linking (through Foucault and Butler) the critique's methodologies to democratic ideals as a theorizing of means to negotiate conflict and as an interrogatory or investigatory conviviality. Conversely, participants might experience the critique process as an authoritarian one, feeling that it is indoctrinating and institutionalizing them to the faculty's viewpoint or at least to those who are most outspoken. However, student refusal, when expressed within the critique and against the perceived authority of the institution, is not radical when it is a refusal to attend to differing views or to having one's own views interrogated. This refusal may cohere around dominant formations, such as of gender, race, and class— either of the student's or against that of the faculty. In such situations, what might typically occur is that participants might not articulate their rejection of faculty views but might simply refuse any kind of critical rethinking of their work, rejecting it as an imposition of an outsider's opinion, thereby remaining entrenched within their unexamined convictions. Typical of this claim to individual sovereignty is the insistence that the work is the unassailable manifestation of the artist's interiority, which no one else can speak to. The critique needs to resist this tendency, and investigate claims to/of interiority, and articulate its affects.

Bad Critter

Since artist teachers regard the critique as a prime, almost sacrosanct, practice of their academic, artistic, and personal freedoms, and conventionally link it to discourses of truth and authentic feeling, institutional prescriptions for critique risk being seen as curtailing individual liberties and individualism itself.

The critique may seem aimless, unaligned, and seemingly dependent on the whims of the instructor leading it, and may appear to have no structure except for the arbitrary ending of the class session. This apparent lack of rules and its celebrated "anything goes" attitude are often its hallmark, a vaunted freedom that—from the points of view of students and faculty—exemplifies the art school experience, though this lack of regulation and accountability may be the bane of administrations. The "anything goes" method tends to reproduce the cults of personality, prejudices, and competition already rife within art industries—and that was its primary justification, that it prepared students *for* art industries. It did so by replicating and perpetuating all the hierarchies and discriminations within art industries, whether class-based, sexual, gendered, or racial. This can foster a pack mentality. As Mary Kelly has described it, it was commonplace to "crit the girls and make them cry."[10]

Critiques might promote the idea of no limits, to push beyond the participants' cursory responses, and to allow for anything to happen. Michael Asher at CalArts, for example, was renowned for conducting critiques over two or three days. It's difficult to do that now—the "professionalization" and goal orientation of current students inclines and pressures them toward immediate answers. Also, students' notions of fairness is that everyone should have an equal amount of allotted time, with no one treated preferentially or given more attention or time.

●

Critiques that are finely attuned to one medium or discipline are necessary to address the particularities and demands of that medium. For example, photography departments will discuss certain "problems" of the photograph, including equipment issues and technical and aesthetic judgments, such as exposure settings, tonal gradation, color balance, and so on. While necessary, these critiques can, however, produce their own restrictions. Their consistent framing of discussions within the perceived limitations and possibilities of the medium as it is taught and practiced by the participants within the critique tends to build a frame for the critique itself as well as establishing a consensus of what the critique should address and resolve. It also produces the participants as a certain kind of practitioner and viewer with orthodox judgments and values, and perspectives and goals of what that medium could and should be. This shared perspective is useful to identify questions, problems, and possibilities from within a discipline. It can also restrict what those questions, problems, and possibilities might be.

This orthodoxy might not and usually does not translate well to another medium or even to a different method of photography that is derived from a different set of values, intentions, and judgments. This one hypothetical group of photographers trained in their particular critique methods might find themselves unable to apply their methodologies to artwork of another medium. Similarly, they might defend their method against a group of painters, say, trained in a method specific to *that* discipline, even to the extent of closing off their respective disciplines from "outside" intrusion.

Medium-specific critiques can prove inadequate for the interdisciplinary ideas, sources, and practices of much contemporary art, which might require critiques that are more fluid in their discussion, more open to contradictory viewpoints, less willing to arrive at evaluations of good and bad, more attendant to the process and criteria adopted by the critique through which meanings are formed, and more willing to process multiple meanings.

Some practitioners have positioned critique as, in the words of James Elkins, a form of rhetoric, "since it is not concerned with consistency or even content as much as it is in the art of persuasion."[11] The critique forms I advocate invert this equation to ones that are less concerned with persuasion than they are with sowing doubt, to shift the student toward investigating what they already (think they) know and experience. Here, one can consider the artwork (its medium, its form, and its aesthetic choices) as an unsolvable crime scene, as it were, and the investigation is conducted upon it, not to establish who did it (the artist, and the wider culture) but to track how it comes into being.[12]

·●·

Critiques can replicate the therapy or support practices that have come to be known as "encounter groups," and of their very opposites (the critique that requires subsequent therapy). Such critiques might be led by authoritarian leaders (rather than facilitators), who can range from the benevolent (relying on charismatic personality, telling students what is good and bad, what works and what doesn't) to more immediately destructive effects (humiliating participants and their work, and goading others to do the same). Conversely, participants might be implicitly supported and celebrated regardless of their work, often incorporating language around "appreciation," "honesty," and "bravery." Other methods of the encounter group include personal revelation (and confession), and the attempt to psychoanalyze participants with the goal of understanding "hidden causes" for the artwork or for participants' responses to it. The focus of these kinds of critique is generally weighted toward the artist and participants, rather than upon the work and how *it* functions.

Like most social behaviors, the bad critique is a deliberate, purposeful practice that endures because someone and something benefits or is kept in place through its continuation. In these cases, the most immediate beneficiary is the petty authority of the instructor, who might also be inflexible in their views and uninterested in anything beyond their area of specialization.

A supplemental beneficiary is the institution, which is replicated through the next generation of artists/teachers who have been inculcated into its value systems.

If these coincide with the student's own work, these may be good critiques for that student, but it may be training the student to remain within that one particular area of practice. This may suit some students, but its outcomes are already known—we begin the critique knowing in advance what constitutes good and bad, and simply slot the work into prescribed categories. This method promotes and replicates work that is already known rather than the students being pushed toward the not yet known.

●

James Elkins proposes "five allegories for critiques: they are like seductions (they're amorous); they are like different languages all spoken at once (theoretical 'discourses,' studio talk); they are collections of stories (they are narratological); they are like battles (they're warlike, people fight); and they are like court cases (people argue, judgments are expected)."[13]

These might accurately describe common critique practices: that some are seduced, some are rejected; that it is a free-for-all battleground, dominated by the most forceful; that meaning is personal and individual; that no one is responsible for what happens; that a person or artwork is on trial. They may be common, but they are obsolete for addressing the social and political demands made by every liberatory social movement since the advent of modernism (feminism, decolonization, Civil Rights, gay-, queer-, trans-liberation, and disability rights, to identify a few). They are, in fact, *deliberate* in training against liberatory education.

These kinds of critiques might act upon and act out the myths that art functions beyond language; that art cannot be examined (through language), only experienced; and its opposite, that art can be accessed *only* through language, and has no affect upon the body; that art is ineffable, transcendent, and beyond meaning and purpose; that art can be evaluated only through already accepted criteria of quality; that quality is unbiased and objective; and that art functions universally.

I am not dismissing these as potential values and as possibilities for art to pursue, only pointing out that the rhetoric of transcendence, quality, freedoms, and universalism is, in practice—and I mean as an applied practice—a perpetuation of the kinds of art and teaching that are already known and that serve narrow interests. Making judgments about good and bad art *without examining the judgments themselves*, who makes them and the basis on which they are made, and whose interests those judgments serve, might be typical of much art discourse, but it is also symptomatic of self-perpetuating authority.

Doubt

Doubt, the operation of "discontinuities and interruptions," is necessary for making or thinking through artworks. Doubt resists the tendency to settle upon immediate resolutions, a tendency that forecloses further investigation and other solutions.

The critique necessarily casts doubt upon the ability of preconceived ideas to account for continuing experience and information. Notwithstanding that preconceived ideas are prerequisites for engaging with art, the purpose of critique is forward looking rather than establishing what is already known/believed. The critique tests, questions, discontinues, interrupts, and, if necessary, reformulates received ideas to attend to and investigate experience, and to open up and pursue possibilities activated in the encounter with artwork.

This pursuit ties critique closely with art making and doing. While critique might open up fissures of how the artwork is experienced, the artist who returns to their work after it is critiqued may further investigate those fissures through the disciplines and materiality of the work.

The doubt that I am advocating is a radical skepticism that is turned toward constituting discourses. When turned inward, this doubt is employed not to *judge* the self but to evaluate how that self has been constituted. This doubt accepts that there are other, equally valid perspectives, forms, methods, answers, and questions than one's own. And when these are applied and tested against the work, they form a fuller account of how the work might function with different audiences: which is to say, how the work will function *in/with the world*.

Doubt is also a necessary attribute, or rather, consequence, of attempting to work in the present, since one doesn't have the foresight of what the outcome will be. History provides lessons in probability, much like theatrical rehearsal: *if I do this, this is the likely outcome*. But to act without rehearsal is to invite unknown, potentially destabilizing outcomes—an attitude that is at the core of performance art and that has become almost its foundational guideline. The caveat to this is that we never fully escape history's precursors and probabilities, in the same way that we can never begin from clean slates and "open minds." We cannot function without preconceptions, since preconceptions are the prior knowledge and imagination that enable us to situate ourselves in/with the world and in time, and that provide the ground from which we can make sense of any new encounter. Making and experiencing art are fully dependent on abilities to conceptualize based on prior knowledge and experience. An "open mind" is a vacant mind, uninformed by history, even by that of its own memory, and is therefore a mind that spirals out of time. Destabilization and momentarily snatching us out of linear time are some of art's most provocative potentials—and ones I do not discount. But such potential, even to discuss if and how it can happen, requires an engaged mind, and an appropriately expansive and critical set of tools, including that of language.

Doubt's role is not to eradicate or diminish belief but to allow for belief to adjust to changing experience, circumstance, and information. Doubt's allowance for these changes marks it as categorically different from and opposed to denial.

In the actions described above, doubt is similar to the "hermeneutics of suspicion" espoused by Paul Ricoeur, and elaborated within literary critique by others, such as Rita Felski.[14] I would add to "suspicion" the actions of being suspect. People of color will already know on a daily basis what it means to feel suspected. I'm suggesting that prejudicial tool being redirected toward a critical purpose, suspecting in its dual inferences of detecting and dissenting, with these actions directed to authorities without and already incorporated within.

●

Self-doubt manifests differently, and can mean the debilitating self-doubt of "shyness," which female students, particularly, may offer as reason for not speaking in critiques. In smaller groups and with their female peers, they are more likely to speak openly. This points to chronic silencing by dominating male voices, and the *normalized*, everyday circumstances in which gendered and racialized subjectivities are marginalized *as* subjects. While the critique is not able to address pathologies of shyness, it can respond by interrupting the social habits that enable some to dominate conversation, and others to feel silenced by that domination. If unaddressed, it remains a constant impediment, not only for the individual concerned but for the group, since valuable voices from different experiences are unheard.

Another example of "shyness," or at least reticence, is when white students become uncharacteristically "mute" when confronted by the work of a student of color, or by work that they perceive to be from a "different culture" or about a person's "cultural identity." They don't want to say the "wrong" thing, that is, to be perceived as being racist, and therefore will clam up. I use this example because it happens too often, with the cumulative effect on the person of color being the perception that their work doesn't matter to anyone. Here again, valuable intersections with the work are lost.

Those who don't speak are not acting neutrally, nor is their silence merely an absence of voice. Their silence can act as a bloc of acquiescence for whoever dominates the conversation, or as a bloc of withdrawal from whoever makes themselves vulnerable, perhaps by speaking against a prevailing view. Those who don't speak are already participating by their presence, and their silence can act eloquently *against* their views and interests. Speaking, then, becomes a responsibility and a caring for one's own interests, and here it is instructive to remember that a root meaning of "curate" is to care for.

Graduate Critique Course Description (Extracts)

Students can present work in any medium, form, or discipline, but are expected to be critical and interdisciplinary in their *thinking*; that is, they will approach any given work through the history of that medium but also by applying insights from other disciplines and through a mobility of ideas across "fields" of knowledge.[15]

We will examine the critical process itself and how meaning is accessed and/or constructed. Students are encouraged to apply information and theories gained through art history and critical studies classes to their own and other students' work. Emphasis will be placed on what the work "does" within culture, in contrast to personal likes and dislikes.

The critique's intentions are to examine how the work functions as a manifestation of culture, and within culture, in relation to both the historical and the contemporary, to other art and artists, and to broader cultural forms, whether advertising, cinema, comics, TV, and so on. Any aspect of culture can be brought into the conversation.

We examine the encounter that we, as a group, have with the artwork. We assess its formal properties, its materiality, its context, and its conceptual and historical references, and we examine our own responses to all these properties. We use different analytical and theoretical tools to help us do this—for example art history, visual culture, feminist perspectives, postcolonial studies, queer theory, and screen theory.

We do not psychoanalyze the student, since the focus is on our encounter with the work. Even where the work reveals personal aspects of the student, we approach these as intentional artistic strategies, including the possibility that what might seem to be revealed is fictional. We try and glean all this from the work itself.

The student presenting work is not placed in a situation where they have to justify or defend their work.

We never arrive at a fixed meaning for any artwork, since meaning is constructed through and dependent on the encounter with the work. Meaning, therefore, is always in the making, always provisional, and always contested.

CHAPTER 5

HOW ART CAN BE SPOKEN
A Glossary of Contested Terms

Many of the following compiled terms originate from other disciplines and are used in slightly different circumstances within art. Where relevant, I have provided brief summaries of their sources and focus mainly on their art usage or how they might be repurposed within the critique. My purpose is less to examine the "proper" meanings of terms and their genealogies, and more to consider the various values they convey and withhold in the present. The glossary is therefore less a dictionary and more a field study conducted through and upon the living medium of art speech.

My discussions are modeled on the form and in the spirit of the critique, with each topic approached from various perspectives (differentiated by paragraph breaks), drawing upon different theoretical, art historical, and popular cultural sources. Many of the terms will have already been written about extensively by others, and will be approached here as brief, working ideas. Each offers entry points on how to think about art. Tangents may be followed to suggest further discussion rather than attempting more complete theses; discussions are open-ended, without arriving at definitive meanings, and hopefully build toward more expansive arguments by means of returns and repetitions. Each term—much like other aspects of art as a working practice—should be read as overlapping, cumulative, and relational rather than as isolated categories.

About [#Translation]

An artist might occasionally be asked, "What's your work about?" Answering this can be a productive exercise to condense one's interests into an easily absorbed narrative. It does, however, presume that individuals and artworks function through linear narratives and thematic closures. Most art doesn't function like that, even though we expect such narrativized "themes" in artist statements and gallery press releases. While themes cannot fully account for artworks, they might provide necessary entry points for viewers.

However, should viewers be told what the work is "about" (by the artist, the gallery, the museum, the critic)? Or should they evaluate the work themselves? Can individuals make such evaluations without drawing upon broader collective, cultural, historical evaluations? Can an evaluation be made without access to other forms of information? Is the artist a reliable informant on what the work is "about"? Can art's excessiveness be articulated by saying what it is *about*? [#How *Art* Can Be Thought]

Is what the work is about necessarily visible within the artwork? Can the artwork be about something else, through inference, allusion, suggestion, metaphor? Is the work a depiction of one thing that informs us about another? Is an abstract work about or at least derived from something? And if it is, does it remain abstract?

Making art might already be an example of that which it is supposedly about; in other words, art is a cultural practice, with the artwork a manifestation and function *of* culture rather than it being "about" culture.

The artwork is always primarily the "thing itself," before being about something else. It may direct the viewer in different ways and to other references, but it is also about itself, narrating its own coming into being, revealing (or intentionally concealing) and sometimes overtly displaying the histories, concepts, materials, processes, and techniques that led to its making. More easily legible examples might be a painting that displays traces of the chronological sequence of its marks, the types of gesture that left those marks, the layering and consistency of paint, the initial drawing if there was one, the over- and underpainting, and the use of certain technologies, such as spray aerosols or acrylic medium. Or a clay sculpture that leaves indentations of fingerprints or of different tools. While these are more or less visible material traces that constitute forensic evidence, other evidence can be similarly tracked to reveal an object's conceptual and historical lineage: developments of abstraction, for example, or of a certain technique. And the same can be done with the history and development of ideas, with a comparison over time of social objects as material witnesses (the tracing of these being roles of art histories).

However, Duchamp's example of the readymade suggests that an artwork is more than just the thing itself, and that the thing becomes an artwork when it enters into artistic discourse (and not simply when it enters into the artistic space of the gallery). Duchamp's (or Elsa von Freytag-Loringhoven's) *Fountain* (1917), then, is "about"—or we can say that it comes into being and into circulation through—its own objecthood plus the historicized discourse that constitutes it as not just a urinal but as art.

This "objecthood plus discourse," what I have already subsumed within my earlier discussion of *process*, has further implications for critique, in that the examination of constituting discourses (through history and theory) does not detract from the objecthood of the work nor from the viewer's encounter with it, but adds to our understanding of what happens *through* that encounter.

Abstract/ion [#*How, Now*, Rothko?]

Abstraction is generally understood as "nonrepresentational," that is, an image or object that does not look like something that already exists. This doesn't preclude "representing" ideas or emotions, nor the viewer's ability to free-associate to their own memory representations. After all, it takes only a horizontal line to suggest a landscape. Given this associative ability, it is difficult to produce an image that has no mimetic associations and is indeed abstract.

Euro American abstraction has developed in divergent, sometimes oppositional, relationships to the historical weight of representational art. In contemporary art's increasing acceptance of an artwork as "the thing itself," that is, as not representative of something else, abstraction has lost much of its modernist impetus to be freed from figuration. This is not to devalue abstraction's current possibilities but to point to the need for different language to examine abstraction's complexities, breadth of content, aspirations, and formal choices.

The following propositions are equally valid and can simultaneously coexist:

1. Artworks are always abstract: artworks are always the things themselves (their own materiality and conceptual form), before they are representations of something else.
2. Artworks are never abstract: artworks are never fully autonomous in that they always embody physical, conceptual, social, cultural, and

historical narratives of their own (and their makers') coming into being, narratives that situate and contextualize them against any possibility of their autonomy. In that sense, artworks are always already representations of themselves and can never be "abstracted" from those representations.

Despite the above arguments, and, in fact, deliberately flouting and flaunting them, abstraction continues within many genres, popularly pursued as highbrow language for depicting the intersection between the artist's interiority (and consequently, collective interiorities) and the external physical and spiritual world(s). Even if one were to accept this premise, the "abstract" work still faces the charge that it is a representation of that interiority or of how that interiority feels. The ploy of depicting how the artist feels—which no one else can dispute—resists evaluation by social, political, and historical criteria, enabling the work to be aligned with authenticity and universality, and as being beyond language and temporal limitations. These humanistic, apolitical, and experiential qualities—indeed, how quality might be evaluated—are also in line with marketing values and the camouflage of "tasteful neutrality," as the artworks that can be found in hotel corridors and corporate lobbies testify.

Given this devaluation, how do we account for the continuation and current resurgence of "innovative" abstraction? One response is that abstraction now constitutes our prime experience of reality, in that so much of our interaction with the external world is through images produced and selected by corporations (as mass media), and that are encountered out of their context and away from the location where they were produced. Communications, friendships, entertainment, education, and access to news and information are increasingly occurring online through technological mediations, interruptions, and removals. Viewers are likely to encounter art online, including on sites such as Instagram, and through museums digitizing their collections and offering virtual and real-time online "tours." Growing up with the digital realm as their primary mode of interaction, it is no wonder that (younger) artists use this infinity of digital imagery—*already abstracted from its temporal and physical locations*—as source "material." When imagery is already abstracted as so many pixels in a succession of pixels, it risks losing its local and cultural specificity and (political) weight. For some, this represents a previously unknown measure of artistic opportunity; for others, this lack of differentiation between images is the ultimate in consumerism, the choice of proliferating difference that makes no difference. [#Democracy]

Certain recent manifestations of abstraction, especially within painting—what has become known as "zombie formalism"—are the epitome of late capitalism and reflect that system to itself. Those artists who claim this glut of disconnected imagery as individual freedoms might be seen to be not only of their time—a continuous, ahistorical present—but also *products* of this political and economic time. Artists are inevitably of their time, but these artists are charged with operating according to the instantaneity of (and quickly forgotten) market time. This is in sharp contrast to abstraction being otherwise posited as transcending time.

•

One way to think through abstraction (or any other visual language and artwork), other than through or by repudiating its truth claims, is through what Rosi Braidotti calls "figurations" or "cartographies of the present." In her description, cartography is "a politically informed map of one's historical and social locations, enabling the analysis of situated formations of power and hence the elaboration of adequate forms of resistance."[1] I mean to apply Braidotti's use of figuration not in its artistic sense but as a *configuring* of how an artwork comes into coproductive relationship with the viewer. [#Authentic/ity]

Academic [#Intellect/ual]

The popular view of "academic" artwork is that it is too intellectual, while the intellectual view of "academic" artwork is that it is too conservative. In the former case, those who bemoan artwork being "too academic," or who rail against "the academy," do so in the guise of raging against the machine, placing themselves outside of it, even as they might suffer amnesia of their location *within* it. The latter use of "academic" as conservative derives partly from the academies of yore with their emphases on display of technical mastery and subject matter that maintains social stability. Avant-garde movements sought to break with the past and with what they saw as the collusion and complacency of art institutions, whether the academy or the museum. Contemporary artists, increasingly produced through "academies," are nevertheless prone to the Oedipal romance of this vanguardist legacy.

That was then (though it is a past that lingers). The ideal (and much of the rhetoric) of the present-day academy and of contemporary art's turn toward education is where new and old ideas may still be examined, disputed, tested, refuted, adapted, and applied without fear of punishment and ostracism; where artwork can be generated from the clash and clatter of these exchanges; and where the misfit can find a place of affiliation. It might not often work in practice, but few other institutions claim such ambitions. Whether the academy is held to those ambitions is another matter.

However, institutions that still call themselves "academies" (instead of "institutes," "universities," or "schools") often do so in order to locate themselves within an imagined classical past, with its fabricated ideals of beauty, truth, verisimilitude, honest labor, and creative expression—ideals, or rather values, that might in the present sense be aligned more with conservatism (and profit) and with anxieties against difference and change.

Another, less partisan distinction:

Academies might align with beliefs and practices that promote skill(s) as the foundation from which creativity (and employment) will proceed, and through which talent can be manifested.

Institutes might align closer to a history of the avant-garde and the notion that creativity (or "engagement") proceeds from ideas and actions (though this, by now, has become its own tradition—rooted as it is in avant-gardes of the past).

◗●

Art students (and art faculty) notoriously tend to situate themselves outside of, and in opposition to, the art world, and see the art school as the indoctrinating entryway even as they might pay exorbitant tuition fees with the hope of gaining precisely said entry.

Like the myths of the Wild West, or nostalgia for the antebellum South, art schools might harken back to mythologies of male outlaws and of white privilege—rugged individualism as a holdout against bourgeois (or northern/ New York) conformity. Those holdouts might now perceive schools as being overrun with intellectuals, bureaucrats, and diversity (worst-case scenario: all these positions occupied by Black women). Art schools, however, provide current jobs and entry to future jobs, so the outlaws can no longer take to the hills. Instead, they circle the wagons, don the hoods, and continue to rail against the academic. The necessity for schools is not to deny or tame the potentially radical impulse of the rebel but to unshackle it from the mythologies that bind it to conservative status quos (hierarchical masculinity, for example) and that render it only as a *performance* of radicalness.

Art students (and occasional faculty) bemoan the imposition of academic expectations of talking and writing about their work or, goddess forbid, having to write essays on critical theory. What they fear being imposed upon and threatened is the emotional, experiential, and spiritual triangulation between the artist, nature, and their work. The academic here is seen by students (and popular culture) to replicate a misrepresented, gendered, Cartesian mind/body separation, as an inhibiting/censoring mental interruption of the artistic body's direct, authentic experience.[2] [#Gender] And if this authentic bodily experience is what is valued by art industries, what is the point of having to read, write, and talk about art?

Howard Singerman, in a study of the development of US art departments, particularly those in Southern California, aligns art *with* the academy: "The project of art is the promise of the university—to advance knowledge, to further the disciplinary field and its questions."[3] Artists and art departments within universities might never be seen to be academic *enough*, being viewed instead by other departments as makers and decorators, with non–art majors taking art classes as easy grades. University art departments might find themselves fighting for recognition as being research, critical, and conceptual disciplines, in ways that align with other, more text-based academic departments.

What might be meant by an artwork being "too academic"?

- It's information-based rather than being experiential [#Didactic/ism].
- It's an illustration or diagram of an idea, rather than being the idea itself.
- It's too informed by theory, or in the extreme it *is* theory and not art.
- It's political.
- It's unintelligible, that is, it doesn't operate through conventional experience- or information-delivery systems, such as paint or representation.
- It doesn't speak to the average viewer; that is, it requires specialized knowledge or an education.
- It's elitist (see above; many viewers, including those art school–trained, claim pride in not having specialized knowledge to understand "difficult" art).

- It takes too long to understand or experience; it's too demanding.
- It tries too hard.
- It incorporates or consists of text.
- It employs an artist's statement to explain it.
- It's too serious; produced by the brain, and with no heart.
- It's no fun (there's no pleasure, no feeling).
- It's not escapist or recreational.
- It's too distant, too withholding (of information, of experience, of pleasure).

Aesthetics [#Affect; #Beauty; #Politics]

Aesthetics in its primary, broadest sense is the philosophy of the encounter between interiority and exteriority, between the body's sensory systems and their interface with the worlds beyond.

From its initial broad scope of a philosophy of sensation, aesthetics developed more as a philosophy of beauty, that is, by focusing on the body's sensory encounters with the more restricted palette of pleasure. More narrowly, aesthetics has now come to mean not those encounters themselves but their depiction and invocation through the arts, with each art form having its own set of codes. Through each step of this cultural narrowing, something is discarded: first the discomfiting stimuli that cause pain, fear, anxiety, and disgust; then the body itself, in all its messiness, is cut away so that we might be left with only innocuously nice things. One might say that aesthetics, as a philosophy of beauty, has anaesthetized us to articulating a full spectrum of sensation.

By excising differences of specific bodies, how each person experiences differently—differently at different times, and under different circumstances—aesthetics is led toward more generalized principles. One can't, however, have a general theory of aesthetics, since different disciplines, such as sculpture, architecture, painting, music, drama, poetry, dance, and so on are produced through their own aesthetic practices. These, however, cannot be fully isolated, since they are each defined in relation and sometimes in opposition to others. All of them have permeable, mutating boundaries that engender new fields of operation, which extend, reconfigure, and sometimes cause those media to retreat into themselves. The aesthetic theories of one might be translated and applied toward another, or two or more disciplines might be reconfigured, but these create new forms with their own aesthetics (the basis of interdisciplinarity).

While aesthetics might still be broadly proposed as a philosophy of beauty, by which is meant it is "a guide to beautiful things," aesthetics is also the means by which the viewer is trained to view those things. Aesthetics, then, produces the viewer *before* and *while* it catalogues what is to be viewed (beautifully), and trains the viewer as cataloguer of what constitutes art.

The hierarchical production of *how* and *which* art is experienced, and the ability to historically constitute and categorize art, are the most political of aesthetics' functions, since they establish philosophical, moral, social, and economic values. Aesthetics' political strategy to establish these values is through its claim to be apolitical, that it has no bias or partiality, that it serves no special interest group but is concerned only with the universal human condition. This is often referred to in terms of unmediated experience or aesthetic purity. Aesthetics is, moreover, typically presented as incompatible or opposed to politics, with artworks assessed along the spectrum between the two.

●

In complex relationship to the "ever-presentness" of social media (see below), aesthetics historicizes our social lives by delineating a formative history of beauty. Most typical of what one might call a "pedigree of good breeding" is the express-line invocation of the ancient Greeks as progenitors of (our) civilization. A common art history syllabus (as taught within studio art departments, at least) draws this through-line from the Greeks (with brief asides to Mesopotamia, China, and the Indus Valley), through Renaissance Italy, French Baroque and Impressionism, German and Austrian Expressionism, Franco-Spanish Cubism, Italian Futurism, through Duchamp (obligatory in some accounts, but circumvented in others) to American Abstract Expressionism and Pop art, where the account usually ends. From a slave economy to a market one. This regionally specific (let alone selectively gendered and racialized) aesthetic vocabulary is woefully inadequate for the global present, and for present forms of art.

Many schools take steps toward teaching broader, more intersecting histories rather than a single linear one, but these tend to be in the form of addenda. An undergraduate student might still be taught that singular narrative for their required art history credits, which they might be able to supplement with "global studies" courses. These might offer some corrective, but tend to leave the singular narrative largely unchallenged.

From these "traditional" aesthetic narratives, we may rethink ones for the present that derive from multiple lineages and locations, and that intersect between aesthetics and politics, locality and global forces.

●

The emotionally descriptive language of aesthetics parallels the "benevolent" aspects of a market economy—as a buffet of experiences and sensory pleasures. The emphasis on the personally *felt* camouflages aesthetics' political maneuverings, making it seem a natural arbiter of our inner and social lives. Subject formation through sensory experience is similar to what Guy Debord describes as the society of the spectacle: "THE SPECTACLE IS NOT a collection of images; rather, it is a social relationship between people that is mediated by images"[4]

This "social relationship" is now hastened and expanded in previously unimagined ways by the (re)circulation of social media and online imagery, including the "artistic" archiving to sites such as Instagram, in which the ever-unfolding present of the self, "friends," the "news," and infotainment are the material and fix of our social lives *as* consumption.

●

Specific formations, such as "feminist aesthetics," or "Black aesthetics," generate much discussion about how they might be defined and implemented, whether they constitute necessary correctives to mainstream omissions or form separatist enclaves. As Joanne B. Waugh asks, "if 'feminist aesthetics' is treated as a special topic within aesthetics, then should we infer that the rest of the time we do masculine aesthetics?"[5]

A cultural movement such as the US-based Black Arts movement (circa 1965–1976), for example, could claim influence through a range of art histories, whether African, African American, Third World, or European.[6] From 1968 through the present, artist groups such as the Organization of Black American Culture (OBAC) and AfriCOBRA (African Commune of Bad Relevant Artists, originally COBRA, Coalition of Black Revolutionary Artists) have formed in pursuit of a Black aesthetics, a broad umbrella that followed different political directives of resistance, separatism, autonomy, internationalism, pan-Africanism, and Black nationalism, each of which produced its own aesthetic signifiers.

These aesthetic coalitions share common goals of what the filmmaker Isaac Julien has referred to as "aesthetics of reparation" and which he describes as "the undoing of a very forceful regime of dominant effects, which are quite a bombardment for any person of color growing up or being part of a generally dominant white culture. . . . Making work is about how one can produce the aesthetics of representation, which is about creating and sustaining spaces for different images to exist of Black subjects, of queer subjects, of working class subjects."[7]

These aesthetic coalitions and reparations are akin to the different avant-garde movements within Euro American modernism. Although these latter necessarily developed within localized, geocultural, and temporal frameworks, their various calls are ultimately to usurp the authorities of the past and of the current dominant, and to renew *all* art practice. Strategically necessary in order to identify omissions, the long-term goals of aesthetic coalitions might include their own demise as their discourses become centralized. In this spread of aesthetic politics, to "aestheticize" means to represent for the senses, or rather, through the senses, to generate thinking and feeling as actions. Despite its popular connotations of "shallow beauty," aestheticization is an intrinsic aspect of all art, and can be directed as much as a call to action as a call to pacification. Whether or how this call takes affect can be steered by artists but is not under their control since it is as much a function of historicized, geolocated viewers, and the prevailing political discourses of viewing.

Affect [#Aesthetics; #Feelings]

"Affect" is usually used to refer to the feelings induced by an artwork within or upon a viewer. Feelings, in general, are generally taken to be a more honest response than intellectual or verbally articulated ones, partly because of a perception of what the sequence of responses are, from feelings arising first, to thoughts forming after, finally to verbal articulation, with each successive response presumed as being mediated by its predecessor.

Affect theories examine what happens when two or more subjects, or subjects and objects, come into contact. In this sense, affect coexists with aesthetics as a generalized codification of those encounters. These questions of encounter, and how they are codified and reexperienced from *within* their codes, are exactly what the critique investigates, how the different constituents—artwork, artist, viewers, location—are reformed and reproduced as new subjects through their encounter. Similarly examined is how meaning is produced through the physical encounter between the artwork's materiality and the participants' sentient bodies. Thus, affect theory helps us track and think through what sensory feelings are registered by the body, how they are processed and translated, brought into language and into meaning, shared with others, questioned, negotiated, discounted, validated, and historicized, and what happens when these actions are collectively performed by critique participants.

Crucial to understanding affect is that it is temporal, historicized, and geoculturally located. The way each one of us feels is embedded in where and how we have been raised, where and in which era we live. This is to sketch out the broadest strokes, since we are subject to an unspecifiable complex of biological and social forces that impact our most deeply embodied, most intimate feelings and responses. [#Identity; #Subjectivity] Earlier, in #How *Art* Can Be Thought, I have given an example of the exhibition *Affecting Presence and the Pursuit of Delicious Experiences*, in which the artwork's affect is dehistoricized, as is the agency of the hypothetical viewer. This dehistoricizing of both parties, artwork and viewer, functions in an abstracting manner, similarly to a frame around a painting or a pedestal beneath a sculpture. Its purpose is to ascribe cultural and ideological value to the artwork, and to isolate the exchange between artwork and viewer from other contexts. What is prioritized, then, is the affective exchange between artwork and viewer as a transcendent relationship unmoored from history and geopolitics.

●

One of capitalism's means of replication is to elicit affect by manipulating and temporally fulfilling desires, and performed in the guise of providing transcendent experience. Specific kinds of affect (pleasure, joy, anxiety, horror, and compassion) that can be predicted, produced, managed, serviced, and repurposed (through entertainment, culture, travel, and leisure industries) are some of late capitalism's primary commodities. One can point to the growing political industry of *psychographics*, mining and examining personal data that have been posted online, for example in the form of Facebook "likes." Psychographics has extended targeted marketing to targeted voters in order to influence the outcome of elections.[8]

Mass communication's terminologies of clustered affect—"breaking news," "amber alert," "war on drugs," "climate of fear," "terrorism alert," "financial crisis," "migrant crisis," "clash of civilizations"—are fully incorporated as regulatory measures within everyday life. The mass regulation of affect is a primary means of control, for example, through the *production* of crisis as a normalized state of emergency against the lost idyll of normal life, enabling the suspension of mobilities, rights, and freedoms. The production and manipulation of feelings, straight from the handbook of authoritarianism, remains a point of suspicion within critical art practices. It's not that we should dissociate emotions from artworks but that we can suspect and examine the economies for which emotions have been mobilized.

Agency

Agency can be understood as the capacity to act in and upon one's environment. If we think loosely of discourse as the (language and other) systems through which we conceive of ourselves and through which we participate in the world, as well as how we are produced through those same systems, then agency may be conceived of as the ability and means to participate in discourse in ways that might intervene in its application upon oneself and the ways in which one functions in the world.

Agency in this sense is understood as being able to act in one's own interest, rather than as an avatar for another body or interest [#Discourse]. Artistic agency is not necessarily understood to produce changes *in* the world, as we might demand from political agency or activism. Artistic agency might be taken as being able to redirect the artistic language that one uses (see my discussion of *langue* and *parole* in #How *Art* Can Be Thought).

Since dominant mythologies of art are built around individualism, artistic agency is generally centered on the individual artist. Other social theories, such as Marxism, posit agency as collective, as, for example, through the mobilization of the working class. Individual and collective agency might then be seen to be in conflict, or at least in service to different class interests. How to separate from the individualism of the bourgeois art industries and create alliances with working-class organizations has historically been an issue for politically motivated artists.

If we consider the interrelation between individual and collective agency, we might ask to what extent artistic agency depends on other individuals, institutions, and collectives, including the art school, gallery, art magazine, critic, dealer, curator, collector, museum, funding bodies, and so on. To what extent does an individual artist have agency outside of these producing and disseminating bodies? Typically, exhibiting artists would have some kind of symbiotic relationship to these individuals and groups, and the artist's agency would be linked to the support they receive from these other bodies. Agency, then, would most often function through linked networks rather than through any one individual.

Additionally, agency can be considered through a history of artistic intervention, principally as an aspect of performance. Intervention might emphasize unilateral action on the part of the artist, and may involve action against other aspects of that art network, particularly those that represent establishment power, such as museums. Even here, though, this kind of work, often falling within the rubric of institutional critique, becomes incorporated, collected, or assisted by the very institutions it might have set out to oppose. [#Intervention]

Agenda [#Intention]

Artists are sometimes asked "What is your agenda?" This can be akin to asking "What is your intention?" It can insinuate that there is something hidden, secretive, even sly, as if the artwork were a Trojan horse to implant the artist's fiendish plan into the viewer's unsuspecting mind. "Agenda" tends to imply an already suspect social or political scheme. Works that seem to function only aesthetically rarely face such questions. One never hears about an aesthetic agenda (the "aesthetic coalitions" I have mentioned are considered as having only political agendas). It might, however, be a provocative question, especially to an artist who believes that their work is neutral or universally available. [#Aesthetics]

Ambiguity [#Didactic/ism; #Message]

Artists sometimes talk about their works as being intentionally ambiguous, that is, open-ended and without being tied down to specific meanings (while assuming that meaning is a form of restriction rather than one of understanding). This parallels artistic suspicions of certainties and absolute beliefs as dogmatic and authoritarian.

Ambiguity has become art's response to the rest of the world's craving for answers. While I have been insisting on context and against absolutism, it remains questionable whether artistic ambiguity is a sufficient response to others' certainty. People might be drawn to religion, to political fundamentalism, and to advertising's promises because they offer answers. Art and the art critique's insistence that there are no answers—only further questions and ambiguities—fail to address the desire/need for answers. This failure risks relegating art to the sidelines. I'm not offering an answer here (and my apologies for playing a similar game). I'm only pointing out that ambiguity fails to address that there might be something at stake that requires a more *unambiguous* response.

Ambiguity is similarly positioned as a counter to didacticism, with the artist refraining from, withholding, or rejecting taking a "position." This apparent subverting of authority (even if it is limited to the artist's own authorship) might be generously offered as a democratic impulse to provide agency to the viewer.

While describing one's work as ambiguous might be intended to suggest having multiple meanings whose specific application depends on context (presumably provided by the viewer), it might be more indicative of the artist's own lack of understanding, commitment, and/or direction for their work. Ambiguity is different from ambivalence, a simultaneous pull of desire and push of anxiety, an oscillation of opposing forces whose bringing into visibility can provide multiple possibilities for the viewer. This is not dissimilar to Hans Hoffman's ideas about the spatial harmonics of color, the visual "push and pull" of painted forms as they appear to recede or advance. This is not ambiguity but the viewer enacting the process of the painting's visual dynamism, understood as a visual equivalent of the opposing forces of ambivalence.

Angry, Aggressive [#Emotion; #Victim]

These terms may be used against "political" art, with the implication that the work's "message" is conveyed too forcefully or too directly, the desire being that the viewer shouldn't be *told* (i.e., hectored or lectured), but should have the prerogative of their own response. [#Message; #Political]

"Angry," "hostile," and "strident" tend to be used more often against the work of those seen to be outside of the majority, whether by race, gender, or sexuality. This is especially so when an artist's work is read as autobiographical or speaking overtly of *their own,* and not *universal*, experience, as though not feeling included is what makes them angry. Similarly, students (and they may well be female) will likely refer to essays by women, and particularly those perceived to be feminist, as "angry" or "hostile."

These attitudes toward "angry" art tend to mirror larger social attitudes toward political activism, and toward stereotypical images of "aggressive women," "uppity blacks," or "hissy gays," as though these were biological traits that are barely sublimated and always latent.

One way to pursue a discussion of these terms (apart from pointing them out as *projections*), is to consider that there *is* something to be (that we should all be) angry about. Why shouldn't an issue or anger be subjects for art (especially if art is supposed to be so connected to emotions)? What else is at stake in maintaining the semblance of an anger-free status quo? What are the distancing mechanisms that enable anger to be isolated from the experience of the majority? What vulnerabilities might female students, for example, experience *as* women when feminist "anger" is discussed? What are the classroom conditions that make such vulnerabilities so latent?

Anger tends to be conflated with hatred, for example, the notion that feminist anger is really a mask for "man hating." Artists will say things like, "I want to be motivated by love, not hatred," even though love in this case might be a euphemism for being "properly behaved," and hate is actually dissent.

"Aggressive," overlapping with "angry," might be used differently and more synonymously with masculinity and assertiveness as valued qualities, such as "an *aggressive* (or muscular) handling of paint."

Appropriation [#Culture; #Democracy/Democratic; #Derivative]

Appropriation, a supposed hallmark of postmodernism, is popularly linked to a dearth (and death) of originality, and viewed as a fancy term for stealing. It's what artists cynically turn to when they've run out of or never had their own ideas. Legally, it is an enormous gray area mired in copyright infringement and artistic fair use laws.

Given the glut of objects and images, artists may in fact question the desire to produce more "stuff," and may turn to a (re)evaluation of the already existing. Appropriation may be critical of art's cult of originality and its demand for the new.

Appropriating an already existing artwork may stem from an artist's sustained thinking about that work, their investigation of their relationship to it, their understanding and enhancement of the pleasures they receive from it, the ambivalence they might have toward it, its effect upon their development as an artist and for what that work might mean in the present (these are all typical pedagogical methods for looking more closely at historical works).

To give one example of artists supposedly copying work (and in this case, the word "appropriation" was never used, since appropriation implies an element of making something one's own): before the twenty-first century, African and Asian artists were routinely accused of merely emulating Western art. Departing from the obvious racist presumptions that such artists are incapable of originality, how does this emulation function if reconsidered as appropriation, whereby elements of "Western culture" are taken *back* to not only *speak* back but to speak *across* from different locations and different historical perspectives?[9] We might consider these through practices of translation, and, most importantly, as decolonizing practices to replay what that work newly does across multiple, transnational subject positions. [#Translate/Translation]

Appropriation, then, can be purposeful, a repositioning, re(e)valuation, or examination of the preexisting, perhaps to develop counternarratives or counterpositioning.

Articulate

The frequency with which this term is used as supposed affirmation of students of color, particularly Black students, has made it an easily identified stereotype to the point that it has become a cultural joke. Given this frequency, it can trigger an angry response that typically dumbfounds the student who thought that they were using it as a compliment.

The racist background to the term's use is the conviction that the darker the person, the further they are from language use (and being "civilized"). In the Americas, this is of course a specific legacy of slavery, during which the many prohibitions against slaves' use of spoken and written language were deliberate forms of control, isolation, and punishment. Slaves' fear of talking (back) and writing is taken as an inability to do so, and used as evidence to justify continued dehumanization.

Artists' lack of articulation is paradoxically seen as a sign of integrity and depth of feeling; and if they do write or talk (articulately), it's because they're not fully committed to or not very good at making art. In this era of expansive art practices, it seems archaic to not include speech and writing as essential to an artist's repertoire.

◦●

In my end-of-semester course evaluations, students invariably describe me as "articulate." I'm not sure what else they expect from a university professor. I can only hope that this book lives up to their description.

Artist [#Creative/Creativity]

A historical lineage of who and what is an artist might include a commissioned or salaried artisan, often within a guild, or a self-motivated, poverty-embracing, compulsive individualist, or a financially successful entrepreneur, a "creative" who employs artisans to produce luxury branded goods under the "brand" of the creative.

If one were to assume—reasonably enough—that a place of/for art is a museum, then one might reasonably extrapolate that those whose works are within the museum are artists. Wandering into a historical, modern, or contemporary art museum, and based on average demographics of whose work is exhibited, one might come away with the belief that to be an artist is to be most likely male, almost exclusively white, and likely with the cultural capital of a certain class (even if financially poor). The continued reinforcement of these demographics in museums and galleries of who gets to be an artist is bad news for those art students who don't fit those demographics.

Momentarily putting aside social exclusions, what constitutes an artist? Is it something that one *is*, or something that one *does* (perhaps as a profession)? Art schools tend to be ambiguous about this question; they can't accept the former, that one is born an artist. If that were the case, why go somewhere (and pay fees) to "learn" to make art? If it is the latter, something that one does, then presumably anyone can be taught to do it.

The art school tends to hover somewhere between: being an artist has to be something that one is or has (talent), combined with something that one becomes or develops and acquires (skills). There has to be the seed that sets one apart, but a seed that requires proper nurturing—if everyone is an artist then there's nothing special about it (and one wouldn't pay fees to become one). The myth has to be that of possibility but rarity. Everyone has the potential to be an artist, but not everyone is going to make it. And that's what's worth paying for, to be one of the few who do make it.

Is the art student already an artist? This question tends to determine how students are treated. One idea within schools is that undergraduates are examining the possibilities of becoming artists, of learning what that might mean as a long-term endeavor, as a profession. Graduates might have already made that decision to be an artist, and begun to put that choice into practice (though the reality remains that many, after leaving school, will discontinue thinking of themselves as artists and will stop practicing anything named as art).

●

Joseph Beuys famously asserted, "Everyone is an artist." Beuys said this in the context of his proposition of "social sculpture," of individuals acting cooperatively and creatively to address and alter social structures. The quote is commonly heard within the critique situation as a foregrounding of individual autonomy, and as a refusal to accept others' opinions—an attitude of I'm-already-an-artist-and-no-one-can-tell-me-otherwise.

One way to qualify Beuys's dictum is through Antonio Gramsci's observation, "All men are intellectuals, one could therefore say: but not all men have in society the function of intellectuals."[10] What, then, is the function of the artist? And can distinctions be made between "everyone" and those who deliberately take on these functions? Everyone is "artistic," but not everyone chooses to act upon that as a vocation, a profession, or as a political action.

●

If one considers an artist to be someone whose primary income is from making and selling artworks, then one would have to discount teachers, and all those (Van Gogh included) who are unable to survive from sales of their work (Van Gogh nevertheless received substantial support from his brother, Theo). This definition of artist moves emphasis from what artwork does to what the market does and how the work sells within it. The market becomes the defining factor on who is an artist, a contradictory factor, since viewers want artists to not be driven by the market, and denounce them when they are.

Being an artist might be primarily a matter of being identified by one's works. Can one be an artist without attributed work (whether one makes it oneself or has assistants make it)? Is being an artist primarily a matter of identifying as one? Does one have to remain productively *making* art to continue *being* an artist? I make, therefore I am? Can one say, "I *used* to be an artist"? Is that equivalent to "I stopped being creative"?

It's worth mentioning the myth of the suffering artist, who dredges their soul to produce true art. The isolated artist, especially the "outsider artist," is one whose isolation is an absolution from responsibility. Their isolation is displayed as proof that creativity arises from individual, heroically mute suffering. Art industries, in their idealization of emotions, are all too happy to address suffering, but only if it is socially and existentially isolated. To track causes of suffering, however, is to enter the realm of politics, and therefore to exit what is considered the territory and scope of art. A challenge for the contemporary artist is to be attuned to the sufferings of *others*.

●

Art's turn to the social is not to discount the importance of the removed space and "quiet time" of the studio. Artists, like anyone else, need time to process experience. I'm not advocating the Socratic dictum "The unexamined life is not worth living" but suggesting that reflection and processing are necessary for the *political labor* of delving beyond immediate façades (including those that form the self). When a demand is placed on art to function politically, this seeming withdrawal to the studio seems difficult to justify. The critic Ben Davis, for example, was disappointed when an artist he met at a demonstration opted to work in his studio rather than attend a follow-up organizing meeting.[11] Admittedly, the studio can be an escape, but it is also a place of two linked practices, politics and work. Most artists pursue other paid employment, and don't get enough time for what they consider their real work, which is devalued because it is unpaid. Artists are therefore constantly expected to give up their time, and since their main work is unpaid and therefore not seen as real work, they are expected to perform other kinds of labor, such as exhibiting, writing about art, participating on panels, teaching, and so on, without being paid, being compensated below minimum wage, and, in the case of many juried exhibitions and conferences, having to pay to participate. These common forms of malpractice (justified to artists as providing them with "exposure"), are compounded by devaluing cultural work as apolitical.

The collective participation and visibility of the street demonstration is a necessary but different politics from the studio and other artistic labor, with each functioning within its own spheres of operations and influence. Because artistic work never seems to have political urgency, it is deemed to be expendable and easily deferred to the urgency of activism. What Davis is requiring is that the artist he met goes on strike. That's a different question.

Art Market, Art World, Artworld

"Artworld," as one word, was coined by Arthur Danto to describe the institutions and discourses that identify what art is: "To see something as art requires something the eye cannot decry—an atmosphere of artistic theory, a knowledge of the history of art: an artworld."[12]

Elaborating on Danto, George Dickie proposed, "A work of art in the classificatory sense is 1) an artifact 2) upon which some person or persons acting on behalf of a certain social institution (the artworld) has conferred the status of candidate for appreciation."[13]

While it is appropriate to consider the artworld as a highly mobile, discursive system, to imagine it as monolithic—where Danto seems to arrive in his article's closing capitalization, "Artworld"—risks imagining a false cohesion that masks its fractionalism and its more antagonistic interrelations.[14] It might be necessary to think of art worlds, or, as Pamela Lee suggests, perhaps it is time to "forget the art world" and address the more complex multiple, overlapping, and rapidly mutating systems that currently operate within/as the cultural formations and engines of globalization.[15]

To speak of art worlds, in the plural, serves a similar function as speaking of modernisms, feminisms, or nationalisms, each specifically located rather than melding into a singular overarching form. These specifics need to be examined from within their own terms, and as variously overlapping and variously incommensurable, sometimes aligned and sometimes conflicting. One might go as far as to say that for every existing and future artwork there is a constitutive art world. We are speaking then of infinity, a veritable multiverse of art worlds of varying sizes, masses, and gravitational pulls, with varying degrees of habitability and intelligent life. While maintaining this understanding of overlapping and usually conflicting multiplicity, it might still be politically useful to consider at least the façade, if not the actuality, of a singular, provisional artworld as a cultural front for the multinational ambitions of a global market.

Popular culture is bombarded with critical, celebratory, and bewildered attitudes about this artworld, at once elitist and subcultural, as though it were a perennial outside to "real life."[16] This artworld encompasses students (despite how distant they might feel), artists, artworks, art histories, art criticism, museums, galleries, auction houses, art fairs, publications, blogs and social media, schools, dealers, collectors, and curators, and their social, intellectual, and financial networks. It is more accurate to identify this "world" as a conglomeration of art industries, a complex of institutions and individuals not dissimilar to what we are more willing to call the "fashion industry" or "entertainment industry." In calling it a "world" rather than an "industry," we downplay its increasingly difficult-to-ignore economic aspects and suggest that it is driven more by lofty ideals than by commerce. We downplay its global marketing and emphasize its universalism. We want to believe that it crosses all social boundaries rather than building the cultural and economic capital of the wealthy classes.

The flipside of this is that art institutions do face economic and political pressures to function *as* industries: the art school has to justify and professionalize what it teaches in relation to job placement for its graduates. In turning toward corporate models, senior administration salaries increase as faculty salaries stagnate. Tenure may be eroded as being incompatible with innovation and market-driven change (as well as a way of cutting faculty costs and faculty governance). Similarly, the museum has to maximize ticket sales in order to stay open; curators need to be business administrators rather than art historians;

galleries limit their exhibition risks in order to pay the rent; trade conventions, aka "art fairs," become the principal sales events; the primary means for artists to gain visibility, attract critical attention, and maintain a living wage (without second and third careers) is through sales of their work by establishing themselves as small businesses (though international visibility requires a model closer to that of global corporations).

●

Allan Sekula expressed deep skepticism about the art world as "a small sector of culture in general, but an important one. It is, among other things, the illuminated luxury-goods tip of the commodity iceberg. The art world is the most complicit fabrication workshop for the compensatory dreams of financial elites who have nothing else to dream about but a 'subjectivity' they have successfully killed within themselves."[17]

What should artists do in light of this depressing scenario, one in which they are completely entangled and complicit? As a professional artist, there is no extracting oneself from this mire, even for the class-conscious Sekula. One might "speak to power" from the position of being caught *within* the art industries' machinations, and from those machinations already operating within oneself.

An artist such as Tino Sehgal is evidence of the discursive systems of art industries generated from its more material transactions. Sehgal creates "constructed situations" rather than objects, and allows no documentation that can circulate as product.[18] He might seem to function outside the material, commodity system and, in fact, is celebrated for apparently doing just that. But it is the market itself that celebrates him and celebrates that he doesn't produce anything so crass as commodities.[19] However, we are long past the age of physical product: it is the brand itself as discourse (as well as the branding of discourse), the artist's name as genius rebel, as "artistic subjectivity," that is the commodity. This is, after all, the logic of the label; it's not the jeans themselves that matter, it's the sticker on the ass.

●

"The art world is full of pirates, rogues, eccentrics, bullies, and snobs, or, if you prefer, passionate aesthetes. It is, infamously, the last big unregulated industry, full of shady dealings and questionable practices, unwritten and often broken agreements, forgeries and price manipulations, wild tales of fortunes made and lost."[20]

Criticism or last refuge? This emphasis on the unregulated, the underground, alternative, DIY, pop-up, or subcultural network is part of the façade and self-image of art industries as being propelled by ideals, altruism, passion, and creativity rather than by management or corporate interests and regulations. It is not unusual to hear institution presidents and directors, CEOs and CFOs, effectively, refer to themselves as infiltrators working from within "the system." In art industries, it seems, everyone wants to be a well-connected outsider, a rebel with an income. In this sense, there is no "mainstream" art world, since everyone within it, it seems, thinks that they are radical infiltrators. The mainstream as outsider trading for insiders (with eager hordes of outsiders banging on the walls hoping to become insiders).

Artists generally (and I mean *very* generally) might be motivated by factors other than profit—factors such as independence, creativity, and spirituality. These are qualities associated with artistic integrity, and it is for this prime reason that the same qualities are heavily commodified and form the rhetorical values through which art is marketed.

During times of market buoyancy, art industries lose the pretense that art is "above" commerce, and one may see a more naked pursuit of commerce. Some of the most visible contemporary artists necessarily have to embrace commerce (as the engine of their visibility) and not just as subject matter (which might have been a previous rationalization or an actual critical position). Art is likely now produced *as* commerce, with the model less of a (at least early period) Warholian "alternative" bohemian factory, and more the (late Warholian) model of the global corporation with its own international branding, marketing, production, and outlet sites. Much like other forms of capital, the galleries, publications, art fairs, and auction houses increasingly function as the distribution arms of an interlinked system. However, despite or because of the centralization of capital and power in megagalleries, such as Gagosian, or Hauser and Wirth, it is pertinent to consider multiple markets, and to emphasize the impact of art workers rather than market values and products. A focus on workers' labor and compensation can help rebalance an otherwise overemphasis on product and monetary value.

Art industries have become transfused with the terminology of entrepreneurialism. Not only does "entrepreneur" carry a hint of French cultural cachet, it suggests a person driven by initiative and risk, the very qualities admired in artists. Typically, art industries' entrepreneurs are not just commodity and fund managers, they are celebrities, innovators, "taste makers," and "trend setters," the movers and shakers on best-of lists, creating (or sometimes, destroying) artist careers. Business acumen is considered to be synonymous with the ability to assess the true, hidden value of artworks, and to translate that value into financial terms (although those financial aspects remain masked by façades of culture, innovation, radicalness, quality, and taste).

Audience

There are different ways to think of audience, the most conventional being audience as customers. These are not required to "buy," but viewer numbers are part of how artwork circulates, and constitute—in marketing terms—the work's advertising. An artwork's notoriety, for instance, will increase its audience, even though it may decrease its critical value. Such work is often, and wrongly, dismissed as "shock art."[21]

Audience can be considered as participants. This is most obvious for social practice or community art, where participants might be required to enact the work or bring it toward fruition. Some artworks are not addressed toward viewers external to the work but come into being (and doing) through the presence or actions of audience/participants. This would never be a closed system, since documentation, or subsequent hearsay or reading about the work, would produce other "nonparticipant" audiences.

More to the point, however, is that *all* artworks require viewers to bring them into meaning and into discourse, even if it is only as advertisers. Audience, then, can be thought of less as passive *recipients* of artworks, and more as active *coenactors*, brought "into being" in overlapping ways as artworks are, through preexisting discourses of art history, popular culture, and advertising. Audiences are already produced, but they will also be changed by their encounter with artwork, continuing to "coform" each other, altering existing discourses and producing new ones.

●

"Blockbuster" exhibitions by the marquee names of art history have readymade audiences, on whom museums depend for revenue. Most other contemporary artists will depend on their name recognition accrued over their careers, beginning with their immediate social networks and extending outward through the industry's discursive mechanisms, such as gallery advertising, sales, exhibition reviews, scholarship, and so on.

Students and artists at the beginning of their careers might face the question "Who is your audience?" This tends to be directed to work that the questioner doesn't understand, or that for various reasons is seen to be "marginal," and therefore presumed to be not for a general viewer but for those that identify as being similarly "marginal" (I've heard this most often used for work that addresses gender and/or race). This assumes that artists automatically want acceptance and assimilation into the mainstream, and want the biggest audience possible. This is also the logic of the market economy, which is predicated on both rarity and mass appeal, or rather, mass desire, rewarding the "uniqueness" of artworks (rarity) that attract the largest viewing (mass appeal), perhaps by notoriety. The more buoyant this economy, the more power it has to designate what is and isn't audience-attracting art, and the more it collapses the separation between art object as cultural practice and art object as commodity fetish or luxury or investment commodity. [#Universal/ism]

There's a related question of reaching *diverse* audiences. The market makes the "commonsense" demand that artworks function "universally" for different audiences. This again is an assimilationist attitude. It is more challenging to require viewers to do the work of overcoming *their* aesthetic gated communities in order for *them* to engage intersectionally with different artworks, rather than requiring "international styles" for mass, global audiences, as biennales have been accused of producing.

The critique trains artists to become their own initial audience. As student artists discuss the work of others, the discussion methods are absorbed and can be applied to their own work. One method of gaining critical viewing over one's own work is through internalizing the voices of one's peers and faculty, with these internalized (and imagined) opinions becoming a primary audience through which differing opinions and responses can be tested.

Authentic/ity [#Honest/y]

Except for issues of provenance (whether art historical, commercial, or anthropological), this is of limited use for assessing art despite how frequently it is used. One major assumption (by artists, critics, museums, collectors, and such) is that a copy is automatically a lesser version of an "original." Artists may deliberately oppose presumptions of originality and authorship, and may instead propose the copy, the simulacrum, the readymade, the plagiarized, the pastiche, and the multiple. Each of these needs to be assessed on its own, different terms.

Authenticity can be used to mean "authenticity of expression," as though the artist has revealed some interior essence in an unmediated way. The making of an artwork, whether conceptual or "expressive," entails an amalgam of learned behavior, invention, and translation into form, all of which are complex, highly mediated processes. Translation in itself is a necessarily hybrid process, constantly cross-referencing and reevaluating—and though it strives for an accurate interpretation of what is being translated, it can be seen as a form in itself, and one that is by definition variable and open to further interpretation.

Authenticity may be used in relation to one's "core being," as evidenced by the popular phrase "being true to oneself." This truism is seen as an ultimate quality for the making of art—a quality that claims to transcend the market yet which represents an artist's prime marketability. Being "true to oneself" often manifests itself in repetition, where the artist has found a formula for making work and remains within it as the façade of the "true self" (though the art term for this repetition is "consistency").

Authenticity is often a prime lens through which artwork by a "marginalized other" is measured, of how "true" the work is to viewer perceptions of the artist's culture. The critic may not feel they themselves are sufficiently authentic or have legitimacy to discuss the work in question. One constantly sees this handwringing in reviews of "multicultural" exhibitions in which the critic questions their own ability and even right to assess the work but might then continue to dismiss or celebrate it (and the artists concerned) in terms of their in/authenticity.[22]

Authenticity in the above examples, at best, does a disservice to the complexity of the processes it presumes to describe; at worst, it's propagandist in its claims to fixity and judgment.

In a critique, authenticity—that for various reasons the artwork, keeping it real, *has* to be the way that it is—might be used as a defense against criticism. Without suggesting that criticism is necessarily right, others' experiences and responses, when different from one's own, might serve a necessary function of casting doubt upon one's own surety and "realness," and might open up other, unconsidered possibilities. The purpose of accepting criticism here is to move beyond one's own armored casing to find intersections with the experiences and perceptions of others.

Despite the above, there are ways to allow for authenticity in its "keeping it real" guise. I've mentioned that "an artwork is a declaration of being in the world from the very particular perspective of an artist's historicized, positioned, embodied, enculturated subjectivity." [#How *Art* Can Be Thought] This is one productive way to conceive of authenticity, that an artist strives to work from the very specific ways that they have been located within the world. This is not autobiography but a criticality from one's location and being located by others, also akin to what Mary Louise Pratt proposes as an autoethnographic text, "in which people undertake to describe themselves in ways that engage with representations others have made of them."[23] This is counter to conventional ideas of authentication, since it is engaged more with intertextuality and performance. This use of "authenticity" is a practice rather than a noun or fixity; it can be the process of coming into fuller being, similar to how Freire considers freedom "the indispensable condition for the quest for human completion."[24]

Autonomy

Autonomy proposes that artworks function independently of social or political forces; that they transcend temporality; that they exist independent of mimetic reference to anything else; that they are unaffected by criticism and changing tastes; *that they just are.*

Once an avant-garde aesthetic position, the autonomous art object is now a market device. Any continuing claim made by artists for the autonomy of their work has to be considered in relation to advertising and branding. The object is desired for itself and for who made it, not because it serves any other function.

There are, however, different "independence" positions that might be useful for artists. The Black Panther Party (BPP), for example, believing in "proletarian internationalism," didn't pursue separatism—contrary to popular media representation—but wanted Black people to control their own means of production and distribution. The *autonome* political movements in Europe, particularly in Italy, Germany, and France, and connected to art principally through the Situationists and subsequent anarcho-punks, emphasize collective interrelations and self-governance rather than what might be strictly understood as independence and self-reliance. While adopting a working-class perspective, autonomists don't prioritize labor but may adopt the refusal or rejection of capitalist labor relations, thereby separating themselves from other leftist groups that might seek to ameliorate labor conditions while sanctifying the centrality of labor itself. Compare this to art's "uselessness."

A shift has occurred in contemporary artistic discourse from autonomy to the relational. Rather than works functioning "independently," we are as likely to now consider how they work in relation to other works, to viewers, to their surroundings, and to history. Artists might see the consideration of these relations as necessary responsibilities but also as impositions that restrict their "freedoms" to not have to be responsible for what their work does; freedoms that others might see as privileges.

Bad/Good; Excellence [#Entry Points: e/Quality]

Typically, "good" and "bad" are applied broadly, but to be practical, one would need to know the criteria—what *makes* it "bad" or "good." Any evaluation is specific to its criteria, although multiple criteria are usually in play, including the work seeming un/skilled; contradicting/supporting what is found tasteful; too familiar/surprising; seemingly dated and repeating earlier styles / seemingly innovative and contemporary; and seemingly ignorant of (art) history / propelling (art) history into the future. None of these criteria is absolute, and all are subjective and variable. Under different criteria, good can be bad and bad can be good. A work that seems unskilled might be deliberately made to fall apart over time; it might be a repudiation of "conventional" taste and values; it might reject the authority of history, and so on.

How would one know if evaluation is being conducted about the work itself, rather than being a symptom of the viewer's taste and bias? Similarly, a work's emotional, social, or discursive affect might be so dependent on the viewer that those criteria can't be applied to the work itself.

If we accept that art is a form of knowledge of being in/with the world, can there be excellent/good/bad knowledge, or is all knowledge equally valid (if not equally relevant or differently consequential)? Is a bad artwork one that fails to exhibit knowledge about its own coming into being, its history and location within art histories, its material properties, and its possibilities? Is a bad artwork one that is too closed in upon its own regimes of truth and ignorant of what it means to be more widely operational in the world? One that a viewer cannot connect to their own knowledge of being in/with the world (or does this make for a "bad" *viewer*)? What are the relationships (and outcomes) of a good/bad work and a bad/good viewer?

"Bad" and "good" are final judgments, and one method of critique is to defer judgment since the work's meaning is always context-specific, or circumstantial, and one therefore can't arrive at any kind of final judgment. Some viewers might find it almost impossible—mostly through habit—to examine an artwork without passing judgment. If a typical statement is made, such as, "I don't think that color is working," one can and should ask for clarification. "Why is it not working? According to what criteria? What does 'to work' mean?" Rather than simply being an unsubstantiated opinion that could be based on personal taste and that can only be agreed or disagreed with, the discussion may now continue to examine those criteria, whether they apply in this case, and what other criteria might be operative. This allows for choices, and is thus a productive form of argument, rather than one that leads to only dis/agreement and the assertion of the most dominant voice.

While I would suggest that the critique is *not* the place for assessments of bad and good, no such restrictions apply within art industries in general. The discussion (whether within or outside of the critique) of how such evaluations are habitually made is therefore an important one. Dominating criteria for valuing artwork are its market value and marketability, including the provenance trappings of which gallery promotes it, if it receives reviews in the right magazines, who owns it, its proximity to celebrity, and so on. The absence of other criteria allows the market to decide what may be "good" (or "bad").

●

We think of art as benevolent, as uplifting, as being somehow "good for us." Is this borne out by any evidence or does it amount to a matter of faith? Or perhaps a matter of desire, that we *want* art to be good for us, a desire that is self-fulfilling and self-sustaining? We *want* it to be good for us, therefore it *is*. This want might serve a therapeutic role, in a similar way that urban parks are meant for the public good by providing a calming escape from life's frustrations. A different critique would suggest that the urban park is deliberately pacifying, providing a rehabilitating appeasement that makes for greater disciplinary control and worker productivity. From this vantage, art might be a socially productive (and lucrative) pacification of potential dissenters—otherwise known as artists.

Art might be "good" for us by being in service to or aligned with religion or patriotism, and might be evaluated according to how well it represents or promotes their ideas *as* personal experience. Similarly, art might be linked to status and wealth, of how it represents my/our/their place in society or the world (or the cosmos) or how it makes me/us/them feel about that placement. If certain forms of art represent a particular social group and those who aspire to it, that group might furthermore have the social power to disseminate the idea that "their" art is good for everyone, and is therefore "better" than anyone else's art. Those groups with limited social power to disseminate "their" art, on their terms—for example, as "Black" art, or "feminist" art—have to contend with the implication that "their" art is only for them. And if "great" art is predicated on being universal and for everyone, these "ghettoized" forms of art are seen as lesser forms until they can be assimilated into the fold of the universal.

•●

A goal of any art school is "excellence" across all its operations. Criteria for measuring excellence—instrumentalized to attract new students and funding—might include the school's national rankings, alumni careers and average salaries, graduate school placements, and faculty achievements (exhibitions, publications, awards and grants, and notoriety). Aside from "achievements," which typically are listed on an artist's CV, there tend to be no measurable criteria for artistic excellence.

Grading is another educational scenario in which bad/good and excellence comes into play. Faculty might grade on a curve; some might grade application, effort, and development over a period of time; some might indulge their biases and grade on personality, on gender, on race, or on how gregarious or "attractive" the student is. Faculty may demand excellence from their students, and declare being uninterested in anything else. [#Mediocrity] Review committees, faced with a form with columns for "excellent," "good," "average," and "poor," might encounter a high degree of arbitrariness on where the X is placed. Does "excellent" really mean better than all others (not everyone can be excellent, because then they would be average)? In the top 1 percent or 5 percent? Tried really hard? Developed considerably from the beginning of the year? If the student is already "excellent," then presumably it makes no sense to suggest or ask for "improvements." A student might be marked as excellent when they are about to graduate and it is "too late" to offer them advice.

How are students to be prepared for excellence? Do schools and faculty habitually act on the presumption that only *some* students will be excellent? Does the focus on excellence produce a tiered system, in which excellence is facilitated, promoted, rewarded, and empowered, and those less than excellent taught separately but unequally? Excellence presumes a hierarchical, competitive system (that some will be *better* than others). How is such a system compatible with the art school's parallel rhetoric about art's equalizing, liberating powers? Do tiered systems promote different (and self-fulfilling) *expectations* of excellence from different rungs on the hierarchy? Should schools operate on varying expectations of excellence mitigated by the unequal entry points of students to art industries? Can one have the same expectations of excellence from a financially poor student who works part-time jobs and who has a child as from a student from a wealthy background who can afford to not be employed, who can attend gallery openings and evening lectures, and who can spend all their "free" time in the studio?[25] These might be questions that are impossible to answer beyond specific cases. But they point to two primary issues for education: the difficulty of unquestioned notions of excellence, and that excellence is ultimately a question of ethics.

Beauty [#Aesthetics]

Beauty has been celebrated historically as the defining characteristic, or at least aspiration, of art; good art was beautiful, bad art failed to be beautiful. This beauty (extrapolating from Kant) might be considered the pleasure produced by the simultaneous or almost simultaneous contemplation of a pleasurable sensory experience. It is the identification and contemplation of the experience rather than the experience itself. Strictly speaking, then, it doesn't make sense to talk of "beautiful" objects, sunsets, people, or places, except as shorthand for the stimulus that provokes the pleasure we name "beauty." In order to name it, we need to be able to identify it, which means that beauty as the stimulus and the response are most likely to be already known and previously experienced. Important to acknowledge is that beauty is neither simply the stimulus nor simply the response. It is a *transaction* between the stimulus that provokes the experience and the person who has the experience. It is this transaction that is invested with political and cultural value. The stimulus is similarly valued by "being" beautiful, being rare, being expensive, providing pleasure, and so on. The experiencer gains value by participating in or owning the rare stimulus of beauty.

Beauty, it is argued, supposedly makes us predisposed toward good; it makes us feel good; it's good for us and makes us want to do good; and therefore it's good for society. Beautiful art is therefore good for us. At best, these are simplistic propositions. Beauty can just as likely produce feelings of anger, hatred, and resentment if the beautiful object belongs to someone else or is otherwise unattainable. In contrast to such popular sentiments, to experience beauty is to be destabilized and made vulnerable to one's own desires and passions. Vulnerability can create defensive mechanisms, reasserting protective barriers as well as responding violently. In a common scenario of pulp fiction, a male character may resent the unattainable, beautiful woman, and seek to destroy her and those who have "access" to her and who thus reveal his own inadequacy. Unfortunately, such scenarios are not relegated to fiction, as was the case of Eliot Rodger, who went on a gun rampage against the women he felt rejected him and the men they associated with.[26] While this is an extreme example, much of the discussion following the murders centered on the underlying and eruptive misogyny that is one more aspect of the objectification, or "beautification," of women.

Does beauty reside in the object (or person, or view), or is it a response from or experience of the viewer (as above)? Are there degrees of beauty? Is one thing more beautiful than another? Is there anything that is devoid of beauty? How do we assess beauty? Without ways and adequate language to address these questions—and aesthetics, the philosophy of beauty, has provided us with no definitive answers—the category of beauty, in its innocuous forms, is communicable more as platitude or as a previously agreed upon standard. In this case beauty can be applied only to forms that are already familiar, which, in turn, is more likely a shared experience of kitsch. [#Kitsch] When talking about art, these questions become even more unanswerable.

Photography, for example, can make anything look beautiful, partly because photographs accrue beauty as they age, acquiring the auratic quality of the unique object from a past time (is the photograph, as object, beautiful, or is what is depicted beautiful?). Given the interest in "abstract" photography, there is no such thing as a "bad" photograph or one that is ugly despite its subject matter. Even photographs of extreme suffering and poverty can have a veneer of beauty, such as those by any number of photojournalists, including Dorothea Lange or Sebastião Salgado, to name only two.[27] As Susan Sontag notes, "Nobody exclaims, 'Isn't that ugly? I must take a photograph of it.' Even if someone did say that, all it would mean is: 'I find that ugly thing . . . beautiful.'"[28] If nothing else, this aesthetics of violence requires an expanded vocabulary to distinguish it from other forms of aesthetic representation.

Beauty is conventionally equated with truth, and when the two are linked they require no justification or explanation. They just are, which is justification enough, becoming an artwork's only reason to exist. This is similar to how Herbert Marcuse speaks of "decontamination" as a ploy of bourgeois culture, whose fantasies of order and civility were segregated from the realities of labor and the violence of oppression that made such fantasies possible. "The medium of beauty decontaminates truth and sets it apart from the present," he writes. "What occurs in art occurs with no obligation."[29] Art, in its beauty (and truth), becomes autonomous, and absolved of ethics.

●•

I'm not disputing that different artworks have different pleasurable (and anxiety) affects upon the viewer that might be thought of as responses to "beauty."

But one person's experience is never qualitatively or quantitatively the same as another's, so we can never have measurable or equivalent experiences of beauty. When we do try, we speak of beauty only in the broadest and sometimes in the most banal terms (though beauty spurs some to veritable flights of language).

The sentimental connoisseurship of beautiful things, artworks, and people can create intolerance of anything that does not provide the same stimulus. Beauty can just as easily create a disposition toward cruelty and injustice toward those that fail to be beautiful (according to whatever criteria are enacted).

Surrounding ourselves by beauty and separating ourselves from the ugly (as many self-help books advocate) probably makes us oblivious, dismissive, and repelled by what we might consider ugly. Any ethical link to beauty makes us almost morally disinclined toward "ugliness." The history of that link, especially in relation to the human body and to cultural artifacts, is strongly linked to regimes of violence against the "ugly."

Beauty, particularly "perfect beauty," might be conceived of in terms of order, or a kind of "perfect order," including as a manifestation of the divine. Thus beauty—and beautiful art—become (utilized as) uplifting moral forces, even or particularly when the "ordering" can and sometimes does take totalitarian forms, as enforced order.

Beauty *as* a moral force has become a central concept in the "culture wars," that highly politicized debate that is less about art and more about morality, as well as about religious and economic values. [#Mood] Those who insist upon a "return" to depoliticized beauty (*make America beautiful again?*) have turned beauty into a public political battleground, attempting to ban works that fail to be beautiful (ugly, depraved, debased, immoral, sacrilegious . . . all the antonyms to beauty). These returns to imagined previous eras of ideal beauty were the hallmark of the Nazis' control over all aspects of culture, with their demands for a pure German art, and denunciation of "mentally ill, racially impure" degenerate art.[30] In these insidious forms, beauty is deployed as a call for highly politicized values, and ultimately for social mobilization and containment. Its appeal to transparency—that we *know* and *immediately experience* when something is beautiful—is part of its ideological arsenal, and one that plays ultimately to an authoritarian politics.

An artist intent on making something beautiful does so within the already accepted codes of what constitutes beauty—what I've referred to above as "kitsch"—and would therefore make something that is already familiar and known. The new, the unknown, might be considered ugly by present standards. One needs only look to art history for examples of works that are initially denounced but which later become flag bearers of beauty. History indicates that beauty is surprising, shocking even, as yet uncategorized, and transforming—in that *we as viewers* have to undergo a transformation in order to begin to experience it as beautiful.

•

To Dave Hickey—an advocate of a return to beauty—"beauty is and always will be blue skies and open highway."[31] In other words, beauty as longing for masculinist escape, for freedom from responsibility and restrictions, social ties, and obligations. Freedom from necessity, from physical need, from hardship. Presumably Hickey is not walking that highway, since a Harley or Porsche Spyder is almost implicit as part of the desired fantasy.[32] This is the revved-up, horse-powered myth of the western cowboy, and of the colonialist dream of empty land.

While talking of cowboys and their ilk, I might mention that beauty is considered within modernist and contemporary art to be suspiciously feminine, with its attendant connotations of prettiness and decoration. The acceptably masculine form is the sublime, with *its* attendant connotations of the heroic and powerful (and fatalistic).

A recent renaissance of beauty (with Hickey at its vanguard) followed and was in partial reaction to a perceived multicultural "takeover," as exemplified by the Whitney Biennale of 1993, which supposedly valorized art that was merely didactic and political without the ameliorating, universalizing force of beauty. This is exemplary of the political role in which beauty is placed, while being claimed to be beyond politics.

Beauty, in its linking to morality and ethics, is spoken of by artists as though there were a balance. By bringing a beautiful artwork into the world they cl/aim to offset the weight of ugliness, thus contributing to world peace and the cure for cancer. Artists talk about beauty as a gateway sensation, a means to attract the viewer and hold their attention with the possibility of directing that attention to other questions. One critique of this use is that it is a lure with no obligation for fulfillment of its greater promise. The viewer might not be led further than the experience of beauty, stuck, as it were, at the gateway with nowhere to go except to kitsch, since kitsch is all about the closed surface. What, then, are the ethics of beauty for a working artist? Resist it, refute it, ignore it, consider it irrelevant? Or can it be harnessed subversively as a counter to its currently accepted forms?

Body [#Body Politics; #Desire]

It has become commonplace to speak of the "body" or "*the* body," as though there were only one kind, or as though we all experience "it" in similar ways and that we all understand which "it" is being addressed. Artists may say *the* body when they mean *my* body—but that would make it too personal, and runs the risk of the work being seen as therapeutic, narcissistic, or fetishistic. This resort to a generalized experience can reinstate normativity, presuming that we all share the same racialized, gendered, sexed, and abled bodies. Within the critique, one needs an occasional reminder to clarify exactly which kinds of body we mean, and which ones might be simultaneously excluded.

A work that *depicts* bodies might not be *about* bodies. Bodies are conventional vehicles for other subject matter. A depicted body might be a formal aesthetic device, a metaphorical and narrative device, a sexual device—in which case it is equally about the *mind* of the artist and the body of the imagined *viewer*. One can argue that the ubiquity of the female nude in art history was a means for male bonding, constituting the public sphere as explicitly homosocial, "homoscopic" territories.[33] One might have an altogether different reading of a female nude by a female artist. For example, Jenny Saville's paintings or Laura Aguilar's photographs are more likely to be evaluated through various tropes of "body politics." In other words, depictions of female bodies by male artists are more likely to be naturalized and universalized; and depictions of female bodies by female artists are more likely to be politicized and linked to particularities of female experience, to the extent where such work is considered to be speaking only to "women's experience" or "outside" of male experience. Similarly, male nudes by female artists might be assumed to have a political "agenda," whereas the opposite is naturalized. [#Agenda]

One common "agenda" might be to depict the "marginalized" body as affirmation, evidence, or proof of existence. This has been the case with feminist art, Black art, queer art, and, most recently, trans-art.[34] Self depiction (and depiction of those "like" the self), as evidence of group visibility and politicization, have played important roles, not least of which has been to identify a community to itself. Questions remain, however, about what roles the depiction of the body may play once it is relieved of the burden of visibility and proof.

Body Politic(s) [#Feminism; #Identity]

The "body politic" (singular) refers to the state, comprising the system of government (such as the "head" of state) and its citizens, and likening the entirety to the functioning of a singular human body. The term suggests a commonality, working within and toward the same system, and tends to elide dissenting subjectivities. Similarly, use of the term "public," as in "the American public," suggests a homogeneity, a melting pot of many people becoming one nation, encapsulated by the motto *e pluribus unum* (out of many, one).[35]

"Body politics" (plural) refer to how individuals are categorized by bodily markers to be regulated by societal power, the regulating policies and discourses that flow from that power, and individual and collective resistances against that regulation. The term developed from 1970s feminist organizing around reproductive rights, domestic violence, and the objectification of women. Current usage is indebted to overlapping movements toward liberated subjectivities, such as the postcolonial, Black, queer, disability rights, and transpolitics. Body politics might be played out most visibly through specific issues of labor, health, racial profiling and police brutality, rape, dis/ability, abortion, sexuality, beauty, fashion, and so on, and extend to any and all human activities. In critiques, when we speak of "the body" we might be invoking any or all of these histories and discourses.

◦•

The critique is an embodied experience, in that it is the bodies of viewers that encounter artwork and experience it in spatial and sensory terms. Body politics become particularly apparent and sometimes most avoided when the artwork involves the display of an artist's naked body, during, for example, a performance. An immediate issue for viewers is the proximity of the naked body, especially in the absence of separating frames such as a stage. Apart from invoking desires (which tend to be conflicted, even if only from the vulnerability of them arising in a public situation), the displayed proximate body may provoke anxiety, especially if there is physical contact, including anxieties of contagion or of being somehow dirtied. These can lead to heated discussions, or lack of discussion, since viewers are generally reticent to become so vulnerable as to reveal their desires and/or fears. A general attitude of art viewers tends to be a studied disinterest, as though one has seen it all before. To feel and voice desire, shock, fear, or disgust, as bodily and political responses, is to become vulnerable. Although to respond with anger or moral outrage might be to cover for those vulnerabilities. Students might be reticent to "say the wrong thing," knowing already that it is not "politically correct" to be disgusted, for example, by hair on a woman's body, or by displays of certain desires. The displayed body that does not match current ideals of beauty may invoke disgust. These responses (as *bodily* reactions) of desire and disgust, of dis/comfort in the relations between our own and other bodies, are precisely the intimate arena of bodily politics.

While the explicitness of some body performance or artworks that depict or refer to the body might be where we most think about body politics, they function more pervasively, including when the body does not appear to be present(ed). What are the body politics of minimalism, for example, in which the evidence of the artist's hand as synecdoche for the artistic body is removed? What is the social power of the already legitimized body that can designate its apparent absence as a universalized gesture? What is the social imperative to legitimize and make otherwise illegitimated bodies visible? Or bodies that have been made illegal, as has historically been or is resurgently becoming the case of bodies that perform their queerness, or bodies that have been designated as undocumented?

Boring [#Interest/ing; #Taste]

"Boring" is one of the most damning things that can be said about an artwork, and is usually intentionally used that way. One can dislike a work, but dislike is at least a response (any response is better than none). For a work to be boring suggests that it isn't even interesting enough to provoke a response. "Boring" art may be viewed as an affront, particularly by instructors, as though their time is too valuable for them to be bored.

A perennial student favorite is John Baldessari's video and lithograph *I Will Not Make Any More Boring Art* (1971). Whether Baldessari succeeds in this endeavor (another favorite student discussion) is debatable, but the point is that what makes a work "boring" and what fails to make a work "interesting" are themselves "interesting" points for discussion. Boredom and interest are ultimately functions of the viewer, rather than of the work, and can be linked to taste as a social identification of value and hierarchy. "Boring" may be equated with familiarity and (market) saturation, or with work that "tells" the viewer what they already know [#Didactic].

Boredom can be an artistic tactic, to make work that is disinterested, dispassionate, unspectacular, neutral, that doesn't "impress" upon a viewer but is a site to be activated *by* the viewer. Boredom can provide solace from overstimulation. It might also be a prerequisite for daydreaming, and for jumpstarting imagination and creativity. [#Creativity]

Capitalism [aka Everything]

A general presumption about "political artists" is that they are against capitalism and that their work actively opposes it.[36] "Nonpolitical" artists might be located along a spectrum of dis/comfort within capitalism, with "apolitical" artists driven by supposedly nonpolitical factors such as truth or passion. The popular and art world ideal for artists is that they be indifferent to capitalism, that is, not motivated by "the market," even as art world markers of success are essentially market-based, such as entrepreneurialism, branding, and sales, so that aspirations within the "art world" are inevitably made within capitalist terms. Even the ambition to "gain visibility" is to accrue cultural capital and market share. To tease out some of these assumptions, I will proceed with a simplified overview of capitalism from the perspective of a hypothetical "political artist."

Capitalism is an economic system in which the accumulation of resources—capital—is utilized to accumulate more capital. This is achieved through three prime arenas of control: the means of production, wage labor, and reinvestment of profit or capital to generate further profit.

In this scheme of maximizing profit, ownership of production is in the hands of the fewest possible (bosses, capitalists, the 1 percent); wages and benefits for workers are deliberately kept low to reduce production costs and create surplus value; workers are kept as close to servitude as laws will allow in order to keep them in service for as long/short as the company needs them; workers are discarded as efficiently as possible when no longer needed, or when cheaper workers can be made available; resources are maximized, with issues of safety, sustainability, environment, and human and life value measured primarily in terms of encroachments to profit. From the perspective of its own logic, capitalism is not a cruel, unjust system; it is a disinterested system that rewards those who can make it work for them, and ignores those that can't, won't, or don't. From the (ad)vantage of the rewarded, capitalism is a competitive game with inevitable winners and losers. From the disadvantage of the dispossessed, capitalism is an already stacked system.

To maximize profit, the majority (workers, the poor, the 99 percent) is *required* to accrue negative capital. Their systemic and systematic capital deficit is the required ground and balance for the accumulation and hoarding of capital by the few. The hoarding, *e pluribus unum*, occurs on a global scale and as a global system of resource theft, disinvestment, and tightly controlled labor. This "negative capital of oppression," accumulated transgenerationally in the very bodies, psyches, and memories of people, historically prescripts who will win, and who will continue to lose, the latter majority required "to become minoritarian."[37]

Various forces intersect with and temper unbridled capital accumulation and deficit:

1. Worker activism and demands toward equity, typically enacted by unions or for unionization, by tactics of go-slows, withdrawing labor, pickets, strikes, and sabotage.
2. Market competition. Companies regulate each other, for example, over wages, since if one company lowers or raises its wages it will lose or attract workers from other companies. Companies therefore tend to operate along class alliances (which tend to trump gender and racial alliances) to maintain profits and reduce costs (just because a woman or person of color is at the helm of a company does not make it less capitalist).
3. State and government regulation, such as minimum wage laws; gender parity; race relations; child labor restrictions, work limits, and conditions; sick leave and health care; parental leave and child care; laws restricting monopolies; taxes; environmental laws; nationalization. This regulatory function is in conflict by the fact that governments are likely to be run by the same group of people (capitalists) who run the companies. At its more blatant, it is referred to as "crony capitalism," even though this is capitalism's default mode. In most cases, even with degrees of separation, governments will side with companies against workers, for example, invoking the "rule of law" to end strikes, or raising the specter of economic collapse to compel worker compliance.

The outline above is complicated by further interactions. For example, advertising entices everyone toward constant and constantly increasing consumption to satisfy the demand for new profits. Advertising is aligned with ideologies that induce us to value the "honesty" and "dignity" of hard work. These "indoctrinate" workers into a sense of self-worth and self-image of success by acquiring the "appropriate" possessions of house, car, spouse, children, pets, clothing, leisure goods, and entertainment machines and filling their "leisure" time (time that allows recuperation in order to return refreshed to work) with consuming the services, labor, and products of other workers: dining out, going on holiday, watching movies, going to sports events, and so on. We do all these things because *we* enjoy doing them—after all, we've worked hard in order to be able to enjoy these "fruits of labor."

This scant overview might be considered outmoded, even quaint, drawing as it does on the image of localized companies, bosses in plush offices, and workers on factory floors. The present reality of capitalism is a highly networked, global system of multinational conglomerates entwined with national governments, their militaries and policing forces, and their international regulating organizations, such as the World Bank and the International Monetary Fund. US President Dwight Eisenhower referred to "the military-industrial complex"—a term that has come into popular use, particularly on the Left—to describe the close financial, ideological, and policy ties between congressional government, the armed forces, and the weapons industry. This complex is pivotal in maintaining political and financial power, and to maximizing profit, such that wars—when this complex is most active—might seem to be a "necessary outcome" and intended consequence of capitalism. War, for capitalism, is a reboot button, the equivalent of "pass Go and collect $200 [billion]."

Capitalism is a totalizing system, regulating all social and political exchanges, eradicating any possibility of "authentic" existence, including from the most "private" aspects of subjectivity and selfhood. Entire industries are built around generating "intimate, private" desires, and to gratifying them. Because capitalism is locked into a trajectory of expanding consumption/production, it is unsustainable since it needs ever more resources and ever more markets. As resources run dry, and markets are oversaturated, it would seem that capitalism's demise is built into its own success. As resources are exhausted, the globalization of capital threatens the demise of the planet itself.

Capitalism is so ubiquitous and normalized *as* everyday life that it can be mistaken for a "natural" system inherent to the competitive realities of "human nature." It might be counterargued that humanity survives because of social *cooperation* rather than competition, and that competition has become naturalized as a *consequence* of capitalism.

●

How does all the above apply to artists, art schools, and within art industries?

ARTISTS: Artists, *as artists*, might feel that they do not participate in waged labor (except unwillingly in their day jobs). They might see grants and commissions as "alternative" forms of payment, somehow divorced from the other circulations of capital. They might see sales, and their "representation" by commercial galleries, as an alternative economy fuelled by altruism. They might indulge the illusion that they are not part of capitalism, and can therefore oppose it from a position "outside" of its operations. Other than seeing themselves as outside capitalism (perhaps spiritually, humanistically, or altruistically), artists might not think about it, might feel resigned to it, or might take the position of being anticapitalist.

A linked question is that of cultural capital. This is transmitted generationally as much as is financial capital, and consists of nonfinancial assets, such as class privilege, education, knowledge, intellect, style, speech, social networks, being male, being white, being straight, being cisgender, and so on— all factors that can enable social confidence and mobility (themselves forms of capital). While defined as nonfinancial, like other social constructions and transactional relationships, these can be and are highly monetized. Education, for example, has increasingly become a down payment and mortgage on an accrual of cultural capital and future employment. The "right" education enables one to meet the right people, and, as importantly, makes one feel that one belongs *to* and *with* the right people, since education can provide the means and values to dress, behave, and speak as though one belongs. Cultural capital can come down to something as seemingly banal but socially complex as knowing when and what to laugh at, so that one's laughter marks one as part of the group and not the butt of it.

One aspect of cultural capital in which artists are highly implicated is that of gentrification. Artists, in their search for cheap live/work spaces that others of their class and racial demographics might forsake because of the lack of amenities and services, can act as the *avant-garde* for financial incursion, attracted by the artists' now visible cultural capital (cafés, clubs, galleries, and craft stores).

Marxism proposes that individuals (in cooperation with other individuals) gain the means and fruits of their own production, thereby overcoming the alienation (the passivity) imposed by capitalism's redistribution of ownership into the hands and coffers of the few. One might think of artists as exemplary in owning their own means of production, and this is certainly one aspect of the "freedom" claimed by artists. However, even as artists "intervene" to oppose capitalism, they might in fact be exemplary capitalist workers, performing the paid labor of "day jobs" to fund their own otherwise unpaid work, doing it willingly in the belief (or capitalist ideology) that it is their calling, an inner compulsion.

Artists might "oppose" capitalism by infiltrating existing institutions, creating new ones, joining political campaigns, ameliorating social conditions, community building, applied design, social interventions, pedagogy, civil disobedience, nonparticipation, and beautification projects (murals, etc., although the very notion of art might itself be a beautification project).

Artists might operate by envisaging the "end" of capitalism, imagining and instituting other systems. A commonplace of "social practice" is for artists to instigate barter systems, some of which are similar to time banking, based on time as currency as a more equitable system of exchange and investment.

However, even as artists might focus on capitalism as subject matter, they might not desire an end to capitalism if they are adequately rewarded by it. This might also represent the art industries' self-awareness and built-in ability to critique themselves and carry on as normal.

Artists can therefore come to serve opposing forces. On one hand, they epitomize ideals of individual liberties and free expression. On the other, the rhetoric of art industries is that freedoms are already available and individually held, achieved by "talent" and "hard work," rather than rights that need to be collectively fought for. Separating art from politics and maintaining art as a competitive field ensures that the "artistic freedoms" of the rights to one's own production can apply only to "successful" individuals rather than being available to the "masses." The "depoliticizing" of art is therefore purposeful, serving to pacify dissent and promote "apolitical" art through artistic authenticity, as expression of individual liberty. These artistic freedoms—perhaps necessary allowances—become representative of the aspiration for *all* freedoms under capitalism, and substitute for freedom *from* capitalism.

And yet . . . the act of performing self-motivated, minimally consuming, unpaid labor that might never be market productive (this is the case for most artists) might offer a desire—if not a method or a system—for something beyond capitalism. Artists are regularly faulted (especially by political activists) for being elitist, for being individualist, for providing luxury goods and cultural capital to the wealthy, and for not offering anticapitalist models. But perhaps there is already power in not being motivated by what capitalism has to offer and for seeking—however naively—to function beyond it. Not every artist has to be a political activist, nor be political in the same ways, but in seeking something better (I'm being deliberately vague), artists can choose how and with whom and what to align themselves, even if they do not participate in ways that can be demonstrably "political."

How do artists estimate financial value for their works? A gallery might set prices based on their marketplace tracking. For beginning artists, one method is to consider one's level of training (formal education, apprenticeship, work experience, and life experience). What would be a wage/salary for a skilled worker with comparable training and experience, a doctor, for example? How long did the work take to produce, including intellectual and emotional labor? What were the material costs of the work, including paid assistants/fabricators, framers, and so on? What other costs are included, such as childcare, health benefits, research and networking (going to gallery openings), distribution, insurance, marketing, display, and shipping? Some of these costs may be borne by a gallery, for which they generally take 50 percent of the selling price, but these are nevertheless costs of the work. What would be appropriate compensation when these factors are brought together? What amount would enable you to invest in future work? What amount would produce profit and enable you to be a functioning capitalist?

ART SCHOOL: The art school, even if it is a public institution (and these are being increasingly privatized), is a hierarchical structure along class and corporate lines, with those lines delineated by cultural capital (one's standing in art industries) and wage differentials. Senior administrators are paid the most, followed by senior staff, tenured or full-time faculty, other administrative staff, part-time faculty, blue-collar staff, and students who pay to attend, with complex hierarchies positioning each grouping. Art schools provide training and entry into the intellectual, social, and networking arenas of art industries. Competitive against each other, schools are dependent on their gateway status, marketing their location (e.g., New York City), the visibility of their faculty as artists (rarely as teachers, who possess little cultural capital), and/or the perceived success of their alumni (measured in terms of movie-star celebrity). Even knowing the names of current art stars (and dropping those names into conversation) is necessary cultural capital.

GALLERIES: Most commercial galleries operate along the lines of "small-scale" capitalism and are essentially single-owner businesses with one or two employees, with exhibiting artists as outside contractors supplying specific services/works, and compensated accordingly. Another tier of "megagalleries," such as Gagosian and Hauser & Wirth, operate along the lines of multinational corporations, with multiple international locations and direct supply lines to auction houses and museums, and "poach" artists from smaller galleries much like a Walmart's putting smaller grocery stores out of business.[38]

Artists might own their own means of production, but they generally don't own or control the means of evaluation and distribution (critics, publications, curators, galleries, art fairs, auction houses, and collectors). This capitalist economic model constitutes the *culture* of the artworld. With its global reach and constant acquisition of the new, it is a culture to which there is no "outside."

Challenge

This term more likely occurs in artist and gallery statements, as in, "The work challenges the viewer to . . ." It may often be accompanied by "and forces the viewer to . . ." These are overreadings of any agency performed by an artwork, and downplay the agency of the viewer. In most cases, the viewer can simply walk away, unchallenged, unforced, unconcerned. In any case, "challenge" is overused, and suggestive of the (mildly) subversive but with little or no examination of how the challenge is being enacted. How could one know, especially in advance, if, how, and by what someone is being challenged?

Another word used to similar effect is "question," as in, "These are works that question our ability to navigate the continuum between a functional physical space and abstract pictorial space."[39] Usually, no such questioning ever occurs. Less common, but similar in effect, is "incite," though it has slight overtones of criminality and coercion, as in, "the jet from a sculpture-fountain stops flowing when a spectator approaches, inciting them to move to the centre of the work."[40] Or the more genteel "invite," as in, "The resulting works of art invite us to contemplate their content while pointing to the chemical aspects of their creation."[41]

In all such examples, the important implication (and marketing ploy of a convention of radicalism) is that the works are not passive. They are active entities, provoking reaction and doing something rather than being uselessly inert.

Chaos

Artists commonly talk about their work "making sense of" or creating "order out of" chaos. What this chaos might be is usually not specified, since it is assumed to be a general condition experienced by all, and can refer to conditions that are both interior (e.g., emotional turmoil) and exterior (e.g., social instability). Specific conditions, such as illness, or political unrest, are generally not specified, since "chaos" here refers to an inescapable human condition that is more akin to an existentialist angst of not being in control. The "making sense of" or "creating order from" is not meant literally, nor as a social solution, but as a generalized psychic condition that functions more as an analogy.

While art does not provide order, it does produce (visual) organizational systems in time and place. Even when thus situated, art can suggest the "beyond," as an idealization, an aspiration, a critique, or a movement toward possibility or purpose, which in turn can activate emotion, organize thought, and provide direction. Art performs these by enabling partitioned narratives, neatly framed and separated from the bustle of the nonnarrated existence we call life. No matter how seemingly chaotic, these narratives, like literary ones, provide the semblance of order, partly through formal organization and readability, as though there were beginning and end, as though there were cause and effect, segments and sequences that we could trace if we only followed the right clues and paths.

Common Sense [#Political Correctness]

Although this phrase is less used, it underlies and structures much of art speech. "Common sense" is a form of knowledge that seems so already known, so transparently obvious, and so commonly held that it doesn't require discussion or examination. It masks its prejudices so well that they remain uninvestigated. Its hegemonic power lies in its seeming obviousness, providing an indoctrination that is so already complete that it has become invisible *as* indoctrination. Already tested and "traditional," it can be a deeply conservative, closed, self-perpetuating form of knowledge that by its structure and circulation preemptively deflects the "newfangled" ideas and "buzz words" that might bring it into question.[42]

Common sense manifests orthodoxies or the solidification of thinking through which power is mediated, which Roland Barthes refers to as "doxa." Examples he gives are "Public Opinion, the mind of the majority, petit bourgeois consensus, the Voice of Nature, the Violence of Prejudice."[43]

In the critique, since information, experience, and meaning are being investigated, it helps to not assume that information is commonly held or that perception and experience are commonly evident.

Communication [#Propaganda]

A common belief is that art is a communication system. However, since art is also an affect system dependent on the viewer, what gets communicated cannot be predicted in advance, in contrast to, say, the intentionality of advertising.

Art can certainly be used as propaganda and as advertising, and—given the historical evidence, for example, art in service of totalitarian regimes, or Pop Art as "capitalist realism"—one could make a case for these functions being inevitable aspects of all art and cultural production. In general, however, art's lack of specificity makes it an unreliable communication system (but see below).

Communication, rather than information delivery, might suggest a two-way process, an exchange akin to dialogue. Artists will blithely talk about their artworks in dialogue with the viewer, as though this is a built-in function, and as though dialogue is commonplace between humans and inanimate objects.

There is one sense in which communication does occur. While the viewer brings the artwork into meaning, a reciprocal affect of the artwork is occurring upon the viewer. In short, viewers are changed, adjusted, or confirmed by their encounters with artworks. This two-way, mutual coproduction brings into question the detached, imperial gaze of the meaning-generating viewer that relegates the artwork to "voiceless spectacle."[44]

However, the means and methods, economies and technologies of communication take on different meanings when we implicate communication industries as imperial devices and practices of globalization. In art industries, this might be played out particularly in the production of internationalism—its vaunted transnational mobility, its larger budgets that enable more spectacular (and therefore "better") art, its production of the local for a global viewing marketplace (and here I would include the production of local resistances, as outsides to be incorporated, as themselves attractions for the global market). What might be communicated to the viewer is a desire for and growing dependence on spectacle, a self-congratulatory worldliness, a hankering for newness, a political distance or consumption of local politics as a cross between conscientious tourism and news consumption—war photos from over there, a well-digging project in a different there, women's rights in yet another there, with the here being the gallery or museum space of viewing (itself likely a tourist site).

These are the communication economies that artists would prefer to not be implicated in but that necessarily form the ground conditions on which they function. Michael Hardt and Antonio Negri write, "Communication not only expresses but also organizes the movement of globalization. It organizes the movement by multiplying and structuring interconnections through networks. It expresses the movement and controls the sense and direction of the imaginary that runs throughout these communicative connections; in other words, the imaginary is guided and channeled within the communicative machine."[45]

It should be remembered, then, that communication is not neutral or innocently benevolent but is fully implicated in other systems of exchange and control. Nor does communication necessarily occur under the direction of the artist, nor through the agency of the viewer. And while communication might appear to enhance their access to information, it does not necessarily act in their interests.

Concept/ual

"Conceptual" in its most simplistic form tends to be used to imply that there is an idea behind the artwork. Sometimes one hears, "What's the concept behind the work?" "Or what's your concept?" [#Meaning; #Message]

No artwork is devoid of ideas, even when the idea—which might have been derived through a prior historical moment—is not consciously known to or generated by the artist. This is another way to say that all artwork derives from ideas and continues to generate them. In that sense, all artwork is conceptual, though some forms of representation (landscape, say) might have become so accepted that their formative, conceptual ideas have become normalized to the point of invisibility. [#Common Sense] The conviction that all art is conceptual helps avoid these false divisions between theory and practice, thinking and doing, concept and representation.

●

Philosophically, a concept is generally understood as an abstraction derived from experience and observation. To use Nietzsche's example, the concept "leaf" applies to forms that share "leaf-life" commonalities but that might vastly differ as individual forms.[46] No two leaves are identical, and we may identify their differences, but we can still link them through the concept of "leaf." A concept is therefore an abstraction that collates differences to recognize commonalities, with the intent of making understandable those commonalities, whether as identifiable categories (of things), experiences, and/or as ideas.

Art is a concept. Given the variety of contemporary art, one might be hard-pressed to "recognize commonalities." One way of avoiding defining "art" is by naming the commonality of *where* we encounter it, such as the museum and the gallery. We are then prepared, literally so in the sense of being made ready, to conceptualize whatever we find therein as art.

Any artwork can be described in conceptual terms. Edvard Munch's series of works from 1893 to 1910, titled *The Scream*, are "expressionist" works that might be seen as antithetical to any notion of conceptual art. Yet they each collate complicated maneuvers whereby the world outside—the colors of the sun and the sky, the proximity of other people, the moving reflections in water—seem orchestrated in ways that mirror feelings of individual anxiety and mortality. These are typically expansive intersections between observations, experiences, ideas, painterly techniques, cultural and peer encounters, art histories, and memories (including, in this case, Munch's likely viewing of a Peruvian mummy that resembles the figure in his paintings' foregrounds; or a reference to his sister's manic depression). We, as viewers, have learned such complex conceptualizations so well that we can now have what we might think of as an unmediated, visceral response to these works without having to tease apart and reconstitute their conceptual components. What we are partly responding to in encountering *The Scream* is the prior knowledge that constitutes the discourse that produces and circulates around it. And it is this prior knowledge, a knowledge that produces us as its potential receivers, that is a further conceptual aspect of the work. Any art movement similarly derives from and produces a language that viewers learn to apply to works that use overlapping vocabularies ("it speaks to me"). Any artwork can be addressed using procedures similar to those above and shown to perform conceptually.

In addition to a general application to any art, "conceptual art" can refer to a specific artistic period and set of practices during the post-Pop 1960s and 1970s, and denotes a practice in which ideas or concepts take priority over materiality and aesthetics, or where the latter are direct consequences of the former. Sol LeWitt famously wrote, "The idea becomes a machine that makes the art." Part of this emphasis on dematerialized ideas arose as criticism of the commodification of the art object, and partly (at least in North America) in reaction to the deliberate alignments by Pop Art with commodification and consumption. However, commodification and the art market (including for conceptual art) do not require an actual object; the marketplace has itself become more conceptual in what is sold.

While conceptual art may be distinguished by its emphasis on addressing questions about what constitutes art, what forms it can take, and its relation-

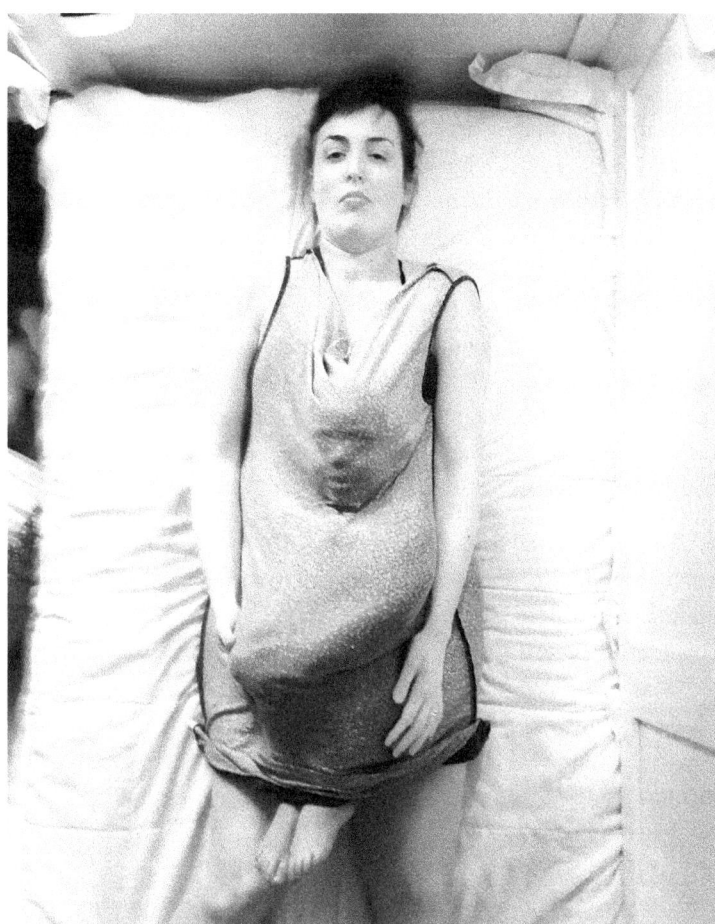

Fig. 5.1 • Megan Wynne, *Untitled (Postpartum Nightgown I),* 2016. Digital print, 9×12 in. Courtesy of the artist.

ship to the viewer, these are necessary questions for any art form that seeks to locate itself within and remain continuingly relevant to the complexities of the contemporary world and to the contemporary viewer.

On occasion, "conceptual" is (wrongly) used to suggest a (physical) lack, or is used in opposition to materiality, as though an object cannot be material and simultaneously conceptual. In this case, the unspoken subtexts are that materiality and labor (of the body) are honest, and that the conceptual (of the mind) is dishonest, distanced, untested intellectualism.

Contemporary

In popular parlance, "contemporary" is used loosely to mean "in the present." It can refer to art of the present and of a recent past as a category distinct from modernist or postmodernist art. It is art that emphasizes its presentness through various material, formal, and disciplinary choices. The term is also applied to art that examines the conditions and forces of contemporaneity. Contemporary art, as it has come to be displayed and circulated through biennales, art fairs, and contemporary museums, is more closely linked to globalization. While sometimes critical of globalization, it might also be the art that most exemplifies the forces of globalization.

Some observers locate the contemporary as originating from 1989–90, a year marked by profound political events with global repercussions.[47]

Some of these events include:

- The USSR withdrawal from Afghanistan
- The fall of the Berlin Wall, marking the end of the Soviet empire and communism as a global force
- Prodemocracy protests in Tiananmen Square, China
- The *Satanic Verses* controversy and the fatwa issued against Salman Rushdie
- The consolidation of the US-funded Mujahideen, and the spread of global jihadism
- The US invasion of Panama
- The dismantling of South African apartheid
- The period between the First Palestinian Intifada of 1987 and the signing of the Oslo Accords of 1993
- The immediate aftermath of Reaganomics and Thatcherism (Ronald Reagan was in office from 1981 to 1988, and Margaret Thatcher from 1979 to 1990)
- The AIDS crisis
- The beginning of GPS satellites
- The launch of Microsoft.

These and similar events caused enormous, worldwide changes that in many ways marked a shift away from semiautonomous nation-states toward a more networked global system, marked by increasing financial flows, instantaneous communication, cross-border conflicts, and the economic, political, military, and health interdependence of nations as well as their increasing dependence on multinational corporations as new global powers. These amount to what we might posit as the global military-backed finance-industrial complex, a complex that, even as it seeks to consolidate its total power, is countered by surges of popular protest movements, such as the Arab Spring, the Occupy movement, and so on, as well as by resurgent extremist, fundamentalist, and xenophobic forces.

One might speculate—as others have—that, since 2001 (post-9/11) we are in a postcontemporary moment. That 9/11 integrated (and fractured) the world in previously unimagined ways. That the global war on terror was in fact the initiation of a new global terror that would not be contained within national boundaries, and was/is a fundamentalist, fascistic response to the previous global terror of colonialism. This postcontemporary moment is in fact overly marked by desired returns to imagined pasts, such as of mythical caliphates, or of "making America great *again*." It similarly leaps ahead to postapocalyptic futures, whether Rapturous, postdiluvian, or monsterized (aliens, zombies, vampires, and mutants). In such cases, this postcontemporary is saturated by other-temporal imaginaries.

●

In art schools, disciplines such as new genres, new media, and new technologies might be designated as *more* contemporary than others, with an emphasis on newness and futurity. They might be differentiated from other departments that emphasize history, tradition, or continuity with a past (printmakers and painters, for example, provide the example of handprints in Paleolithic caves as the earliest forms of their medium, with photographers suggesting that this "shadow work" is a precursor to photography—although conceptual artists could similarly claim this as a conceptualization of indexicality).

Temporal separation between media is conceptually problematic, suggesting that "new" technologies don't have histories, and that "older" media are not engaged with the present or future. There is a similar reconsideration needed of visual languages. For example, abstract expressionism might be seen to be rooted in the 1950s, though many painters use its language in the present. The problem is less about whether to use the language, and more about how to make it relevant and functional in the present. In other words, simply replicating its stylistics can lead to pastiches of a past moment, but considering what roles that language can play in the present makes it *contemporary*.

Context/ual

Like the term "text" to which it is related, "context" is a weaving or joining together. As within a text, the context of a word, sentence, or paragraph is provided by what comes before and after, and which influence its meaning or affect. I have been insisting that meaning is not absolute but provisional and produced through context, that is, through a confluence of multiple factors of location, temporality, subjectivity, culture, and discourse. This mutability would suggest that meaning can never be settled, is always deferred, and that meaning produced in one set of circumstances cannot apply *in the same way* in different circumstances; that meaning, while nomadic, does not travel lightly. Meaning is not touristic, as it were.

This endless permutation is enough to drive us in the opposite direction toward a desire for some kind of fixity, toward something meaning more than and beyond its immediate, locating factors. We crave some foundations of meaning in order to act in the world. One way to proceed through the miasma of possibilities is to locate meaning through power. Each one of us is a subject, that is, constituted through and enabled by our geocultural histories and locations; we are also subject to external authorities. These are our context, which apply not only individually but collectively. It is through this back-and-forth, with ourselves and with each other, with interiority and exteriority, that context and meaning are produced in multiple, overlapping, and contradictory ways. Context continually changes, and meaning changes accordingly. One function of culture is to produce temporary and temporal pauses, foundations, snapshots, representations, artifacts, discussion points, documents, elucidations, provocations, and analyses that are subjects of and subjected to/by/within these flows.

Similar to Freud's analogy of the mind, a fruitful image is of ice floes within larger flows: more or less temporary, melting, flowing into one another, reforming new floes, slowing and/or speeding different flows, emerging and remerging.[48] Like a berg, much of the weight and action is submerged, gradually lightened and revealed only as the berg melts, dissipates, and eventually (through state changes from solid, fluid, and gaseous back to fluid and solid) reforms into stabilities, ice packs and ice shelves that might appear stable, monumental, and frozen but are volatile and flowing. Occasionally there might be dramatic fissures and ruptures, perhaps cataclysmic changes, or increasing, cumulative climate changes that might seem to irreversibly alter directions and factors, producing new contexts, and new imperatives on how or whether we respond or whether we continue to respond to older, previous contexts and information that may insufficiently account for the new contexts or that may even no longer apply.

Broadly, then, context is the historically accumulated information and experience of the moment, but with an understanding that it is produced within and by these constantly shifting, temporal flows.

Creative/Creativity

To have one's work or oneself described as "creative" is to be paid one of the highest artistic compliments (though see "Creative Class" below). The common perception of creativity as originating something new is linked to the early Christian-derived idea of divine inspiration, and the later Renaissance idea of creativity being the attribute of great men and genius (the Greeks, before that, did not link creativity to the arts, seeing artists as imitators of nature rather than as originators).

If we problematize newness and originality, as I have within this glossary, then we need other ways to conceptualize creativity, especially in its relation to pedagogy (after all, how does one teach newness and originality?). Is creativity an "innate talent" (conventional art histories and exhibition demographics might lead us to believe that "talent" is unevenly distributed across race and gender)? If it is not innate, can it be nurtured or taught? If it is an ability available to anyone, what conditions does it require to blossom?

Art history has tended to answer (or evade) such questions by attributing creativity to natural ability, hard work, and mostly to white men (the attributions being made mostly by white men). The conditions for it are either greatness (again, innate or inherited) or extreme struggle (and suffering), through which greatness can be acquired, much like a rite of passage. To leave creativity unexamined is to risk continuing such legacies of exclusivity, which art industries are generally happy to do.

Creativity can be considered as a universal attribute, one of the factors through which we provisionally recognize what it means to be human (while acknowledging that being human has not been and is still not universally attributed to all peoples). In this universal application—and we can insist on it being universally *applied*—we can consider creativity as the manifestation of sentience. I am being deliberately broad, in order to suggest that creativity is an ability available to everyone (as well as—why not?—to nonhuman sentient beings). The creative act is an affirmation of being, and in this it can rebel against constraint, and be empowering of the self, even when its manifestations are destructive to its enactor or to others. To insist on the autonomy of creativity is to allow for acts that may be otherwise repudiated as misguided, irresponsible, criminal, hateful, destructive, or violent—an allowance that is one of the consequences of a blanket insistence on "artistic freedom" or "freedom of speech." In practice, no society allows such license; each society negotiates or imposes which speech acts are taboo, hateful, and/or criminalized (and subsequently censored, legislated, or banned).

One answer to these questions is to consider creativity in relation to ethics, not only in consideration of the prevailing social consensus of what is offensive, taboo, and/or criminal, but to test (and sometimes refute) those limits and the reasons for them being (made) offensive/taboo/criminal. [#Politically (In) Correct]

While creativity is strongly bound to individualism, it is entirely dependent, especially within an art context, on the collective. [#Agency] Only others can designate whether an individual or artwork is creative. This designation is always contextual to the group (or class) who make that assessment, even though some groups have more power than others to have their designations and assessments of who and what is creative enshrined within Art History.

•

"Creativity: Today I will make something new and different and thereby change the world for the better."[49] This is the first on a list of motivational "promises" for budding entrepreneurs. Creativity—and here it refers specifically to generating a new, different *product*—is equated with progress, and progress with amelioration of the world. This model of creativity, the making of "something new and different, and *better*" is now directly harnessed to consumerism, and turns artists—producers of high-value, one-of-a-kind products—into the perfect paradigm for the market.

Unlike "suffering artists," the "creative class" is a market-driven class described by economist Richard Florida.[50] He breaks it down into three main groups: the "super-creative core," the "creative professionals," and the "bohemians" (as likely successors to hipsters and to David Brooks's coinage of "bourgeois bohemians," or "bobos," as socially tolerant and economically corporate). Florida's core group consists primarily of research scientists, engineers, and computer programmers, with subsets of artists, designers, and media workers. As knowledge and cultural workers, this creative class boosts economic growth through innovation, and works across education, health, business, and finance as "problem solvers" to streamline practices and create greater efficiency. Identifying factors include the rewarding of talent, the celebration of individuality, and an expectation of tolerance and diversity—although the former two easily override the latter two. Similarly, tolerance and diversity might amount to little more than the availability of different restaurant menus.

Talent, individuality, and tolerance are the public face of art industries and art schools, and "creatives" might increasingly see themselves as artists, though being somewhat better paid. Florida also speaks of the importance of what he calls "street-level culture," the bohemian-*like* social and cultural consumption of cafés, bars, galleries, farmer and artisanal markets, boutiques, and bistros. These "fauxhemians" overcompensate for their temporary financial lack with the visible markers (dress, tastes, hangouts) of their subcultural cachet. It's an added bonus that these very markers provide feeding frenzies for art industries. This creative class might see itself as socially and ideologically affiliated, like-minded individualists, and it's this individualism that sets them apart (at least in their own minds) from other classes and from the idea of class itself. They might see themselves as uniquely privileged in their class mobility, in their chameleonic mobility across classes, to be culturally wealthy and therefore able to hobnob with and be the darlings of the rich even as they might be financially poor (at least the artists, not the "creatives") and therefore ideologically (again, artists, and again, in their own minds) affiliated with the working class.

Culture [#Identity]

Culture is the complex of relations between people and their discursive and materialized histories, ideas, and experiences. To this we can add the systems that service and circulate these material relationships, that define producers and consumers as individual and collective nodes within networks of interactions, which are themselves productive, material, and virtual. Broadly then, we can think of culture as the totality of life as lived by people, with that "totality" evidenced through analyzable fields of material artifacts, behavior, dress, food, art, and so on.

Typically, this overview of culture is broken down into many cultures, as though they are distinct, and separable, despite the history of human culture being primarily a record of interaction, of influence, confluence, exchange, and theft. Despite how habitually we do so, it is impossible to specify cultures by their limits, as this would suggest an inside and an outside to each one, with strict boundaries separating them. Culture/s are much more porous and fluid, temporally as well as geographically, and we may consider them as coinfluencing, coformed through discursive and material exchange with other cultures. Identifying cultures, then, is more accurately an identification of clustering, of characteristics in common (and sometimes in contrast).

Since we are formed and operate from within culture(s), our ability to "see outside" or "from outside" has to be in question. We can never know, for example, to what extent our understanding of "another" or even our "own" culture is already determined *by* culture.

Identifying *within a culture* entails a complex of political alignments and practices. A claim to culture is through identification with a group, though a common tendency is to naturalize one's belonging, for example, as a racial identity, with its culture as an intrinsic part of that identity. In this example race and culture are seen as one, with a tendency to biologize both.

It might be more useful to examine coproduction, the ways in which we are produced through culture and the ways in which we (re)produce culture in a dialectic of acting and being acted upon. [#Performative]

Artists speak of "my culture" principally in terms of discovery, affirmation, recuperation, maintenance, and opposition. Culture might be thought of in terms of loss of something that has been erased or is being threatened, with artists undertaking salvaging operations of maintaining culture. This may also entail the tactic of using cultural specificity as the site of opposition. Claiming proprietorship over a specified culture leads to other forms of policing, most notably in relation to purity and authenticity, and to who has rights of access to and representation of that culture. While I fully understand the impetus to hold on to what little one might claim as one's own, this claim to a slice of culture—while tactically necessary at times—runs the risk of the artist being locked into these operations—salvage/opposition. Their art, required to authenticate "their" culture or provide proof of its authenticity as a culturally legitimate practice, is likely to become a document of the authentic, and becomes locked into and out of time much like the "living" museums of heritage industries. The artist is then expected to speak *only* of their culture—to become a native informant, assuming the burden of representing one's group or culture—usually in roles that can only be uncritically celebratory of one's group and/or oppositional to others.

During the time of writing, various art industry controversies, or rather protests—against Kelley Walker, Dana Schutz, Sam Durant, Jimmie Durham, Joe Scanlan, and Omer Fast—have been occurring over who has the right to speak/represent a culture. While these artists have been institutionally celebrated as transgressive and innovative, their transgressions have been criticized as trespassing into other cultures through prevailing colonial patterns of cultural appropriation. These appropriations can be and have been made as "benevolent" claims, such as through empathy—and here empathy is an emotional claim upon the other *for* oneself—but in effect can be acts of incursion, occupation, and eradication closely tied to other forms of violence. What has been protested is not just the place of individual white artists to represent the experience of others, but the art industries' eager commodification of those cultures and histories—through its celebrity artists—to embody and enshrine omniscient white freedoms of speech (which are rendered white by being simultaneously denied to artists of color).[51] [#Democracy/Democratic]

Culture is a hierarchical system of values—some slippery and some relatively stable—by which people divide into cultured and uncultured—which can be understood as "classy" or "without class," law abiding or law breaking. To be uncultured is to fail to have been properly administered, and to exist outside of what is valued. On a smaller scale, looking at art, for example, we might make distinctions about who "understands" the work and who doesn't, and based on which artists one likes, which ones one despises. To like Salvador Dalí, for example, as undergrads often do, might be taken (by faculty) as evidence that one hasn't grown out of adolescent taste, and that one hasn't become properly educated into mature culture. To unironically like Thomas Kinkade (despite the speculations of him being a performance artist) is to reveal a class-based lack of culture. To like "pretty" things is to reveal a feminine-based lack of serious culture, and so on, so that each one of us might police our own desires in order to fit within a desired social grouping. Our cultural behaviors and wants might conform so tightly to our desired groups that we might never have them questioned.

One occasionally hears a student bemoaning their lack of a culture and envying another student, usually a student of color or an international student, their claim to a "real" culture. This envy of another culture might mask an envy of another's pleasure and a perceived lack in one's own (aka "Protestant envy"), whether it is manifested through food, dancing, music, bodily decoration, or forms of worship. This envy of another culture is often spoken of in terms of the authenticity of that culture [#Authenticity].

Dark/ness; Light/ness

White (light) is generally understood as normative (and is therefore invisible in its normativity): the blank paper/canvas, the white pedestal, the white wall, the white cube . . . the white artist; these are abstracted, supposedly neutral grounds, from which all other colors, including black, deviate (colors might also produce anxieties of encroaching onto white space). Darkness, within this pantheon, is inherently deviant (and invasive).

Darkness is experienced as both presence and as absence. As presence it contains menace: the face of fear, horror, and anxiety. As absence, it awaits filling or dispelling by light. Darkness is a space of waiting, and a space that itself waits—predatory, engulfing, obliterating. We speak of being swallowed up, ingested by darkness, and of being filled by or immersed in light. One *falls* into darkness, an unending descent; one is *lifted* up into light, a passageway to promise. Darkness is death, light is awakening. Both are conditions of potential, one of annihilation, one of fulfillment. One is bodily—digestive and excretory; one is ethereal and spiritual.

Conceptually, darkness/lightness are too tainted by these binaries of good and evil, racial categorization, moralities of purity (again racialized and gendered), and populist assumptions about the sub/conscious. To spell it out baldly: "white" does not mean "good"; "black" does not mean "bad." [#Bad/Good]

Artists such as Kerry James Marshall and Lynette Yiadom-Boakye enter these binaries to produce other possibilities. Marshall, for instance, uses "unadulterated" black paint to depict his characters. He plays upon visual black as an absence, aligned with racial invisibility within art history. His characters read as both visual voids and impossibly embodied. Yiadom-Boakye, employing a constellation of painterly browns, creates convincingly historical, that is, "authentic," portraits of imagined Black characters, her "impossible subjects" positioned between fact and fiction.

Decoration/Decorative

"Decorative" is often applied to the art forms of the working classes, to women, to gay men, to the marginalized, and the colonized, dismissing them as outsider, kitsch, domestic, women's work, craft, tribal, tourist, and airport art. These might all be used to decorate one's home, particularly following the touristic escape to exotic locations, but not considered serious art (for a museum), worthy of representing national cultures, or subject to serious art historical investigation. These dismissals of work suggest that the makers of the work are themselves seen as decorative, frivolous, excessive, and dispensable. Decoration might suggest enhancements of beauty, but these are considered excessive adornment that serves no serious purpose, or that detracts and distracts from the true essence of a work. Adornment is suspect, as though it camouflages a work's lack of depth. Decoration's surface, excess, and frivolity are marked as feminine in their lack of seriousness and depth—these being masculine, even phallic enterprises. Masculine beauty resides beneath the skin (the ripple and hardness of muscles, for example); and feminine beauty *is* the skin's surface, which can be easily enhanced by makeup, thereby masking the truth beneath. In these scenarios of gender hierarchy, feminine beauty is deemed to be false, a diversion, a mask, alluring, deceptive, scheming, and dangerous. Roman and Greek mythologies, for example, are replete with warnings of these dangers of the alluring, grotesque feminine, whether Medusa or the Sirens (though they are usually vanquished by a heroic male).

There are other ways to consider decoration instead of chauvinistically. Decoration comprises complex geometries beyond art's disciplinary conventions of the rectangle, the cube, and the grid. Arabesques, curlicues, waves, and spirals may be more attuned to (depictions of) complexity, multiplicity, pleasure, energy, exuberance, and *jouissance*. Similarly, one can think of pattern as complex forms of organization that are more pertinent to conditions of chance, of physics, chemical and organic structures, transmission, temporality and duration, excess, expanse, the uncontained, the networked, the discursive, the societal, and the relational. The rectangle and the cube have been art history's primary isolating devices, whereas pattern (and decoration) offers possibilities for reconnection beyond such frames.

Democracy/Democratic

Rather than political democracy, I want to address the confusing rhetoric of "artistic democracy." The former is engaged with structures for negotiation of social power, though perhaps phrased as the negotiation of collective freedoms and responsibilities through equal participation. Artistic democracy emphasizes individual (the artist's) freedoms, and tends to elevate the individual artist above collective responsibilities. The two democracies might in fact be incommensurable. This is most evident in cases of controversial work, which tend to become polarized into arguments of artistic freedoms (or freedom of expression) against collective standards of morality.

Artists can be glamoured by their access into globalized culture in which images from all geographical areas and historical periods are readily available, and equally consumable. Since the global market is invested in capital and ethically disinterested, its freedoms and mobilities are extended primarily to the circulation of goods, of which images now constitute a significant part of knowledge, culture, and entertainment industries. Images, like capital—and artworks have become emblematic of capital made visible—are celebrated as being infinitely mobile. A "democracy of images" has become the fetishization of highly mobile, decontextualized, commodified culture.[52] Access to this cultural economy might be a necessary way to consider privilege, which, favoring one or a few over others, undermines political democracy of people.

⚫

The Internet is celebrated as a primary democratizing medium of interaction and participation. Though it is now unprecedentedly accessible, one might argue that, given the simultaneously restrictive and fluid parameters of social media sites, whether access is the ability to have a voice and to represent oneself, or whether it represents a massive disciplinary power, as much of participation as it is of incorporation into global marketing. Similarly, it might mark a previously unknown expansion of surveillance, including the mass data orchestration of psychographics. [#Affect]

Different media make different claims to democracy, for example, printmakers might claim that the dissemination of prints through books, 'zines, posters, and pamphlets is more democratic than gallery exhibitions. Similarly, photography (and its digital uploading and online circulation) might be claimed as a current democratic medium, available across the globe. Again, we may ask to what extent there is a disciplining and homogenizing of aesthetic choices and social behavior when the photographs one might take (and upload, and customize) as emblematic of one's personal life fit within specific genres and look like everyone else's (for example, as grouped on Instagram or as "beautified" through phone apps such as Meitu).

Claims of democracy have been made for certain photographers, for example, for Wolfgang Tillmans or William Eggleston.[53] The supposed democracy of Eggleston's practice—that anything and everything merits photographing—is a proliferating tendency toward the banal, which Roland Barthes suggests is almost intrinsic to photography: "Photography, in order to surprise, photographs the notable; but soon, by a familiar reversal, it decrees notable whatever it photographs. The 'anything whatever' then becomes the sophisticated acme of value."[54]

This "anything, whatever" is offered as evidence of photography's democratizing practices, or perhaps elevating practices in that it renders anything, whatever, equally beautiful or equally deserving of attention. In contrast to the vernacular of Eggleston, we might consider Robert Mapplethorpe's "classical" treatment of everything he photographed, whether a white lily or a black penis. One might make a claim that both photographers *elevate* their varying subjects to similar heights of edification, though it's debatable whether this complexly in/discriminating impulse is a *democratic* one.

●

Artists (and others) cherry-picking from democracy espouse its highest principle as the freedom of expression. When does espousing freedom of speech become advocating for the freedom to *take* as one's own? When are these freedoms the façade for an imperial overseeing, like the figure in Caspar David Friedrich's painting *Wanderer above the Mist* (1818)? Panopticon-like, he surveys all below him, even as he is absorbed in his self-reverie (the mists metaphorically blinding him to lives below). How might this freedom be rethought as responsibility to speak, not only from one's position, but to speak on behalf *of* (not *for*) those others whose freedoms have already been curtailed?

Artistic freedom and artistic responsibility are not in opposition. One *can* exercise artistic license by making work about any topic one wants. One can also expect to now hear from those whose voices have been historically muted, silenced, and punished for speaking about *their own* experiences, and who hear once again their experiences voiced *back to them*, even if that voicing is intended *for* them. Those who claim their freedom to *speak as* others, and to *take from* others because that's what imperial culture is, can expect to now have those imperial justifications challenged. This is the cost, and the promise, of democratic and artistic freedom *for all*.

Derivation/Derivative [#Appropriation; #Democracy]

"Derivative," on par with "boring" as an artistic insult, has been applied to the artistic output of entire peoples and nations. [#Boring] African modernisms, for example, have been routinely dismissed as derivative of European modernism. Conventionally, charges of derivation flow in the wake of other systems of power, whether cultural, economic, or military, so that those hierarchically lower in those systems are deemed to be derivative of those higher placed, and those higher placed seen to be *inspired by* or *universalizing* the marginal

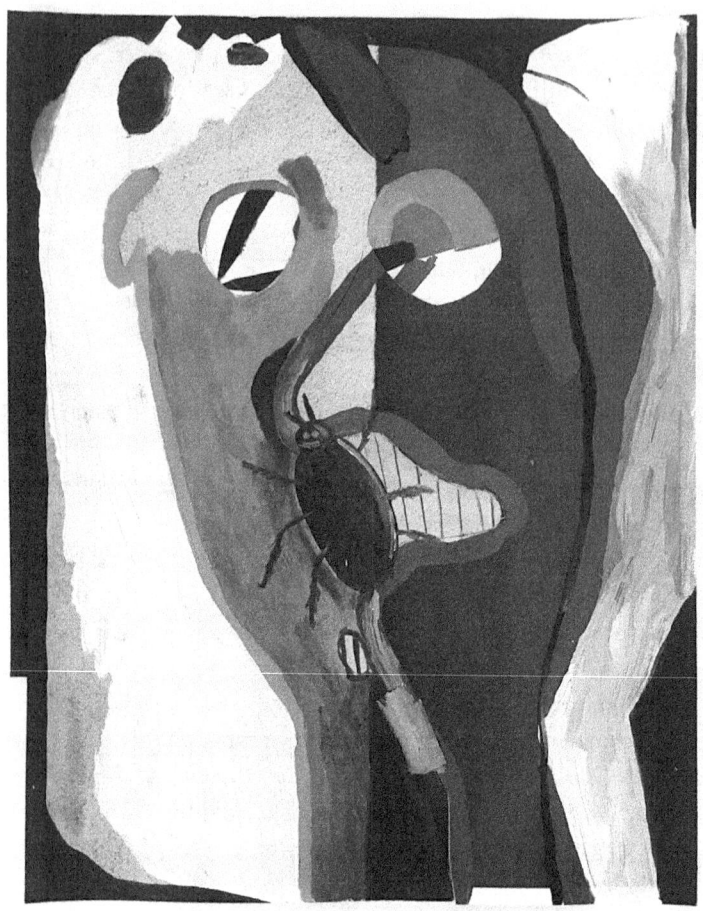

Fig. 5.2 • Isaac Vazquez Avila, *Figure with bug shaped birthmark on face*, 2017. Oil on paper collage, 11 × 9 in. Courtesy of the artist.

identities, difference, and tribalism of those placed lower. Contrary to this civilizational and art historical hierarchy, for example, Pablo Picasso's *Les Desmoiselles d'Avignon* (1907) is not the culmination of Fang masks but an event along pathways that continue into the present through a broad swath of influence and intention, including Romuald Hazoumè, an artist (from the Republic of Benin) who quotes Picasso in order to provoke critical readings of European ingestion of the primitive. In contesting hierarchies of value and originality, we might consider instead that all artworks are derivative in that how they come into being proceeds through multiple genealogies. Derivation, then, is misleading in that it might gloss over a range of strategies, intentions, and quoting practices.

Design [#How *Art* Can Be Thought]

Art schools have increasingly adopted the phrase "art and design" as a single utterance. This suggests as inseparable what might once have been seen as two distinct disciplines and professions. It used to be that artists (Magritte, Warhol, Lichtenstein, Kruger, etc.) were designers in their day jobs, with their "real" work being making art. Design versus art remains a career-guided, financially motivated, ideological discussion, since design represents the more professionalized "creative" sector of what is perceived to be useful, fundable, lucrative, and employment-oriented, compared to art's image (and actuality for most artists) as impractical and financially precarious.

Various presumptions divide art and design:

- Art is culture; design is economics.
- Art is a calling; design is a profession.
- Art is done for oneself; design is for others.
- Art is done for love (or compulsion); design is done for pay.
- Art is interiority made manifest; design is engineering made social.
- Art is expression; design is promotion.
- Art is innate; design is learned.
- Art proceeds from talent; design, from skill.
- Art inspires; design motivates.
- Art springs from instincts; design, from instructions.
- Art is feelings; design is facts.
- Art generates feelings in the viewer; design generates usage by the user.
- Art is interpreted; design is understood.
- Art produces multiple meanings; design communicates single (applied) directions.
- Art communicates meanings; design transmits messages.
- Art is beyond purpose, function, use; design is purposeful, functional, useful.
- Art is transcendent; design is applied.
- Art produces viewer responses; design produces user behaviors.
- Art motivates reflection; design motivates consumption.
- Art is a plan that exists for itself; design is a plan for usability.

- Art transcends commodity; design enhances commodities.
- Art creates the new; design communicates the already existing.

Many of these mythologies of both art and design have no bearing on actual practices. However, between each of these chasms lie gray areas that could apply to both design and art, gray areas that make any division untenable. Within the expansiveness of contemporary art, artists design usable things. Designers make aesthetic objects that serve no other purpose than their own existence. Designed objects are displayed in museums. Art is applied directly within the world. The language of design, however, is naturalized within commodity discourse, whereas art constantly strives to justify its role and value against and beyond commodity culture. [#Creativity]

Design-y

"Design-y" is a colloquialism that is used against artworks when the speaker can't quite articulate their criticism but wants to cover a multitude of possibilities. If a design is a plan, then for an artwork to be too "design-y" is for it to display too evidently or even ostentatiously its plan or schematic. A plan suggests that an object can be made from it, or that an action can proceed from it. If the plan or design is too evident, presumably it isn't yet the object or the action, or that the object/action has not been sufficiently brought into being. This meaning suggests incompleteness.

Another meaning is that the work is too distant, in that it bears insufficient or no mark of the artist. It could have been done by an assistant or by a machine. This lack of the artist's own hand suggests a lack of the artist's bodily and emotional investment. A similar meaning is that the work is too clean, by again not bearing the imprints of its processes of making or the emotive gesture of the artist. This again suggests the rote or the machine-like, devoid of personality and emotion.

The romance of the artist studio is that it is freed from social inhibitions and strictures, where social desires for stability are contested. A design studio is viewed as a place where social desires are perhaps reinscribed and gratified.

Desire [#Male Gaze]

The frequent artistic declaration "My work is about desire" might seem particularly hazy. It is a phrase that is most commonly offered in relation to sexual desire, and within the context of sexual identities and sexual politics, as, for example, queer desire. Presumably, the artist means their own desire, but they are enabled to make that description within and *by* a social, politicized context, resulting from previous political struggles to speak and make visible different forms of desire.

Conversely, as in the case of life drawing from a model, the pretense is that there are no messy desires involved since the work is supposedly an exercise of disinterested skill, where the model is not nakedly or discomfortingly revealed, but *nude*—a euphemism for denial and propriety. While the life model might be the object of scopic, if sublimated, desire, a work about desire need not *depict* the object of desire but may instead depict the artist's own body as both desiring and desired, the faculty of desire, or the engine of the "desiring machine."[55]

Desire is not a personal feeling insulated from other bodily motivations and inhibitions, nor from other social forces. Intrinsic to desire are anxiety, aversion, sublimation, and repression—of desires unmet, redirected, deferred; desires fulfilled only to reveal other desires; desires that create shame, humiliation, inadequacy, frustration, terror, rage; desires that mock, that imprison, that enrapture, that kill.

Legal, moral, and economic structures (of the state, religion, and market) control messy, unbridled desires, curbing and redirecting them toward more manageable and lucrative forms. Entertainment and tourist industries, shopping, alcohol, drug, and sex industries produce, redirect, and attempt to fulfill desires, such that desires might be trained to be satisfied only through the particular routes these industries offer. Art industries can be reconsidered as sensory histories of desire and acquisition, similarly training us as do other industries to what we find pleasurable, beautiful, valuable, covetable, self-affirming, and self-aggrandizing. Who are the trained "we" whose desires art history depicts? Who are depicted as only the objects of desire . . . and as causes of anxiety, aversion, sublimation? Who are shamed, humiliated, excluded?

Even under regimes of constraint (and there are never not such regimes), desire is unruly, irrepressible, excessive, bursting into visibility often through codes of gesture, metaphor, insinuation, association; the glance askew, the tilted head, the stretched foot, the curled finger, the blossoming flower, the ripe fruit. Some might be overdetermined, farcical if only they didn't still carry such cultural weight, still able to determine social value and behavioral roles.

What are different viewers' investments in an artist's desires, and how do those responses change in varying circumstances? In a hypothetical critique, there are two similar sets of photographs of women's breasts. One set is by a straight man; the other by a woman, her sexuality undisclosed. Still hypothetically, the man's work might be seen as sexist and the woman's as feminist; the one conventional, the other breaking new ground. One might be seen in terms of violence toward women, reducing their complexity to sexualized body parts; the other might be seen to naturalize women's bodies in all their complexity. The male photographer is attacked for his fetishizing, sexist depiction of women; the female photographer is lauded for her bravery and honesty.

The critique participants are clearly not responding only to the works themselves nor to their own (sexual) desires but are influenced by peripheral information about who made the work, their understanding of each photographer's intentions and desires, their own complex desires for how they want the works to function, and their anticipation of who else will look at the work. Their immediate public, visible responses might also be different from their private or deferred responses.

We could add titles to the works: one set is called "Prostitutes," the other, "Mothers."[56] Again, our readings of the works will change. We may learn that both students placed ads for their models; one student paid sex workers their working rate; the other solicited mothers but didn't pay them. Does this information alter our reading of the works? Is one group exploited, though paid? Is the other ennobled, but unpaid (we might pursue an argument that motherhood is the most exploited form of labor)? Would the works function differently in relation to our desires and inhibitions if they were encountered in a gallery, in a "men's" magazine, in a "women's" magazine, in an art magazine, in a gender studies class, in a hospital, on billboards? Are desires activated differently in public and private spaces and by who else (we think) is looking, and by who else is looking at *us* as we look? Are publically stimulated desires deferred until the "safety" of a private space (as might be fantasies or revisualizations for masturbation)?

Given some of the above variables, we don't *ever* respond only to works themselves, since our engagement with works are already contextualized in multiple ways that I have expanded on elsewhere. Our desires for the works and the manner in which those desires are activated are directed by our reading of the works' context, our knowing who made the work, and our consequent understanding and investment in how we desire the work to function.

The broader art-historical context in which the two hypothetical sets of work function is that there is a long, dominant, and naturalized history of the depiction of women's bodies as receptacles for male desire. For a contemporary male artist to perpetuate that lineage serves different critical purposes than a female artist trying to counter it. It's insufficient to reduce these questions to only ones of artistic or viewers' freedoms to desire. It's more helpful to consider them in relation to expanding the possibilities of art beyond the conventions of the past, and to have art respond to the expanded debates and possibilities of the present. Viewers' desires (investments) for fantasies of unbridled pasts, of prefeminist sexualized and pre–Civil Rights racialized power, will inflect how they look at art, and what kinds of art they will support. Others will find threatening the artworks that contradict their desires for a moral society formed in their own image (these artworks might be denounced as immoral, as obscene, as blasphemous, as degenerate). Those who seek future-making possibilities where desires are unshackled from the subjugation of others will be drawn to certain works, and might view other works as caught within the politics from which they seek escape and which oppress their desires.

Didactic/ism

Didactic work is that which is intentionally informative, instructive, or educational, whether by direct means or through metaphor or analogy. Art speech uses "didactic" to dismiss anything that is information based rather than experiential, and/or that is seen to be "preaching" to those already informed. Didactic artwork is seen to be manipulative, directing viewers immediately to the artist's intentions, as though the work allows no viewer choice and is programmatic on how to respond, either emotionally or intellectually.

These views presume what art "should" be, that is, primarily experiential. This forgets that our abilities to experience and interpret experience are based on already learned behavior or prior experience; in other words, that art-viewing is learned behavior.

Even though one might be already informed, there might be a valid, even necessary function of having information, opinions, or experience didactically confirmed, especially in the case of marginalized or oppositional subjectivities.

Dismissals of didacticism need to be examined for other forms of bias (that reveal the *viewer's* position rather than an examination of the artwork itself). For example, I've experienced a number of critiques that react against work (and here I will paraphrase): "looks like '70s feminism"; "it's telling us something that we already know"; "we've done that already and we've moved on." In the next session, the same critique group will celebrate work that reiterates the language of abstraction of the 1950s but will talk about it in terms of individual freedom, spirituality, and universalism. The difference here is not that one work is didactic and one isn't, but that the group reacts against a claim to an oppositional subject position and a politicized language as "didactic," and celebrates the claim to individual liberties as not about information but the experience of "all of us." The universalist cause is posited as experiential—that all of us can experience if only we were open to it (those who are not open are philistines—literally closed-minded). Meanwhile, the cause of an oppositional practice is dismissed as "been there, done that."

Fun exercise: try insisting (in a critique) that an abstract or gestural painting is too didactic. Point out that its visual vocabulary is too familiar, too derivative; that its operating claims to individualism, artistic freedom, and to spirituality are politically motivated and overly signposted, to the extent that it can be read as a didactic compilation of signs from the history of painting rather than anything that can be physically or emotionally experienced in an ongoing present. Adapt the same arguments to different media.

Discourse

Too often "discourse" is used to mean a conversation, rather than—as elaborated by Michel Foucault—speaking to and of the generative attributes and functions of practices that construct systems, whose networked organization is *systematically* in service to forms of authority and power. Discourse and discursive formations denote the languages *and* the institutions, structures, and practices that organize and circulate knowledge. Into this broadly indicated outline one may throw in a mix of beliefs, customs and conventions, cultural patterns of imagining, formal and bureaucratic languages, hierarchies and social relationships, patterns of monetary flows, and so on. Artistic discourses include quality, truth, and beauty, which maintain certain institutionalized forms of power, and which produce certain forms of art, display spaces, language responses, and monetary exchanges.

To provide a highly simplified example of a cycle that is already in process: paint is applied to canvas, displayed in a privatized "public" space. The object is named as a painting or a work. If the maker has sufficient brand recognition, the work may be known by their name, for example, "a Rothko." It is written about in specific publications, sold/bought, displayed in a larger public or privately owned space. Viewers are drawn to look at the work, now influenced by what has been written. Subsequent and concurrent acts of applying paint onto canvas are performed by different makers, more or less influenced by the discourse around the "Rothko," and the process repeats. Each of these steps transpires through a complex history of ideas, exchanges, and practices, producing subsequent acts that respond according to fluctuations along each step. Each step is imagined *prior* to its execution, and also responds to prior imaginings and practices. It can be seen that this *discourse* of thoughts, systems, and practices is self-generating, and is thought and practiced from within its discourse, and thus from being already constituted by it.

If we extrapolate this loosely outlined interplay, the artwork is a nodal complex within this system, a node that produces discourse, and that is itself constituted through that discourse. One may apply similar principles to the formation and functioning of an artist, and equally to viewers.

Documentary [#Authentic/ity; #Truth; #Us]

"Documentary" refers to certain modes of photography or film/video that are popularly assigned unmediated veracity. In its role of witnessing, documentary may bear a burden of accounting for, or bringing an event or its perpetrators *to* account. It may be required to provide the impossibility of a full, impartial version ("the whole truth"), even though it can never present how things are. Instead, documentary presents information through historical, technological, cultural, and aesthetic narratives. Even though any account is partial, from a vantage, and mediated through multiple frames, it may provide sufficient evidence to overcome "reasonable doubt." Documentary's aim, then, might not be to provide unadulterated truth—an impossibility—but to be convincing.

Documentary practices might act in different interests. They might be driven by conventions of realism, depicting life without romanticization, "as it really is"—or actively work against the grittiness of realism, for example, by romanticizing the glamour of the wealthy and famous. Documentary practices might provide evidence and truth—or counterevidence; act for inclusion or representation of marginalized communities—or celebrate the rulers; act in the interests of the state or an occupying force to control and archive a subjugated people—or document resisters and dissent. What we see is not *the way things are* but the choices that culture, politics, technology, and opportunity allow us to make, underscored by the different group and individual interests served. These choices, as formal devices, can be more or less deliberately made to determine the viewer's response.

Documentary's "framing devices" are *styles* and *practices*, which can be examined for how they have been historically formed, how they continue to respond and change in relation to a present, and how they imagine or produce a future. Framing can take essayistic or novelistic forms, crafting arguments, perspectives, or poetic narratives through the disciplinary qualities of the medium.

Susan Sontag notes the "sustained look downward" of "class tourism," of the more privileged classes documenting the poor, even if their intentions are benevolent or to promote social change.[57] This downward look is also emblematic of anthropology, and the archiving of the "lesser," the colonized and the incarcerated—whether in reservations, camps, ghettos, or prisons. Aside from intentions of individual documentarians and the institutions they work for, these forms of documentary play a wider role of division, between "us" (viewing) and "them" (viewed). They reinscribe the dynamics of the racialized viewing of double consciousness, and the "looked-atness" deployed by the gendered gaze. [#Male Gaze] Certain bodies are already marked to be looked at, and others privileged to look. The effects on those looked at is a prevailing "pessimism," a confinement of what those bodies can be, and what they can do. The term "Afro-pessimism," for example, refers to the framing of Africa as inherently unredeemable, depicting it only through famine, violence, and poverty.[58] Those "pessimist" arguments are more prevalent, as can be seen in the depiction of the Middle East as also irredeemable. Their implications are that Western intervention, no matter how altruistic, is destined to failure, since the people in these areas are themselves faulted—for example, by being almost genetically disposed toward "ancient, religious feuding." Conflict and war photography, while providing necessary human rights evidence, also reinscribes the larger script of hopelessness, partly by failing to expose the international relations that cause conflict, and redepicting those who have already been marked to be looked at—under surveillance—rather than redirecting vision onto those who watch and perhaps profit. Images of war routinely distinguish between which kinds of traumatized bodies can be depicted. Mangled bodies of the "enemy" might be shown, images of Madonna-like, wailing (enemy) women are routine since the rationale of invasion might include "saving their women," whereas the bodies of "our soldiers" are withheld.[59] The wider effect of this scripting is to render some bodies with agency, others as perennial victims—and also as dangerous, since they pose various threats (terror, sickness, crime, reproduction) to "our" social body. "Us" in this case is the normative social body that the presumed normative viewer identifies with. If the viewer is African, Arab, Asian, or female—in these examples—their viewing marks them, by association, as "dangerous victim"—these two terms, together, defining the foreigner—to be also placed under surveillance. [#Victim]

Documentary negotiates these complex questions of who is looking, who is looked at, directional looking, of distance and proximity, outsider and insider, safety and danger. How close is too close, how far is safe yet close enough to (make the viewer) feel something? What are the conventions of closeness, in the sense of both proximity and intimacy? What are the risks of transgressing these? And who are put at risk? How much time did the documenter spend with the subject to "gain their trust," with trust as the anthropological gateway that also ameliorates viewers' moral anxieties about intrusion, privacy, and revealed intimacies?

"Documentary" might be historically burdened, but artists can use its methods with an impetus more toward creating material and discursive "documents of social relations" rather than the façade of telling the truth.

It might be timely to consider all artworks as documents of social relations.

Dream [#Expression; #Unconscious]

Artists often claim that ideas for their work appear in dreams. This can be a wily strategy for critiques, since if the work is directly from a dream, and one wants to maintain the authenticity of the dream and its insights, then the work can't be changed or improved. Critiquing such "dream work" is faith-based, with the critique group accepting, on faith, that the student actually did have the dream and that the work is an accurate depiction of it. No point critiquing the work's color palette or how convincingly a figure may be drawn, because that's how it might have been in the dream. The dream as critical escape clause is an intriguing strategy, but it doesn't work. The critique is directed to how the work functions within culture, regardless of the work's origin claims, though those too are subject to scrutiny. Even if the dream is accepted as source, it could be a reworking of received ideas, or a partial remembrance of artwork previously seen. Yet the claim is nearly always made that the dream is a conduit to or an artifact from the unconscious. Following Sigmund Freud, dreams are popularly considered to be enigmas or riddles to be unlocked. However, if, as Freud suggests, the dream—like memory—is in fact a "psychological structure," a convoluted fiction designed to frustrate interpretation, the only way to unlock it is through the psychoanalytic practice of a sustained investigation of the history of the dreamer. It is not the dream itself that interests Freud but the wish fulfillment and fantasy that *cause* the dream, or that which the dream represents. This fantasy and desire are always part of larger processes of repression and censorship, which create the coding and perhaps unintelligibility (to the dreamer) of the initiating desire. The Surrealists however, while indebted to Freud, turned toward Jungian ideas, to consider dreams as constituting their own realities. Their artworks, then, are proffered as representations of interior but collective realities. This is the trope that artists still tend toward.

It might be timely to reassess the value and role of dreams to contemporary art at a time when information saturation makes "dream time" seem like an escapist luxury. During daily routines when we might once have daydreamed, we might now be jacked into electronic devices, filling our attention with information and social media rather than allowing our minds to wander or process what we have previously absorbed. This globalized mediascape, a technological "dream world," now most closely matches Jung's description of a collective unconscious:

> In addition to our immediate consciousness, which is of a thoroughly personal nature and which we believe to be the only empirical psyche (even if we tack on the personal unconscious as an appendix), there exists a second psychic system of a collective, universal, and impersonal nature which is identical in all individuals. This collective unconscious does not develop individually but is inherited. It consists of preexistent forms, the archetypes, which can only become conscious secondarily and which give *definite form to certain psychic contents.*[60]

See also Frantz Fanon's rejection of a collective unconscious as "the sum of prejudices, myths, collective attitudes of a given group," and his countersuggestion of "collective catharsis."[61]

Emotion [#Affect; #Expression; #Mood; #Moved]

Artworks are commonly understood to embody the artist's emotions and express them to the viewer. Emotion is equated with unmediated, honest reaction. Art's assumed ability to "transfer" emotions is what popularly distinguishes it from other consumer products, which in general erase the emotions of the workers who produced them (consumers are complicit, for example, in preferring to ignore workers' conditions and low wages). Artworks are the only commodities that venerate the suffering of their producers (Van Gogh, and expressionists in general, as prime examples).

Artworks are emotionally experienced through conventions of color, shape, texture, and line. However, these *vocabularies of feeling* are "read" in ways comparable to texts, with the "reading" experienced as emotion. Rather than allowing that emotions are the end result, we might ask what emotions *do*.

"How does it make you feel?" might be an opening question to elicit discussion about an artwork, but this discussion is about the viewer, not the artwork. Artworks, generally not being sentient, don't have feelings. Good feelings, or just the experience of feeling, are valued as rewards or benedictions bestowed upon us by good art. The way it makes you feel, much like a Michael

Jackson song, is art's marketable power. While a Jackson number, following James Brown, might make us feel good, it has an ambivalent form, speaking to us of other feelings of repressed and unrequited desires (who exactly is the *you* that *turns me on*?).[62] This should indicate to us that feelings, even at their "simplest," are complicated, that we might recognize and acknowledge only their most immediate and identifiable aspects, or the aspects that make us feel good, while repressing others.

Art industries routinely make distinctions between good and bad emotions. A typical attitude is reflected in this curator's selection statement: "'I knew one thing would disqualify a photographer—anger,' he said. 'It was important to look at Israel without complacency but with compassion. I believe art has a power to address questions that an ideological perspective cannot.'"[63] Anger is located as ideological, political, and partisan, whereas compassion is the universalized human emotion. We may well question whether this apolitical front (of art as nonideological compassion) is being utilized, instrumentalized, for the specific political purpose of not criticizing Israel but appearing to depict it with unbiased eyes. Emotions are not just to be experienced but are also put to use. Emotions cause us to attach and detach to/from things, people, political beliefs, and communal identities. Are these *attachments/detachments*—for example, hate, anger, compassion, disgust, or love—the emotions, or the *products* and *manifestations* of emotions? In any case, emotions are powerful tools and weapons in the work of social formation, of group affiliation and disruption. We might say that emotions are sectarian.

There is an inherent slippage in how art-related feelings act in the world:

artists feel = artworks are embodied feelings = artworks create feelings in the viewer = feelings are the true experience and meaning of the artwork = the viewer's feelings are true, real, and are therefore facts = artists create facts.

The Everyday

It is commonplace for artists to situate their work within the everyday and/or banal. This may derive from a cocktail of the following:

- An antiheroic impulse
- A desire to validate and value the ordinary
- Seeking the unusual (sometimes spoken of as the "strange" or the "magical") within the usual
- A desire to meld art with "ordinary" life.

These are valid motives, but they might be misdirected energies. The ordinary is not the focus or result but a means. In the way that doodling "distracts" the brain to free-associate, ramble, *and* focus, the ordinary may allow a sheltered time and space for creative thinking and activity. It is *where/when* the work may happen, rather than *being* the work or the work's subject.

Melding art and life presumes the two are already separate, and further presumes that this separation serves elitism. While artists link this valorizing of the everyday to a democratic or a counterheroic impulse, without a historicizing or social context, or a more politicized imperative (for example, of Dada, Arte Povera, or photography's New Topographics), it runs the risk of being only a sanitized stylistic choice that masks conservative normativity.

The everyday can presume stability, continuity, repetition, and duration, and preemptively mourn their possible interruption and demise. The everyday can therefore be an aesthetics of the status quo. In this, it can be proffered as an island against the rapidity of technological and social change, and as an antidote against the brutality of terror and the anxieties of social unrest. The everyday, as Susan Sontag notes, can be "unremitting banality and inconceivable terror."[64] If we're lucky, these might be mediated by the palliative of entertainment. The everyday is not an antidote to terror, nor is shock (and awe) a remedy for the banal, despite the proclamations of Dada, the Futurists, the Viennese Aktionists, and various ruling administrations. This might be a necessary lesson for those students who feel the need to shock their peers and the institution of the school out of its perceived (b)anality.

Like common sense, the everyday can provide a façade for, if not the "banality of evil," at least the casualness of discrimination, whose very familiarity acts as camouflage and provides its sustaining strength even as its effects accumulate.

A focus on the everyday does not automatically result in making art more accessible. If anything, viewers might expect art to transcend the everyday and the mundane. The mundane as subject matter might be perceived as producing bad, boring, mundane art, which might not even be seen as art. Its mundane attributes might make it incomprehensible to the viewer with expectations of something more unusual, transformative, dramatic, and difficult.

Experiment

RULE 4: Consider everything an experiment.[65]

Sister Corita Kent's rule should apply as an attitude, rather than to objects. In other words, be experimental in one's thinking and making, but what one ends up making does not require the justification of "being an experiment." This justification is often proffered in critiques as an excuse, an apology, as a deflection against criticism, or against the work being "taken too seriously." The authors of *The Critique Handbook* advocate using this "my work is an experiment" line as a delaying or deflective tactic to soften the instructor.[66] When used intentionally in this way, it assumes the instructor hasn't read the same book.

An artwork always has an element of the experimental, even if it copies every step of a previous work or the artist knows every step of a work's progress and outcome. The act of repetition can itself be experimental. The viewer, then, should always expect some degree of experimentation.

Express/ion; Expressive/ness [#Self]

"To express myself" is possibly the most common reason given for making art. The implication is that an essential, fully formed, unchanging aspect of the self is the "truth" of each person, and it is that truth that is being expressed. Those students for whom this truth is a matter of unshakeable faith should know that art schools tend to perform a secularizing function. James Elkins, for example, advises "neo-expressionist students to drop out of school."[67] Elkins suggests that the expressionist artist, in order to remain stubbornly authentic, must *not* learn. The Die Brucke artists he cites as examples might not have attended art schools, but they did study (and copy) the work of others, including gypsies, the mentally ill, and so-called primitives. Contrary to Elkins, contemporary expressionists *need* art pedagogy in order to stop making pastiches of German expressionist pastiches of "primitive" art.

If the self that enters as a freshman is the same self that leaves with an MFA, then presumably nothing was learned, since to learn is to acquire new ideas, new skills, new desires, to become, in effect, a new person. If one compares the work of any given student from when they first entered art school to the work they do when they graduate, there are usually, and hopefully, marked changes. The initial work is more likely to be—and unknowingly so—derivative of museum marquee names from before the 1960s (impressionists, fauves, surrealists, expressionists, et al.). The student might speak of the work in terms of self-expression, even though it is clear to other viewers that the work is absorbed from other sources. The work of that same student upon graduating might not yet be freed from the above limitations, but the student (ideally) will have expanded their repertoire of visual languages, and their critical, conceptual, and technical skills. They will hopefully have gained some knowledge of art history that will help them resituate their work and their interests in how to imagine and pursue their future work. The student will more likely see their artwork as *work* (no matter how compulsively pursued), and less so as *expression*. Their references will likely be more within the contemporary. If still derivative, the net for their work will now be cast wider, and the references might begin to coalesce in ways that haven't occurred before. If still pastiches, they are more likely to be knowingly pursued.

Some students *do* resist what they see as indoctrination, preferring to hold on to their own "truth." It might be that the student needs to gain the skills and techniques that will enable and not impede the flow of whatever is within. But this too doesn't allow for a fixed, unmediated self, since the tools and languages through and with which one works define both the maker and what is made. Skills and ideas are never neutral, and can't be acquired without acquiring their historical and conceptual weight. As one acquires new ideas and skills, one acquires a new self.

If a student needs to be *taught* how to express herself, then she will be expressing what has been taught and not her self. Expressing the self also presumes that the self doesn't learn. These are dilemmas faced by art schools that trade on self-expression but can't unravel the paradox of claiming to teach it. Given these unquantifiable complexities, self-expression, even at its supposed simplest, is one of the thorniest questions within pedagogy.

●

Let us assume, for the sake of argument, that an artwork might express the emotions and thoughts of its maker (the God reference is deliberate). Viewers have no access to that "primary" source. All they have is the artwork, as an artifact (in an archeological sense or as residue from a performance) and as a translation. A translation is necessarily a hybrid form, between one text and another, one language and another. Add to that the translation from the artwork to the viewer's responses, and the exchange is further hybridized. The fact that viewers have access to their own responses (to a greater or lesser degree) doesn't mean that their response is the artwork's meaning, and it certainly doesn't mean that their response is equivalent to the artist's expression or intention.

A more productive way to examine a work's meaning lies not solely within viewer response (though that is often a necessary starting point), but instead considers how the work functions within and as culture. Rather than an artwork expressing an individual, it's more applicable to examine how it manifests and generates cultural discourses, and therefore how it intersects with viewers.

For many students (and artists), however, this approach is less than gratifying in that it doesn't celebrate the(ir) expressive self.

For these and other reasons, art industries still love the romance of untainted self-taught and "outsider" artists, the more isolated from the rest of the world, the better.[68]

●

A way to rethink expression and expressiveness is as means to bring forth the experiences that have not yet or that have been insufficiently manifested, circulated, and valued in the world. This might be undertaken as part of a collective self, for example as a member of a marginalized group. But this "burden of representation" raises its own questions. [#Culture]

Expression of the self can be pursued as performance, following the idea that the self is *already* a performance. [#Performance; #Performative]

Another constructive way to consider expression is as a consequence of an *impression*. Sara Ahmed, for example, speaks of emotion being imprinted: "An impression can be an effect on the subject's feelings ('she made an impression'). It can be a belief ('to be under an impression'). It can be an imitation of an image ('to create an impression'). Or it can be a mark on the surface ('to leave an impression'). We need to remember the 'press' in impression. It allows us to associate the experience of having an emotion with the very affect of one surface upon another, an affect that leaves its mark or trace."[69]

Failure

Students are consistently told that to continue as artists, they have to learn to negotiate failure. That negotiation already operates within the school, which is most likely predicated upon systems of success and failure, with methods of judgment being typically opaque. Given the predominance of merit-based institutions predicated on success and their ritual humiliation of failure, art school—with its variable and sometimes contrary criteria—can allow other pursuits. That which is deemed to be shameful, humiliating, failing—which is otherwise hidden away and kept unspeakable and unspoken—can be made the subject of artwork, and open to further inquiry. Centralizing and normalizing failure rather than constantly marginalizing it is to reconstitute what success means.

One consequence of an emphasis on process over product is that there is no resultant failure, since the process—whatever its outcome—constitutes the work. Similarly, subjectivities, experiences, and behaviors that may be otherwise stigmatized as nonnormative can be addressed without further shaming to become vital sources for artwork. Different perspectives, or rather, perspectives of difference, can endorse these as not only valid but necessary for *all* constituents in a pluralist society.

Strategies such as these can interrogate sources of shame (not fitting in, being bad at drawing, failing at being a good artist, not being the favorite), and can turn shame against itself to open up other possibilities of inquiry. To follow Eve Kosofsky Sedgwick, failure can initiate liberatory transformation: "At least for certain (queer) people, shame is simply the first, and remains a permanent, structuring fact of identity: one that . . . has its own, powerfully productive, and powerfully social metamorphic possibilities."[70] Since *all* identities are constructed through and in opposition to experiences of shame (and likely manifesting as pride), the art school bears the possibility and responsibility of not further shaming its students by attempting to squeeze them out from a single mold.

Declining the will to success (the triumph of the will) and eliminating the work from artwork does not mean adopting what may seem to be their antitheses—laziness; deskilling; lack of initiative, rigor, application and ambition—a general slacker mode that is already associated with art schools. Lessening the burden of success allows for other possibilities of the not-yet-known, that one's energy, time, and labor are less instrumentalized toward profitable production to allow for "something else." Though we wouldn't yet know what that something else might be.

Feminism/Feminist

"Feminism" can be defined as "a collection of movements aimed at defining, establishing, and defending equal political, economic, and social rights for women."[71] It may be considered as a gender-initiated, necessarily unfinished, heterogeneous project of theoretical, social, and political possibilities. Feminism takes many forms, especially in regard to race and class, and draws upon many histories (herstories) and geopolitical formations, sometimes conflicting with each other. Womanism, for example, centered on the twinned gendered and raced experience of Black women, arose in response to the dominance of white, middle-class women in 1970s feminism. Other aligned movements, such as for transgender rights, may altogether reject categorizations of "woman," whether biological or socially constructed, but may still insist on gender nondiscrimination. It is more accurate, therefore, to speak of "feminisms" rather than using the singular form, which suggests one set of ideas, goals, and practices.

Feminism(s) still tends to be an f-word in art school, and some see it as a failed or completed movement (of the 1970s). It is not unusual for some to insist that feminisms' aims of equality have been fully achieved, with no reason to discuss them in the present. Feminisms might still be disparaged by some (not only older male) faculty, mourning the good old prefeminism days, "when female students would still get naked" (actually overheard), or before feminist artists intruded to "spoil the fun" (also overheard). Given such a negative context, it is unsurprising that (female) students might use it only in denial—"I'm not a feminist"—especially to preempt dismissal when their work might overtly address gender. Their perception, reinforced by art industries, is that feminism is marginalizing, divisive, excluding of men, speaking only to a limited audience (despite that being 50 percent of the world's population) and . . . the clincher: not conducive to selling one's work. These are all symptoms of the larger separation between what is considered to be art and what is considered to be politics, and symptomatic of the pressures of assimilation into masculine, or rather patriarchal, culture.

Some harbor resentment that women artists "use" feminism to gain entry into sections of art industries that their work wouldn't otherwise attain. This is along the same lines as resentment that some artists use their "race" or "queerness" to gain similar entry. This (largely false) perception that art industries operate any kind of affirmative action affirms the subtext that the straight white male artist is being victimized by not being able to call upon such strategies.

●

Regardless of its naming(s), and who identifies as feminist or not, gender equality and nondiscrimination are necessary foundations for pedagogy, and should not be considered the responsibility of women or applicable only to women. While women might lead its discussions, strategies, and actions, as a movement of nondiscrimination it should be normal practice by all. Within the critique, feminist politics and analyses are applicable to all and any artworks, as important tools to identify and bring into conversation otherwise naturalized gender biases (within both the work and the critique itself). Feminist theories address questions far beyond those of bias, from what might be seen as the more gendered questions of subject formation and theories of the body to "universalist" questions of art histories, global economics, and to any field of inquiry. The exclusion of this scholarship is its own form of bias.

Feminisms might in fact constitute the most far-reaching, *ongoing* art, cultural, and political network of movements, so widespread in their global effects and with so much that they still aim to achieve that they need to be addressed more along the lines of museum space, gallery sales, scholarly scrutiny, and pedagogical attention of the much more aesthetically limited and parochially (and patriarchally) produced movements of, say, Impressionism or Cubism.

•

Do feminist artworks require use of certain aesthetic languages? One occasionally hears the question "Is it feminist?" directed to an artwork. It's impossible to answer, since the question carries too much viewer baggage, too many implications and accusations, and can lead to too many possible answers. One might as well ask of any work "Is it antifeminist?" A lightning rod for such questions—from many contenders—is Lynda Benglis's notorious "advertisement" in *Artforum,* November 1975. Along one edge of a double-page spread, across from a black rectangle, the naked (but wearing sunglasses), slickly oiled Benglis, hip and shoulder thrust assertively askance, holds/strokes a large, realistically "lifelike" dildo protruding from her crotch (and penetrating it, since the dildo is double-headed). A credit line in the black rectangle reads, "Lynda Benglis, courtesy of Paula Cooper Gallery. © 1975." The ad (or is it a "work"?) remains controversial approaching fifty years later, and at the time was seen as both radically feminist and virulently antifeminist, both striking a blow for and regressing the cause of women.

Why is this image still controversial, and to whom, when nakedness, and particularly the nakedness of women, is a convention within art? Or especially when there was also another image of Benglis naked within the same issue of *Artforum*, performing a more conventional version of femininity as subservient and heterosexually alluring? Did the image shock by depicting a libidinal woman who didn't make herself available, not least by cloaking her own gaze with the sunglasses? A woman who was publically parodying the "private" exchanges of pornography, and of masculine desire? And parodying male artists' hypermasculinity?

But did the ad also fulfill stereotypes of "women's lib" aggressive sexuality, man-hating anger, penis envy, and all-around antisocial behavior, creating a backlash and making it more difficult for more nuanced feminist articulations

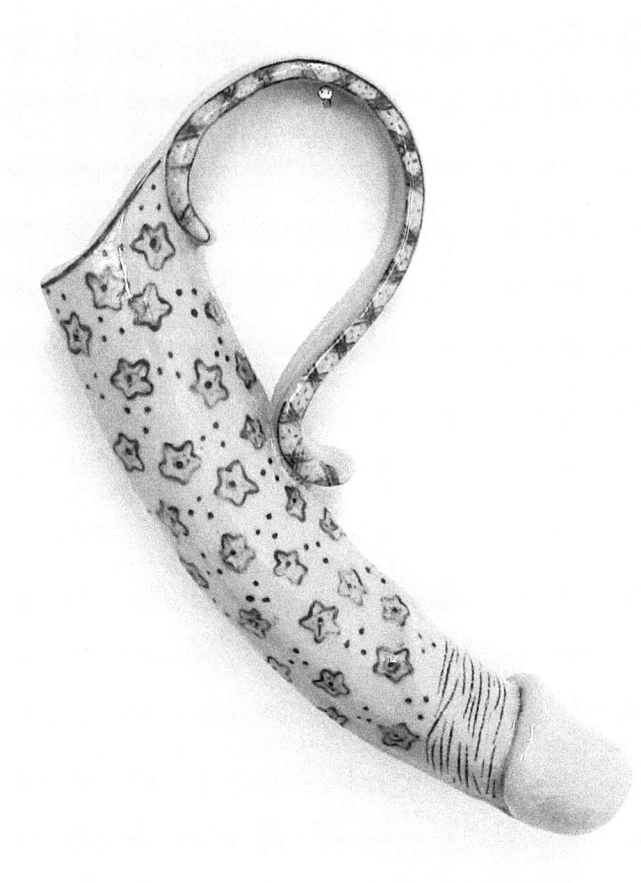

Fig. 5.3 • Nicki Green, *Sex Objects*, 2009. Glazed porcelain, 4 × 8 × 2 in. Courtesy of the artist and [2nd floor projects], San Francisco.

(does "more nuanced" here mean better-behaved)? Did the ad objectify and fetishize the female body (the oil, the tan lines, the model-body glamour)? Did it provoke a different male fantasy of a woman who wants sex as much as a man? Was Benglis trying to enter the male-centric art world by outperforming its masculinity (a demand exacted upon individual women in all careers)?[72]

More recently, artists such as Sue Williams, Barbara DeGenevieve, Kara Walker, Sarah Lucas, and Laurel Nakadate have provoked similarly polarized views. Are their works feminist, exploitative, or denigrating women? A contention is that their works play into both the (feminist) glee and (masculine) anxiety of women enacting revenge upon individual men. In Nakadate's video works, such as *I wanna be your midlife crisis* (2002), the participating men seem to have the least societal power, such that one feels sorry for, even empathy toward, them rather than to the libidinal woman (Nakadate) who teases and humiliates them on camera. The work's feminism is not in humiliating men but in wickedly addressing a woman's place and what is considered proper (lady-like) behavior. Nakadate plays to all the stereotypes of Asian women being submissively available, and turns the tables against the men who are snared by those stereotypes. Some viewers may consider Sarah Lucas's works to be vulgar, derogatory toward women, and incomprehensible as art; others may find her work witty, acerbic in its mockery of how women are already objectified, and crucial to redressing conventional (male) depictions of female bodies.

The many questions raised by such artworks and artists require complex responses, and their inability to be resolved into easy answers adds to the different artworks' provocations. While feminisms can work toward social resolutions of equality and justice, their artistic role in provoking (provocative) questions that have no such resolution is also part of their broader, necessary contestations against how and for whom power and images work.

Form/Formal/Formalism

Formalism prioritizes an artwork's visual, material, spatial, and compositional properties—its *form*—as the sensory, physical experience of the work. This kind of empirical encounter resists translation into words except as a description of the work—often a default method for art history and criticism. Contextual factors—such as the artist's intention or biography, and historical and cultural background, or the viewer's own subjectivity—are seen as secondary, and intrusive on the work's unmediated affect. Exclusive formalism, which posits that everything knowable about an artwork is "contained" within its material presence, tends to emphasize ontology (as a study of being), phenomenology (as a study of structures of experience and consciousness), and a debt to structuralism (as a belief and study of underlying structures that determine all aspects of culture). Formalism, as described, has been a core method for experiencing art and, despite being heavily contested, remains a foundational method. Formalism narrates modernism as a quest for ideal, universal form, beginning with figuration, through various abstracting methods. This ideal form is manifested and experienced as beauty. Form becomes beauty's delivery system, and the continued dominance of formalism, overriding other critical approaches, establishes art's culture as systemic amnesia.

Despite its ahistoricizing blinkers, formal analysis is useful as a beginning strategy within critiques, proceeding from what is observed, a sensory catalogue, as it were, an accounting of marks, lines, colors, shapes, spaces, materials, and temporality, and how these intersect to produce the whole. This is a necessary step for any reading of an artwork, partly as a safeguard against too quickly narrativizing the work in relation to the viewer or an imagining of the artist's subjectivity. These descriptions allow viewers to compare and contrast different works, enabling stylistic links.

Formalist approaches within the critique can take highly racialized and gendered paths, applied by rote to certain kinds of work in which the artist's subjectivity is normative, or otherwise un(re)marked. Conversely, the work of women or artists of color tends to be read biographically, in relation to their gender or race, regardless of the form or content of their work. Since a higher, universalist value tends to be placed on formalism, how and to whom it is applied and withheld can be a symptom of bias. To expose these biases, I suggest turning the tables to read the work of dominant subjectivities through "identity politics," and the work of minoritarian subjectivities through formalism.

Gaze [#Male Gaze]

The ability and freedom to look is closely tied to social power. The ideal of public space is that individuals/groups are free to circulate, to remain, or to leave. They would be able to look freely. But who looks, when and how one looks, and how long one looks are tightly circumscribed by law, political power, convention, body politics, and social circumstance.

The police (and military/security industries) may look, and do so unobstructed by others, who may in fact face charges of obstruction if they interfere with the police's looking. Looking back at the police may incur a response, anything from being questioned to forcible arrest to being shot, depending on one's gender, race, and dress. Racial profiling, for example, determines who can look, depending on the politics of the time. In America, it might be Black men in their late teens to late twenties who are most proscribed from looking (and historically, this has involved the paranoid "protection" of white women). Men who can be profiled as Arab (and this includes South and Southeast Asians, South Europeans, and South Americans) might raise alarm if they are seen to be looking (at pretty much anything) with any amount of interest. A man may not be "caught" looking at another man (especially in heavily circumscribed homosocial arenas such as public toilets), since to hold the gaze of another man is read as either a physical challenge or sexual interest, both of which risk violence. Men expect to look at any and every woman, and expect that women be available to be looked at. Women looking at other women might be taken as being competitive (for men). Women looking at men is invariably understood by men as sexual interest and availability, but if it's an "older" woman looking it may be read as predatory. The above are all dependent on assumptions of heterosexuality, and all may result in violent responses. For anyone lesbian, gay, bisexual, trans, or read as such, the risks of looking while in heteronormative spaces are exponentially increased. Looking is already implicated as action, and as the precursor to further action.

All the above indicate that "public" space and who is able to look are highly regulated in favor of obedient citizenship, maleness, heterosexuality, mental health, able-bodiedness, and whiteness (at least in Europe, the Americas, and the white-ruled former colonies; other regions don't escape this, but may enact localized, sectarian hierarchies of class, caste, and light-skinnedness). Essentially, these are questions of which bodies "require" regulation, and which are deemed likely to cause infection and disruption of the body politic.

●

A convention of art viewing is that if a figure in a painting or photograph looks directly out at the viewer (or to the camera), that figure is read as powerful, independent, or defiant in their ability to look back. If it is a female figure, this might be read as a feminist, returned view of the male gaze. Since the male gaze is presumed to be predatory, or at least scopophilic, a female figure displaying the agency of looking (back) might be taken to be acting provocatively libidinous, as for example, in Édouard Manet's painting *Olympia* (1863). The model, Victorine Meurent, gazes imperturbably out to the viewer, presumably male. This direct gaze, coupled with her naked body, was deemed scandalous at the time, and could be interpreted only as the gaze of a soliciting woman, that is, a prostitute. The figure in *an image* looking back is, however, not the same as an actual person looking back. There is only the fiction of a returned gaze, and the figure remains within the relations of being looked at. The figure looking directly into the camera might create "trouble" (Butler) for the photographer who is "caught" looking, but the third-party viewer of the photograph is untroubled, since the figure has been already fix(at)ed into and as the print object. If anything, the image/object provides permission to look, with the added, invasive thrill (for some) of the figure knowing they're being looked at.

What is it to participate in looking at someone who is being viewed against their will? In Michael Wolf's photographic series *Tokyo Compression*, subway commuters during rush hour are pushed up against the doors and windows.[73] They can't turn away from Wolf's camera as he photographs them from the platform. The most they can do is close their eyes. A few manage to place a hand on the glass to shield their faces. One man looks directly at the camera and flips his middle finger. The condensation and scratches on the glass lend an aesthetic, dreamlike, rapturous effect to the faces pressed behind. With their eyes closed, some individuals seem in religious ecstasy. But these are projections from art history that viewers enact onto the images, and have no connection to the physical discomfort and now personal intrusion experienced by the individuals photographed.

Wolf's photographs are tempered by their aesthetic vocabulary, and remain familiar to city dwellers. They can even be humorous (though the joke is on the commuters). They are quantitatively different from other photographs in which the camera is but one step of the violence being done to those photographed. How do we look, for instance, at the photographs taken by Marc Garanger of Algerian women during the war of independence?[74] Garanger photographed women in internment camps under French military occupation and forced to remove their veils for identity cards. Garanger has spoken about wanting his photographs to document the women's resistance, even in their impossible situation. Their faces scowl at the camera, evidence of the rage, humiliation, and violation they are experiencing. How do we view these photographs now, in the context of France currently enacting laws banning women's veiling? How we do we comfortably view photography's complicity in making the other knowable through violent surveillance?

How do we look at photographs of Cambodian prisoners at Tuol Sleng prison who were forcibly photographed before being executed by the Khmer Rouge? Or Iraqi prisoners at Abu Ghraib, ritually humiliated, tortured, and killed by American soldiers?

What does it mean for different viewers to view these already violated faces and bodies in art exhibitions, where these photographs have all been displayed? They, as others like them, provide necessary historical evidence against the denials by their perpetrators, but they are nevertheless acts of violence. They cannot be condoned by the offensive cliché of "looking into someone's soul," as though we, as omniscient viewers, though so removed from the brutal circumstances of how these photographs were taken—and here the photographic nomenclature of "taken" is applicable—can once again know these individuals, even as their imprisoners sought to know them as vanquished statistics.

Gender [#Feminism; #Identity; #Performativity]

Gender, especially since feminist clarifications of the 1970s, has come to mean social categorization through performances and assignations of masculinities and femininities. Gender is linked to, but does not necessarily coincide with, sex (as biologically argued categories of male, female, intersex) or sexuality (as forms of desire).[75] Each of these categories produces a politics of relations that does not fully coincide with the others. The term "cisgender" applies to social and biologically argued categorizations that do coincide to produce dominant, socially approved forms, for example, masculinity + male = man; femininity + female = woman. The masculine male is the social norm, the site of an abstracted, universal subject, from which femininity is considered lacking or deviant. Masculinity, inversely proportional to femininity, and vice versa, become organizing societal principles, argued as natural, god-given, and immutable. Variance from this fully institutionalized binary, man/woman, is demonized, criminalized, medicalized, and pathologized.

What are the art organizing implications of such categories, for example, under the rubric of exhibitions of "women artists"? Judith Butler notes, "It is not enough to inquire into how women might become more fully represented in language and politics. Feminist critique ought also to understand how the category of 'women,' the subject of feminism, is produced and restrained by the very structures of power through which emancipation is sought."[76] In what ways does such an exhibition prescribe a biological or social category of "women," as well as what work such a subject might produce? Does the category of "women" presume to speak to/for *all* those who female identify, across other categorizations of race, sexuality, class, and gender? Women-only exhibitions might be necessary to counter the ongoing exclusion that women face, and to expose the still normal but undeclared practice of men-only exhibitions. But the women in women's exhibitions do not represent other women, "womanhood," or "women's art," nor should they be required to. The same argument can be made for national identifications, as, for example, an exhibition of "Indian artists" does not represent "Indianness" or the "arts of India" (nor does "Indian art" represent Indian artists). Perhaps such exhibitions are necessary to push against and confound existing categorizations, although they risk producing their own categorizations.

In broad terms, exhibition practices need to be transformed to make gendered selections obsolete, and beyond that, to enable artists and art practices to function beyond the institutionalized categories of gender, and, beyond *that*, to refuse gender itself as an organizing, disciplinary principle—we are not there yet, and any current claim to gender-blindness is suspect. Instead, justifications for such exhibitions can be to recuperate histories, to investigate social and artistic commonalities, such as when gendered experiences or interrogation of gender form the curatorial focus and require artists with shared histories and socialized subjectivities who address those questions *in their work*, rather than only premised on those who might fit a bodily profile. However, a curatorial examination of, say, "masculine painting" does not require the work of male-identified painters, since masculinity—as femininity—is a floating attribute, attachable to and inhabitable by differently sexed/gendered bodies.[77] Exhibitions along the lines of those suggested here may furthermore provide the discursive foundations for their own future obsolescence.

●

While trans activism has substantially repudiated gender binaries, and points toward the refusal of gender as a disciplining factor, it has also made representational claims to another gendered category, no matter how inbetween or fluid. The popular narrative of "being in the wrong body," for example, presumes the "rightly" gendered body. The burden might be placed on a wronged body to make itself "right" so as not to be further wronged. Or a corrective emphasis might target the forces that wrong bodies. Does the fight for gender equality—by identifying, organizing, and representing un(der)represented gendered identities *as* gendered—undermine or reinforce forms of gender categorization? To what extent does equality of categorizations maintain those categorizations? Butler's following questions remain foundational to curating feminist or gender-specific exhibitions:

> Is there some commonality among "women" that preexists their oppression, or do "women" have a bond by virtue of their oppression alone? Is there a specificity to women's cultures that is independent of their subordination by hegemonic, masculinist cultures? Are the specificity and integrity of women's cultural or linguistic practices always specified against and, hence, within the terms of some more dominant cultural formation? Is there a

region of the "specifically feminine," one that is both differentiated from the masculine as such and recognizable in its difference by an unmarked and, hence, presumed universality of "women"?[78]

Art, as histories and politics of representation, is fully implicated in the reproduction (as perpetuation and representation) of gender normativity, though it is also replete with what might be considered gender queering, whether through hidden codes or overt representation. While the depiction of women has historically presumed male viewership, its gender moralism can be undone by female, trans, and feminist interpretations. This ability to be misread, and unread, cuts to the instability of gender itself, and its social pathology (and these equally apply to art). If gender consisted of stable categories (woman, man), it wouldn't demand the anxious policing of its boundaries and codes, the criminalizing of anything but its binaries. This pathology points instead to gender's political and labor functions, to categorize populations into those that can be made subservient, and those that will be served.

Great/ness [#Entry Points: e/Quality]

Greatness is rarely defined. It is assumed that everyone knows it when they encounter it. Referring to artworks, it can be used to mean any of the following: size, permanence, transcendence, monetary value, technical skill, virtuosity, spirituality, timelessness, daring, bombast, ambition, innovation, genius, talent, rarity, distinction, eminence, old, and masterful.

"Greatness" might feature particularly in conversations with gallerists, dealers, and collectors, all of whom, unsurprisingly, wish to be professionally linked to and are invested (literally) in greatness. In art industries, it is hard not to think of greatness as effective marketing, and in that context it means little more than fame, celebrity, topicality, or even notoriety.

●●

A collector once asked me, "What is it that makes Matisse great?" The question took me by surprise, as though it were asked not only in a different language but from a different era. It came with its own set of understandings and beliefs that I no longer shared—though like most art students, Matisse was drummed into me as some kind of deity. The question assumed it was a given that Matisse *is* great. I lamely answered something about Matisse being a "pretty good" painter in that he was adventurous in how he (re)configured color values. I didn't say anything about his borrowing heavily from North African architecture and textiles. His greatness lay in his acquisitiveness and historical timing. Though from another perspective, his was part of the larger acquisition and timing of France's colonial occupations of Algeria, Morocco, and Tunisia, occupations that provided access (and occupations) for French artists. Did Matisse's greatness lie in that he was a particularly effective translator, perhaps pacifier, of colonialism? To have had that conversation would have struck at this collector's core values, and would have labeled me as not only a philistine but as some sort of cultural terrorist or barbarian (literally, as someone outside of any known civilization). I readily admit that Matisse is an exemplary artist in that he incessantly pushed against formal aesthetic boundaries.[79] However, there are greater boundaries at stake. Greatness is the manifestation of civilizational aspirations and achievements. What does this mean when the civilization in question is a colonizing one? When its occupant cultures perform the role of *civilizing missions*, of making colonialism aesthetically palatable, even tasteful? While these are highly provocative (and polemical) questions, greatness is a loaded term that is of little use for discussing art. It tells us more about the person using it, about their aspirations and affiliations, and about how they locate themselves aesthetically and politically. As such, it is an aggregate of foundational, civilizational values. Its use deliberately leads us away from questions about *how* and *to whom* artworks matter.

Gut Feeling [#Emotion; #Instinct]

Indigestion.[80]

History [#Memory; #Narrative]

Memory causes us to be historically minded, literally so, locating us and those around us within time's passage. But memory is notoriously unreliable, easily altered by physical, social, and emotional factors, by vested interests and even through the act of recall. History is equally malleable, responding to changing circumstances and interpretations. As a professionalized (and variously academic, militarized, nationalist, constraining, and potentially liberating) discipline, History manages—in the bureaucratic sense—the tasks of recording and representation. History creates narrative fictions, selecting—and judging—which individuals and groups, speeches and actions, moments and events, will be remembered, and therefore which will be assigned value and importance.

Or one can record histories oneself. In contrast and sometimes in intentional opposition to the certified versions of History are the un- or less-certified genres of oral history, people's history, counterhistory, herstory, genealogy, palimpsest, autobiography, conspiracy theory, art, speculative fiction, and so on. Each of these forms produces its own questions of reliability, accuracy, and evidence, but what might separate them from certified History could be primarily matters of degree and definition. Are conspiracy theories not histories of anxiety and distrust? Is speculative fiction not history of the unknown and the as-yet-to-come?

These counterhistories, now aided by strategic use of communication and recording technologies, and distributed through social media, have interrupted the reach of and dependence on professional History, and certify in previously unimagined ways who can now be a historian and documentarian of history *as it happens.*

An earlier example of this interruption—though one still horrifyingly resonant within memory—was the video by George Holliday of Rodney King being beaten by LAPD officers in 1991.[81] It provides vital counterevidence that what had been happening before, happening since, and recorded again in more frequency is a historical pattern, known all too well by some, dismissed by all too many others. Like so much else about histories, whether this pattern and its recognition become official, certified History is a political question. How might we rewrite histories if we think of them as the recording of human desire (for wealth, power, potency, for the subservience of others, for escape, for equality, for justice)? If we consider History as a hierarchy of desires, how would we record the pursuit of desires by some groups in relation to the denial of desires to others?

Given the above, if art practices are reconsidered as history practices, or as counterhistories of desire and the imagination, some conventional divisions blur, collapse, or are at least brought into question: private and public, memory and history, personal and political, individual and collective. We may well ask what mechanisms maintain separations between histories and politics, between private memories and histories, and History.

Another way to produce history is through techniques of genealogy or archeology, which, as Foucault proposes, are particularly applicable to those "truths" that appear to have no history, such as art's value systems of quality and universality.

Within pedagogy, how could histories be taught that value their intersections with the desires, memories, and lived experience of students? Perhaps one of art and pedagogy's primary functions is as lived practices of people's histories.

Honest/y [#Authentic/ity; #Expression]

A viewer describing an artwork as "honest" suggests that the work connects with them in an unmediated way. Others can't know whether this is a self-fulfilling desire *for* connection rather than actual unmediated experience, or whether the honest artwork triggers the viewer's latent nostalgia, even mourning, for an imagined simplicity, or an unadulterated past when artworks were apparently immediately understandable.

"Honesty" might be read through a vocabulary of signs that are aligned with the viewer's literacy: evidence of the artist's hand, for example, a gestural brushstroke, or a sculptural imprint as an authentic mark, as unmediated transference and synecdoche of the artistic self. In this logic, there is a descending hierarchy of authenticity that is escalating in distance from the artistic soul, from the hand itself, to the handheld prosthesis—the brush, the carving tool, the manual camera, all of which are described by artists as extensions of their bodies—to the human assistant, the machine, the computer, and so on. We might instead consider all of these, including the hand itself, as tools, and question how reliable any of them are as indicators of an artistic self (let alone of a soul).

Analogue photographic prints, especially black-and-white, are seen to be honest, whereas digital, color, and high-gloss prints are seen to be less honest. This is more to do with associations of intimate, creative labor—the photographer hand-printing in the darkroom—and color photography with machine printing, and with advertising and/or mass-marketed populism. Black-and-white photography is seen to harken to an earlier, less adulterated, more artistic, even timeless period—temporal distance abstracts the photograph from its era's social indexicality. [#Time]

"Honesty" often refers to earnestness, a sincerity of intention and belief in what the work is and how it functions. This sincerity might seem like naivety, or a delusional misunderstanding of the historical formation of ideas and practices. Artists may unwittingly sound like politicians. The more they speak of honesty, the more you should look for the misdirection, the mythology, the prescripted—including when the artists themselves believe in their own sincerity.

What would be a "dishonest" work? A common answer is work that panders to the market. If the market is seen to be the tainted commercial aspect of art, then artists are placed in the absurd position of proving their honesty by rejecting the very profession and field in which they operate. To be an honest artist, in this thinking, is to operate in isolation, to work against what are seen to be current trends, and to reject or ignore critical assessments of one's work. For art students, this can be a double-bind: how to be "true (to themselves)" and still adapt to criticism. Occasionally, students will reject any criticism of their work except that which is affirming of its current form, and will interact only with those faculty members who might work in similar ways. Undergraduates, especially, have been known to create two lines of work: one for presentation in class, and one—their "real/honest" work—that is made in secret and which they will fully return to beyond school. [#Outside/r]

Honesty, equated with the already known and the familiar, rather than the innovative and unknown, can operate within art discourse as a moral force, as arbiter of usually conservative values. As a moral value, and therefore a restrictive criterion, since it presumes that making, looking at or evaluating art are moral acts, honesty proceeds from a desire for art to do something *for* us. If it affirms or serves our interests, we evaluate it as honest. If not, it's dishonest.

Hybrid/ity

Hybridity is often uncritically celebrated as the ability to cross boundaries, and to occupy multiple spaces and times. This meaning can be applied equally to the colonizer, the multinational corporation, and the global operations of capital. Despite this broad contradictory sweep, hybridity remains a valuable tool to think between, within, and against binaries (us and them, high and low art, global versus local, etc.) and the vested interests staked on such essentialisms. Most importantly, hybridity applies to *practices* rather than to people and objects. In other words, it doesn't apply to the body, history, or identity of an artist (as it is so commonly used). But it can apply to certain discourses through which that artist and their work may operate. Art practices, objects, and events are intrinsically hybrid, polyphonic (in that they are brought into meaning through multiple voices), and never arriving at finite meaning.

Hybridity enables us to think across culture, across time, across locality or cultural inheritance. While diasporic artists are frequently celebrated as border-crossing and global, within nationalist discourses they are ultimately marked as not hybrid but foreign, and less valued when pitted against the also essentialized authenticities of local, nation-representing artists. A similar binary is produced between interdisciplinary artists and those who define themselves by medium-based ideologies, such as black-and-white photography, abstract

painting, experimental film, or conceptual art. These forms are easily essentialized as pure and unadulterated, unless historicized as already hybrid and constantly evolving.[82]

Identity [#Culture]

Identity is first and foremost a formulation for political power. A dominant,
normative identity would be cis-male, heterosexual, white, and able-bodied, or
at least a (self-)perception of all these. Because this compilation is normative,
it can remain cloaked as an identity. The term "identity" may then be applied
only to those who deviate from normativity, who are rendered less visible as
individuals and silenced to lesser or greater degrees by their "deviations." They
are, however, rendered simultaneously hypervisible, or rather, hypersurveilled,
as deviating, collective identities.

Artists often say, "My work is about my identity," presuming that identity is
unchanging, and even genetic (a recourse to biology is often made). [#Instinct]
Identity is better considered as an active, social *process of identification*, with no
fixed division between interiority and exteriority, formed partly in relation to
those one resembles and in contrast to those one does not. Like memory, it is
in constant flux and in constant formation. It is always relational, responsive
to temporally experienced stimuli and information. That which is experienced
as most intimate, most personal, that most strongly represents or embodies the
"I," that which might be held on to most dearly, is where "external" power is
deeply embedded, and where the embodied is most in play *as* the self. To use
Derrida's term, the "constitutive outside," the "interior" of an identity is formed
through, by, and *with* its "outside."

Not only is identity necessarily hybrid, constituted across membranes that
have no fixed boundaries, it is nomadic, continuously dis- and relocated, adaptive even when its adaptations erect isolating walls. These are the very qualities
that ostensibly fixed identities are threatened by and vigilantly oppose. The migrant, the political radical, the gypsy, the foreigner, the foreigner within, the
ethnic other, the libidinal woman, the "homosexual," the transgender, the insane, the pervert, the unclean—none of which are equivalent. Each threatens
differently, though it is no coincidence that these were targeted by the Nazis
and by other totalitarian fantasists. These boundary figures shimmer (Barthes)
at the edges of visibility, alluring while threatening, destabilizing the supposedly fixed and stable identities of social normativity.

The long-term goals of the politics of identity (I will get to "identity politics" below) negotiate various forms of visibility beyond asserting different

identities onto "seats at the table" or to attain "slices of the pie," to use two common phrases. Visibility can extend to bringing back into the world those experiences, memories, histories, forms of knowledge, and skills that have been systematically denied, incarcerated, medicalized, and otherwise made to disappear. This is consistent with goals of critique, to bring forth that which is not yet voiced rather than what is already compulsively reiterated.

Identification is dynamic. As one factor changes within its relational network, other factors adjust in a constant process of (re)articulation. Artworks, similarly, are articulatory nodes through which identifications are made. Absolute forms, such as *Truth* or *God* or *Beauty*, exist outside such relational, articulatory networks, and are therefore unresponsive and inarticulate. Absolute forms cannot provide evidence of their own existence (except as miracles), nor can they be brought directly into meaning, though artworks are often made to speak for them (with the meaning and the speaking for remaining mysterious).

• •

Identity tends to be applied to and by those who form a speaking site (an identity) from which they may organize for recognition and rights that approach those already available to the normative. The corollary to this organizing is the normative complaint that "minorities" are demanding "special treatment." Identity as a site from which to speak offers at least the semblance of a stabilizing platform in otherwise unstable conditions. A limitation of occupying pre-named positions is that they are already spoken *for*. One risks being fixed into those sites by others, to speak only *from* and *to* those sites. To speak "as a gay man" or "as a woman of color," for example, excuses others to hear one's speech *only* as a gay man/woman of color. While identity can and does speak to such specifics, it operates more broadly in ways that can't be fully contained within any of those speaking positions. A question, then, is how to act and speak multiply, yet specifically, without recourse to the humanistic "we are all the same."

To claim a national or "ethnic" identity is to claim a line of descent from a shared past. Claiming "Americanness," for example (unless one is Native American), is to accept, to some degree at least, the mythologies of the nation, and to link to those others (or rather, similars) with sufficiently overlapping affiliations. The more one feels that one's identity is "the real you," the more threatened it is by boundary crossers; the more precarious it feels, the more one seeks to defend it. Such attachments and their accompanying precarity can be supremely utilized. For a nation to have its citizens willing to fight and die for it, for example, its citizens must be made to feel that the nation and their own sense of personal identity are inextricably one. For a nation to exist (and maintain its borders, and occasionally extend them through war), a nationalism that will bind its citizens to it is of utmost importance. (In)fusing a populace with a national identity is achieved by deploying the language of an identity under attack, and is activated through its readily identifiable symbols of flag, social markers, and religion, as well as art.

Other political coalitions may also be formed on the basis of identity, most commonly through affiliations of race, sexuality, class, or gender. [#Self] To be Latinx (and Native American) is to identify with a complex of trans-American linguistic and cultural formations that are also already in place before one's affiliation, and with a much longer lineage than the nation-state. Even as these national, intranational, and counternational identifications may be invented and experienced within the present, and imagined and acted upon as future-making, they draw their character from pasts that, however invented, may be perpetuated through ritual commemoration (Independence Day, Day of the Dead, Pow Wows, etc.)—with the identification itself creating narrative through-lines between past, present, and future.

These are some examples of what I mean by "identity is first and foremost a formulation for political power."

●

The self (identity) that speaks in the present is still in formation, even though it imagines itself as an enduring form, much like the imagined timelessness of artworks. In practice, any artwork that purports to reflect its maker's identity, in the present, is always already out-of-date, always of a past moment, and necessarily incomplete. The *failure* of an artwork to reflect its maker's identity as a totality might in itself be a worthwhile, if unending project, but that would be more about the impossibility of adequately rendering identity or the Self (see, for example, On Kawara's *Today* series, from 1966 until his death in 2014).[83]

While the above speak to the difficulty, even impossibility, of adequately translating a process—identification—into a (generally more) static form—artwork—there is a converse approach to these questions. An artwork is *always* evidence of its maker's points of identification, including the racial-, sexual-, or class-based, though it doesn't necessarily reveal other aspects of who that person "is." "What you see"—to refute the iconic statement by Frank Stella—is not *how* you see, since we see from and through particular historical, political, artistic, and intellectual junctures.[84] It is these aspects of "seeing from and through" that the artwork may reveal—despite attempts to remove illusion and allusion. What we see, then, is not the artwork revealed, let alone the artist revealed, since what is seen is screened by *how* we see.

Artwork about identity does not automatically mean a license for self-affirmation, nor necessarily a confessional trope. These could, indeed, be the forms it takes, and can serve important functions, but there is a larger field of operations that stems from a politics of examination, exposition, critique, opposition, and reformulation. One example is the formative feminist slogan, "The personal is political."[85] Its *political* project was to expose and repudiate the forms of (often violent) sexism that occur in supposedly private realms, such as the domestic workplace of the kitchen and the bedroom (sex, particularly within marriage, might indeed be contractual labor): the privatized realms that form walls of shame, silence, and invisibility. It is a slogan that has specific historical and social groundings and that is adaptable and responsive to political and social changes. It is useful to consider it as a politicizing process whereby social constructions of the personal are revealed and *brought into* the political realm, the private *into* the public. It is not fixed dogma whereby any aspect of the personally experienced is of equal political or even of artistic value.

•●

A different aspect of identification is the viewer "identifying with" the work. This identification is the basis of art histories of any nation, including Euro American art history that has become globalized. It might be most apparent in works that are religious or patriotic, but applies in more hidden ways to work that is formally abstract and that appears to be autonomous. Art history, as learned, is essentially a cataloguing of identity formation, and an archive of identity politics. [*#How, Now*, Rothko?]

Identity Politics

While this overloaded, overbearing, and overused term is best left out of any critique discussion, I will offer some clarification. [#Politically (In)Correct]

Below, for example, an exhibition statement typically misreads the political goals of identity politics as being only to gain visibility and a slice of the social pie. With such goals now apparently achieved, identity politics are relegated to the past:

> Various groups in society have, during recent decades, defined themselves along political, economic or social lines such as race, ethnicity, gender or sexuality in order to enhance their visibility and overcome marginalisation. After this established discourse of identity politics, often associated with the art of the 1980s, artists are once again considering notions of identity and what they mean in the contemporary world.
>
> Having outgrown theoretical and visual modes that were too often focused on representations of the self or the body, and that more than anything expressed a desire for social visibility, artists today seem to be more interested in identities (in the plural) as part of an overall understanding of complexity—which the art system has not always been able or willing to accommodate.[86]

While the statement does take some steps to relocate the political project of identities in the contemporary moment ("in the plural"), it replicates other problematic subtexts, such as the infantilizing use of "outgrown" and the implied narcissism of "*too often* focused on representations of the self or the body." In contrast, it is important to note that the larger political projects pursued by identity politics are not toward visibility (these are *strategies*, not goals), but to change the terms of what it means to be visible and fully participatory, and to destabilize (and perhaps dismantle) majoritarian, dominant subjectivities and their institutionalized capacities to remain dominating. These critical *politics* of identity politics are the aspects that are the most commonly elided by institutions that still maintain and practice the politics of assimilation.

Contrary to their general use in popular discourse, identity politics are most effective when they are invisible, when normative identities are equated with success, power, knowledge, creativity, and access. In an art context, for example, a group exhibition might include only white men; or one walks into a room of artists, or of professors, or of art students, and all of them are white; or one attends a conference panel, and all the speakers are male. No one seems to notice or think it unusual—partly because these are such common events. These occurrences, *and their acceptance as normal*, are where the normalized, transparent (meaning unseen) identities of whiteness or masculinity—in these examples—are consolidated in the most seemingly innocuous, everyday manner. No one gets angry, emotional, hysterical. No one riots. This is the everyday, *passing* life of identity politics. If a person of color or a woman enters those spaces, and draws attention to the fact that everyone else is white, or male, then they might be accused of playing the "race card," or being a divisive feminist, or of perpetuating (their own) identity politics, leaving intact the identity politics of the dominant.

We need remember that political identifications—for example, Blackness or feminism—organize in opposition to the discriminations and violences *already* done to those identifications. Those identifications—Black, woman—have already been made by those who *enact* the discrimination and violence. For example, our alleged "card player" above might speak from that position because they've *already* been excluded by having been racialized or gendered.

Similarly, though on a different scale, when a white policeman, already activated by *his* (and I emphasize the masculinist) attitudes to Blackness, shoots an unarmed Black man, or slams to the ground a Black woman for "talking back," that is the policeman acting upon *his* and *dominant society's* identity politics. These latter cause all of us, police included, to racialize and demonize a whole group of people—with the police further supported by the institutionalized identity politics of all those who think the fault *must* have been that of the unarmed Black person.

Sometimes the fantasy in the room is that all the white, or all the male, or all the cisgender, heterosexual people—because they are well-meaning—*do* represent all demographics. This is the apogee of normalization, when everyone else is cast into invisibility. This is not to insist that any particular grouping has to include every demographic or that no homogenous group should ever meet, hold exhibitions, panels, conferences, and so on. But if and when they do (and they might have valid reasons for doing so), they should know that they don't speak for anyone else, that they do not represent a "universal" voice, and that their works, views, discussions, criticality, and imaginings are necessarily limited by and likely consolidated by their identity politics.

Any criticism made against identity and identity politics—and these criticisms may include charges of it being self-indulgent, apolitical, and/or overly political—needs scrutinizing that it does not spring from or align itself with reactionary positions of reestablishing normative forms of discrimination and dominance. My own ambivalence about the use of the term "identity politics" is due to its sole placement upon those groups who resist being othered (e.g., racialized or sexualized or, conversely, deracinated or desexualized)—leaving "normal" situations, as described above, of dominating identities unquestioned and intact.

At the time of writing, there is a resurgence of identity politics, which are most powerfully wielded by separatist, pack formations of whiteness, of xenophobia, and of walled-in fundamentalisms and nationalisms.

In opposition to the mutually hostile formations above, is an insistence on intersectionality, the idea that oppressive structures and practices (racism, sexism, etc.) are linked, and that their discriminations cannot be examined or resisted in isolation for/by only one demographic group (leaving other discriminations intact or strengthened).[87]

Imagination [#Inspiration]

In biological terms, the activity of imagining, such as during daydreams, may function as a kind of reset button, the brain allowing for thoughts to be processed while temporarily escaping the onslaught of incoming data. While daydreaming, it's as if one switches off part of the brain, the mind allowed to drift, the senses that link us to our immediate environment seemingly turned off. Imagination allows us to test the limits of what we deem to be reality, and to understand it from perspectives that are less rooted in sensory evidence and previously acquired knowledge. This is imagination as play, "letting go," or "flights of fancy" of the unencumbered mind, perhaps in pursuit of "what if . . . ?" questions, which are the foundation of imagined narratives—fiction. Such fictions, as myths (or religion), novels, cinema, and television, help us test, translate, and understand in social and personal terms questions that may otherwise feel overwhelming in their scope. They also provide pleasures, confirmations, and escapes beyond the constraints of our own lives. [#Unconscious]

Imagination, as the process of creating new mental images, is popularly celebrated as a prime prerequisite for artistry, with art generated by the spark of inspiration, the fuel of imagination, and the engine of hard work. Artists might consider imagination as one aspect of purposeful, necessary labor. Contrary to society's romantic celebration of artistic imagination, "normal" socialization constrains the imagination in ways that are repressive, inhibiting, and censoring. We might be so habituated to "the way things are" that we can barely imagine how things could otherwise be. Imagining "beyond," under repressive conditions, can therefore be an act of dissent or of world making.

We imagine, and bring that imagination and what is imagined into some kind of form, which we may call art. That bringing into form requires language—whether verbal, visual, tactile, or gestural—and the further structure of a discipline and its history, such as literature, painting, or dance. These are the initial structures through which we can activate, translate, and develop imagination. Secondary and tertiary enabling structures are the school, the gallery, the exhibition, the publication, the Internet, and so on. These are as necessary to imagination as it is necessary for imagination to resist them as disciplinary frames. If we don't resist them, we become derivative, repetitive, stuck—all the terms artists don't want to hear about their work. In other words, artists may need these frames and disciplines since they help ground imagination in the world. But that grounding and training is always from a past moment, so artists need to imagine beyond these frames in order to keep up with the present. Artistic imagination needs structures that are reasoned and contested, in order to function within any social sphere. Artworks need shared forms of dissemination and, to some extent, shared language, for example, the exhibition, which is a necessary framing device, even as artists might resist its disciplinary aspects. It's this perpetual realignment of imagination with structure, thereby remaking structure and imagination, that allows for cultural development.

Our abilities to imagine, what is imagined, and the forms that these take are both enabled and constrained by language, culture, genre, and the period in which we live. Paradoxically, imagination is the means by which we may extend beyond those forms of inherited, learned, and lived experience. Within disciplines defined as genres of imagination, such as science fiction, the imagining needs to follow "rules" of science or of the already known in order to convince the viewer to believe the fiction. We police the imagination, then, to function within socially or artistically acceptable parameters, though the popular figure of the artist is a person who skirts the boundaries of the socially acceptable. This allows possibilities for art beyond other cultural forms of theater, cinema, or music, whereby art can utilize those media and disciplines but evade their expectations, for example, to be entertaining in any conventional sense. This ability to operate outside genre conventions also creates the slippage in the popular imagination between the artist and the criminal deviant. "Unconstrained" imagination is always suspect. If what is imagined is violent or sexual, or runs contrary to or outside of societal mores, the person doing the imagining runs the risk of being ostracized or punished as a criminal or a pervert. If what is imagined does not equate with other "rules of reality," or how others experience reality, the person imagining might be identified as mentally ill or socially dangerous. "Deviant" forms of imagining, or misaligned or entirely nonaligned imagining, in tandem with the inability to distinguish between them and exteriority, will tend to follow recognized patterns that will likely be grouped within certain pathologies—such as the sociopath or psychopath.

While contemporary art draws from historical examples of activism, such as the Situationists, a major recent change (at least within art industries) is toward collective or social imaginations, over the modernist prioritizing of the individual imagination. Social practice, "artivism," community art, and artist collectives to some degree aim to activate collective imaginations through participation. Artists may take the role of "activation by imagination," initiating or organizing participatory events toward subsequent acts of dissent, civil disobedience, or insurrection. The imagining may take the form of creating the conditions for reconfiguring social relations through cooperation, barter, or negotiation. Other historical trajectories can be drawn through the broad spectrum of feminist art or Black art, whose practitioners aimed for major structural change, whether against patriarchy or white supremacy. Rather than being relegated to past moments or movements, they can be considered within the present as unfinished projects, not least of the imagination.

Inspiration [#Appropriation; #Imagination]

Inspiration still carries some of its archaic, residual meaning of divine intervention, as though the inspired (literally, breathed into) are the medium through which the sacred is transmitted—the artist as Saul/Paul enlightened on his way to Damascus. In his Epistle to the Galatians (1:11–16), Paul provides a definitive description of this archaic meaning: "I want you to know, brothers and sisters, that the gospel I preached is not of human origin. I did not receive it from any man, nor was I taught it; rather, I received it by revelation from Jesus Christ."

Contemporary artists voice secular versions of this, that ideas came in their sleep, from dreams, from nowhere, from something fleetingly glimpsed— all as though by revelation. If anything, these suggest unintentional processes such as *confabulation*, the misinterpretation, distortion, or fabrication of memories; or *cryptomnesia*, the reexperience of forgotten memories as though they were new ideas. These are closer to how culture works, as the accretion, reformulation, and redeployment of existing ideas and practices. In this latter sense, inspiration is sometimes used to denote work that is made in response to another artist. While this might overlap with plagiarism, or appropriation, and continues to form a legal gray area, "quoting" practices (quote, unquote) are now prevalent and, for the most part, critically accepted within contemporary art.

Another way to consider inspiration, and which is closer to its etymology, is as activation. In this, inspiration is close to outrage, in that both are activating agents. Most of us might dampen our moments of inspiration and outrage, since the impetus to act outside of our routines might be too much of a demand. And it is a demand. To be inspired or outraged is a demand to be activated in/with the world. Is being an activist to be constantly inspired? Others may feel that an inspired or outraged person puts a demand on *them*, upsetting the routines of *their* lives, and may read the demand as messianic, self-righteous, and likely as evidence of mental illness.

Compare to "expire," as a terminal deactivation.

Instinct/ive; Intuition/Intuitive

While these concepts have complex philosophical variations and histories, whether through Plato, Kant, Freud, or Jung, I will combine them here in the way they tend to be interchangeably used within critique. Intuition, for example, is philosophically recognized as knowledge that is acquired through nonrational means. While I am not discounting the nonrational, nor suggesting a hierarchy of knowledge acquisition, intuition is artists' convenient go-to answer for virtually any question about their decisions. "Intuition" is used as shorthand for not knowing from where/how the idea developed, or for learned behavior that has become so familiar that one can no longer trace its source. It's something that just feels right. [#Gut Feeling]

While intuition might be necessary shorthand so that one doesn't always have to track a mode of knowing or a source of knowledge, it leaves open a tendency to assume knowledge is somehow magical, that it just appears (through individual genius or divine inspiration), rather than through pathways across a broader collective, social process.

Intuition and instinct are complexly gendered, with intuition conventionally attributed more to the female, and instinct to the "feral" male, whose escape from the taming influence of society and return to nature is conquering and heroic, much like Tarzan. "Woman's intuition," however, suggests that women have never escaped the clutches of nature to enter the manly realm of rationality and reason.

Artistic instinct should be separated from any discussion about biology and genetics or even Freudian instinctual drives. Since art making is a cultural practice rather than a survival mechanism in the biological sense, the terms "instinct" and "intuition" as generalized sources for decision making don't help to clarify how a work or decision was made. They might instead leave crucial creative processes unexamined.

Biological determinists suggest that art not only serves evolutionary purposes but is positively Darwinian. The assumed factors that produce a good artist or a good work of art—creativity, intelligence, sensitivity, problem solving, dexterity, and all round "coolness"—are the same factors that attract possible reproductive mates. The argument favors male artists, since animal examples offered as biological evidence, such as the bower bird or the peacock, tend to be male. This dubious argument, with apologies to Walter Benjamin, could be termed "art in the age of sexual reproduction." A prefeminist prejudice in art schools was that female students would less likely become artists anyway since most would take the more direct creative route of producing babies.

•

While "intuition" remains an inadequate term, there might be some possibilities for reclaiming its use as an *intentionally* gendered or decolonizing term opposed to a disciplinary rationalism. This intuition deliberately courts the unexplainable, the unanswerable, and refuses to answer *to* a rationalizing authority. Its forms might resemble those of the absurd, but it remains purposeful and directional, rather than something that just happens.

Intent/ion/ality

In phenomenological terms, intentionality is linked to consciousness, in that it is conscious *of* something, including of itself, with the object of consciousness being the *intentional object*. Phenomenology examines how this object is constituted through and into structures of consciousness. Drawing a loose analogy between consciousness and artwork, we might say that an artwork's primary intention, its "aboutness," is itself [#About].

For artists, to make the work might be the only intent. It's not unusual to hear a painter give as reason for a painting, "I just wanted to make a painting." Compare this to Garry Winogrand's reasoning, "I photograph to find out what something will look like photographed." Yet this tells us little about artists' formal, material, or conceptual choices, about how the discipline or material is *worked*. In Winogrand's case, it doesn't tell us why one thing was photographed and another wasn't. Presumably he makes choices about which things might make for more "interesting" photographs. This choice, of one depiction over another, is intent. And this is where we might want to know more, to identify intent by at least a few of its myriad presets and directions. On what basis are those choices—intentions—made? To ask such questions is not only to be directed toward the thing made (the artwork) but also to question the structures of consciousness the artist directed toward the making, and the viewer's structures of consciousness in posing such questions, including toward their experience of the artwork. Intent, then, is necessarily examined on these three broad fronts: the viewer, the artwork, and the artist, *through* the historical and cultural forces that act upon all three.

We might further break down "intent" to make an artwork into various categories, possibilities, and questions:

- When does intent become conscious (when is consciousness *of* consciousness)?
- What impact does the consciousness of intent have on the process of making?
- Does realization of intent become *self*-consciousness, with a possible inhibition of the continued making of the work?
- Does prior intention close off other possibilities for the work, with it being too quickly directed toward being finished?
- Does prior intent limit the artist *to* their narrowly imagined field of intent (the preset I referred to earlier)?
- When is intent realized (or at least, when does it become known to the artist)? Before, during, or after the work, or some combination of these? Does this sequence matter to the work, to the artist, or to the viewer?
- Did the artist have particular intentions by using certain stylistic forms, colors, and materials?
- Does the artist have intentions for how the finished work will be understood? Or for it to have particular affects? Is there intent for how the work should function in the world?
- How does intention differ from or align with inspiration's meaning of activation? [#Inspiration]

These questions, and the artist's intention, can be given varying importance, from none at all to fully determining the viewer's response and understanding of the "meaning" of the work. We can trace some of this variation to discussions following the "death of the author" and the "birth of the reader."[88] With the deposing of the authority of the author/artist arises the agency of the viewer/

interpreter. Moreover, the viewer's agency is not enacted in isolation but is activated by collective and historical processes.

There are no rules to answering these questions, only an acknowledgment of *how* and *why* we choose to collate meaning, whether and why we as viewers respond solely or primarily to the work, or whether and why we incorporate the artist's own description and intent into our response. There are limitations with any approach:

- By not assessing the artist's *stated* intentions (how would we know these if they are not stated?), viewers prioritize their own experience and responses, and may be insufficiently directed to new information/ critique/forms of experience/methods of interpretation. This might be especially the case when viewing works from subaltern positions that are critical of dominant paradigms of experience and interpretation. Prioritizing viewer responses pushes against the work being autonomous and fully coherent, requiring a response to be "completed."
- To prioritize the artist's intention *as* the meaning of the work is to accept the work as a complete and fully coherent entity. The viewer remains on the outside, as it were, as though the work and its meaning were hermetically sealed off, with the viewer's engagement relegated to a mode of acceptance. Viewers might respond to a *description* of the work, the artist's stated intention, rather than to the work itself.
- Is it possible to distinguish a work from its description (and the discourses in which it operates)? Art historical discourses (through which viewers are already constructed) might limit their engagement with other kinds of work, disposing them toward comfortably engaging only with the already familiar (the "I know what I like" of popular art viewing).

Despite the varying importance we may give to an artist's intention, it is still one of the popular means by which something is identified as art. Intent suggests purpose beyond practical use. A work's meaning, then, is sought through understanding its intention and purpose, even if that purpose is apparent only to its maker or is as elusive as the "artist expressing themself." One of the goals of the critique is to denaturalize intent and bring its processes back into visibility and scrutiny.

The seeming lack of intent beyond the technical demands of producing a "good" photograph is one reason for the delayed recognition of photography as art. The transformation from the scene/seen to depiction seems too immediate, too mechanical—or now, too electronic—to allow for anything so incremental as intention. We tend not to wonder what a photograph means or intends unless what it depicts is unrecognizable, such as in abstract photography, or in photomontage. That is, unless the photograph uses techniques and forms associated with other, more artistically validated media, the less it looks like what we expect of a photograph. With photographs that look the way we expect photographs to look, that is, their indexicality seemingly duplicating something that has happened in the world, we tend to think that it is the camera that does the seeing and the "work" of manufacture. Strategies that photographers use to delay these mechanical immediacies include the photo essay or the series, where intent might become apparent through narrative sequencing or reiteration of stylistic elements.

When, as preselfie tourists, we ask someone to take our picture, that someone ceases to exist for us once the picture is taken. We don't ascribe intention to them. If we attempted to ascribe authorship to them by asking their names, they might wish to rescind their agreement to take the photograph, suspecting that the transaction is no longer an everyday one. Intent in these cases, if ascribed at all, is most likely ascribed to ourselves, the ones who initially asked for the photograph to be taken. Even here, the intent might consciously extend only to the technical, wanting the image to be reasonably well lit, in focus, close enough to see our faces, far enough to show our location. Intentions beyond the technical, like the ruse of having our photograph taken by others as a means to examine the social performance of photographing and being photographed, are what might turn "holiday photographs" into "art."

In the above example of tourists taking each other's photographs, intent might be so enculturated as to no longer be apparent *as* intent. We have been so well trained to photograph, be photographed, and share expectations of how the photographs should look that the training is no longer visible to us *as* training but is now part of who we are. Intent can be so ingrained that it now seems natural behavior, and no longer intent. [#Instinct/Intuition]

For some artists, intent acts like a weight of artistic authority that intrudes upon the viewer's encounter with the work. Donald Judd, for example, wanted to remove all marks of the artist so that the viewer isn't directed by the artist's authorial traces on *how* to experience the work. For Judd, this was a politically motivated act to liberate the viewer by allowing them their own agency. John Cage, in relation to his composition, *4′ 33″,* didn't create a piece that was silent but instead created a piece that surrendered his control in favor of accidental, ambient, and audience-produced sound. The piece is never the same each time it is "played" but is dependent on the soundscape of its location and audience. We can think of these as precursors to more contemporary social practice works, activated or "completed" by viewers. In such cases, *control* is deferred to the viewer/audience, though the degree to which control is relinquished is debatable. Intent *for* the work is still ascribed to the artist.

Interactive Art/Interactivity

Generally understood as artworks that require some kind of participatory doing to enable the work to proceed, such as by pressing buttons, tripping sensors, providing voice instructions, scrolling through virtual spaces, eating, and so on. These are proposed as distinct from artworks whose activation or completion is not determined by the viewer's presence or response. The artist's intention might be that the work function as a rehearsal or staging for other forms of social interaction. The work may be intended as a metaphor of political action or civil disobedience.

Artworks, however, are constituted through discourse as well as by one's experience of it. It *becomes* art through an active and discursive engagement that *precedes* the physical or virtual contact of any mode of interactivity. "Traditional" modes of artistic encounter—viewing, listening, feeling, thinking, questioning—are already active modes of interaction and staging. Considering these as only passive modes follows from a condescending presumption that viewing can only be passive. It should not be presumed that physical interaction (pressing buttons, answering questions, and so on) is necessarily activating a viewer's agency, since the parameters of interaction are for the most part prescribed by the artist or by the artwork itself. This can be compared to forms of entertainment or diversion that may pacify its participants since it provides the semblance of agency, in which the participant is acted upon as much as, or rather than, being activated.

Interest/ing

One of the most frequently used terms in artspeak, and one of the most useless. It's an articulate stutter, a stalling term until one has something more to contribute.

Donald Judd's statement that a "work only needs to be interesting," begs a number of questions, including on what or whose terms is it interesting? Interesting to whom? What constitutes interest?[89] Interest can be brought to the work by the viewer, and can be influenced, even generated, by factors such as the viewer's comfort and confidence, their prior knowledge of art history or of the artist, marketing, the artist's fame, where the work is encountered, the prestige of the gallery, the market price of the work, and so on, rather than factors intrinsic to the work itself.

A practical rule in critique is that "interesting" should not be used to complete a sentence or conversation, as in, "That's interesting." Period. One needs to continue the conversation, at least on what makes it interesting and on what terms. Invariably within the critique, a work gains interest as the critique develops, as the group considers different aspects to the work and their own different approaches to it (though different works will have higher or lower interest rates, depending on viewers). Interest in this case is generated by engagement. *How* the work gains interest, and what factors bring the viewer into the "sphere of interest" can themselves be subjects for discussion.

Sometimes faculty members declare their lack of interest in a work or a particular medium, especially if it is not one in which they themselves work. This might mask their lack of knowledge about the work's medium or content. They might feel that the student's lack of engagement, or what they see as the work's poor quality or hasty construction, doesn't warrant their attention. Or it might be a provocation for the student or her friends/peers to defend the work and generate interest in it through the process of critique.

The political sense of "interest," as in "US *interests* in the Middle East," might be useful within the critique. We find something interesting because we have some kind of investment in it, even if that investment is not (yet) apparent. What are our investments in and expected payoffs from the work? What are these expectations based on, and how well do they intersect with the work itself? Or are our interests misaligned with the work? The critique may instead employ a strategy of disinterest, a deliberate distancing with no investment in any outcome for the work, nor expected payoff from it.

Journey

To describe one's process or work as a "journey" suggests a transition from a known position or state to another that is previously unknown. The journey itself is meant to be purposeful rather than aimless, though open-ended and without a destination in mind. The implication is that change occurs, with possible encounters with difference so that the traveler undergoes some kind of personal growth through the experience. The physical journey "out there" is companion to an existential one "in here." It all sounds profound and heroic, and is generally used as synonymous with a medieval-style quest or colonial expedition that overcomes all manner of obstacles. In most cases, however, there is little at stake. The term is so overused by artists that it's as banal as saying, "I took a bus."

Kitsch

Mostly used dismissively, to suggest that an artwork's attributes are any of the following: shallow, sentimental, shiny, gaudy (whether of color, pattern, or surface quality), lowbrow, cheap, mass-produced, and/or unsophisticated. The qualities of a kitsch object reside on its surface, almost as paradigmatic of a lack of seriousness and depth. These qualities render kitsch as a failure to emulate the seriousness and depth of high culture.

Clement Greenberg, in his infamous essay *Avant-Garde and Kitsch* (1939)—an essay he later partly recanted—encapsulated the supposed opposition between an avant-garde and a rear-guard, between "serious culture" and its cheap imitation for those who are "insensible to the values of genuine culture": "Kitsch is mechanical and operates by formulas. Kitsch is vicarious experience and faked sensations. Kitsch changes according to style, but remains always the same. Kitsch is the epitome of all that is spurious in the life of our times. Kitsch pretends to demand nothing of its customers except their money—not even their time."[90]

Even if we momentarily put aside Greenberg's class disdain—a disdain that surfaces despite his otherwise Marxist leaning, antifascist arguments—in which the "insensible" and "ignorant" are victims of their own lack of discernment [#Taste], an artwork might intentionally incorporate the attributes of kitsch, or deliberately mimic the faked, spurious, shallow, sentimental, and so on. It might set out to revalue those attributes as qualities; it might deliberately be critiquing what might be seen as cultural or political biases against these supposedly base sensibilities. Artwork might be recuperating marginalized attributes associated with the working class, women, the "primitive," or the supposedly uncultured, those whose products are commonly dismissed *as* kitsch. All of these are, in effect, strategies that can be linked to Pop Art and what distinguish it conceptually and politically, let alone stylistically and visually, from the Abstract Expressionism that Greenberg espoused.

In his essay, Greenberg speaks repeatedly and disingenuously of "true," "authentic," and "genuine" culture, which is infiltrated, undermined, and contaminated by mass-market-driven kitsch. For Greenberg, kitsch is "synthetic art," a predigested visual effect that saves viewers from the labor of their own engagement.[91] It might be these very qualities that are employed by an artwork as a deliberate façade, or to mimic the affect/effect of much popular culture, as a Trojan horse to infiltrate high culture with everyday lived experience.

There is an overlap between kitsch and camp, though not all kitsch is camp, nor vice versa. Both kitsch and camp emphasize surface over depth, though camp emphasizes artifice as pleasure, whereas kitsch may mistake artifice for beauty. For camp, it is the *pleasure* of artifice that is beautiful, not the artifice itself.

Labor [#Capitalism; #Work]

(Good old-fashioned) hard work is equated with honesty and self-fulfillment, although hard labor is invariably a punishment. Artwork that is "too easy" (that is not *work*), not providing evidence of labor or of struggle, is seen as being somehow unworthy. Having work made by an assistant or professional fabricator, despite being a ubiquitous practice, is popularly seen as cheating and dishonest. Labor is valued differently if equated with "creative" labor, or if it is a form of endeavor rather than menial, repetitive, or paid (outsourced or assistant) labor. The more contact the work has with the artist's hand, the more it is valued as creative labor. Intellectual work is considered as inspiration rather than labor. Work is valued according to how much training it requires, how hard it is, how long it takes, how much it is paid, and who does it. There are the 3 D's of blue collar and migrant labor that no one else wants to do: dirty, dangerous, and demeaning (or difficult).[92]

Parenting is a good example of the contradictory criteria for labor, with the perception that it requires no training, just practice and biological predisposition (or contraceptive failure). Prospective mothers go "into labor." Parenting is unpaid, 3D, 24/7, lifelong labor, but is its own reward, even a "gift." It is generally done by women, especially poor women, who are also likely to parent other people's children. It would be a mark of an enlightened society if parenting were paid.

◗●

While idealistic, the artist's pursuit of useless labor, or their withdrawal of labor, is ineffective when conducted on an individual basis. Despite the occasional calls for artists' strikes, no one perceives artists as supplying necessary services whose withdrawal might produce any disruptive effect.[93] The ineffectiveness of individual labor withdrawal is that the individual can be easily replaced— and in the case of artists, each withdrawal might not even be noticed, or be seen as an "artistic performance" that is incorporated into the artist's oeuvre (for example, John Baldessari's act of burning his paintings, or his refusal to make any more "boring art"). Artists' anxieties about being forgotten, replaced, or ignored makes them pliant workers who will work for free or even pay to work (exhibition fees and other uncompensated costs).

•●

Claire Bishop observes that audience participation in artworks is a form of voluntary unpaid labor that dovetails neatly with the age of both reality television and the service industries as cultural and subsequent economic capital, and, "far from being oppositional to spectacle, participation has now entirely merged with it."[94]

Like/Dislike [#Taste]

"I like it" is a standard opening gambit of viewing an artwork and exposes a typical tendency in critiques of narrating the viewer's tastes and opinions rather than examining or deciphering what the work *does*. It can be a generative entry point but remains elementary if maintained only at that level of likes/dislikes, and can be a way of evading further engagement. Is it important (to the viewer, to anyone else, to the artist) that one likes a work? Is it important to the artist that their work is liked? And strange as this may sound, is it important to the work that it is liked? In other words, what purposes does liking serve? These questions have been inflated online, where what one likes and the number of likes may constitute one's personality profile, one's social standing, and artistic currency. Being liked online has become equivalent to a stock portfolio.

Within the dynamics of a critique group, to tell the artist that you like their work might be more an affirmation of your social relationship, the sort of thing one's friends and family feel obliged to say as encouragement. Likes/dislikes are not fixed and may change over time and circumstances. Disliked artworks might have the most lasting effect, and through that (perhaps irritating) effect we might come to like them. Likes and dislikes are also becoming increasingly conditioned responses online. These instant and instantly gratifying responses absolve us of further engagement, since the communal display of our tastes and presence as modes of belonging has been served.

Male Gaze [#Gaze; #Gender]

Invariably, the reference here is Laura Mulvey's pivotal essay *Visual Pleasure and Narrative Cinema*, a standard text in critical studies courses.[95] While the essay may now be criticized as being too sweeping, and without accounting for class, racial, or sexual differences, it is nevertheless more complex than how the term "male gaze" tends to be used in critiques: as a monolithic formula that all men look and all women are looked at. Some students use the term earnestly; others use it with accompanying air quotes. Most seemed to consider it archaic, though it has had a resurgence following the rash of publicized sexual harassment and assault cases in all areas of social life, including in academia, in the film and entertainment industries, and in politics.[96]

Mulvey builds upon the cross-racial (non)identifications of double consciousness and objectness proposed by W. E. B. Dubois and Frantz Fanon, respectively, to analyze cinema and the ways in which women are depicted.[97] Her scholarship applies more broadly to other areas of culture, particularly to advertising. In both cinema and advertising, the presumed majority audience/ viewer is male, heterosexual, and white. The depicted woman's role is therefore to provide sexual allure to capture and maintain the attention of the male viewer. This is most explicit with advertising of "masculine" products such as cars, motorbikes, and power tools. The accompanying woman bears no relationship to the actual product, except as a kind of promise or reward of masculine accomplishment for the potential purchaser. Such examples do not exclude the viewing habits of women, since women participate also, to be "looked at." The (heterosexual) female viewer's point of identification is to see herself *as* the woman depicted, as the potential promise, reward, and rival for the male purchaser. She sees herself as an accompanying product, as accessory. Women, therefore, might constantly view and evaluate themselves through a male's eyes, even when no man is present. Similar effects and identifications occur in horror or crime films in which the depicted female is the terrorized victim of the killer/monster/alien. The female viewer's point of identification is as victim and, if she's lucky, she may be rescued—again as promise and reward—by the film's male protagonist, who is the point of identification for the male viewer. This complex of women being seen is what Mulvey refers to as "looked-atness."

Such are the broad strokes of the male gaze, although, of course, identifications are never that straight(forward) or predictable. Furthermore, while such overdetermined narratives and depictions still continue within cinema and advertising, both industries have adapted to attract (new) female viewers/consumers in more complex ways.

In art, the most obvious application of the male gaze is to the female nude. Who produces these images? Who have these images been for (historically)? Who is given permission and presumed to be the one to look at and to consume? Which viewers might feel themselves on display alongside such images? Do such images only "document" social and sexual relations, or do they also assist in their production and maintenance? What competitive ideals and standards of beauty do such images document, maintain, or produce? What fictions of passivity and "a woman's place" do the female nude assist in producing? And here, I'm thinking of the Guerilla Girls' poster *Do Women Have to Be Naked to Get into the Met. Museum?* (1989).[98]

While the above questions are directed toward the nude, they apply more broadly to all forms of representation, as coded forms of social relations. Despite some of its limitations, questions about the male gaze form a useful means to discuss ever-present gendered viewing and readings of artwork.

Mediocre

This is one of the most damning comments one can make to a student or any artist. [#Boring] In the competition for excellence, no artist wants to be mediocre. If the comment is directed at the work—"This is mediocre work"—then the student can improve, and it is sometimes used as a spur for just that. If it is directed at the student—"You're a mediocre artist," or worse, "You'll always be a mediocre artist"—then the suggestion is that you might as well give up. The term itself might never be used, but students are told this in all kinds of ways, including by the expressions, body language, and apparent boredom of the faculty. One sees similar uses by critics, for example after an artist's retrospective, when one can more fully assess an artist's life work. To be judged mediocre at this point is a kind of historical execution, to be escorted out of the pages of art history and into deaccessioning sales.

Everyone is mediocre until one does something exceptional. And even then, one can return to mediocrity, resting on one's past laurels. Good ideas and happy accidents can happen to anyone at any time, though the means to implement those ideas might require other resources, thereby favoring those with better means of support and access to resources. It's the role of educators to prepare the conditions for good ideas *to* happen, and to provide the resources to implement them, rather than the more common disciplining into categories of excellence, mediocrity, and failure, likely based on poor pedagogy and dubious value judgments.

●

"Mediocre" also operates as the language of discrimination, directed—often systemically—against artists of color and/or against women. It provides rationale for why, apparently, there are no great women artists, or why there isn't a black Picasso—to rehash arguments one still hears. When women or artists of color do achieve success, they might be dismissed as unfairly gaining it because of their "minority status" rather than through the excellence of their work. When institutions and individuals link intelligence, criticality, enterprise, and success to whiteness and heterosexual masculinity—as they often do—they act as though the mediocrity of "others" is biologically determined and can never be overcome. "Mediocre," even if never spoken, becomes the commonly understood background to group exclusivity. In this, the use of "mediocre" reverts to its word origins, meaning "halfway up a mountain." If civilization is imagined as a vertical, racialized hierarchy, with white Europeans (Aryans) at its peaks, the mountain's lower levels are where "others" might reside (see again Caspar David Friedrich's painting *Wanderer Above the Mist* (1818). See also the genre of German, proto-Nazi "mountain films" of the 1920s–1930s emphasizing verticality and heroic conquest).

Meditation/Meditative

Meditation is generally considered a benevolent state of deep focus and engagement, in contrast to daydreaming, which is tainted by a connection to laziness, escapism, and avoidance. Applied to artwork, a meditative response suggests a continuing focus upon the work, while daydreaming suggests the work is quickly left behind as the mind wanders to other, presumably less lofty things.

Though the artist might intend meditativeness to slow the viewer down from the fast pace of metropolitan life, the artwork is not wholly causal with the viewer passively acted upon. The viewer has varying degrees of agency in how they respond. A Mark Rothko painting might provoke a deeply spiritual, meditative response from one viewer, while another might see it only as unsettling, fuzzy blocks of color. In neither case is the work itself meditative. If there is a meditative effect, it could not be said with certainty that the cause is the painting. The viewer's predisposition or desire might be projected onto the painting as an appropriate stimulus. [*#How, Now,* Rothko?]

An artist may think their process of making the work is meditative. Another artist may experience the same process as catatonically boring. Similar questions of predisposition and desire may apply here.

The terminology of meditation, and the often-mentioned idea of slowing down the viewer, are familiar within Euro American modernism and contemporary art, in which a primary mode of understanding the world is in terms of increasing speed. The Futurists, on the other hand, wanted to speed up the human body to meet the demands of the machine age. Within certain legacies of avant-garde art, from Fluxus to Minimalism, the perceived need to slow down is partly derived from the huge impact of Zen, particularly as taught by D. T. Suzuki in New York in the 1950s, and disseminated further to artists by people such as John Cage and Alan Watts. Since then, and more recently, there have been continual influxes of South Asian gurus introducing other forms of meditation, with a current ubiquity of yoga-related meditation. The discussion of meditation, then, cannot be separated from an orientalist yearning for escape from the rigors of the contemporary. Meditation is increasingly appropriated into individualistic privileges of being able to escape through self-improvement, much like yoga and spa vacations, and correlating with art being good for us.

Medium [#Message]

A necessary entry point for engaging with an artwork is through its medium. Some critiques, however, never get beyond this, instead becoming fixated on technical data or on the material properties of the medium. [#Form] Critique discussions can be entirely taken up by f-stops, printing paper, camera lenses, or by thickness/thinness of paint, titanium white versus zinc white, or six inches into a corner or six further out (for photography, painting, and sculpture, respectively). These are necessary discussions within instruction and tutorials but not the purpose of critique as I have discussed it earlier.

Conversely, more immediately tactile media, such as clay or paint, might be regarded in similar ways as a spirit medium, as conduits into emotive, dream, or otherworldly realms.

We can extend Marshall McLuhan's catchphrase, "the medium is the message," that meaning is embedded within and conveyed through the materiality and technology of a medium.[99] Art itself—its histories; its affects; its expansive, discursive practice; its marketability; its social consequences—all of these extend from an individual work's materiality to become the *broader medium* through which the work functions. The individual object/action provides access points to these other questions.

Memory [#History]

Memory, the archiving of the self, consists of multiple, complex processes with different aspects and functions: acquisition, processing and encoding; storage; and recall. These are highly dynamic and continually responsive to each other, with temporal and "conscious control" differences. For example, clinical tests suggest that "sensory memory" consists of automatically acquired sensory data that begins degrading within a second of acquisition. If this were not the case, we would be overloaded by constant sensory input that we wouldn't be able to forget. These processes are notoriously unreliable, affected by suggestion, (mis)information, correlation, dramatization upon recall, and emotional significance, to list only a few factors that affect their variability.

Anyone who has crammed the night before for an examination knows that there are big differences between short-term and long-term memory in terms of what gets stored, how it gets stored, and what can be recalled. Short-term memory has more limited capacity, and will be forgotten within a minute without some kind of reinforcement or mnemonic aid (the convention of grouping telephone numbers into three-four clusters, e.g., 345-6789, is a memory aid). Long-term memory may be more episodic, in that we tend to remember specific events or episodes (e.g., birthdays, the year I went to college, my first concert, etc.) as markers in time and as gathering points for related memories. This kind of memory serves as formative moments for our sense of self and our place in the world, that is, as markers of space and time, of personal geography and history. Long-term memories and their vivid recall can be heightened by emotional connections, especially by fear. These sometimes overwhelming, repetitive, and uncontrolled fear-related recollections are a central experience of trauma. Memory is necessary for both aspiration/desire and punishment, to remember what one is seeking and to remember why one is being punished. The mythical Sisyphus, even though compelled to his eternal task of repeatedly pushing the boulder up the mountain, is driven by aspiration and therefore has a glimpse of a desired future where he succeeds. If he didn't remember his previous labors and failures, his task would not be a punishment.

○●

It is commonplace for students (and many artists) to describe their work in terms of memory, or to simply state, "My work is about memory." They don't mean computers, or storage capacity. They mean something inherently and distinctively personal. What values are being given to the past? What is being remembered, and for what purposes? What is the relationship between history and memory? Between the artist as an individual and the artist as representative and "voice" of a group? What value do we place on tradition, and how do we define ourselves in the present in relation to the past?

While memory is overused as (pro)claimed subject matter, it bears further investigation, since artworks *always* engage with memory. Objects exist in the present, but they have pasts, in the literal sense of their material and conceptual coming into being. In order to engage with both the present and the past of an artwork, we require abilities to read the past and the passage of time, whether this means being able to trace material development over a period of time to the work's present, bringing to the encounter our own past likes and dislikes, our previous viewing of artworks, or our memory of contextualizing art history. We are incapable of comprehending something entirely new, as though we were blank slates to be freshly imprinted. Much as we entertain the self-help mantra of "living in the moment," we can't do it, and wouldn't want to. A continuous present would be a kind of limbo, a goldfish never knowing that it is swimming in circles or, worse for us to anticipate, Alzheimer's. Or it would be the traumatic saturation of sensory memory, as mentioned above.

Message [#Ambiguity; #Communication; #Design; #Medium]

The specifics of a message might be seen as diametrically opposed to the open-endedness of "ambiguity," but neither addresses the more complex means through which artworks actually function. "What's the work's message?" is an unproductive, even lazy approach that bypasses the potential complexity of any work. It reduces the unquantifiable possibilities of art—excess, contradiction, multiplicity, the unknown, the undisciplined, imminence, and so on—into a linear, finite statement. If art were knowable, containable, and reducible to that extent, artists would put up written statements *instead* of the work. This is not to be confused with the written statement *as* the work, nor the use of a written statement as one means to direct a viewer. If the intent of the work is to function *as* a message—as a specified set of information—then it should use an appropriate message-delivery system, whether a placard, billboard, announcement, TV, or infomercial. Even with these, questions of style, form, medium, and history operate in excess of any message.

Modern, Modernism, Postmodernism [#Contemporary]

"Modern" is popularly used to mean the present, but it can be confusing to students when used in conjunction with modernity, modernism, postmodern/ism, or the contemporary. I will offer brief—albeit idiosyncratic—starting points here. It is important to remember that, in sketching out histories, I am participating in fictional narratives of linearity: that there are beginning and end points, that one thing led to another. [#History]

"Modernism" does not mean "modern," nor does it mean "modernity," the condition of being modern. Modernism is a philosophical and ideological belief system responding to social, technological, and material factors and with its own array of consequences. Most commentators locate the beginning of modernism (and by this is meant *European* modernism) sometime in the mid-to late nineteenth century, as a direct outgrowth and response to industrialization (the Industrial Revolution "began" in the 1760s, with a Second Industrial Revolution in the 1850s, marked by the beginnings of steel production). Modernism, then, correlates to the mass social changes following large-scale industrialization: growth of cities, technological advances such as factory-scale textile production following the invention of the cotton gin, the invention of sheet glass, steam power, the invention of cement, iron (and later, steel) manufacturing, gas lighting, and the building of railways and roads. These caused seismic shifts from the previous feudal system of agricultural peasants and landowners toward the building of intensive factories, with denser housing for new workforces, and more efficient transportation of goods and people to and from the centers of manufacture. This led to the rise of a merchant middle class (the bourgeoisie), as well as a concentrated urban working class. The changes in social relations were accompanied by changing intellectual and political analyses. The new economic and resultant political systems sparked developing theories of capitalism (Adam Smith), and socialism (Karl Marx). The physical proximity of large numbers of different peoples (within cities) also propelled the social sciences, including the biological (Charles Darwin) and, later, the psychosocial (Sigmund Freud).

This, as far as it goes, is a fairly conventional background for the development and concerns of modernism as an aesthetic system. We might also equate modernism more expansively with the period and ideas following the European enlightenment and maritime expansion (rounding out, say, from the 1660s to the 1960s). I will similarly situate postmodernism in relation to decolonization and postcolonialism (from, say, 1955 of the Bandung Conference rather than the more common Eurocentric version of Paris, 1968).[100]

Within these timelines and frameworks, modernism projects a set of beliefs and practices formulated on linear progress, development through technology, the ideal of universalism, and an emphasis on individualism as a site of agency and creativity. These worthy beliefs and practices nevertheless allow for slavery, colonialism, world wars, and a universalism that, rather than universally applied, was/is actively denied to different groups based largely on their class, race, gender, and physical and mental ability. The preamble to the United States Constitution, "We the People . . . ," is a case in point, the "we" applying initially only to white men of property.

Within the arts, a similar sense of linear development holds sway. Art history is celebrated as a singular narrative of individual geniuses, with artistic movements coalesced around them, one movement leading to another, each one more "modern" than the previous, and with little accounting for alternative or contradicting locations, practices, and timelines.

Modernism is also understood as a break with the illusion of naturalism, a break that makes the act of viewing self-conscious and that, to some degree, makes the viewer self-aware of their looking, as in Cubism, for example, with its naturalism-disrupting mechanisms being already put into place by Paul Cézanne and others.

Édouard Manet's paintings *Olympia* (1863) and *A Bar at the Folies-Bergère* (1882) have been identified as similar turning points that precipitate modernism (as is the much earlier Diego Velázquez painting *Las Meninas* [1656], with *its* complex interplay of viewing). At the center of *Bar at the Folies-Bergère*, a woman looks directly out to the painting's viewer. Her reflection in the mirror behind shows her to be attending to a male patron at the painting's edge (who is only seen in reflection) rather than to the external viewer. The external viewer and the depicted patron are intentionally conflated, marking both as male in contrast to the female attendant (understood as attending both). The painting's "impossible" visual pyrotechnics of mirror reflections and angles of view anticipate Fredric Jameson's description of the Bonaventure Hotel in Los Angeles a century later.[101] Art historian Albert Boime's description of the painting could apply equally well to the Bonaventure, as well as to any number of postmodern hotels, department stores, malls, and casinos: "The new public space is viewed as a magic-lantern show of dazzling optical illusions that deceive the crowd by blurring the boundaries between consumption and production."[102]

In these scenarios, viewer and viewed are constructed through their environments, and all are indicative of burgeoning change (though women remain depicted as handmaidens to this masculine-driven change). Viewing becomes emblematic of postmodernism's totalizing spaces and as allegory of global capitalism. [#Male Gaze]

Despite the examples here, and their precursors, it is difficult to make a case for an originating moment for modernism. There will always be precursors and lines of influence. It is much easier, then, to think of modernism as a system of

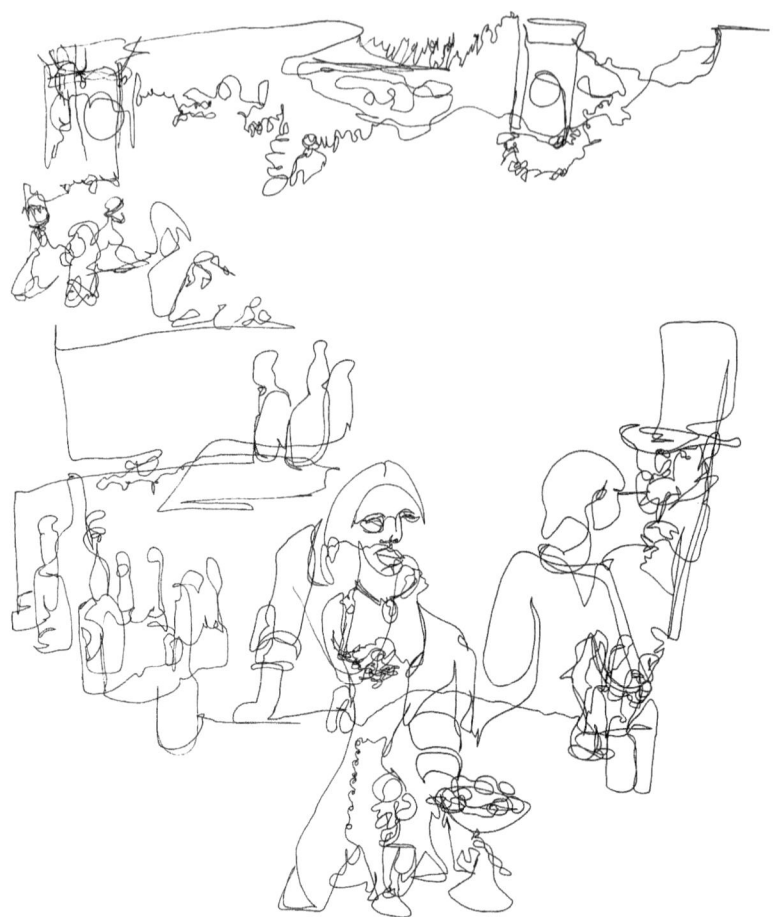

Fig. 5.4 • Paige Davis, *Reflecting Woman at Bar*, 2017. Ink on paper, 34 × 29 in. Courtesy of the artist.

accelerating, aggregated ideas and practices that gain dominance, rather than being period-specific.

•

American critics and art historians tend to narrate the beginning of postmodernism as a kind of culture rupture, instigated by Pop Art, and particularly by Andy Warhol. Arthur Danto, for instance, situates it with Warhol's Brillo Box multiples of 1965. Seeking originary moments from which everything else follows, however, is already a modernist endeavor, and to situate global shifts with a single artist, and in a single city (New York), is again to locate origin myths within the trajectory that postmodernism critiques.

In the broad way that modernism temporally, ideologically, and economically aligns with colonialism, postmodernism aligns with the collapse of certain forms of colonialism. I say "certain forms," since although we are in a period following the national independence of countries that were once colonies, we now inhabit a global postcolony, one less occupied by national powers than by national debts and globalization operated by multinational conglomerates, including multigovernmental concerns such as the International Monetary Fund. [#Capitalism] The "post" of postmodernism is misleading. We live in colonialism's aftermath, as we do in modernism's aftermath, but we are also living in their widespread continuation. It's a mistake to imagine that modernist ideas have been fully superseded by *post*modernist ones. Modernist ideas persist and remain alluring within the classroom and within art industries in general. And it's important to keep in mind that artists are willing to maintain modernist mythologies of artistic transcendence because they *benefit* from them, at least in the short term.

Postmodernism coincides with the loss of faith in linear progress, and relocates emphasis to acknowledge the validity of multiple and sometimes contradictory beliefs and perspectives. It conceives the individual not as an isolated person but as a subject formed through social and collective forces. Postmodernism arises when speakers of those supposedly forgotten histories have sufficient access to and through the disciplines created within modernism. Antagonism between modernism and postmodernism can take the form of a clash between what has been forgotten and what is being remembered. One can think of postmodernism, then, as operating *within* modernism, as the remembering of what has been dismembered. In many ways, that is how this book operates. The artists I refer to in this book are mostly associated with modernism, and the book's last section focuses on Mark Rothko, who might be seen as both a terminal stroke and a crescendo of late modernism. My readings of these artists are, however, postmodernist.

Rather than follow the usual dichotomy between modernism and postmodernism, where the latter might be presumed to have superseded and followed the former, I consider them as coexisting sets of practices, and as highly adaptive, complex systems of ideas and their implementation. Modernism is not a failed ideology superseded by its postscript but has succeeded all too well in becoming the dominant, cohesive system of ideas and practices, especially up to and including undergraduate education. As one marker of this success, students tend to enter art school programs as fully formed modernist, individualist subjects; that is, as subjects whose claims to truth (especially being "true to oneself"), and to being as yet unadulterated mask any ideological formation, and through which ideologies are unquestioningly perpetuated. Students may undergo art school's notorious "breaking down" and reformation as born-again modernists or reconstructed as protopostmodernists (I use "proto" because the restructuring is never complete, these in/complete subjectivities themselves being ideological markers).

Art departments often split into opposing modernist and postmodernist camps. These might be generational, but they will also occur periodically with new administrations or new faculty hirings, with the "new" postmodernists pitted against the "old" modernists. Since critiques and reviews are likely the only times when different faculty will overlap in teaching situations, their opposing stances are likely to be on raw display—often to the confusion and sometimes entertainment of watching students.

Instead of a singular modernist dogma, what is needed within art pedagogy (and art industries in general) are intra- or transmodernities, if you will, the application of modernisms to postmodernism (and what might be now post *that*), and vice versa. We need to examine how each asserts and reasserts itself in response to the infiltration of the other. I use "modernities" in the plural to emphasize that European modernism is one of many national or regional modernities. Each requires its own account, but an account that is relational to others, especially given that artists and the dissemination of their work—not to mention that cultures in general—have always been transnational, and cross-temporal.

Mood

A common question in critiques is "What mood does the work have?" Strictly speaking, since mood is a product of sentience, inanimate objects such as artworks don't have moods. Viewers instead link elements within artworks to their own or collective memories and to cultural associations that are already associated with moods. Mood is also a way to talk about affect, of how the work is "felt" by the viewer. This is similar to how tone and inflection in speech add to or sometimes override the words being said.

After *sustained* viewing, color might affect the mood of a viewer (the basis of color therapy), but the color itself is not a mood. To say that a color is "moody" is shorthand for its potential to produce a mood in the viewer. But mood is generally a prolonged emotional state, rather than one produced in response to the specific stimulus of an artwork—unless one is locked up with, or in, that artwork for an extended period, but in that case, such a mood change is more likely to be the effect of being locked up.

There are, however, ways in which artworks are linked to partly responsive, partly imagined collective moods, as, for example, a group identity or a national mood as a disposition or prevailing sentiment. Artworks may reflect and per-petuate, as well as instigate, collective sentiments, such as at times of war or religious fervor. They may become rallying points either for or against moral attitudes, for example, around sexuality. These might validate or run foul of the orchestrated, highly politicized "public mood," and can have major so-cial and artistic consequences. One example of this are the conflicts between conservative and progressive values in the 1980s and 1990s that have become known as the "culture wars," when artworks were heavily policed as violations of public morality. Thus instrumentalized, mood is a mode of identification, of social value and morality, of linking to others who one imagines feel the same, and in opposition to those who don't.

Moved [#Emotion; #Gut Feeling]

Emotion can be thought of in terms of bodily mobility, with "positive" emo-tions moving us outward from our bodies and toward what prompts the emo-tion (associated with love, empathy, and desire), and "negative" emotions moving us away and into ourselves (associated with fear, anxiety, and disgust). Emotions cause movement, and they are themselves migrant, producing sensa-tions and symptoms in different parts of one body, and transferable between bodies. We deploy emotions onto others, whether love or hate, and desire or fear their deployment onto us. Other bodies are not final destinations, nor are they where emotions permanently settle. Discussing the organization of hate, Sara Ahmed notes that emotions "circulate in an economic sense, working to differentiate some others from other others, a differentiation that is never 'over', as it awaits others who have not yet arrived."[103]

•

To reconfigure the cliché—one *is* moved by the experience of engaging with art. I mean it in the sense that one can be moved out of one's self, literally relo-cating one's thoughts, emotions, prior conceptions, and so on. Looking at art is an encounter in which both parties, art and viewer, are reconfigured, and perhaps moved out of their present intellectual and/or emotional stabil-ity in which they might feel safely located, to a state that is more unstable and even threatening.[104] In this case, being moved is to be cast into a state of precariousness, which, like the sublime, is inherently destabilizing and potentially threatening. To be moved, then, is not a casual affair and, as noted earlier, is a means to deploy emotions as differentiating and discriminating.

Though it is precarious and threatening, we tend to tame this sense of being moved by imagining it as similar to a plant turning toward the light. With no discernible physical movement, we might still be drawn, blossoming toward pleasurable stimuli, and toward stimuli that produce different emotional responses almost as a pleasure of feeling *something*. This curtailing of the full threat of being moved brings it more into the realm of the sentimental, what Oscar Wilde described as the desire "to have the luxury of an emotion without paying for it."

What other potential might this moving have, or is it an end in itself? What is it to be taken out of oneself, and toward what? One possible, if slightly idealistic consideration, is that one is moved toward another. The potential to be moved is a potential toward empathy, to see, think, and experience from another's location and point of view. We might not know exactly what the artist sees, thinks, and experiences, but the artwork might provide a portal for the viewer to see, think, and experience from another position outside of their own. It's worth noting that empathy is not a substitute for political action. Empathy may make the viewer feel good about *themselves* empathizing with the predicament of another, rather than doing anything about that predicament. Empathy—being moved—can be its own reward, and entirely self-serving. [#Culture]

Feeling moved presupposes that artists are intentional, benevolent, and altruistic, that art is good for us. The opposite may occur: an artwork may confirm our own thoughts, views, and experiences to the extent that it moves us further into alignment with the selves we have already (had) constructed, and moves us away from alignment with others, thereby strengthening the construction of them *as* other. An artwork might move us toward the traumatic, the repugnant, or the profane, regardless of the artist's intention or lack thereof. Artworks may have come into being with no intent other than their coming into being, and any subsequent "moving" on the part of the viewer might be entirely unintended or even contrary to the artist's intention. As viewers, we might refuse to apply the nomenclature of art to those objects that either fail to move us, or that move us all too well to positions of instability and anxiety. As with most discussions of art, the opposite may apply, in that we may equally use the nomenclature and terminology of art as distancing mechanisms to reduce or prevent its destabilizing potential ("it's only art, not the real thing"). In other words, we may desire art to have an emotional, destabilizing effect (the "move"), but one that is not *too* destabilizing, that doesn't move us too far.

Narrative

From the Latin verb *narrare*, "to tell," "narrative" is generally linked to the idea of telling a story. This is why it's considered such anathema within modernist and contemporary art, since the expectation is that art should be *experienced* by the viewer rather than related *to* the viewer—much like a beginning lesson in creative writing, where budding writers are told to "show, don't tell." However, every artwork narrates its own presence and its own coming into being. If we act forensically, we might even track how a work is made, for example, its materials, the mark of the artist, the tools used to make it, its influences, its relationship to other works: all of these "tell stories" about the work itself, before it begins to "tell a story" about anything else, that is, before it becomes a representation of anything else. [#Abstract/ion] *All* artworks, even immaterial ones, are narrative to this degree.

I've suggested above that the work itself tells or at least contains a story awaiting its telling. However, a *person* (or people) tells the story, and in relation to stories previously told, so any narrative occurs through the network between the teller(s), the told, the telling, and the previously or simultaneously told. Intrinsic to the telling is the mode of address. Through what disciplinary and historical forms, what tools and technologies, what materials is the telling conducted? These might be so enmeshed within the artwork that there appears to be no telling outside of the object's material properties. This however, *is* the telling, much like the liar's "tell."

Nature/Natural

Nature is assumed to be a category identifiable as distinct from the human or the cultural. Its depiction in art might instead serve a range of very human interests and be considered as legacies of received ideas, whether spiritual or religious (especially of nature as divine manifestation, whether Christian or earth goddess), or territorial and property values, or cartographic and exploratory, or of colonial and imperial expansionism (such as Manifest Destiny or "terra nullius," supposedly empty land that is awaiting occupation), or, more recently, as environmental awareness and activism—all of which may overlap rather than exist as separate endeavors. Some will be explicit in their interests, others well disguised, some seeming outside history—but all of them deeply historicized. Empty land syndrome, for example, in all its colonizing and frontier discourses, nevertheless produces a repertoire of unbounded magnificence, with sweeping expanses, dizzying heights, and cascading depths that seem to be about only the "wonders" of nature (see, for example, Thomas Cole, or Ansel Adams).

In describing the central role of photography in "nature safaris," Susan Sontag observes that "nature has ceased to be what it always had been—what people needed protection from. Now nature—tamed, endangered, mortal—needs to be protected from people. When we are afraid, we shoot. But when we are nostalgic, we take pictures."[105] Like Roland Barthes and other commentators, Sontag goes on to note, "Photography is an elegiac *art, a twilight art.*"[106] An art that mourns and seeks to preserve, if only as image, what is already past. This mourning narrative of lost nature all too neatly overlaps with a mourning for primordial, authentic, and similarly beleaguered experience, such that this particular construction of nature becomes a conduit to a search for unmediated interiority, a search that in itself is representative of metropolitan narratives of loss and melancholy.

The desire to be "in nature" presumes that we are otherwise "outside" and cannot be separated from a desire to escape the social. The "amount" of nature that we desire to be in, or our proximity to and distance from it, is determined by the visible *absence* of the social, which also determines our degree of escape, comfort, enjoyment, and threat, from indoor pots and pets to outdoor gardens, parkland, zoos, wildlife parks, "wilderness," and "jungle." It's worth remembering that the word "jungle" is from the Hindi *junglee*, meaning "uncivilized," "uncouth," "dirty," and enters the English language through colonial relations of contamination. These are only a few examples of how "nature" is perceived and experienced *already* in relationship to the human and social, and as therefore never an independent category.

Nature is often used to describe landscape. "Landscape" is, however, a depiction of a section of land. As a form of representation it is therefore a *cultural* invention. "My work is about nature" is more accurately amended to "My work addresses (my) cultural understandings of the category of 'nature' and its representation" (though few artists are likely to say this).

"Nature" might be used in the context of "human nature." While science posits that we are products of both genetics and socialization, of both "nature and nurture," we are not able to identify or specify to what degree each operates. If anything, prioritizing a polarity of either a genetic or social cause is usually politically motivated. For the sake of equanimity, I might declare that cultural forms and practices, such as art, can be compared to verbal language, which is biological in the sense that articulation of sound is physically produced, but cultural in the particular ways that sound is used for communication and understanding. If language and art were natural, each one of us would understand any and every human language and artistic manifestation. [#Instinct]

Artists' common recourse to nature might be linked to ideas of originality, since to draw upon culture risks plagiarism. The myth of originality can be maintained only by sustenance from outside spheres—nature, the divine—that are not already tainted by the human and cultural.

There is an entirely different set of imperatives for reconfiguring our relationship within nature, not least because of catastrophic climate change. Its answers lie beyond the romance of the urban garden, or the privileged village of the urban "farmer's market." To develop a new "aesthetics of nature" is to know that disaster is not ahead but already here, man-made, and whose gale force is already behind, propelling us faster forward. A new aesthetics of the natural opposes the havoc already wreaked by unsustainability, war, impoverishment, pollution, deforestation, and desertification. To turn toward nature is to oppose the deskilling and deeducation of peoples, and to provide healthcare, choices for birth control, and childcare. These "aesthetic" turns toward nature are future-making, rebalancing the human *in* nature.

Original/ity [#Self; #Inspiration]

Originality is a foundational concept of plain-speak, with artists advised that they need only "follow their hearts" to achieve it. Originality prioritizes individuality over collectivity or the relational. It is fully entwined with the proposition of a fully integrated, independent self, implying that the work has no predecessor, that it arises not through discourse and culture but through some wellspring of inspiration. If inspiration cannot be traced back through culture, then it must be divine or at least untainted by the civilizing strictures of society. This outsider status is also romanticized through alcohol and drugs, or through emulation of the insane, the "primitive," and the childlike.

Discussing Gauguin, Abigail Solomon-Godeau notes, "Common to both the embrace of the primitive—however defined—and the celebration of artistic originality is the belief that both enterprises are animated by the artist's privileged access, be it spiritual, intellectual, or psychological, to that which is primordially internal."[107] This desire for the primordial—that which prefigures culture—links the primitive, the divine, and nature to the artist's interiority as sites for activating artistic genius. Hence the claim to biology and biological determinism ("primitive" means "first formed"). This desire for a return to the primordial can be seen in relation to a crisis of representation within European modernism, related to the crises of culture and society in a Europe riven by wars, a desire for a return to innocence.

Contrary to what we might wish, if a work *were* completely original, it would be nonsensical—and consequently not identifiable as *art*. It would not be grounded in any discernable or understandable historical or aesthetic form. We could examine art history for such breaks or ruptures, when work with this sense of originality appears, but if we research further, we usually find precursors and conceptual tracks that lead from various directions so that a work never just appears "out of nowhere."

Similarly, originality as something new that never previously existed applies to every living thing and to much of technology, and in fact to most things in the world, since nothing now exists in precisely the same form and in the same system of relations as it might have before. In this sense, *everything* is original, but this renders originality as a hopelessly useless category precisely because it does not categorize.

If a work's originality (the Benjaminian aura) cannot be reproduced, then originality cannot be represented (since that would involve its reproduction). If it cannot be represented, it cannot be identified (though it can be alluded to). This is not saying that originality does not exist, only that we can't know if it does since we can't identify it. Originality is therefore a matter of belief, or faith.

"Originality" might be easily critiqued as a maundering modernist mythology, but other terms, such as "radical," "rupture," and "intervention," stand in for some of its implications. All of these, in different ways, suggest a break with the past and the beginning of something new. A little more careful is the use of the term "turn," as in the "turn toward social practice" or the "turn toward pedagogy." This more nuanced use, as orientation, suggests a preexisting but nevertheless mobile terrain, the terrain or the mapping itself being shifted as it is navigated in the way that a GPS map moves as one faces and moves so as to constantly relocate oneself.

Originality is no longer an operating factor for many artists, nor indeed for much of contemporary art, whose intentions and functions may develop through different discourses of pastiche, parody, interactivity, critique, political efficacy, sociality, and affect.

Despite the above, the question of originality remains central, if largely unexamined, within art education. The underlying impetus for most art schools is that they will provide the ground from which students will discover or enhance (and learn to market) their creativity. Here, "creativity" is meant as originality, since to be creative is to be innovative, to think and make independently. Yet creativity cannot happen too independently, because then the student would have no need of the school. Therefore, creativity has to be nurtured, whether by instruction or by association with or even through proximity to the already creative (the model being the faculty). Nurturing, however, runs the risk of the students becoming imitators of their nurturers, thus defeating the school's claim to enabling creativity/originality, and instead leading to a perpetuation of its house styles. It is this continuing claim to originality that almost requires faculty to repudiate the academy, to see themselves as infiltrators subverting from within. [#Academic]

I have been consistent in proposing that artworks are meaning systems akin to language or that they are themselves forms of language (nothing original in this proposal). A consequence is that art (making) is a collective endeavor learned and conducted by individuals through, with, and against each other. There continue to be advancements, changes, losses, and alterations, but these tend to be collective or by individuals speaking to, speaking across, and speaking against other speakers and other speech. We may rush to identify who said what first, but we can also track genealogies of thinking and of speech, of where, when, and how these are manifested and what turns they take. The great fear is that if we don't pursue originality, then we lose individuality. Collectivity doesn't mean we lose abilities for independent thought or action; but it does provide social contexts for how that thought and action can come into being and can continue to function and resonate.

Performance [#Performative]

Without the conventions of theatrical performance, such as a program, a stage, rows of seats, a curtain to announce a beginning and an end, and lights, what constitutes (a) performance? Does it have to be identified as such for it to be experienced *as* performance? How is performance distinguished from "everyday life" (if presuming that everyday life is not performed)? Performance *art* may expand on such questions. It may proceed from sculptural and installation questions about spatiality, about the body and objects occupying space. It may proceed from the gesture of painting, or dance, from how bodies move within space. It may draw upon photography, film, and video to examine the body/object in time/stasis/motion. Drawing upon histories of social and institutional disruption, performance art has tended to emphasize the act/ion itself, rather than presenting fiction, as does conventional theater. Purists may insist that performance art be live, happening in real time, unrehearsed, and unrepeatable—with no script or preceding version. Its documentation is *not* the work, even though it might be the only remnant by which the work becomes known. Performance might also seek to expose, ridicule, or disrupt the performative reiterations through which normative patterns of behavior are produced (see, for example, Martha Rosler, *Semiotics of the Kitchen*, 1975).

What are the implications of considering *all* art forms as performance, and as performative? Art in any medium is an event, of which the object, if there is any, is a record or a trace. A Pollock painting—to take a celebrated example—is a record of a gesturing body and a gestural happening that is the "thing itself," as well as a restaging of its discursive forbears, including Navajo sand painting and the mythic and neoprimitivist cannibalizing of/by European surrealism and expressionism.[108] Painting becomes an archetypal performance of ingestion, digestion, and discharge. Similarly, the photographer Henri Cartier-Bresson's famous dictum about the "decisive moment" is not a natural outcome of the photographic apparatus but, like all photography, choreographs forms, light, and actions, and perhaps a restaging of the language of painting (*photo-graphy* = drawing with light). Sculpture may perform and display the conditions of its materiality, making, and spatiality. These—contrary to performance purists, and the ideology of originality—are all borrowings, prescripts, in performativity's sense of being acted upon.

Artworks in any media can be rethought through the performance of gesture, of skill, of value, of originality and authenticity, of various modes of ingestion and excretion, and of history and of ideology. Every medium and discipline comes with a script (cf. *langue*), and for the artist, performer, and curator, that script needs to be made explicit as to what degree it is being followed and to what degree it is being rewritten (cf. *parole*). [#How *Art* Can Be Thought] In all instances, artworks arise out of a conjunction between performativity and performance, as both encryption and translation (rewriting), constraint and

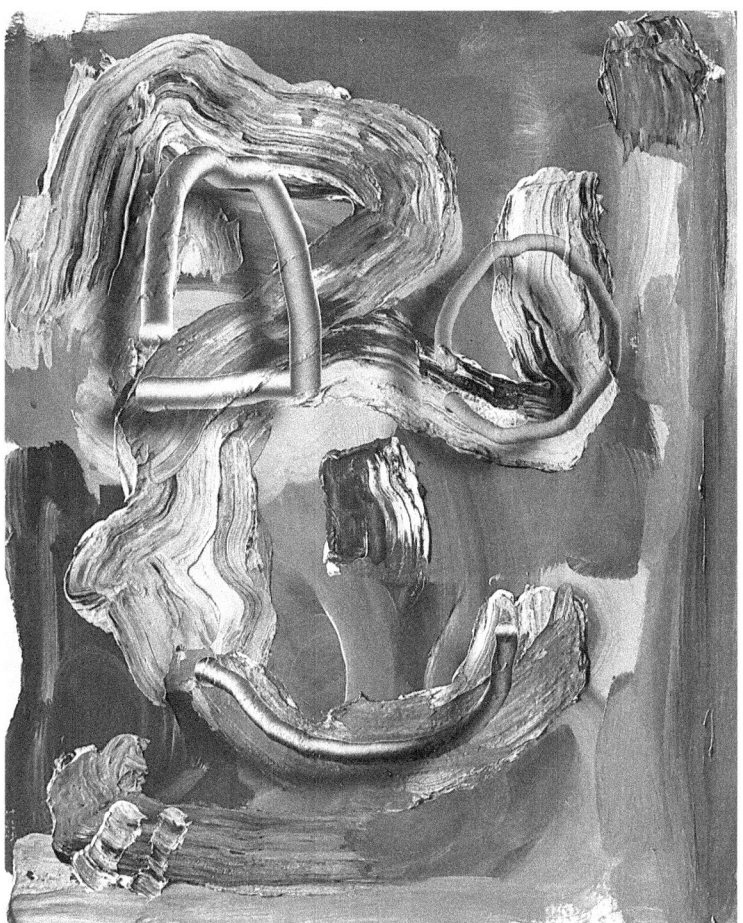

Fig. 5.5 • Matt Smith Chávez-Delgado, *Frankenpainting*, 2016. Acrylic and acrylic ink on paper, 17 × 14 in. Courtesy of the artist.

possibility. We too easily forget these conjunctions, and instead fetishize the artwork as object. Where we do allow for performance, our tendency is to fetishize it as spectacle, and as marker of the heroic, for example, the thrown lead work by Richard Serra, *Gutter Corner Splash: Night Shift* (1969/1995). We might compare the performance (in their work) of heroic yet mournful white masculinities of Serra's working-class body (and its invocations of the steel-worker), with the paint/alcoholic emissions of Jackson Pollock—particularly the "black paintings" of 1950: *Number 28*; *Number 31 (One)*; *Number 1 (Lavender Mist)*; and *Number 30 (Autumn Rhythm)*. [*#How, Now,* Rothko?]

Performance can take the form of interventions, which are generally anti-commodification and antiinstitution. "Intervention" has the particular sense of "coming between," whether between people going about their ordinary lives and what *constitutes* ordinary life, or between an institution—such as a museum—and its audience. In both cases, intervention interrupts the preexisting scripts of institutionalized life. Typically, this coming between has meant interruption, perhaps an act of property damage, or sabotage of an institution's regular functions, or an absurdist gesture that exposes the rationalization of institutions. Artists bring to attention how everyday life is itself performative, both in the sense of being performed by individuals going about their everyday lives, and in how those individuals are themselves being performed upon and produced as disciplined subjects by the seeming everydayness of life.

The field of intervention includes pedagogy, which is now legitimized *as* art. Artists give "performance lectures." They can display their students' work as aspects of their metaprojects. They can even put their students on display as the raw material and outcome of these metaprojects. These might all be considered performance. But it is complicated *as* intervention when it is sanctioned or promoted by the museum. Some might see this as success, whereby the institution and its resources are corralled into the broader intervention of public education. Others might see the institution as co-opting and pacifying what might once have been radical acts of interruption.

Intervention can take the form of activating museum dead space, such as the work of Tino Sehgal, though this might be closer to what used to be called "live sculpture." Do commissioned, brand-name artists who are promoted *by* the museum challenge viewers' passivity, or do they now model the museum as entertainment spectacle? To what degree do such actions extend or intervene into how the *institution* performs, and into how the institution performs through *us*, as its figureheads, members, participants, representatives, audiences, and possible stooges? Intervention toward social equity is, after all, the ambition of much performance art as well as of theater, whether it is drawing upon the radical prototypes of Allan Kaprow's *Happenings* or Augusto Boal's Theater of the Oppressed as rehearsal for political action, or the direct activation of groups such as the Guerilla Girls, ACT-UP, Occupy, or Black Lives Matter. These are more pressing questions of the impact of thinking performance than simply adding performance to a schedule of events.

Performative [#How *Art* Can Be Thought; #Culture; #Identity; #Performance; #Self; #*How, Now*, Rothko?]

Within linguistics, J. L. Austin proposed "performative utterance" as that which is already the action rather than speech that describes an action. His examples include the judge's "I sentence you . . ." and the marriage affirmation "I do."[109]

Judith Butler extends this meaning in relation to gender, as "that reiterative power of discourse to produce the phenomena that it regulates and constrains."[110] Gender, then, is compulsively repeated performance that produces and authorizes the gendered body through its performance, and whose reiteration is what enables the identification and categorization of gender. More broadly, we can apply performativity as compulsive inscriptions that produce subjectivity within normative power relations.

Performance art may employ these aspects of performativity to make visible the scripts through which bodies are "written," particularly in relation to racialization, gendering, and sexuality. Applied more broadly to processes of art making and viewing, performativity acts upon the artist, artwork, and viewer, producing them within already defined societal and art historical modes of behavior.

Poetic [#Politics]

A Western lineage of poetics dates back to Aristotle and an understanding of how the different elements of a work act upon or produce effects upon the viewer. Aristotelian poetics formed one branch of aesthetics. The other branch, rhetoric, was the art of persuasion, including logic, and which was linked more to philosophy and law. The Greek etymology of *poiesis* links it to making, creating, and composing, and ultimately to the making of citizens. These links to the making of a viewer and audience might be more helpful for artists than the more populist notion of poetry as solipsist. Poetics, in making viewers, not only references individual artworks but also points toward curating artistic encounters and modes of display.

Contrary to poetics' political making of viewer/participants, it is usually proposed by artists as a foil to and transcending politics. Gray areas may be proposed, such as by Francis Alÿs's exhibition in 2007, *Sometimes Doing Something Poetic Can Become Political and Sometimes Doing Something Political Can Become Poetic.*[111] The exhibition included the work *The Green Line,* performed in Palestine in 2005. The piece was a "redo" of his performance in 1995 that created a blue line in São Paulo. The different circumstances of each performance determined their reception as variously poetic or political, and the later work in particular has become a somewhat smug mantra for other artists to invoke poetics as intrinsically political while dodging the label of being a "political artist."

Poetics might be conceived as complementary to hermeneutics, which is the theory of interpretation and an inquiry into a work's meanings. On a spectrum of agency of how meaning and effect are produced, poetics is weighted toward the work's affect, and hermeneutics toward the viewer's interpretation.

Political/Politics [#Propaganda]

The word "politics" is derived from the Greek, with its primary meanings of city (especially the independent city-state), citizenship, and the social body of citizens. It has come to stand for that which is of, for, or relating to citizens, including systems of governance or participation within the governance of a state, and the means (including war) through which relations are conducted between different states. These meanings already pose a morass of what constitutes citizenship, who is barred from it, and the relationships between different states. Given these complexities, this is not the place for that expanded discussion. What might be considered is how art enters into a relationship to citizenship that can enable art to be thought of as political, initially in these primary meanings.

Art can, and does, address what it means to be citizens, and the complex ways that citizenship is daily negotiated. As crucial as the art of dissent and protest, art also addresses what it means to be more than a citizen, that is, more than what is negotiated with the state. It is in this excess, in the possibilities of what could exist beyond the social contract or an imaging of a better contract (better for the citizen, that is) that art can extend the immediate meaning of the political as "of, for, or relating to citizens."

Imagining beyond (the social contract) is art's prime rhetoric. This imagining can be energizing and radical, but it can also be placating and conservative. The vocabulary of transcendence has become the means through which art is apparently depoliticized, proposing instead a universal humanism that is always *for*, but never against, speaking to all people but in the vocabulary of the dominant, speaking the language of love (e.g., "love trumps hate"), but failing to recognize that the rhetoric of love for oneself (e.g., "love for the white race") can be employed as the basis of hate for others. And yet this art that is only for good, that appears to be neutral, or concentrates on the poetry and joys of daily life, that doesn't announce itself as political is unavoidably political in being "of, for, or relating to citizens" by participating in a culture of removal and escape. It would seem, then, a paradox that art's strongest ideological power, as both progressive *and* conservative, lies in its claim to be beyond politics. In this beyond lies art's political efficacy as a future imagining, even when this imagining might be deeply reactionary—for example, imagining a future in the mold of a discriminatory past. [#Transcendence]

A broader use of "political" refers to all human relations as conducted through social networks and institutional structures, including those of "private life," while noting that the claim of the private is that it is an inside—of domesticity, corporeality, mentality, spirituality—uncontaminated by the outside of politics. As social and socialized beings, we are constructed through these various systems, with politics encompassing all aspects of our lives. While this suggests that everything is political, political work proceeds from identifying and analyzing how these human relations operate, in order to be able to act with, through, upon, and against them.

Perhaps it can be restated thus: art is not politics, but it is always political. On one hand, a case can be made that all artworks and all art making are political in the broadest sense of politics. On the other hand, one can make a case for political art being art with a political *intention*. Between the two lies a minefield of presumptions and viewer subject positions as pertinent as anything in artworks themselves. My interest here is not to define a separate category of political art but to consider the broad scope of art, all art, as cultural politics.

In the *broadest sense*: even the most disinterested decision to make an artwork as something that is purposefully useless, that has no other intention than to be made, has political implications of rejecting or opposing capitalist culture in which everything is designated purpose. This is exemplified by the very political decision behind performance art, say, to avoid producing commodifiable objects. Though ideologies and economies are subsequently reconfigured around the useless to provide it value and therefore bring it back into the fold of the useful (as has happened with performance art), it does not negate or entirely overwhelm that initial call to uselessness. This uselessness might be manifest as "radical negation" against all systems of meaning or the "negative commitment" of apathy and nihilism (the "No Future" slogan of the punk movement). Or it may manifest as (sometimes parallel) strategies of interference and disruption—not to create new social or aesthetic orders but simply as interruptions of an existing one.

Art, by its aesthetic choices and visual languages, can manifest, confirm, reject, or oppose existing or new values, and since values are highly contested as cores of society, civilization, and humanity itself, art in all its manifestations has intrinsic political implications.

If the political in political art is thought of in terms of dissent and intervention against hierarchies and orthodoxies, and toward universal applications of rights and justice, art can be thought of in similar terms of dissent and intervention against prevailing orders of how individual and collective experience, knowledge, and affect are produced and *managed*. Approached this way, notions of genius, uniqueness, and the demand for the new are all rendered problematic if not irrelevant.

Political art, "artivism," and social practice function politically in ways that are qualitatively rather than quantitatively different from a landscape painting, say, or a photograph of flowers. Not only can social practice intervene into social space in what might be seen as political ways, it can manage the social as obedient or aligned with service and tourist industries. Its effect can be as activating or as pacifying as any other art form. Passivity is a practice, adapted to any medium or discipline, and the form that the artwork takes does not fully determine the viewers' or participants' responses. Participation in participatory art can take the form of being entertained, of being unpaid labor for the artist, of acting dutifully under instruction, whereas an inanimate sculpture can activate a viewer into social protest. Viewing can be active, critical, and energizing, as much as participation can be pacifying and indoctrinating. If we do accept that all art is political, the most helpful way to proceed is to examine how it *functions* politically, through what systems, and through whom.

The political effects and consequences of an artwork are dependent on and enacted through the systems in which it operates (or in which it is represented), including through the viewer's encounter with the work and how that encounter is contextualized by where and how it occurs. The work's political meaning, effect, and consequence cannot therefore be identified in advance or through the work in isolation. In this sense, the "politics" doesn't occur in the artwork itself but in the encounter between the viewer and the work, and in the various forms—the gallery, the academy, the media—through which the work is disseminated and enters into discourse. While the artist and the work can point toward certain directions, neither controls the encounter nor the political effect upon the viewer. The political, then, needs to be assessed in its continuing affects and effects. Such a task would not only track the art object/event but also would track the art industry through which it comes into being and into circulation, through art history, education, artist, viewers, gallery, publication, dealer, critic, and so on—a task impossible to complete.

If we reject the association between art and the political, and dispense with this argument altogether, then we have limited ways to proceed with what art *does*, and how to follow the effect it has upon viewers or within the world, since these all occur within the social (and therefore the political). Without the political as part of the open discussion, critiques tend to defer to abstractions or to forms of authority, for example, with the instructor decreeing what is good and bad, that is, with that authority being passed down to the next crop of future authoritarians.

⋅●

The term "political" is often used in similar, negative ways as "didactic," with the implication that political art is temporal, localized, and reactive, whereas art is presumed to be transcendent, enduring, and disinterested.

To be a political artist can pose a paradox. Some artists, and those compelled by social justice, might feel the inadequacy of their art practice to enact social change. They might stop making anything that can be called art and become more directly involved in political organizing with various campaigns and direct action. For them, the art industries' separation from "real life" and an emphasis on individual, aestheticized material production mediated through galleries does not allow for effective political work—however effectiveness might be quantified. From this perspective, those who make political art within art industries have turned politics into aesthetics whose political effect is the *appearance* of radicalness while maintaining and extending the grasp of commodity culture and the service industries.

This stance particularly affects those who might feel already distanced from the "art world" by their class, gender, or race, with a result that those potential artists (and scholars, critics, and gallerists) with a pressing sense of social justice and responsibility are the very ones who vacate art industries, leaving them as more diluted fields of what it means to be political.

Politics is situational, or in art terms, it is site- and discourse-specific. It responds to specific locations, sets of circumstances, and to specific forces. Art industries are megasites of political practices, and to be politically engaged with these is to be engaged within specific arenas, rather than to be dissociated from the world. Similarly, the gallery is a political site, and to abandon the gallery—as much radical art proposes—is to abandon an operational site. The gallery space is no less radical or influential or populist than "the street," as street artists sometimes claim. Conversely, the street is not *more* radical. Its claim to be a public space counter to private galleries elides how controlled and surveilled it is. [#Gaze] It's a *different* site, with its own terms, its own possibilities and limitations. To abandon the gallery means only to withdraw one's own engagement with it, hence leaving it to others. Unfortunately, no one seems to care much when artists withdraw their presence or labor from *any* site.

●

Political art is often dismissed as ineffectual or naïve, in that it fails to change society or at least a particular issue. However, to effect political change is not necessarily the purpose of political art. Its purpose might be to participate in the formation or continuation of a politicized *culture*, a culture that fosters elements of analysis, reevaluation, and criticality. The burden of change is upon the wider culture, including viewers, not upon individual artworks. Artworks' roles might be to help sustain, reflect, provoke, and/or extend political culture. In this sense, artworks tend to be ineffective activists in that their effects and functions are not geared toward direct change but serve instead as activations within broader discourses.

Artists might choose to focus on selective and diverse arenas of culture rather than prescribing that art address every political cause. Similarly, art need not perform the political work that might best be served by other activities. Art need not necessarily operate at activist "frontlines," where it might be seen to do so ineffectively. However, it might be more of an imperative that art adapt to and occupy a range of arenas. It can do so without insisting that *all* art do so. Art that chooses to not engage politically needs to recognize that it too is discourse and site-specific within *its* political spaces.

Politically (In)Correct [#Common Sense]

Historically fluid, highly contextualized term used by both the Left and the Right to suggest social control by "the other side." Its use tends to be pejorative, accusatory, and denunciatory, and it is occasionally used sarcastically about factions within one's own political spectrum. Generally, it is placed in opposition to "common sense." There's common sense, and then there's political correctness.

This glossary might be seen as an example of political correctness (PC). The term "PC" is generally used to denounce the "liberal agenda" of generative connections between language and thought, language and behavior, language and knowledge, and language and culture—the connections that this glossary espouses. My focus on language as the medium through which critique is conducted is not to impose a new orthodoxy—a political correctness—but to examine the tools with which we dismantle existing orthodoxies that have proven inadequate to investigate, decipher, and advance contemporary experience. My interest is not in policing other people's (or my own) language but in examining how habits of language already curtail how we think, and how thinking or its lack (by depending on default terminology) enable or restrict how we might imagine beyond the habitual. At the risk of being PC, the term in any of its forms has no place within the critique. This is especially so in the context of the term being weaponized by right-wing forces to quash critique and dissent, and to justify returns to discriminatory policies and reactionary ideology, language, and behavior. This reactionary use may even adopt the language of Civil Rights and feminism to recast itself as victimized by the supposed tyranny of leftist political correctness. A typical example might be a male student dismissing criticisms of sexism in his sexualized depictions of women's bodies, suggesting these criticisms are a political correctness that impedes his freedom of expression. [#Desire] He might even view his work as metaphors for his own marginalization, and call upon art history's many similar depictions as justification of his own work being unrecognized as radical. In other words, he feels victimized because he no longer has the freedom to treat women the way that men (like him) used to. Racists, homophobes, and ableists enact similar narratives, and sometimes they will be elected to political office on these platforms, with the hope that they will advocate for their fellows. This is the danger posed by the politically incorrect, as they create pathways to totalitarianism in which they can't be criticized, and where they can return to an imagined glory of everyone else's subservience. [#Democracy/Democratic]

Practice

Art practice, like musical practice, literalizes the habitual, long-term nature of learning through doing and making. Practice switches the emphasis from the art object as an independent entity to it being part of a broader continuity and network, as a manifestation and generator of discourse. It emphasizes the conceptual and the process-oriented, expanding artistic work from only the finished object to the intellectual and preparatory labor that the artist does, and to the "labor" that the artwork does as it circulates in public. It also indicates to a viewer that there is more to a work than the single object they are viewing.

Conversely, "practice" is criticized as a term of professionalization, similar to a dental or business practice. "Practice" doesn't sound like the rebellion that art is expected to embody.

The art critic Peter Schjeldahl, complaining about contemporary art rhetoric and the ubiquity of the term practice, winces, "Artists don't make works any longer. They maintain practices. Like dentists, only less honourably. Or like musicians trying to get to Carnegie Hall. When do you stop practicing something and do it?"[112]

Just do it: art as a sneaker commercial.[113]

Preconception

Artists and art viewers often state a desire to avoid preconceptions, both in making and in looking at artworks. However, since making and viewing are learned behaviors—"prior knowledges"—a necessary preconception for both making and viewing artwork is, in fact, making or looking at artworks. The viewing of art is dependent on the central preconception that it *is* art, and the subsequent preconceptions of how and what makes it art.

Preconceptions are received ideas or assessments based on past experience, abstracted to their generalities and reapplied to newly experienced, even altered, circumstances. For them to remain applicable they require continuity between past experiences and those newly encountered. Avant-gardist and contemporary art often set out instead to break away from the past, to function through disruption or redirection. In these cases, preconceptions that are based only on previous models might no longer be practical navigational tools. Preconceptions, therefore, require constant updating as preparation, and as preknowledge for what may lie in the future.

Process [#How *Art* Can Be Thought]

"Process-based work" is that which emphasizes the procedures, methods, choices, systems, and duration of its making or coming into being. It may emphasize these to the extent that there is no "finished" work other than the process itself and the changes that may be in continual play.

Process entails two primary approaches:

1. A conceptual or procedural system as a set of instructions or intentions (that may or may not be subsequently enacted)

2. A loose methodology that is more responsive to choices and changes during the process, and that may be linked more to the (instinctive or expressive) persona of the artist as ongoing decision maker.

Process-based work that proceeds from a system or set of instructions (1), may do so from an intention to undercut the myth of the expressive artist. Nevertheless, the artist remains as originating author, even if the "work" is carried out by assistants, machines, the audience, or mass production, or by exposure to time and the weather.

It is this *intention* to undermine the authority of the artist that can lend process-based work its democratic gloss, even if no such undermining actually occurs. An emphasis on process can, however, radically change the terms of engagement with art.

Propaganda [#Political/Politics]

All information and all representation are intrinsically propagandist in that they proffer viewpoints with claims to be believed. Representation convinces us (to various effect) that something like this exists, even if primarily as metaphor for something else, or as evidence of a complex of relations. Propaganda is the dissemination of viewpoints or information with which one disagrees. If one agrees with it, it might be viewed as confirming the truth.

Some state-sponsored or official art might be explicit in their propagandistic functions. These direct (the limits of) what and how citizens should know and experience, in ways similar to what Julien Benda refers to as "the organization of collective passions."[114] Most obvious are the vast pageants celebrating dictators and military juntas. But these might be less effective as propaganda because they are obvious, and because they follow a now overly familiar script, one exemplified by Leni Riefenstahl's *Triumph of the Will* (1935), which revels in the adoration of fascist aesthetics, accentuating mass rallies as political art that are febrile in their organizing of collective passions.

Propaganda's intention is misleadingly understood as conveying messages (the script). The legibility of messages makes them ineffective *as* propaganda, since they can then be counterread. The primary role of propaganda is to produce social effects, and ones that are not so easily traceable back to the propaganda machine. Its use value is in not being recognized *as* propaganda but as already truth.

Art's truth claims become primary delivery systems, reinforced by the popular language used to discuss art—the inalienable truths of universalism, individualism, quality, beauty, and so on. A notorious contention of the deployment of "sm/art" propaganda was the CIA's Cold War–era "Operation Long Leash" promotion of Abstract Expressionism as emblematic of American freedoms, and counter to the "oppressive uniformity" of Soviet social realism.[115] Since then, propaganda has become more dexterous. David Levi Strauss notes, "The Vietnam-era generals in charge of Desert Storm recognized from the beginning that modern communications technologies make it impossible to wage war in the open. Today, war must be hidden behind an impenetrable propaganda curtain—no images of death and destruction, no fields bloody with carnage, no dismembered corpses; no orphans, or gangrene, or naked napalmed little girls; and no body count. The surprise was how readily, and how completely, the American public acquiesced."[116]

This screening function is a major part of how contemporary propaganda functions: not to *convince* us of something but to prevent access and thinking about something. Its function is omission and redirection so that we will not know, cooperatively ignore, or forget the omission. This is also how art can function as propaganda—as screen, as omission, and as redirection. Propagandist functions of art (and art industries) are the perpetuation of what I earlier referred to as *white suprematism*, the most pervasive art movement for the ideological, cultural, and economic gain of dominant class-based, gendered, and racialized subjects. While there is substantial (though not enough) pushback, through calls for diversity, inclusion, and visibility, these generally demand expanding the field in ways that easily segue with expansion of the market. Pushback less commonly rejects the rules of white suprematism, thereby allowing it to remain propagandistically intact, and ever expanding.

Quality [#Entry Points: e/Quality; #Bad/Good]

Quality is one of those ubiquitous but unexamined values that are constantly conferred upon or denied to artworks and artists. Like beauty, quality is a value that one is supposed to intrinsically recognize/experience when one encounters it. It's a value that art schools also espouse, and again in ways that are usually unexamined. One sometimes hears faculty say things like, "The work is not of graduate quality." If art is only subjective, then there is no shared measure of quality. If the term is used as a common measure, it assumes some kind of collective evaluation. It's a standard of some kind ("graduate quality"), but of what? How exactly is it measured? And what is the threshold point for its lack?

Artworks may take on the *appearance* of quality via an emphasis on technical and formal virtuosity. Skilled fabrication of expensive materials with an emphasis on surface finish goes a long way toward looking the part, at least superficially, of anything we may discern as being of quality (consider Jeff Koons).

Real/Reality [#Representation]

Thinkers throughout Western history have postulated that we are unable to directly access the "real," perceiving only a shadow of it (Plato), or that reality under capitalism can be experienced only through the distortions of ideology (Marx), or that we are unable to escape the disciplining linguistic structures through which we access and process information, and therefore experience the structures rather than reality itself (Lacan). Though we may not be able to experience or know reality directly, or know if we have in fact experienced it, it exerts a strong pull over us primarily as ongoing, unattainable desires for truth, and for unmediated and authentic experience.

When an experience does feel real, we likely turn it into a narrated fiction and compare it to being in a movie. We turn it into a representation of itself in order for it to become comprehensible. When an experience is overwhelmingly real, usually through extreme violence or its threat—what we might term "trauma"—we might become locked into it, compelled to relive its immobilizing force as the only thing that feels real.

●

Walter Benjamin (and others) would suggest that our experience of reality is through its reproduction, that is, as representation. Reality is experienced through the *technologies*—or apparatus, or medium—of reproduction, such as the camera or the computer. We remember family or other histories partly through still and moving representations (photographs and film/video, whether as family albums, national archives, TV reruns, slides, home movies, Facebook Timelines, etc.). Memories are (re)presented and (re)produced through the particular technologies of (re)production, (re)presentation, storage, and dissemination. In that sense, memories that we may consider so personal and intrinsic to our individual histories are made similar, and collective, through the form of their representation and the technology/apparatus used, so that, say, Super 8 films, Polaroids, tintypes, Betamax videos, inkjet prints—regardless of the content of what they depict—tend to have visual affinities within their particular medium that set them apart from other media and that create certain period-specific "looks" to our memories. The "real" of our own lives, then, is highly compromised by these technologies of (re)production.

In art terms, "realness" might be a reference to mimesis, that something that looks real (that looks like a preexisting entity) is taken to be more real. Paradoxically, what might be the thing itself might not be attributed the quality of realness: an actual chair might not be attributed the quality of realness, whereas a photograph or a painting of a chair, or even a sculpture that looks like a chair but does not perform the function of being sat upon, might. Realness, then, does not have to refer to the thing itself, its objectness, but may indicate its ability to convincingly suggest or represent the object.

In popular slang (though I am deliberately perverting and expanding its usage), "keeping it real" refers to the ability to "represent," as in standing up for one's neighborhood, people, community, and so on.

Representation [#Abstract/ion]

A representation (an image) does not have to look like the thing represented; it needs only an agreement that it stands *for* the thing. A drawing of a tree represents a tree not because it looks like the tree. If that were the case, one could say that because the tree looks like the drawing the tree is a representation of the drawing, which is clearly not the case. The drawing is the representation because it is a cultural agreement that it is, even to the extent that a circle with a line descending can be understood as a representation of a tree. There is also a temporal factor, but not a determinant, of which came first, the tree or the drawing. If I made a drawing of something which didn't yet exist, or which I hadn't seen until after the drawing, we would still consider the drawing only as the representation, and not the other way around. We would have to come up with another explanation for how the drawing came into being, such as through a dream or that I might be clairvoyant.

Representation is often contrasted with abstraction. This can be misleading, since, as discussed above, a representation does not have to look like the thing alluded to. An abstract work may represent the intangible and nonvisual, such as ideas, emotions, or beliefs, and that is usually how abstraction gains meaning beyond its formal and material qualities. For example, a red shape with two bulbous forms at the top and a point at the bottom can stand in for a heart, which can stand in for romantic love. A color, by cultural agreement, can represent a certain emotion. Similarly, a broken, smudged, or jagged line, by convention, can be expressive, while a straight line represents order.

These representational agreements overlap with the legal and political uses of representation, of having one person (a lawyer, or an elected candidate, a *representative*) stand in for and speak on another's behalf. These are representations to power. Who/what is being represented, to what purposes, and to whom? The medium of representation is language, particularly legal and political language, whether written or spoken. It is the interpretation of what has been previously written (e.g., the law) that advances representation. One might say that art functions similarly, through its medium-based languages and their interpretation and advancement of what has come previously.

One of the tensions of art making is the correlation between the artist's mental image (imagination) that prefigures the work, and the work made to match that mental image. Artists also apply this to emotions. An artwork is always therefore a(n attempted) representation of the artist's prior mental imaging (or emotions). One of the legacies through abstraction and minimalism is an emphasis on the artwork being the "thing itself," as something originary, without a prior mental imaging. The notion is that the work comes into being through the *process* of making, the artist responding in real time to the medium, rather than acting in a time delay from the mental image. This is the *event* of painting, rather than it being a representation. [*#How, Now,* Rothko?] However, the artist's mental imaging or emotional state cannot be known by the viewer, except through what is interpreted from the work. What the viewer acts on is how the work corresponds to cultural agreements of representation, of how one or a combination of things stands in for other things. In addition, the viewer responds to how the artwork intersects with their own mental imaging and emotions. Artworks, and viewers' internal imaging, continue to circulate as representations and as imaginaries after the encounter with the artwork. This "afterlife" is where the works come into extended meaning, and intersect with already circulating collective representations. This afterlife not only determines the meanings of works—what they come to represent—but determines what kinds of works have a prolonged currency within an economics of cultural representation.

Representation, then, performs as a sequence of temporal operations, of cultural codes, and of individual and collective interpretations. These are far from the truth claims made for art, although they can approximate the "tracing"— the correlation between representational artifact and mental imaging—made by the maker and viewer, and experienced by them as truthful. Rather than fixed operations, these are continuously in flux, like imagination itself. Therefore, the representational properties of artworks, their meanings, their affect, are also in flux, and dependent on the full range of social forces that act upon individuals and the codes they use.

One aspect of representation that is not usually connected to artworks can be borrowed from its association with (trans)gender presentation. What are the external markers of gender, such as clothing—a blouse or a shirt, tailored or straight jacket (no pun intended); makeup or not; facial hair or not; protuberances at chest or genital levels? Do these external presentations coincide with the person's perceived gender, even though there's no biological or "natural" reason for them to coincide—though we habitually demand that they should? Similarly, we might ask how an artwork presents. What aesthetic and social assumptions are made because of external markers of materiality and scale? Clay or bronze, oil paint or embroidery, matte or glossy, somber or bright, gigantic or miniscule, slow or frenetic? What differing values do we ascribe to these markers? How can these markers' stereotypical conventions be interrupted?

Presence and presentation are intrinsic to representation, and point toward physical properties of the thing itself, as outward manifestations—presenting—of an inner self, the materiality of the artwork that represents itself before anything else. [#Abstract/ion]

While representation can be a game played between artist, object, and viewer, it is never neutral, never just a game. It produces social relations in similar ways as legal representation arbitrates and governs social relations. Guy Debord, in *The Society of the Spectacle*, theorizes the endgame of representation within capitalism: "THE WHOLE LIFE of those societies in which modern conditions of production prevail presents itself as an immense accumulation of spectacles. All that once was directly lived has become mere representation . . . The spectacle is by definition immune from human activity, inaccessible to any projected review or correction. It is the opposite of dialogue. Wherever representation takes on an independent existence, the spectacle reestablishes its rule."[117]

Self/Subject/ivity [#Culture; #Democracy/Democratic; #Identity]

The self is popularly conceived of as an individual's authentic, immutable essence, like a secular, humanist version of the soul. Humanism's aspirations of universal reason and liberty as an abstracted "human nature," while worthy, simultaneously allowed for hierarchies of the self, with categories of the subhuman to which those universalisms were not applied. This hierarchy provides pretexts for colonialism, slavery, and expansionist wars. This history of the self, even as it may be idealistic, or perhaps idealized, locates it instead as economically and politically motivated, and culturally constructed, what Pierre Bourdieu refers to as "structured structures predisposed to function as structuring structures."[118] To "express" that self is to intimately iterate the structural workings of culture, economics, and politics.

Despite Euro American modernism's collusion with hierarchies of the self, it celebrates the self as the romanticized driving force for artistic creativity. If a central tenet is individual agency, but that individual agent is a manifestation of (political and economic) culture, then the individual is a host body for the survival of the parasite of culture. If colonial culture is indeed parasitic, how are these individual and collected selves, these cultural agents, complicit? How might they work against their complicity, which has been reinvigorated through global capitalism, whose practices are legacies and continuities of earlier, colonial forms of expansionism and subjugation?

The self is a prime cliché of popular attitudes toward art: "finding oneself," "being true to oneself," and so on. In practice, one never knows what is the "true" self, even though one may retreat to it and cling to it in the face of conflict or opposition. Artists often speak in terms of expressing their deepest self. In such cases, it is more useful to examine how a self is brought into being, into representation, and into doing. Identifying, constructing, representing, and activating a self are performative acts rather than authenticating ones, since the self is perennially a future formation rather than one that is perpetually past.

The self can be understood in relation to alterity, as a reciprocal formation with otherness. The identity of a ruling class, for example, is dependent on having an underclass against which to measure its separation. Recognizing that which is not-self (in order to distinguish that which is self), also allows the possibility of recognizing alternative viewpoints and experiences. Though here, recognition is not a guarantee of equality but may enable forms of cultural appropriation while maintaining the societal distance between the self and the other.

The turn from the humanist self toward more complex examinations of subject formation includes how individuals and their collective alignments are subjected to disciplinary authority, how they are acted upon, and their social agencies of being able to act. The encounter with art, for example, can be examined as a site of subject formation, through the intersection between artist, artwork, viewer, and their framing institutions and discourses. Disputes over an artistic or viewing self as an abstracted, universal "overmind," *or* an embodied, historicized subject who intersects with the artwork in complex, mutually subjected ways—who has the right to make what—are played out regularly in the guises of freedom of expression versus "identity politics." How might one perform the labor of bringing one's self into being (which is equated as individual freedom) in ways that don't restrict or climb upon the selves of others? As Sara Ahmed notes, "When being freed from labor requires others to labor, others are paying the price of your freedom. That is not freedom."[119]

Seminal

A favorite word of art critics, meaning "of importance" and "highly influential." Its etymology, however, is from "seed" or "semen," thereby equating importance with the distribution of patriarchy.

Shock Value [#The Everyday]

Usually used derogatorily to dismiss work that depicts contentious material, particularly of a sexual and/or violent nature, with the implication that such visual impulses are purely market- or fame-driven, attention-grabbing strategies. A further implication is that beyond its immediate visual impulse, there is little or no content. All surface with no depth. This correlates to kitsch, which may be similarly dismissed as not being serious.

As an artistic strategy, we can partly blame Charles Baudelaire's oft-quoted "Il faut épater le bourgeois" (One must shock the Bourgeoisie). This is closely followed by the general inclination of any modernist avant-garde to usurp its predecessors. Baudelaire's "shock" tactic, however, has a more nuanced intent. His target reader was highly urbanized, in a constant state of distraction by the burgeoning technologies—the noise, the speed—of the city. This distraction was a necessary, trained response, acting as a screening device against the city's constant barrage of sensory incursions. To shock the viewer, then, was to penetrate and embed the work behind that defensive screen.

Given that we now function in a different historical moment, with a mass public and private availability—almost onslaught—of potentially "shocking" imagery, that imperative to shock and get behind viewers' defenses might no longer carry transformative potential. Shock (and awe) might not only no longer shock the bourgeoisie, it might be a form of bourgeois entertainment, and economic gain.

◦•

In my critique experience, the term "shock value" is casually used as a form of dismissal, with the person using it often clarifying that they themselves are not shocked but are imagining the shock on others' behalf. Used in this way, it is not a critical term but a moralistic and moralizing one.

Spirit/ual/ity

We can consider spirit/uality in two primary ways. First, as a supernatural essence or being that is coexistent with and animating the physical, a matter of belief and foundational to religions. Second, as the prevailing tendency, set of beliefs, and ideals of a given period, as a zeitgeist (time spirit). [#Mood] By definition, "spirit" itself cannot be rendered as visual or tangible form, since it would then be material and cease to be spirit. At best, art can represent conveyances for cultural beliefs and conventions *about* spirit. Spirit can be depicted, or rather, inferred through symbols that stand for and narrate its different qualities, such as winged beings—doves and angels—for aspiration, and as intermediaries or messengers between states of being. Water, for example, may represent spirit's flow and life-giving properties. Fire might represent spirit's transformative, activating properties. Natural phenomena might be personified as spiritual beings, such as Oshun, the Yoruba deity of rivers and fresh water, whose qualities include pleasure, sexuality, fertility, and beauty. Typically, such spirit figures are part of larger pantheons that are themselves cosmologies, which locate the human in relation to the totality of existence, visualizing the different natural forces and activations of physical matter. Other, less animistic belief systems might prohibit such personifications as idolatrous.

If one does believe in spirit, presumably the spiritual experience occurs in the viewer rather than in the artwork (one would otherwise have to believe that the artist is a divine conduit, and that the artwork is a divine vessel [#Inspiration]). The artwork might function as a focus or conduit for such experiences but in itself is not spiritual. Wassily Kandinsky, however, influenced by theosophy and anthroposophy, considered artworks as harmonic conduits, akin to the esoteric idea of *musica universalis*, the "music of the spheres."[120] The artwork, attuned to this celestial harmonics, visually *vibrates* its affect to the viewer.

Camille Pissarro, reworking Marx's famous phrase, considers the desire for spirituality to be manufactured for politically pacifying purposes: "The bourgeoisie, frightened, astonished by the immense clamor of the disinherited masses, by the insistent demands of the people, feels that it is necessary to restore to the people their superstitious beliefs. Hence the bustling of religious symbolists, religious socialists, idealist art, occultism, Buddhism, etc., etc."[121]

We may interrogate the political purpose served by the spiritual, as well as examine its effects and consequences. These consequences may be pacifying, as well as politically progressive, as in the cases made, for example, by radical theology or by "engaged Buddhism" for spiritual practices that enable a more principled, compassionate, active participation in collective life. It's not spirituality itself that is liberating or restrictive but the ideologies and practices to which those claims lead and to which they are put into service. This is equally true for art's claim to spirituality. Despite spirituality's supposed transcendence of the worldly, it remains highly political in what kinds of future imagining and present action it produces. Art's relationship or claim to the spiritual is its potential to suggest, imagine, mediate, access, or depict the not-as-yet-known, the unknown, and otherwise unknowable. The potential to imagine and to provoke further imagining is crucial to any discipline, and it might be one way to center the range of practices that we name "art."

Statement [#Message]

Artists tend to be resistant to statements, preferring the cliché that the work "speaks for itself." However, artists are required to describe their work for residencies, grants, and exhibitions. In nearly all cases, exhibitions will have some form of introductory, descriptive statement, though gallery or museum staff tend to write these. Rather than denouncing statements, viewers have a choice in whether to read them.

An extended statement might be required as part of a candidate's final thesis on completing an undergraduate or graduate program. This can be pursued as autoethnography, not in the sense of revealing the facts of one's life, but as a form of "self-positioning," locating the artist aesthetically, historically, politically, and geoculturally.[122] The statement may evaluate one's ideas and practice within historical and contemporary contexts, including to other artists, social movements, theoretical models, and so on. The statement can be a research document (as a more conventional academic format) on some aspect or question that is relevant to one's studio practice; it may also include proposals for or speculations on a life or work (allowing for possibilities of fiction, performance, and scripting).

Although it may be a school requirement, the statement is for the benefit of the artist, to help them understand their own work. It also demonstrates to faculty the student's level of understanding and their abilities to translate that into words.

I want to suggest some possibilities for the artist statement within the school situation, for example, during end of semester Reviews by the faculty:

1. It is a self-evaluation of the semester/year's work.
2. It identifies material, formal, conceptual, thematic, and (art) historical questions that the work seeks to address/resolve.
3. It begins to identify the long-term consistency of ideas, methods, and genealogies. #2 can deal with individual works, while this identifies connections and constants across many works.
4. It considers next steps and near-future ambitions (for the work, not for one's career!).

These can all be adapted for application and gallery statements, though gallery statements will tend to focus more on #2, with a little of #3.

Students might need reminding about some general writing guidelines:

1. Don't overstate what your work does, or make grand claims that are not borne out by the work itself.
2. In the educational setting, you're not promoting your work but conducting an inquiry into how it functions (in relation to the historical, the contemporary, to other artists/practices, and within culture).
3. Don't tell us what your work does politically. This isn't known before the fact. You can still talk about your political intentions (if you want), but that is different from what the work does.
4. Don't make assumptions about an automatic transmission of intellect or emotion from you to the work, and from the work to the viewer.
5. Don't make assumptions about what the work's affect is, how it acts emotionally on viewers. You cannot assume that how you experience your work will be how the viewer experiences it. Don't tell the viewer how to experience your work, or what their experience will be.
6. Spell-check.

Subvert/Subversive [#Challenge]

Can mean "overthrow," "disrupt," "undermine," "interrupt," or "irritate." Gallery statements are rife with claims to "subvert viewers' expectations" or "subverting society." There is rarely any indication of how these subversions occur, nor to what purposes. Though it may be heartfelt, the artist's claim to subversion might amount to little more than a stylistic affectation of radicalness. Only by imagining the viewer as being the same as the artist can the artist claim to subvert the viewer's expectations. This is to make work only for those like oneself.

Taste [#Aesthetics; #Beauty]

In popular discourse, personal taste and good taste are prime criteria for evaluating art. Personal taste is a display marker of one's social group, or "taste community," and the manifestation of that group's morality, status, and politics. These groupings cohere hierarchically against the taste markers of other social groupings. Taste, then, is a competitive indication, confirmation, and display of social standing, particularly in relation to class or wealth.

A seasoned "taster" is a "connoisseur" who epitomizes refinement and good taste. He (the character tends to be male) presumably achieves said taste through breeding, experience, and/or education. All three factors are heavily weighted by class, to the extent to which good taste is essentially the taste of the upper classes. While breeding suggests inherited "old money," experience and education can be acquired through application, diligence, and discrimination, that is, by the Pygmalionesque shedding of one's former class markers and allegiances.

In this hierarchy, tastefulness is blandly decent, behaving according to dominant conventions, with everyone knowing their place (everyone/everything in the right place and in the right proportions are vital components of taste). Taste is civilized (civility dependent on knowing one's place). Taste is gracious, withholding ostentation, reliant on those who can read the codes. The display of one's taste is evidence of one's judgment and morality (or their lack). "Tasty" is salacious. "Distastefulness" or "lacking taste" might be euphemisms for "bad," or morally upsetting. Lack of taste is overt display, insistent on labels for the unread.

In addition to the above, individual taste cannot be disassociated from taste-making industries, such as fashion, advertising, and design. Taste may be vintage and classic (the suggestion of old money), or it may reflect demand for the new that drives consumption.

Taste is the arbiter for consumption, in the sense of what is ingested. If the encounter with art is ingested into our subjectivities, taste is the means to control what is ingested. Something in bad taste elicits bodily reactions of disgust and outrage, as though the unpalatable sensation were already within the body. Given the delicate balance of social taste and how easily its systems are upset, artists may easily find themselves attacked for obscenity, immorality, or heresy—all of which are variations of producing a bad taste *in public*. Inevita-

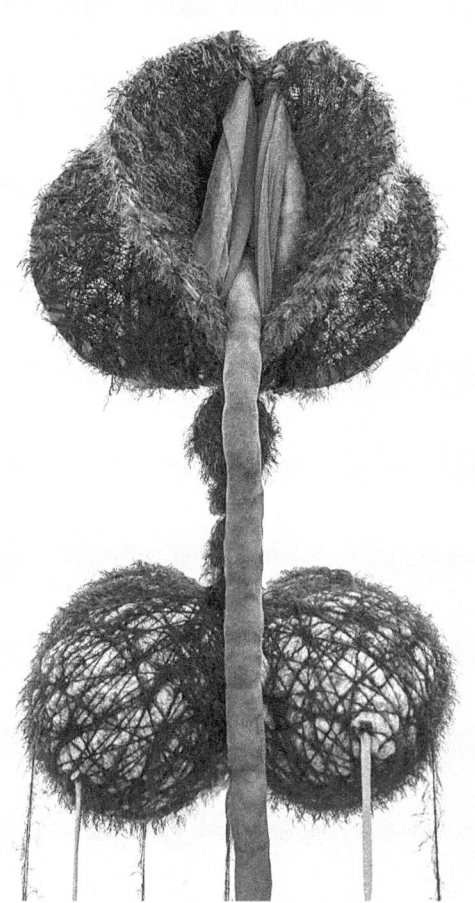

Fig. 5.6 • Behnaz Khaleghi, *In Heaven* (installation detail), 2017. Mixed media, variable dimensions. Courtesy of the artist.

bly, violations of good taste are configured as bodily infractions: an artist reading from a scroll extending from her vagina (Carolee Schneemann, *Interior Scroll*, 1975); an artist's self-portrait with a leather whip protruding, taillike, from his anus (Robert Mapplethorpe, *Self-Portrait with Whip*, 1978); a crucifix in blood and urine (Andres Serrano, *Immersion [Piss Christ]*, 1987); a black Madonna with elephant dung and collaged female genitalia (Chris Ofili, *The Holy Virgin Mary*, 1996); a female artist's naked self-portrait at a "last supper" (Renée Cox, *Yo Mama's Last Supper*, 1999). Note how many of these are body infractions against religious edicts.

Artists might intentionally pursue tastelessness and bad taste, if only to examine and enjoy what wriggles beyond the conventional. Pushing against taste extends aesthetic boundaries, and can develop new categories for beauty. More importantly, countertaste can expose the collusion between taste and forms of power. Countertaste can bring (back) to visibility what good taste deems immoral and perverse, and what should remain hidden. The "cunt art" (the naming itself is in deliberate *public* bad taste) of the 1970s, associated with feminist artists such as Judy Chicago and Faith Wilding, wasn't shocking because it depicted labial or vaginal imagery, stylized as these were. Art history has always included such imagery. It was because *women* were now depicting these images *for other women*, as autonomously pleasurable, assertive emblems of their own bodies and sexuality. The offense, then, was to proprietary male taste.

Text [#Performative]

"Text" has etymological connections to "texture" and "textile," and suggests that previous texts are woven together to form the new one. The implication (e.g., from Roland Barthes) is that a text is necessarily an amalgam of contradiction (as in multiple speech acts), and as in the warp and woof of weaving, two or more threads that intersect to create a whole.

Considering artworks as texts designates them as intellectual, contextual, cultural, and therefore as collectively generated discursive artifacts. This runs counter to modernist ideas about art objects as inherently unique, individualistic, autonomous, and auratic.

To read an artwork is less to uncover a true meaning, and more to unweave and tease apart its materiality, aesthetics, and social context, and otherwise examine how (or if) its many parts coalesce toward a generative whole.

Hal Foster identifies one textual model whereby a "*work* in modernist terms—unique, symbolic, visionary" is differentiated from "*text* in a postmodernist sense," "already written," allegorical, contingent."[123] [#Work]

This book, I hope, is an example of all of the above.

Theatrical [#Performance]

The term "theatrical" is usually used disparagingly to suggest unnecessary excessiveness, whether of form, gesture, or material. It can also mean self-consciousness, as though the artist is trying too hard to produce effects that will engage the viewer; that is, the artist is *performing* their craft for the viewer. These attitudes are partly the less-is-more legacy of minimalism, though see Michael Fried's reading, below.

In performance art, "theatrical" is a prime insult, usually meaning rehearsed, staged, exaggerated, emotive, pandering to the audience, maybe even *too* entertaining. The insult maintains the disciplinary separation between performance (as theater) and performance art. Historically, there is no easy separation, with a strong history of theater *as* art practice, such as Dada cabarets, Futurist, Aktionist, and Fluxus events. However, these were intended less as entertainment and more as disruption, altercation, and alteration.

Theater has a different application through the critic Michael Fried, who used it to describe minimalist art (what he termed "literalist art") as a *staging* of an object. The object's lack of excess, decoration, color, and gesture embed it, site-specifically, as installation within the architecture of its display space, so that the slightest color change, shadow fall, and external movement, as well as the viewer's own presence, registers upon the work and creates its totality. In Fried's reading of minimalism, "everything counts—not as part of the object, but as part of the situation in which its objecthood is established and on which that objecthood at least partly depends."[124] For Fried, this was tantamount to viewing a theatrical event, what he described as the "condition of theater" and which he felt was detrimental to art.

The present expansiveness of art forms and the fluidity with which artists and now art institutions incorporate dance, parades, opera, soap operas, carnival, and parties as their modes of operation have narrowed or closed this— already artificial—separation between theater and performance, between art and the theatrical. In art schools, however, one is still likely to encounter these disciplinary divides, usually premised upon separated departments.

Theory

The term "theory" is derived from the Greek and Latin, and means "to look at" or "to contemplate." Theory refers to a "systematically linked set of propositions, taking the form of a systematically unified deduction."[125] Available information is hypothesized into a set of propositions and likely consequences.

Art theory is an ever-evolving tool kit to *speculate* upon, understand, and *propose* thinking, making, and viewing practices. Theory is the deductions through which we come to understand, examine, and implement histories and experiences, whether individual or collective. I use "speculate" and "propose" to suggest that definitive answers might never be arrived at, might not be intended, and are always anyway provisional in the face of ongoing and contradictory information.

Theory's work of constant reexamination and reapplication, as information, experience, and circumstances change, doesn't necessarily happen, since theory is also a matter of belief, history, social standing, gratification, and political positioning.[126]

Which theories are popularized, which are advocated, and which ones are acted upon are dependent on complex interactions within art industrial branches of academia, art history, criticism, publicity, publishing, and art sales. These determine what kinds of information are acknowledged and allowed into the art industries' framing structures, how that information is understood according to the structures already in place, and how that information reinforces or adapts "unified deductions." A relationship to theory, then, is motivated by self-interest in all senses of that term, rather than proceeding from disinterested conceptual frames built upon objective testable information. This doesn't mean that we abandon theory (we can't; we can only revert to other theories). But it does create an imperative to use theoretical tools to examine how theory is invested, and what and whose purposes it serves. This examination of power is one reason that theory and intellect in general might be sidelined by the very systems of power under scrutiny.

A differentiation is sometimes made of "critical theory," which overtly critiques society and culture. In art, critical theory is most associated with the work of the neo-Marxist Frankfurt School (Theodor Adorno, Walter Benjamin, Erich Fromm, Max Horkheimer, and Herbert Marcuse). Horkheimer describes the critical aspect of theory as a "conscious opposition" and a quest "to liberate human beings from the circumstances that enslave them."[127]

Theory can help think through what happens in the processes of making artwork, what happens in the encounter of viewing, and how the artwork functions in society. It can help artists think and work beyond the constraints of inherited propositions and deductions—which is what artists claim to be already doing.

Much of the language used to investigate art derives from philosophy, literary criticism, and the social and political sciences. Those who rail against the use of theory in art are themselves acting upon earlier theories of what art is and does. [#Beauty; #Aesthetics; #Identity] Typical criticisms are that theorists don't talk about the artworks themselves or the experience of looking but instead talk about politics, about psychology, themselves, about anything except art since—an old theory goes—art has only to be experienced. [#How, Now, Rothko?]

A familiar reticence from artists is that theory is antagonistic to practice, that it inhibits creativity, that artists need to "do" rather than "think," and here, thinking is considered to be "overthinking." [#Moved] This contrast, however, maintains an artificial separation, that theory is *only* thinking and practice is *only* doing, and doesn't reflect theory as a form of praxis that itself has consequences upon the material and the social. There is a complex interplay between theory and (art) practice, with no simplistic causal relationship. In *addition* to verbal or written languages, artists may think through their materials or their medium—what artists often refer to as "being in the zone," when verbal thought processes are not interfering with the immediacy of working the medium. Similarly, one can read faster when one learns to stop mouthing and "hearing" each word. It's not that thinking interferes with making, it's that we're multitasking without realizing. Without romanticizing labor, working one's medium requires concentration and practice. Art practices, after all, are forms of knowledge, ways of knowing and acting, each with their own histories and inheritances. One can be trained in a medium, with one's knowledge inquiries pursued *through* that medium, it being one of many modes of thinking, language, and articulation. Verbal or written language can intersect, parallel, enhance, or be a corollary to this, *without* usurping or destroying it in any way.

The frequent demand for artists to publicly speak about their work can be thought of as multilingualism, and accompaniment (in its pedagogical sense), rather than speech substituting for the art practice. If artists choose to accept invitations to speak about their work, audiences can rightfully expect a degree of facility in verbal articulation rather than a refusal to speak to the work—the oft heard "The work speaks for itself."

Looking and contemplating—the origin of theory—is also the starting point of any critique (though not its beginning, since we cannot discount prior knowledge). Critique employs at least two tendencies that are nevertheless comingled (and here, highly simplified): a hermeneutical tendency that draws from literary theories and is engaged in interpretation of the artwork as a text to be read. This might be limited to what the work means, or, more accurately, the different ways it is produced through referencing other texts, and the consequent ways it/they produce(s) meaning. [#Text] The other tendency draws from political or critical theories, and emphasizes what the work *does* or how it operates within society, as product and as producer (including how it might produce the viewer).

For Arthur Danto, it is theory that provides the ability to name something as art: "[Artistic terrain] is constituted artistic in virtue of artistic theories, so that one use of theories, in addition to helping us discriminate art from the rest, consists in making art possible."[128] He also says, "It is the role of artistic theories, these days as always, to make the artworld, and art, possible."[129]

Theory is provisional, unstable, discourse-specific, and multiple. It is site-specific to where and when the critique occurs and to who conducts it. Hence the common student complaint that each instructor provides conflicting interpretations. That's the nature and the point of the discipline: to train students in a critical practice that includes thinking through what is said about their work, not to train them to do what their instructors say.

Students might be admonished that their work illustrates theory. One sees this when a student encounters a new idea (theory) and makes a work in response. The problem is not the theory but that the theory has not been developed through the medium of the work.

Students of color who use theoretical and critically articulated language might be seen to be stepping out of their place—in short, acting white. Women might be similarly criticized as behaving like men. Their attention to the particularities of language might be seen as an indication of their irreparable contamination by Western (or male) theory, which presumably divorces them from the indigenous (or feminine) modes of feeling and knowing that would connect them to "their" communities. They risk the perception of having sold out by "losing their roots" (or femininity), and deliberately pandering for acceptance by a white (or male) elite.

Time/less/ness

Despite one of its central truisms, art is not timeless (or groundless). The influences and forces that precede an artwork cross time periods and geographical locations, but an artwork itself is grounded in the sense of it being made or coming together at particular moments, within particular conditions and specified locations. When we situate artworks *in* time, we can track developments of materials, ideas, practices, and forms. Timelessness suggests that a work's meaning, affect, and values are unchanging. Since these are partly dependent on the viewer, this argument depends on the absurdity of viewers also remaining unchanging, whoever, wherever, and whenever they are in the world.

Timelessness is instead attributed to artworks as ideological vessels for societal values. Combined with "greatness," "timelessness" suggests a civilizational continuity, for example, between the ancient Greco-Roman world and present-day northern Europe. This linkage becomes a guiding principle for museums as the legacy and archive of civilizational values.

Experience of time is linked to the emotionally affected perception of its passing, with something enjoyable seeming to speed by, and something anxiety-producing or boring seeming to drag. Viewers can maintain attention for longer periods if they can narratively link otherwise seemingly unrelated moments, so that there appears to be consequence, or a story. A viewer might not commit to watching unless they know how long a work is, or how long it will take to get sufficient sense of it—to "get" it. Without the escapist entertainment of TV shows or Hollywood movies—which are already allocated time "slots"—duration can feel like work. Given that attention spans have been retrained to access the glut of information that now surrounds us, we want artworks to provide instant, dramatic gratification. Slowness and duration can feel like wasteful, unproductive time.

Artists might actively work against these expectations, trying to slow down the viewer, partly fueled by beliefs that by slowing down we engage more fully, we enjoy more deeply, we get more "in touch" with our own experience. This is not necessarily borne out by evidence but is partly informed by a general anxiety of the speed of contemporary life—an anxiety that might be a perpetual condition of modernity of any period rather than peculiar to our present moment. [#Meditation]

●

Convention distinguishes between "still" and "time-based" media. While this distinction serves some conveniences, it is more porous than we generally admit. A Jeff Wall backlit photograph suggests cinema, partly because it functions on a scale close to a projected image, and because the light box has some of the visuality of a screen. The Douglas Gordon work *5-Year Drive-By*, a screening of the John Ford film *The Searchers* (1956) slowed down to one frame per twenty minutes so that the entire film takes five years to screen, might be experienced as something closer to photography, or even as an advertising billboard. What attributes would we ascribe to time-based media if we consider them as still, as material objects, and material objects as time-based? What possibilities would open up within each medium if we consider *all* media as material form *and* time-based? We can further consider any artwork as in a temporal process of unfolding, of immanence, during which meaning is produced.

Durational media, such as performance or video, create expectations of a beginning and an end (if the video is on a loop, as soon as we recognize a repetition we think of it as an ending, or the beginning). We place no such expectations on still images, and in that sense, paradoxically, nondurational works don't "end" (unless destroyed).

The still image or object generally doesn't make us think of the passage of time, except for genres such as *vanitas* paintings, which address the nature of change and human mortality. However, all material artworks are in a state of constant decay and entropy.[130] Decay and immanence as durations—from prefabrication to postviewing—apply to any artwork of any medium.

Our experience of duration is dependent on having a timeframe, whether it is the length of a Hollywood film, the length of a human life, or the timeframe of climate change. Our experience of time's passage and duration is especially acute, even in crisis, when one timeframe intersects with and disrupts the expected duration of another. These intersecting durations are what activate the present, and encounters between these multiple durations produce new meanings, new intersections, new durations.

Photography, in its language and practices, is highly revealing of artistic attitudes to time. Contrary to its conventions, photography is a time-based medium that, palimpsest-like, is sometimes durational within the same frame, and sometimes multidirectionally sequential across many frames, like nonlinear cinema. Conversely, text and video, ostensibly experienced as durational, might instead depict or re-create the experience of a single moment—a little like a snapshot—though it could be an oscillating, unstable moment.

The history of photography has created an archive of difference, yet photography's moment or event, the photograph, treats and reduces everything in the world to the same quality of *being* a photograph. One can think of photography as producing categories of sameness, each with their own style, from the colonial "native type" to the glamour shot, from the family album to Instagram, from street photography to staged epics, from the police mug shot to the celebrity selfie. The "essence" of photography is to contain difference, to prevent dispersion, friability, shimmer. To stop movement, and to stop time.

Deviating from the (Barthesian) understanding of difference as the instability of excess and contamination, whose encroaching movement indicates the passage of time, Henri Cartier-Bresson proposes photography as restabilized stoppage and containment. His coinage of photography's "decisive moment," "captured" by the shutter's "release" (the scare quotes denote the medium's conventional, though hardly neutral, terminology), suggests that what is depicted is stilled, to then operate self-reflexively *within* the photographic frame. [#Performance]

The ubiquity of this conception, the *still*birth of the timeless moment (dark-room chemicals "fix" the image, preventing its further "development") belies different temporal processes of the photographer scripting, crafting, orchestrating, choreographing, or waiting predator-like for an alignment of light, form, and action. The viewer, too, can narrativize the photograph as one may a cinematic still, of what might happen before or after. This is not literally (or literarily) as narration, but accedes to the photograph being performative, as a prescripted reiteration of, for example, gender coding, as in Cindy Sherman's *Untitled Film Stills* series of 1977–80 (the reader will have already noted my own coding of photography's masculine conventions as birth envy).

The photograph depicts space with the convention of stopped time and movement (still/ed life, the still), even if the stopped movement is understood only as the halted action of light.[131] The viewer, though directed by the work, determines the duration of their encounter, which also depends on movement and the traversal of space, including the duration of their eyes moving across the details of the photograph. This experience of movement in/across space (of the viewer's body, of their eyes) assists in sensing duration. The viewer might also get locked into the work, zoning out of linear time. This is precisely what photography does: it appears to remove movement; it even appears to remove its own space *as* a photograph. Our tendency is not to view the photograph as a material object that occupies its own space but as the illusory yet utterly convincing depiction of another space, which continues to exist now only in its depiction.

Despite its terminology of stopping time and motion (and emotion), the photograph always exists temporally, that is, historically, its duration extending at least from the time of its shutter release or its making (Ansel Adams: "You don't take a photograph, you make it.") to the time of its viewing. Add to that the duration of influences and references, the preconception or "premoment" that leads toward the making of the work, and the postpartum or "postmoment" that determines its circulation and interpretation. Add to *that* photography's constantly changing technical and stylistic forms, and its representation or performance of preexisting representational codes. We can never fix an originating moment, only make note of a pause midstream. As Karen Archey has noted, artworks have multiple temporally located "activation points."[132]

Photography/art aspires to timelessness, that certain (master)works transcend the temporal (Dorothea Lange: "Photography takes an instant out of time, altering life by holding it still"). If anything, photography commemorates the instant to memory and to history, thereby reinserting it into a more enduring temporality, and without losing its other activation points. (See #*How, Now, Rothko?* for a different reading of painting's relation to time.)

Foundational truisms of video and performance art—to distinguish them from film and theater, respectively—were that they were produced and viewed in real time. This was an authenticating marker, that the real time of the work as experienced by the maker is to be reexperienced in the real time of the viewer's viewing. Duration, marked by endurance, becomes the sign of the authentic, immersive experience, unlike the fleeting fripperies of the shallow and the popular. Endurance is hard (literally), and not much fun. But its reward includes a certain righteousness of *having* endured, with a possible bonus of having been transformed by the difficulty of that endurance.

Tradition/al

"Tradition" usually refers to the beliefs and behaviors generationally handed down or inherited within a specified family, group, or culture. The conventional view is that traditions are fully prescribed, and therefore unchanging. In practice, each handing down is altered by different circumstances, though the general substance may continue. The handing down, or rather the taking up, is reinvention in the face of changing circumstances, a restaging of the cultural group to maintain stability and continuity. Traditions can vary from slight but continuous changes to total invention, as has happened within colonized countries as means to introduce administrative changes. The acceptance of such changes was made easier under the guise of them being already part of "native" cultural tradition. Or an existing tradition would be adjusted to better suit the colonial power. Traditions are also invented as a result of fashion choices, or deliberately to act as identifiers and create cohesion for particular groups, as badges of membership. Tradition is seen as a stabilizing, cohering force, vital to any group's sense of identity, upheld as a means of resistance and endurance.

Tradition is increasingly linked to burgeoning "heritage industries" that have become economically vital aspects of tourism. In fact, tourism is a prime factor for the reinvention of traditions, with the purpose of creating distinguishable localities against the homogenizing forces of globalization.

Tradition can be a highly motivating political force, as evidenced by the rallying cry of "traditional family values." These traditions might be invented precisely to create homogenous, stabilizing power blocs within the perception that society is changing too rapidly, usually because of the perceived infiltration by the new (social progress and political rights), and against the deviant, the feminist, the foreign. The ideological power of tradition here is its implications of being normal, natural, Godly, patriotic, the way things have always been.

•

Critiques might discuss "traditional materials" and "traditional techniques." These nearly always allude to the *idea* of the preindustrial and the handmade as somehow purer and more authentic, even when the materials and tools are now likely mass-produced. With photography's now almost wholesale switch to the digital, the moment seems to have passed in photography critiques when analog, wet, or film photography are virulently defended as traditional, more authentic, and just "better."[133]

A student might claim to be working in or representing their family or cultural group's traditions, usually as a form of respect or as a continuation of something that is otherwise disappearing, or that might be in the process of being salvaged, having already been lost. Cultural responsibility might be prioritized over individual creativity. This can lead to conflict for students, given that art schools and contemporary art emphasize individual creativity and see cultural responsibility as a constraint.

Given the above permutations, it is necessary to tease out exactly what is meant by "tradition," and to consider what purposes its reinvention serves.

Transcend/ence [#*How, Now*, Rothko?]

Transcend's Latin derivation from crossing (*trans*) and climbing (*scandere*), suggests an active, physical overcoming rather than the common application of transcendence to artworks as a spiritual, disembodied rising above, an artistic Rapture. Tugging the viewer along, the artist rises above the banality of everyday experience to something that is beyond society, beyond language, beyond the political, to an experience of what might once have been thought of as the divine. Presumably this rising above is achieved by the artist's mythic struggle, and its manifestation upon, within, and through the artwork. This rising is subsequently emulated by the viewer's spiritual (if secondhand) experience with the work.

A prime example is works by the heroic sufferer Vincent Van Gogh—which are invariably surrounded by selfie-snapping spectators on secular pilgrimages of cultural must-sees. It's not the paintings themselves that cause transcendent experiences; hardly anyone spends any time looking at them. It's the experience of having crossed it off a collective bucket list, which has become a contemporary stand-in for "rising above." Another example is Marina Abramović's brutally demanding endurance piece *The Artist Is Present* (2010). The artist "invited" museum visitors to sit facing her, logging over seven hundred hours of sitting in direct engagement, one by one, with a total of almost 1,400 people. Many viewers were moved to tears by the transcendent intimacy of the experience, if one can describe sitting in the atrium of a major museum watched by hundreds of others as "intimacy." While this transcendence is attributed to intimate connection with a stranger, it is more likely produced through the golden allure of having been part of a crowd in the presence of celebrity and orchestrated production, the "silent opera" as described by critic Holland Cotter.[134] Abramović is a celebrity, which by definition means that she is not a stranger. The fiction is of profound, transcendent human connection to someone we think we already know. I'm not immune to this: Abramović once held my hand for eleven minutes (I timed it), and years later I can still imagine that I feel her transcendent clasp. [#Duration]

Translate/Translation

"Translation," with the same roots as "transfer," and intersecting with "transcendence," means "to carry or bear across." It is generally applied to crossing from one verbal or written language to another. Like diasporic theory, translation considers the site/language "left," the site/language "arrived at," the crossing itself, the migrants/language effects that are translated, borne across from one place to another, and the effects on the places left and arrived at that are translated *by* migrants/language effects.

Applied to art, "translation" can examine the crossings that are otherwise taken for granted:

- How experience, ideas, and stimuli on the part of the artist are transformed into formal, material-based languages
- How these language forms are interpreted by the viewer into other forms of stimuli, experience, and ideas: from the sensory, visual, and affective to the verbal, and back; from the embodied to the social; and from the discursive to the embodied
- How artworks carry existing meanings or accrue new ones as they circulate from one location to another

- How viewers translate artworks from different locations
- And so on, across different flows of artistic experience and discourse.

A translation does not seek to replace the original, nor does it seek to be or do the same thing but in a different language. The translation acknowledges what cannot be carried across from one language to another, and might have to invent language forms that can cross and that act in similar ways in both languages. The production of the same is not translation's goal, which is rather to produce an equivalence or an approximation within the possibilities and limitations of the language being translated into. Thus the artist's experience is not the same as the artwork. The artwork is not the same as the viewer's experience. Speaking or reading about the work or seeing it in reproduction are not the same experiences as engaging the work directly. The experience of one medium is not the same as experience of a different medium. Each of these requires translation. Each functions as intersecting—rather than autonomous—forms and languages. Each generates and influences the furtherance of other forms in this cross-flow of movements.

Translation investigates how and whether what happens within one medium (e.g., paint) can be "moved across" to another medium (e.g., words). Paint can be described through color, texture, and material, but that is not translation. While paint is the medium, *painting* is the language, including its history and its practice. Painting as language is what can be theorized or translated into other languages, such as words or photography. While one language is never the same as another, they can investigate each other. If this were not the case, we would each be locked and isolated into the languages each one of us uses, without the ability to translate between those languages. We would not be able to dance to music, as examples of two related and overlapping but different languages.

When artists insist upon or privilege the truth of one medium over any other, they adopt an essentialist insulation and isolation, a refusal of relationship, a refusal to translate between languages, and a refusal of synaesthetic and imaginative possibilities.

Translation produces the language being translated into, since it introduces new terms, perspectives, ideas, and structures that might not have existed (in quite the same way) in the recipient or hosting language. Thus each stage of these translations—between discourse, artist, artwork, viewer, and discourse—produce each other into new entities.

Truth [#Real/ity; #Universal/ism]

In the era of fake news and alternative facts, when belief is unhinged from veri-fiable information, truth is ever in question, and at stake. Truth can be deliber-ately created and planted, to lead people to take up certain social and political positions. Even if false truths can be disproved by counterinformation, by facts based on evidence, we are already skeptics. We have learned to distrust "the media." If nothing can be believed, then everything is plausible, especially if it fits in with the views we already have. In this scenario, opinions and feelings are facts, the ones we disagree with are conspiracy theories and fake news, and no one can tell us otherwise. Truth is the claim that beats out the opposition. However, truths have consequences, which can be measured by their effects in the world. Which truths we accept and abide by are how we locate ourselves politically in the actions of the world.

As much as truth might be a matter of belief or have become petrified dogma, it remains fundamental for desires for meaning, and to provide a directional focus or a moral compass. Absolute truth might be ideological fabrication to make people conform, but without something equally powerful to believe in, to believe in truth rather than relativism remains a compelling choice. That choice is additionally attractive because it confers social power. For example, truth might be linked to dominant identities, or to the conventions that certain subjects and subjectivities have greater claim to truth. However, this linking of truth to identity might be used strategically as forms of countertruth, as truths that have been historically suppressed, that speak against one's own ongoing marginalization. [#Identity]

Truth might be linked to professional connections to legality (judges, po-lice) though paradoxically, lawyers are considered professional twisters of truth, if not outright liars, and the police have increasingly been called into question—though not sufficiently to be held accountable. Men, through masculine bonding—and a test of manhood is how well one bonds with other men—might consider each other more truthful than women—who are also constituted as those that can't bond as men. Men may truthfully believe that lying to women is necessary for masculine solidarity and dominance. The testimonies of many women may be "disproved" by the denial of one man.

The darker one's skin color, the less one may lay claim to truth, especially if that truth is weighed against the truth of the lighter-skinned (recall House Republican Joe Wilson's outburst "You lie!" to then-President Obama in Sep-tember 2009, compared to the widespread acceptance that President Trump routinely "diverges" from truth).[135] For Obama, the power of being president of the United States of America did not bump the "underpower" of being black.

These examples expose links between truth and power, and specifically the political and institutionalized power moves to have one's truths verified by others, to enact truths rather than being only subjected to them, and to be able to impose one's truths upon yet others.

Against this background, what are the truth claims made by art? These are based less on verifiable information than on beliefs and ideologies embedded in the sacrament of the experiential encounter with art as the evidence, proof, and truth of material presence. We can generally agree, and say truthfully, given all the evidence of our senses, that there is a sculpture in the room; though here, too, our senses might be easily fooled. Another concept of truth is based on shared symbolic and linguistic frameworks, without which it's harder to agree on the sculpture's symbolic meaning or its affect.

Truth, then, is commonly held discourse or shared culture, produced through history and context, and accessed and reinforced through our sensory, bodily encounters. These ideas-in-common become conventions, fixed and enduring over time, regardless of circumstance, regardless of cultural framework. They are presumed to exist independently, beyond the partial perspectives of individuals or groups, to transcend the vagaries of time, place, and subjectivity. If it was true then, it has to be so now; if it is true here, it has to be so there; if it is true for me, it has to be for you. Interpretations based on the evidence of encounter and hearsay become dogma and truth.

These fixed Truths—based on the certainty of belief—lay claim to power, rightness, and righteousness. They impose corrective, disciplinary measures upon unorthodoxies—formal and informal education being prime disciplines. Art, however, is less obedient and less answerable, with fewer singular answers. Art might proffer attitudes of doubt, of uncertainty, of unanswered questions and open-ended investigation, of irresolution and nonarrival. Despite the truth claims made *for* art, its many possibilities defer truth.

Truth, as in an artwork being truthful or revealing truth, is an unreliable value since we can never know if it is in fact true, whether our limited perspective distorts it, whether the artist is deluded, whether the artist is using fictional strategies (intentionally or otherwise), or whether it is a lingering mythology. [#Honesty]

Myth (1): art reveals the truth of the world as it *really* is, beyond mere appearances. Consider whether Bruce Nauman's neon sculpture *The True Artist*

Helps the World by Revealing Mystic Truths (1967) is truthful or a parody or both. It can be read as a true rendition of a commonly held belief, while its storefront flashiness renders that truth as beguiling entertainment.

Myth (2): art reveals inner or transcendent truths about the artist and, by consequence, about all humanity—since:

Mini-Myth: the artist is able to access and reconcile interior and exterior mysticism, or at least reach the parts that others can't reach.

·•

"Artistic truth" can refer to mimesis, or convincing representation—whether of outward appearance or of interior states. Mimesis in art—for example, trompe l'oeil in painting and sculpture, indexicality in photography—is mistakenly viewed as a duplication of the real, but in the confusion produced between the thing itself and its representation, in being life*like*, it becomes more of a *removal* from the real.

The mimetic ability of an artwork hides its own particularity, its own form. In describing a photograph, for example, we tend to speak only of what it represents, what it seems to be an image of, rather than speaking of its particular arrangement of silver halide crystals (analog) or its precise application of acrylic inks (digital). Beyond physical mimesis, the artwork mimics or stages conventions of representation, of form, transcendence, and beauty, each of which are linked to or bring into question regimes of truth. Consider, for example, *To Fix the Image in Memory* (1977–82) by Vija Celmins. The work consists of found rocks displayed alongside their replicas that are cast in bronze and painted, so that the rocks and their copies are indistinguishable.

It might be more productive to consider artworks as works of fiction, comparable to novels. Novels necessarily contain elements of truthfulness in order to be plausible and convincing, no matter how extravagant their imagining. Similarly, an artwork might proceed from the facts of its own materiality (which, paradoxically, we tend to read as *abstraction*), but other propositions can be treated as fictional, whether representational, indexical, conceptual, and/or narrative. These can be more aptly considered as exerting *claims* to truth, rather than descending to calls upon faith. This not to deny that there are operative conventions of truth but rather to examine how those truths are produced.

Golconda (1953), a painting by René Magritte depicting men raining down from the sky (though they might be rising, or hovering, or they are location points mapping the spatial surface and illusionistic depth of the painting)

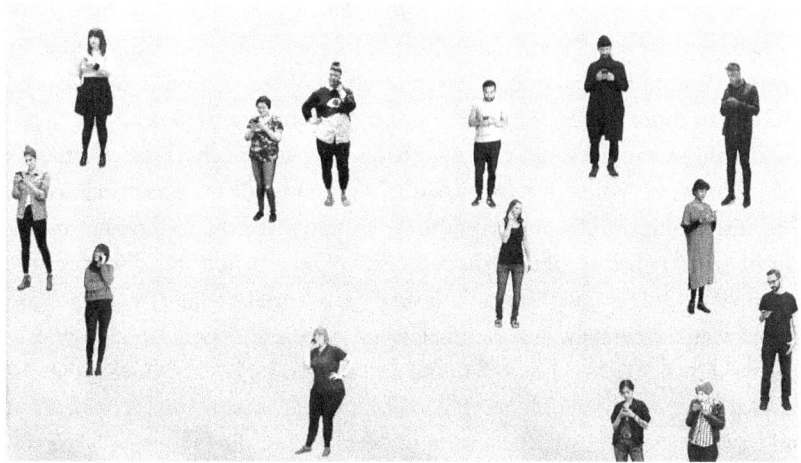

Fig. 5.7 • Laura Hyunjhee Kim, *(Modern)Formations III*, 2016. Still image from video (single-channel), 24 minutes 42 seconds. Courtesy of the artist.

does not present the truth of an actual occurrence in the world, except within the painting itself. The naturalistic, though stylized, representations of Euro everymen convince us of this occurrence as plausible fictions of imagination, or perhaps as the truth claim of the subconscious or of dream states—though Magritte himself vigorously denied any Freudian interpretation of his work.[136] One might claim this as a personal truth, that it reveals or depicts something of Magritte's own history or memory, or of his own idiosyncratic imagination. But it is available to us, to our interpretation, to intersect with our experience and imaginations because it (and art generally) makes a claim toward a more collectively experienced, social truth. Art, then, uses fictional strategies to make truth claims about being in the world. [#Universalism] More overtly, in *The Treachery of Images* (1928–29), Magritte plays upon the fiction of reproduction, with the material truth of the painting as object, and the evident truth of declaration ("This is not a pipe").[137]

Unconscious [#Dream]

When asked where their ideas come from, or how a certain image developed, artists might say from their unconscious, or from their subconscious. Whether there is any difference between these two terms is a matter of debate. Most people seem to use them interchangeably to imply any mental functioning of the brain that is not immediately apparent. "Subconscious" (what Freud referred to as the "preconscious") might be used in a more personal capacity to

refer to memories or things that are individually experienced, including un-
noticed sensory data, but that have been "forgotten" until recalled, whether by
memory stimulus, dreaming, or psychoanalysis. "Unconscious" might be used
to refer to those things that have not been personally experienced and therefore cannot be recalled but that might still exert some behavioral effect, such
as in the use of "collective unconscious" or the idea of the preconsciousness
"primitive brain." "Unconscious," however, does have the undisputed meaning of being comatose, of *being* unconscious. "Unconscious" can also mean the
habitual, or doing something unknowingly as a matter of habit or compulsion
rather than deliberately. The unconscious, as a theoretical model used to explain
the unknown, has become so familiar and so seemingly self-evident (pun intended), that it is invariably accepted as fact. While most mental activity is not
under conscious control, there is no physical part of the brain that is the unconscious, even though we may picture it as the brain's equivalent of a vault,
storeroom, basement, or cellar. Freud likened the mind to an iceberg, with the
greater bulk of it, the unconscious, submerged, and with the preconscious just
below the water line.[138]

Artists use techniques to distract the conscious brain in order to more
directly access the subconscious. Such techniques can be as simple as drawing while talking on the phone; drawing with one's nonleading hand; drawing
blindfolded; painting while stoned, drunk, or on hallucinogens; or copying
from the work of those one deems already less conscious, such as the mentally
ill or the so-called primitive—all of which have been "innovative" modernist
practices.

The "collective unconscious," coined by Carl Jung, "is as follows: in addition to our immediate consciousness, which is of a thoroughly personal nature
and which we believe to be the only empirical psyche (even if we tack on the
personal unconscious as an appendix), there exists a second psychic system of a
collective, universal, and impersonal nature which is identical in all individuals.
This collective unconscious does not develop individually but is inherited. It
consists of preexistent forms, the archetypes, which can only become conscious
secondarily and which give definite form to certain psychic contents."

Artists have pounced on Jung's ideas, and sometimes talk of them as unassailable facts. Their use provides a multiple license: to leave source material
unexamined; to appropriate imagery from all cultures and eras; that artwork
functions universally and that all viewers will be equally affected in equal ways,
even though the viewers themselves may not realize it—it is an *un*conscious,
after all. [#Democracy]

Like much of structuralism's claims of singular, universally applicable systems—deep structures that underlie all social forms—a collective unconscious as an explanatory, workable idea has been largely discredited by poststructuralists. It is important to remember that most popular beliefs about un/consciousness are derived from philosophical speculation rather than scientific evidence.

Unique/ness [#Original/ity; #Truth]

"Unique" is one of the most common terms of popular art appreciation, usually taken to mean "the only one of its kind." When my class of beginning students wrote artist statements, fully two-thirds of them described wanting their work to be unique, reflecting a desire for *themselves* to be unique. This is the crux of what "uniqueness" might mean in our current entrepreneurial model. We're aware that our projected, visible identity is accumulated, performed, and customizable. We have access to and consume the same objects, clothing, entertainment, and tastes, and the only way to distinguish our particular consumption (let alone production) from that of others is through customizing it. Even though our choices of mixing and matching are available to others, the permutations are seemingly so infinite that the particular mix and match we perform can appear to be the only one of its kind. This is one form of uniqueness—savvy shopping that projects individuality and that makes us stand out from the crowd.

In a more general way, "unique" has come to mean unusual, that something is sufficiently different from other things of a similar category. Even questioning how much is sufficient and what is different, we are still caught within the relational, that is, different from what? "*Sufficient* difference" might value individuality while not being overly different to incur social stigma. A desire to stand out while fitting in. This is essentially the logic of branding and a central aspect of marketing, including art marketing, whether by artists or by galleries. To stand above the crowd while being desired by the crowd. Since the nature of the crowd is to constantly incorporate what steps above and upon it, branding has to pursue originality, that is, it has to constantly rebrand itself. Rebranding can take the forms of constancy, tradition, or longevity; in art terms, consistency, history, and maturity—a sameness that accumulates uniqueness over time.

If something were actually unique, one couldn't have previously encountered it nor have preknowledge of it. If a thing is like no other, we have no pathways to recognize, understand, or assess it. In other words, we can only recognize and understand things in relation to other things, in context with other things. The unique thing that stands by itself, that has no comparison or basis for comparison, is a thing unknowable.

In a different understanding of "particularity" (though not uniqueness), things accrue meaning depending on our association with them. I might value a particular mass-produced object because it has been in my possession for a long time. It has accrued history, *my* history, which no other same object has, and so I might be unwilling to part with *my* object for another one that to someone else seems exactly the same. The uniqueness, then, is not in the object itself but in what this particular object has come to represent for me. In a similar way, we invest a different set of meanings and values to what we term "original" and "unique" than to what we consider copies, or multiples.

Artistically, uniqueness might be effective pastiche, the kind of highly mobile, adaptive appropriation that is the hallmark of the new, though it is often criticized as the insincere markers of postmodernism. The *idea* of uniqueness is not only that it is singular but also that it is entirely earnest, a kind of immediately evident and singularly manifested truth. Uniqueness might be, then, a collage that leaves no trail of its appropriations, or that is dependent on its audience not being able to recognize or follow its trails. This claim to uniqueness requires the viewer to be ignorant and/or amnesiac, an agent of modernism's culture of forgetting.

Universal/ism

To be universal is one of the most commonly encountered desires voiced by artists, that their work is accessible to any and all audiences. There are many things that are commonplace, and the ways that viewers experience and respond to them might follow certain patterns, but that is different from the imperial presumption that everyone else experiences things the same way that one does oneself. Global capitalism—through its ideologies, spectacle, and mass consumption—is the closest to universal experience, although that's not what artists mean. Another increasingly possible universal experience is global destruction, though that's not what artists mean either.

"Universalism" is often synonymous with "normativity." Both presume their own mobility and expansion across all boundaries. Richard Dyer, for example, clarifies how whiteness functions: "Whites are everywhere in representation. Yet precisely because of this and their placing as norm they seem not to be represented to themselves as whites but as people who are variously gendered, classed, sexualized and able. At the level of racial representation, in other words, whites are not of a certain race, they're just the human race."[139] Dyer further clarifies: "There is no more powerful position than that of being 'just' human. The claim to power is the claim to speak for the commonality of humanity. Raced people can't do that—they can only speak for their race. But nonraced people can, for they do not represent the interests of a race."[140] Dyer's arguments can be equally applied to other normative hierarchies, such as the ones he mentions of gender, class, sexuality, and ability. These critiques overlap with Édouard Glissant's observation, "The universal is a sublimation, an abstraction that enables us to forget small differences."[141] The claim to universality is a prime tactic in the larger project of forgetting difference.

"Universal" might be used to mean "populist." Populism is assumed to be better than elitism, which is understood as benefiting a small group at the expense of a larger group. However, populism is inseparable from mass marketing, and the ideology and practice of mass marketing is to reroute the resources of as many as possible into the pockets of the fewest. In other words, populism—and its ideology of universalism—might be elitism at its most efficient.

Scrutinizing the meaning and application of universalism peels away its mask of inclusivity *as assimilationist* and power-maintaining. From this meaning universalism needs to be reconceptualized to produce inclusivity *across difference*.

To become actually universal, art industries have to strive to be open to include all viewpoints and experiences, no matter how critical, contradictory, seemingly marginal, or unmarketable. While this can easily parallel the workings and ambition of global capitalism, universalism's main divergence would be to pursue these possibilities against hierarchies of dominant and dominated. Without this parity, there can be no claim to universality. Any artist claiming that their work is universal *in the present* really means that their work is assimilationist, in the manner that supports normativity. Artists tend to declare their assimilation as "I'm not a feminist" or "I'm not a Black artist" or "My work is not about being gay" or "I'm not interested in politics" or "I'm against all labels" and "I just want to be *an artist*." These seemingly reasonable claims can lead to productive discussions about what one might wish to assimilate *into*, and what might be the rewards and costs of that assimilation.

Alternatively, it might be necessary to advocate for universalist and future-making principles, such as "life, liberty and the pursuit of happiness," or "liberté, egalité, fraternité"—what Paul Gilroy refers to as "the ethical pretensions of western civilization."[142] We might aspire to and insist on universalism even as we remain highly critical at its lack of universal *application*. Edward Said suggests possibilities: "Universality means taking a risk in order to go beyond the easy certainties provided us by our background, language, nationality, which so often shield us from the reality of others. It means looking for and trying to uphold a single standard for human behavior when it comes to such matters as foreign and social policy. Thus if we condemn an unprovoked act of aggression by an enemy we should be able to do the same when our government invades a weaker party."[143]

Us [#Identity; #Universal/ism]

The premise of the seemingly innocuous "us," derived from an assimilationist model, is that we are all the same and we all want the same—except for those who aren't, and who don't.[144]

"Us" is the specter that defines the limits of discussion, of whom artwork is for, of what formal languages and stylistic choices it employs, of who constitutes an art public, and even, hyperbolically, what constitutes civilization and to whom it belongs. The critic Peter Schjeldahl provides a primal example: "Is there something excessive about the popular deification of Rembrandt, as of van Gogh, at souvenir shops throughout Amsterdam? You won't think so in the Gallery of Honor, where I had a moment of fancying the almost hundred-and-eighty-five-square-foot canvas as a raft for the self-respect of Western civilization. One of *us* did that!" (emphasis added).[145]

Who is this *us*? Someone Dutch (a possibility, given Schjeldahl's name)? A white Euro American? A man (since only men are mentioned)? Without having to list them, the litany of those excluded is extensive—outsiders to Western civilization, even as they are producers (not least as slaves and laborers) of that civilization. Along with that "us" of "those-like-me," art itself is positioned as evoking nationalist and imperialist pride. *Those*, over *there*, don't have, have never had, and *will* never have a Rembrandt. While Schjeldahl might have meant "us" to mean all of humanity, it seems less convincing that facing, say, a Benin bronze, he would have made a similar exclamation.

In Paul Gilroy's words, "To be recognized as human was to be accorded an authentic kind of historic being. On the other hand, to be dismissed on raciological grounds as bestial or infrahuman was to be cast outside of both culture and historicality."[146]

●●

Any configuration of "us" is predicated on those who are excluded, who are outcast. The outsider, rather than one who is lacking, or marginal, can instead be seen as a central figure of contemporary society. The outsider is a necessary fabrication to enforce disciplinary and punitive laws that define what society is and who it includes, *through its exclusions*. The outsider—however configured and marked—is the figure whose exclusion describes and tests the limits of laws enacted to safeguard us, the insiders. It is the outsider who shores up the bastions of our insiderness, and who also serves as example of what can happen to those who transgress those bastions. It is this setting of an example that provides as much a social function as any claim to justice or punishment. The threat posed by the outsider is provided as justification for emergency or exceptional curtailment of insiders' rights, though once employed, these emergency measures tend not to be rescinded.[147]

●

During critiques of a student who is perceived to be performing their outsiderness or victimhood—whether on the basis of race, culture, sexuality, or gender— the rest of the group may feel constrained in their discussion. They may feel that they do not "have the right" or permission to discuss such work because they do not share that particular outsider status, and therefore cannot speak from that position. Wrapped up in this is the fear of appearing to be racist/homophobic/sexist, and so on, if they were to reveal their true thoughts, or if they were critical of the work. [#Victim]

While this is a general political imperative, the critique allows for potentially radical possibilities of reconceiving notions of "us." It may pursue possibilities that are systemically different from the institutional configurations of inclusiveness and diversity, and, in the words of Nandita Sharma, will allow "us to co-identify and coexist as interaltruistic co-humans."[148]

Victim

"Victim art," a term that seemed to have reached its nadir during the 1990s, still lingers in all its sniffy unsavoriness. It was mostly used as an epithet against "multicultural" art by artists whose primary claim to subjectivity and artistic creativity was through their own supposedly victimized lives. I will draw from Arlene Croce's notorious essay "Discussing the Undiscussable," in which she coins the term "victim art."[149] Croce outlines her refusal to see and review Bill T. Jones's dance piece *Still/Here* on the following grounds that she *as viewer* is made to feel victimized (all bracketed, italicized quotes are from Croce's essay):

1. Exclusion: the viewer feels excluded from the group that has experienced the victimization; that group is then characterized as divisive, as "tribally" cohering around their exclusive experience
2. Emotional manipulation: the art, dependent on empathy for the traumatic experience, circumvents the viewer's intelligent, critical response ["*I can't review someone I feel sorry for or hopeless about.*"]
3. Having to be subjected to a voyeuristic spectacle that parades its own martyrdom while masquerading as art ["*. . . those . . . I'm* forced *to feel sorry for because of the way they present themselves: as dissed blacks, abused women, or disenfranchised homosexuals—as performers, in short, who make out of victimhood victim art*"]
4. "Victimhood" is a mass delusion happening on a society-wide scale, with the viewer/critic in question as a stand-alone voice of reason
5. A sense of betrayal ["*Jones . . . was (in the late '70s) one of our favorites, because he seemed to be uninterested in conforming to the stereotype of the respectable black choreographer*"]
6. They are changing art for the worse ["*It was still possible in the sixties and seventies to unearth values in postmodern dance*"]
7. Having to face aggression and intimidation by the artist ["*With Jones, you were actually intimidated. . . . Politically provocative, accusatory, violent, it was a barely domesticated form of street theater.*"]; in her use of "*domesticated*," Croce invokes bestiality, slavery, and "thuggery" to situate the black body
8. Being silenced ["*No back talk! Anything you say not only will be held against you but may be converted into grist for further paranoid accusation*"] (this list being a case in point)
9. Artworks become politicized, detracting from the viewer's pleasure
10. Artworks become bureaucratized, syphoning off public funding—the "it's my taxes that pay for it" syndrome.

Croce, and similar viewers, experience themselves as being *bullied* by certain forms of art. In this case it was a dance piece about living with AIDS, choreographed by Jones, a gay, Black, HIV-positive man. Even though Jones himself does not dance in the piece, a typical complaint of "being bullied" is that the artist and the artwork are equated as being one. Croce cannot speak objectively about the work because she feels "*sorry for*" and "*hopeless about*" Jones. Jones, then, is the sum of that reduction, a "gay, Black, HIV-positive man" who can never be anything else—not a professional, highly trained, and experienced choreographer, not an intellectual who can have insightful and profound views both on his own experience and on other aspects of life.[150]

The fully complex person is reduced to being a victim. Their art is proffered as evidence of *only* that victimhood. These same maneuvers are enacted by racism, sexism, homophobia, and other forms of reductivism, but critics are generally careful to direct their complaints to the introduction of politics into art, even as they seem incognizant of *their* views being so political.[151]

Since the criticism of victimhood is made through capitalism—victims being unproductive failures who wallow in their failure to be productive—it is useful to understand victimhood as negative capital that is imposed on and accrued by certain subjectivities who are *already* cast as failures. [#Capitalism]

Why do viewers feel threatened and victimized by artworks that don't support their own views? Why do they feel that they are the primary, intended viewers, and why do they feel that those works are directed *against* them? Why does the authority of one offended viewer override another viewer's freedom to view (censorship being a common consequence of being offended)?

Victim art: this book (note my hesitancy in writing a biographical introduction).

Work [#How *Art* Can Be Thought]

What is the "curious unity" that constitutes a work, and how do we distinguish a work from everything else an artist does?[152] Is an artist's shopping list a work? When an artist shops, is it a performance? Is their trash a sculpture? Their home remodeling a painting, installation, or public work? Does their signature on a DMV form designate the form as a work? Is a framed object on a wall more likely to be the work than the wall on which the frame hangs? Is an object on a pedestal the work, or is the pedestal part of the work? How does one know whether a gallery installation includes the wall's air vents or electrical outlets? When does a performance begin or end?

Some signs are more easily readable than others: objects and events encountered in galleries and museums are more likely to be works than those encountered in public restrooms, even those in museum restrooms. What of street interventions or a Fluxus list of instructions? What of a person reading aloud a private letter in public, or holding a sign on a street corner (Sharon Hayes's *Everything Else Has Failed! Don't You Think It's Time for Love?* [2007] and *In the Near Future* [2009])? A man selling snowballs on a street corner (David Hammons, *Bliz-aard Ball Sale* [1983])? A museum attendant hopping (Tino

Sehgal, *This Is Good* [2001])? A column that sinks into the ground (Esther Shalev-Gerz and Jochen Gerz, *Monument Against Fascism* [1986])?

Some factors to consider:

- Where the work is encountered
- What material the work is made from
- Whether the work employs separating mechanisms, such as a frame, a white wall, a black box, a white pedestal
- In the case of a live event, whether there is visible documentation (the presence of cameras)
- Does the work use similar stylistic, formal, and conceptual factors as known previous works (i.e., is there a way to historicize it?)?
- Is the work attributed, even if to "artist unknown"?
- Temporality: Is it a work during its making/doing? Or is it a work only after completion?
- Audience: does the work require an audience?

Part of the trajectory of conceptual art was to investigate these questions of what art is and when something becomes art. We can blame Bruce Nauman for popularizing the notion that whatever one does in the workplace of the studio is work, including thinking, waiting, cleaning, pacing, standing, kneeling, sitting, making faces, and so on. All these activities can be part of artistic labor, *work*. But when they are brought into the public realm of the exhibition space, they become *works*. [#Practice]

For art to be work is to conceive of the artist as a worker, which allows for these terms' class associations. In the contemporary art market, this idea of the artist as affiliated with the working-class laborer seems more of a parody than even the romance or mythology that it might once have carried. A current model of the artist is closer to that of the small business owner or entrepreneur. Certainly more factory *owner* than factory worker. In the art market, it might be more accurate—but upsetting to artists—to speak of a product rather than a work.

Works are the means by which we designate authorship. Can an artist exist without artworks to their name (even if those works have been lost or destroyed)? Can one be an artist if one's works are solely imaginary? To verbally describe the works, to draw or photograph them, to build models, and so on—all these forms of imagining or documenting can be/come the work.

For artists, these questions of what constitutes work, or *a* work, can be crucial in deciding what directions to take, and subsequently what to make public.

Many artists will pursue a repeated set of actions, which become (a) work only through their accumulation—partly because the repetition allows for patterns and artistic intention to become apparent. Would Yayoi Kusama's *Infinity Rooms* be as effective with only five or ten dots? Would Allan McCollum's *Plaster Surrogates* convince as a work if he had done only one (*Surrogate*)? A crucial aspect of artistic labor is to find the logic of the work, which will point toward its appropriate medium, form, materials, and size; determine whether it requires a single or multiple iteration; and assess when the work is finished.

Artists might pursue a number of different ideas and directions, with only a few being publicly shown. With art history predominantly investigating what is shown in exhibitions rather than what is made in private, it is the exhibited work that tends to historically frame the artist. What of the doodle on a restaurant napkin, the sketchbook, the laptop, the unprinted negatives, or the unedited film? There are, of course, many exceptions, particularly in the case of what is known as outsider artists who may never exhibit their work in their lifetimes. How these "preworks" enter the market and discourse to become works is dependent on the art industry and its agents.

HOW, NOW, ROTHKO?

A major reason for reconsidering Mark Rothko—and it could have been any number of his contemporaries—is that he marks a culmination of modernist art survey courses, with all artistic roads leading to the United States, and to New York. Reinforcing Rothko's canonical status is the significant museum display space that he and his cohort occupy. Rothko exemplifies Euro American abstract painting as civilizational destiny/destination. Discarding the excess baggage of representation, he arrives, first-class, at *refinement*, to an aesthetic purity that is equated with freedom, transcendence, authenticity, and spirituality. His travels parallel social exclusivity, dispensing with the fripperies and vulgarity of the *working crass* toward the refined taste and veneer of the *aristoclassy*—a trajectory that might also be associated with the positioning of museums as civilizational destinations. Abstract painting, contrary to its rhetoric of universal access, is deployed as a social filter.

Whose interests these deployments and the museum serve, what they historicize, what they exclude, and whether and how they can be democratized form the background to my viewing of Rothko. I emphasize and examine the viewing itself, although I hope my arguments can be extrapolated toward those more expansive issues, and elucidate some of the earlier arguments made through the course of this book.

I entered the first gallery of the Rothko retrospective as part of a small crowd.[1] By the time I reached the second gallery, I was pretty much the only person in it. Most viewers had given each work a cursory, ticked-off glance (been there, seen that), and had hurried on. This is unsurprising, since museums have become less temples of solitary contemplation and more an amalgam of department store of touristic consumption, and zoo for tamed encounters with the unusual and entertaining. More than a few Rothkos together stop being unusual and entertaining. Judging by viewers' reactions, Rothko had clearly never encountered John Baldessari's dictum of not producing any more boring art.

Yet solitary, prolonged communion is still the idealized encounter for painting, if not for more "participatory" works. Why look at Rothko—and by extension, any abstract—paintings, whether of that period or contemporary? What does abstract painting *do*? How does painting intersect with other aspects of our lived/viewed experience? Is Rothko's work good for us? If it is, and not just because of the authority of the venerated past, *how* is it good (for us)? Rothko, one-time social idealist that he was, himself intended his works to "lift up" the viewer from the commercialism of everyday life. How? And does that uplift work (now)? Facing his paintings, I had similar expectations. What was this hoped-for transfixing, transformative, transcendent effect (I'm using "transcendence" in its popular usage as going beyond individual human experience to a universal humanistic connection—what might also be known as the "human spirit" or the Jungian collective unconscious)?

Rothko paintings tend to be spoken of in sensory and spiritual terms rather than historical ones. His work is exemplary of art's purported quality of timelessness, in the dual sense of transcending time periods and functioning in the perpetual, paused present of a viewer's encounter with it. These are major claims made for art, and for abstract painting, that they create phenomenological encounters in the present that visually, almost haptically, transfix the viewer.

However, a retrospective exhibition produces its own timeline, a narrative arc, an unfolding of an artist's work toward a personal arrival—the mature work. It allows the viewer to trace the development of the artist's language across time, to see firsthand what continues, what adapts, what is abandoned. A retrospective grounds an artist's work back in linear time, even as viewers may be lost in time within each work.

Having never seen them before in person, Rothko's early works (1920s to mid-1940s) are a revelation to me. They help me understand how Rothko had arrived at his particular visual fusion of figuration, landscape, and abstraction. Or, to think it differently, how he suspended physical presence into a visual, almost liquid space. One can read history in any artwork, but Rothko's early work explicitly charts art history, perhaps too explicitly. Our tendency as viewers—and the chronological hanging of the work in the museum underscores this—is to link this explicitness to immaturity, as the artist still learning and acquiring his style. In these early works we can map references, formal vocabularies, and direct influences. To draw together a few of the most immediate references (gleaned from the work itself, from critics, and from Rothko's own writings):

- the historicity and mythological weight of Assyria, Babylon, and Sumer
- the flatness and spatial organization learned from Pablo Picasso (through Fang masks)
- the expressiveness from Georges Rouault, Paul Klee, and Die Brucke (from the childlike, the mentally ill, the "tribal")
- the color vibrations as optic-emotive conduits garnered from Henri Matisse and the Fauves (through North Africa)
- the totemic spirit beings of the Pacific Northwest
- the (neoprimitivist) placement of biomorphic and shimmering geometric forms within dream space learned from Giorgio de Chirico, Joan Miro, Yves Tanguy, Max Ernst, Roberto Matta, and Salvador Dalí (most of whom had arrived in New York in the 1930s); also here consider Aborigine "dreaming"
- liberation from figurative description arrived at through Piet Mondrian's grids (through theosophy, drawing from Hinduism and Tantra)
- the spatial experiments of his immediate American elders, Milton Avery, Max Weber, and Marsden Hartley
- the mythological delvings of his contemporaries, Adolph Gottlieb, Arshile Gorky, Barnett Newman, and Clyfford Still.

Seemingly paradoxical, what links many, if not most, of these Euro American "men of intelligence, faith, and law" is their interest in the primitive, and in non-European mythology and art forms as stimulators for their own inner truth, as though each one, as an individual, is himself the apex of these complex world histories.[2] Their desire to search "elsewhere" is premised on a crisis of faith that "their own" art history had run its course. As the artist and critic (and Rothko contemporary) John Graham condenses it, "The purpose of art in particular is to reestablish a lost contact with the unconscious . . . with the primordial racial past and to keep and develop this contact in order to bring to the conscious mind the throbbing events of the unconscious mind."[3]

Achille Mbembe situates modernist avant-gardes more historically: "In many ways the conceptions of art developed between 1890 and 1945 were deeply shaped by the idea that civilization had exhausted itself. They drew a contrast between the supposed vigor of savages and the exhausted blood of the civilized."[4]

Rothko himself, in a letter in 1943 to the *New York Times* jointly written with Adolph Gottlieb and with assistance from Barnett Newman, plots a manifesto that begins as a colonial expedition, takes Kurtzian turns, and ends by "going native":

1. To us, art is an adventure into an unknown world, which can be explored only by those willing to take the risks.
2. This world of the imagination is fancy-free and violently opposed to common sense.
3. It is our function as artists to make the spectator see the world our way—not his way.
4. We favor the simple expression of the complex thought. We are for the large shape because it has the impact of the unequivocal. We wish to reassert the picture plane. We are for flat forms because they destroy illusion and reveal truth.
5. It is a widely accepted notion among painters that it does not matter what you paint as long as it is well painted. This is the essence of academicism. There is no such thing as good painting about nothing. We assert that the subject is crucial and only that subject matter is valid which is tragic and timeless. That is why we profess spiritual kinship with primitive and archaic art.[5]

∙●

The encounter with art produces bodily experiences. I expect it, desire it—knowing that feeling something is the most commonly verbalized response to artwork, such that we take it as a given. Standing in front of the paintings, I might be feeling something, but I couldn't say what "it" is, nor whether "it" is happening *to* me, or what my agency is in making "it" happen. My belief—and I realize that this belief can inhibit experience—is that the behavioral oddity of prolonged gazing at abstract painting is (collectively) learned behavior, with the learning so continually reinforced that it feels like it comes *from* within. The learning is expansive and flexible enough that it enables me (us) to experience new things that can settle upon and reinscribe the already ingested. This reinforcement provides feelings of truth, authenticity, narrative continuity, and historical importance—which in turn reinforce the embodiment of the feeling. The sediment of small possibilities and reassuring comforts that build to promontories of truth. One might equally apply this as a description of how ideology functions, which is also what makes me suspicious of "it."

But I want to put these beliefs—doubts, really—on hold, and allow myself to be fully immersed, even as I wonder what that immersion might be. Viewers talk about artistic encounters that produce unexpected responses, for which they felt completely unprepared, like they had been picked up and shaken or like a Pauline conversion on the road to Damascus. I don't experience Rothko quite so joltingly, but I *am* surprised by and gain pleasure from his use of bright colors, the gay (in all senses) exuberance of shocking lilac, the pulsating plum, the tumescent magenta that is vivid as a fresh welt. There is an undeniable pleasure in seeing these colors in paintings, which is qualitatively different from seeing them in, say, flowers. I think the difference is that they were *chosen* for a painting, so the pleasure is not only in their visual sensation but also in that someone (Rothko) selected and arranged them.[6] I am drawn to a comparison with flower arranging, though aware that such a feminine-associated practice is not accorded the same value as painting. Flowers die quickly, whereas we protect paintings to last for centuries. Seeing these colors so dominant in the paintings leads me to a speculative queering of Rothko's possible inner desires that he was otherwise not able to manifest. However, while gossip might constitute (sometimes necessary) informal knowledge, that's not my pursuit here, even though the speculation is itself pleasurable. I know I also want to "queer" or at least "feminize" Rothko away from a (hetero)normative reading of masculine genius and spirituality.

The artist Alma Thomas is instructive. Her painting *Breeze Rustling through Fall Flowers* (1968), like others in her *Earth Paintings* series, draws upon flowers and foliage shimmering in breeze. These are not depictions but invocations, the colors, light, and brush marks suggestive of sustained pleasures of firsthand experience of gardens, flower beds, and trees. To the prejudicial eye, the painting might seem too pretty, too colorful—gaudy even, naive rather than serious, intimate rather than the grand gesture of "great art," her mosaic brushstrokes too craftlike, too *feminine*. As an aside, we can map Thomas's brush marks to the modular, black-hair, and gender-related but cross-gender forms of artists such as Mark Bradford (hairdresser endpapers) and Kori Newkirk (pony beads).

How else might we read Thomas's willful joyfulness in contrast to Rothko's melancholia? How does her intended "respitory" function (I *can* breathe; the painting as a momentary space to breathe before returning to the fray),[7] in the midst (emphatically so; Washington, DC, in 1968) of the Civil Rights movement, and now reexperienced by this viewer in the ongoing human rights movement of Black Lives Matter?[8] While Rothko's melancholy emphasizes a break from the imagined past, the tragedy—to use Rothko's term—in Thomas is that the violence of the all-too-real past has *not* been broken.

●

Standing in front of a Rothko painting, *Untitled* (1957), which we typically think of *as* a "Rothko," I slow down and allow my vision to relax into the paint, lulling my mental chatter.[9] The rewards of this are immersion into the paint, whose luminous layers and brushstrokes one can follow as though choreography, the swimming into the optical dream space; an immersion that promises a merging. My eyes float into this space, which *feels* like the miasma of my own consciousness, or rather, unconscious. I can't help interjecting—to myself—that this is another inherited, learned concept that now resides so implacably within my body that I imagine it was always there, a primal, atavistic throwback. It feels like a potentially liberating and affirming space, one so active and activated that it feels more like an event, an event space of being able to drift within it, a twofold experience of coexistence within the painting and within my own unconscious. This particular dual space would have been literally unthinkable in Western art before Freud, and before Surrealism's visual inventions (though, as always, there are precursors). Perhaps, with the ingestion of pop-Buddhism (Budd-lite), meditation, and yoga, we—a contested Western "we"—are ever more adept at entering these dual states.

This dream of drifting within an event space is highly alluring and physically pleasurable, but it *is* a learned concept. Referring to Pollock, Harold Rosenberg spoke of the transformation of painting into an existential drama, in which "what was to go on the canvas was not a picture but an event," and that "the gesture on the canvas was a gesture of liberation from value—political, aesthetic, moral."[10] The action painter becomes an action *figure*, striking a blow for liberty, if not justice for all. (The) painting is where the artist, and the viewer in their wake, encounters liberty—at least metaphorically. This has become a deeply embedded desire for art.

My experience of "floating within" is partly a physical effect of my eyes focusing upon a circumscribed area within the painting. The mechanics of human vision (unlike the camera) are activated by the eye constantly moving. If the eye remains still without interruption, it stops seeing, as it were. A hypnotic, trance, meditative, or dream state—zoning out—can arise. These are consequences of the mechanics of vision, but we make sense of and interpret them through culture. These states probably are good for us, like rebooting the brain. But whether they are caused by abstract paintings any more than by staring at a blank wall or at a candle is a dubious proposition.

A painting (before which one zones out) may add other interpretable or suggestive entry points, of color, of form, of mark and texture. While painting enables a particular, cultivated experience of interpreting the mechanics of vision, it is not unlike viewing "floaters" in one's eyes. Seeing floaters is to see a space that is both outside and within the body, distant and intimate, fugitive and haptic, mystical and material. In an actualizing of Plato's cave metaphor, it is also not to see the thing itself, since what we see are the shadows cast onto the retina by protein and cell debris floating in the eye's vitreous humor. What we *see* is the physical apparatus of sight.

What limits floaters as metaphors for looking at art is that, when looking at art, one is engaging with another's intelligence—and I mean intelligence here very specifically within the realm of art as a complex of cognitive and affective abilities that articulate experience of being in/with the world through any discipline, medium, or language. Applying this to Rothko (or to any other artist) is to approach the work through questions of how it comes into being—historically, materially, politically—including those questions being applied to the artist's subjectivity and agency. And following Rosenberg's description of painting as event, we can examine the work as the *performance* of the artist's subjectivity and agency *through* history, materiality, and politics. Alongside these interpretive methods, one can simply *be* in front of the painting, in an extended present, the same as one can *be* with floaters, basking in the *self*-conscious and self-*escaping*—and immensely pleasurable—experience of vision. But I don't need art for this—I have floaters—which means that I want more from art.

Looking at Rothko, I reconfigure particular b/analities: the b/anality of painting being essentially a stain on cloth (as photography is on paper); the b/anality of art history conferring esteemed value on this staining; the b/anality of participating in viewing and valuing these stains; the b/anality of Rothko's very particular repetitions of stains (illusory rectangles within the solid rectangles of the stretched canvas) as adequate accounting for his experience of being in/ with the world; the b/anality of transcendence—*from* what *to* what exactly, or as merely elitist escapism? The b/anal overuse of the term "transcendence" for the most ordinary of experiences.[11] These various references to b/anality serve to relink transcendence to its inverse of bodily abjection, from which it seeks perpetual escape.

Contemplating a Rothko is for me a little too distanced and knowing for it to produce an actual welling up of emotion, when a knot from somewhere deep within my body—against any control I might exert—might swell outward, or perhaps contract into itself. I don't notice any physical reactions, the muscle action of emotions. They might be fugitive possibilities, like bodily memories awaiting recall. Where and *when* do these emotions originate? Are they bodily responses to the artwork, which suggest that they start from the artwork (outside to in)? Are they already in the body, and "triggered" by the artwork through other associations (inside to out)? Are they between the body and the trigger (as a bridge or an encounter)? That I can anticipate them and feel them as bodily memories would suggest that they are already within, and already known.[12]

Our looking to art to provide emotional experience is linked in complex ways to beliefs about biology and civilization. The sensitive artist (though someone like Picasso is more the bullish artist) becomes a conduit to primal, unmediated emotions (the "timelessly tragic" in Rothko's words), which precede socialization, hence the recourse to the "primitive and archaic." As I have written already, it is this emotional experience, this emotional *connection* that, when experienced within the body, feels as though it cuts across millennia of the socialization that separates us—from our inner selves, from nature, and from what essentially links us all as human. The alignment of what is seen externally with what is felt internally makes the felt and the internal seem truthful. This "truthy" alignment is one reason why we think art is good for us, and why someone like Rothko is exemplary. At least that's the belief. As beliefs go, it's not a bad one. Not quite gospel, but certainly sanctified to its believers. What about the apostates, the agnostics, the atheists, and the heretics (I count myself as all four)?

We can instead consider that emotion circulates as and within an "affective economy" (Sara Ahmed's phrase). Ahmed argues that emotions accumulate (like capital) in feeling bodies and through the repetition of discourse, circulating and "sticking" onto certain signs, objects, and bodies. As biocapital, emotions produce use and surplus political value, which maintains its instrumental economic value and its production of feeling subjects and felt objects. Feeling emotions is a form of reading (experienced *before* the revisit of interpretation). Our emotional experience *is* the reading of the stimulus. I have already elaborated on artworks as texts, and considered that the body is written upon. Emotion, as bodily experience, cannot be exempt from that writing. We think of it as wiring, as in "being wired" in certain ways, almost as if the body is a feeling machine, part of a larger biodiscursive complex. The body's emotional experience is part of a fractional engine of the vocabulary of stimulus/feeling (or, prioritizing the body: feeling/stimulus) that, like memory—indeed, *through* memory—can, in popular parlance, be triggered.

Emotions and stimuli can be thought of as fractions (with the medical implication of mending a fracture or, in linguistics, the double-vowel sound of a diphthong) of mutually attractive forces, as incomplete texts that come into being if not to completion by their meeting. The red-brown subtleties of almost-blacks, for example, in a Rothko painting, *Untitled* (1963), being one fraction of the equation, and my emotional responses being another. Other vital fractions consist of the histories and currencies of how those emotion-vocabularies become attached to and embedded within both painting and my body. I might want my active looking, rather than passively seeing, to be a response *from* me, in overlapping ways that I think emotions operate like *looking*, as something that *I* do, rather than the seeing that my body does. I also cannot discount the performative forces that have already acted upon me to mold the person that I am, as the being who can respond emotionally or otherwise to a Rothko. The only way I can contemplate this separation between "I" and "my" body, is that this "I" is a complex of social relations, while "my" body is a physical entity that is the reservoir and engine of these relations. It's not much of a separation. Though when feeling pain, for example, I can "extricate" my "self" and remotely observe the now-lessened pain that is happening to this not-me body. This ability to extricate the "I" or my "self"—a transferable ego—from my body suggests a floating, mobile self, which in this case can be attached to an external object—such as an abstract painting. This attachment, or rather, "attach-ability"—similar to Ahmed's articulation of the stickiness of emotions—is what we might think of, and invest the artwork with, as shared emotion, as transcendence, as greatness. This suggests that the painting acts as site of transference from the viewer, as the recipient of redirected, otherwise unexpressed emotions (rather than the repressed emotions suggested by psychoanalysis—though this too is probable). The painting becomes a Pygmalionesque, compliant love object (which, disturbingly, might point to why much rhetoric of artistic production is of "sensitive" masculinity).[13]

These overtones of the psychoanalytic indicate that looking at and attaching to art are forms of social practice, literally so. The viewer is socialized *through* the very experience of this looking, trained into believing, *feeling, actuating* that they are transcending the social and the historical. Knowing how to do this looking, feeling, and attaching—pleasurable (or painful) as it is—means that I have learned to do it, unless one believes, erroneously, that looking at artwork is an innate, biological function that is of survival value. I can refer here to Freud's anal stage. Defecating is biological; toilet training is cultural: I will leave the reader to develop this *analogy* further through the outline that follows. I have been acculturated, cultivated, *civilized* into this event-space-act, which is prescribed, and prescripted for me to enact. The space of Rothko's paint-soaked canvas, which is not "out there" but "in here," is by convention a space of (self-)affirmation, of escape, of human connection, and social positioning. It is the event of the "in-here" transferred to the "out-there," and imagining that transference is reciprocated. This escape into "Rothko space" feels simultaneously like a rite of passage, a secret code, an old habit, perhaps like a familiar heat in the lungs from a guilty cigarette drag experienced by a former smoker (I'm speculating, since I've never been a smoker; but I think smoking might be an adequate comparison, in its mode of ingestion into an internal experience, its pleasure, its habit, its guilt, and its current ideology—not dissimilar to abstract painting's—of defiance and assertion of individual freedom).[14] In all cases, this escape affirms me as one of the people who "gets" Rothko, as though entering a cabal of cultivated aesthetes.

The paintings are agents for remaking *me*, the viewer—though to what and in whose image? The scheme of art being good for us is an essential cultural force in a larger civilizing mission. Much as I can indulge, I don't want to participate (any longer) in this particular transferring, remaking, inhaling, or excreting. I want to undo the training, to refuse the script, to repurpose the paintings away from this aesthetic escape and humanistic connection. Instead, I want something as sullied and debased as the conflict-ridden world outside the museum walls (and within my self). I want to grow up. However, rather than entirely repudiate this script, which would be to repudiate so much art—a repudiation undertaken by every oedipally motivated avant-garde movement, which typically, and like Rothko, looked to the primitive, the pre- and uncivilized as antidote—I wonder if there might be other pathways to equivalences of this escape-connection, which I think is what we mean when we speak of transcendence.

Losing oneself into the transcendent, and celebration of the art object that provokes that experience, can no longer be affordably thought of as a selfless communing. Like other forms of commodified experience—it is an art *indus-try* after all—this particular escape into pleasure functions (for me) as a mode of selfishness and mindlessness, its communing with something beyond myself more of an indoctrination into the hierarchies of certain art histories than to anything spiritual. It doesn't feel like an out-of-body experience. To be blunt, it feels like putting on a particular form of (albeit "sensitive") masculinity, and donning the white mask that Frantz Fanon speaks of.[15] Not as a form of mimicry, or of wanting to be white—paler shades of Daniel Martinez—but seeing, from outside, a culture iterating and adulating itself, and my own participation within that complex of (re)formations. [#Refusalon]

However, that description's not entirely accurate, since there is no outside position from which I can look at Rothko. I am part of the globalized culture of which Rothko is a component. One might say that, like all others, I am subject to the rule of the canon (the ultimate gun lobby). Rothko, and all the other "men of intelligence, faith, and law," are in me (in the senses of penetrating and already within). What is required is a Fanonian examination of this penetrative violation: to locate that Euro American individual and collective (masculine) unconscious, that civilizing mission, within my own sense of being. I have to proceed from that historical particularity (which dehistoricizes and dehumanizes as it penetrates), the transcendental event horizon into the universal, which resides within and upon all of us. The apex of whiteness as a black hole into which we are all sucked.

This assimilation provides the only framework from which one can conventionally participate in Rothko. The hegemony of his canonical status doesn't allow any other participation. You get him or you don't, although it is more accurate to say that, like ideology, he gets you.

There are ways, other than the conventional, to participate in Rothko, as there are other ways, histories, reasons, and desires to continue to paint abstractly, for the painting to reference "social and historical conditions through the formal methods of abstraction, producing a point of convergence . . . ."[16]

A driving process of colonialism was/is to syphon all knowledge into and through its bureaucratic systems—the museum being a prime site of art and pedagogy's bureaucratic archiving.[17] If the postcolonial state functions with new leadership but through those same systems, one extremist response has been the attempt to entirely eradicate those systems and return to some fabled precolonial era (hence groups like Boko Haram's core opposition to "Western" education or Steve Bannon's agenda of "deconstruction of the administrative state").[18] My position within this book, contrary to any forms of eradication, is to work within, and adapt the systems we have, and to at least make their knowledge processes more transparent. My focus on Rothko is to consider that syphoning, whitewashing process whereby otherwise erased and denigrated world cultures and cosmologies are interiorized into individuals who are then lauded as emblematic of colonialism's civilization (which is replicated through its bureaucracies, in this case of art history, the museum, and the academy).

•

I backtracked to the first gallery, relooking at the paintings, wondering how they might bring me back to the world, rather than to my interiorized un-self. I needed to rescript the paintings without being assimilated by what they represent. I needed to make them relevant to the world as it is, or at least to how I experience it, even when it is screened—and I mean this in both its Lacanian and technological senses. And perhaps it was this thought, of the world being screened, which led me to photograph details of each painting. Through the camera screen, I viewed the meeting of colors in each painting not as incidences to take me out of myself—as I had learned to want from paintings— but to bring me back into the world.

My use of the camera screens *me*, in that it mediates between the painting and my direct viewing. It allows the viewing apparatus (eyes/brain) to become partially disembodied, redirected through the prosthetic apparatus of the camera and *its* screen. The digital camera enhances this separation more than a film camera since one looks *at* the camera's back screen in a different sightline than the painting/object being photographed, rather than *through* a viewfinder to the painting/object. The operation and viewing habits of the camera, and the digital camera in particular, cut through the illusion of floating within the event space of my brain and the paintings.

What I was seeing—through the rectangle of the camera's viewfinder— was the indelible, also rectangular, viewing of Syrian cities being bombed (and Iraqi . . . before that Vietnamese . . . and here, I'm recalling those in my lifetime that have been most televised and turned into cinematic spectacle), and of the relentless Atlantic and now Mediterranean waves that break over bodies. Rothko's lurid orange became the orange of nighttime explosions seen on TV, the trailing brush marks became plumes of smoke, the shatter-splatter of shrapnel, the foam of waves (and I think here too of Théodore Géricault's *The Raft of the Medusa* [1818–19], or J. M. W. Turner's *The Slave Ship* [*Slavers Throwing overboard the Dead and Dying—Typhoon Coming On*] [1840]).

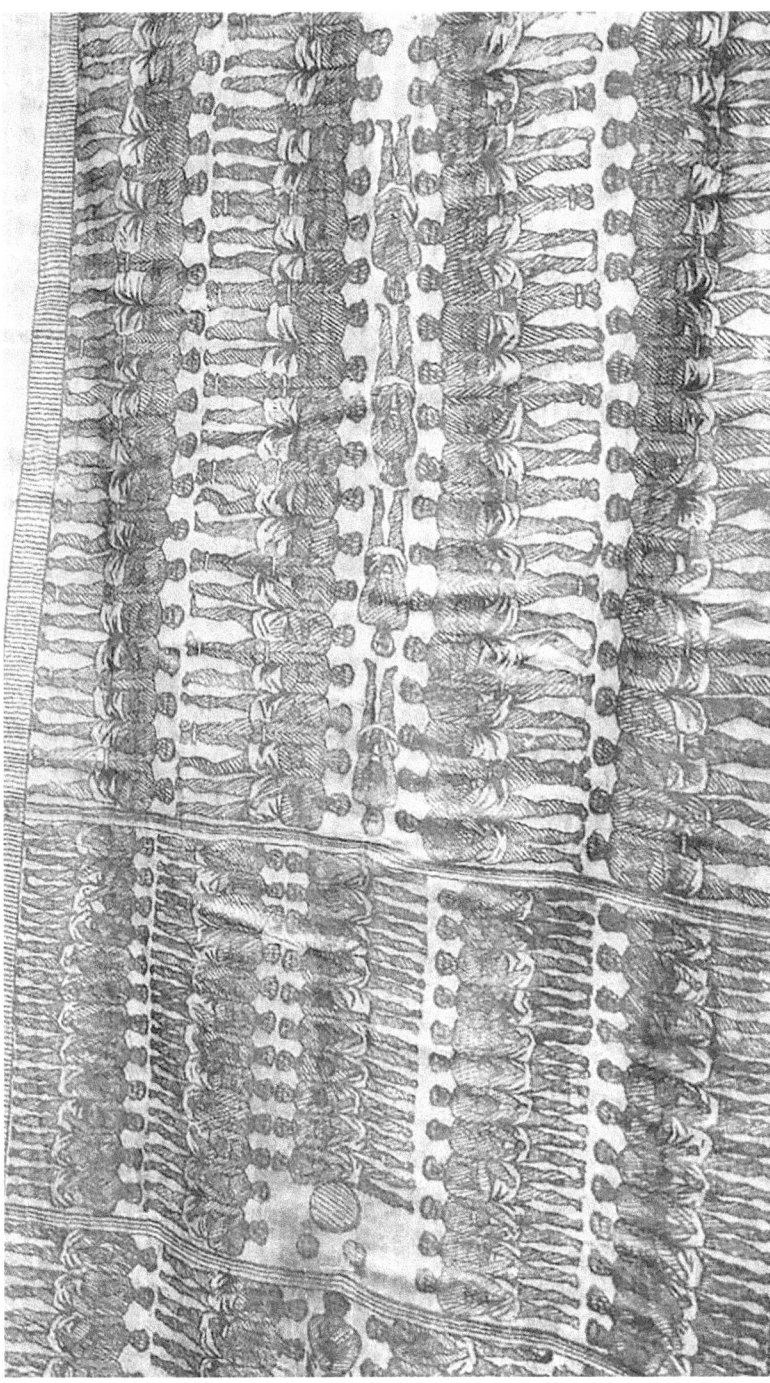

Fig. After.1 • Andrew Wilson, *Ship* (detail), 2015. Cyanotype on cotton, sewn. Courtesy of the artist.

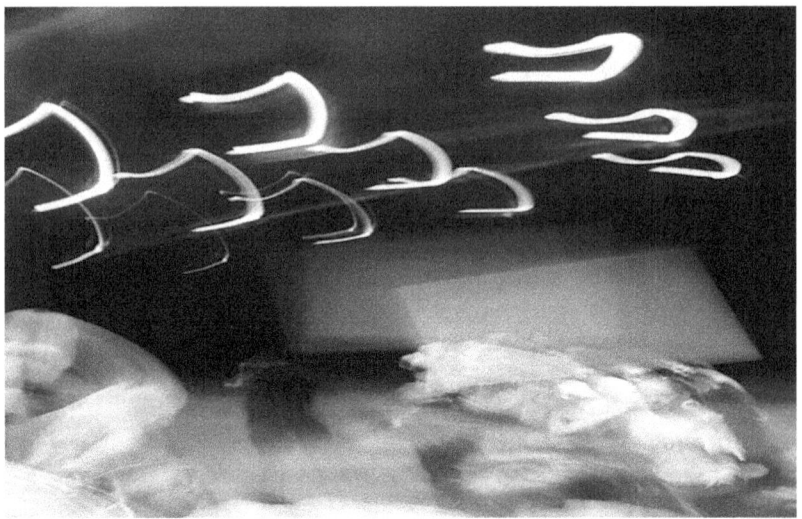

Fig. After.2 • Aaron Hughes, *AHMED: A Selection of Ahmed Jabar Shareef's Photographs*, 2006. Still image from video (reedited and remastered in 2016). Courtesy of the artist.

From Rothko's "borrowing" from ancient Assyria, I am returned to an all-too-present Syria, to its borderless wars, their before and aftermaths in Iraq, Lebanon, Turkey, Kurdistan, Palestine, Israel, Egypt, Libya, Guantanamo, Madrid, London, Paris, Nice . . . I think of the photographs by Ahmed Jabar Shareef, photographs that he will never see but which are compiled in a video by the artist and Iraq veteran Aaron Hughes. The nine-year-old Ahmed, blinded by shrapnel, remembers how to use a camera, pointing it toward sounds ("Ahmed Shareef remembers that the camera is held up to his eye, that the lens is pointed at the subject, and that a button is clicked.").[19] The photographs are both abstract and legible. They have the familiar yellow cast of night shots taken under incandescent light, the blur of camera shake, the proximity of what might be figures and parts of bodies, the rectangular frames of buildings and windows, the repeated calligraphic bursts produced by the camera moving—what, in other, more pastoral circumstances is known as "painting with light."

I am not sketching out a lesson on how to look at Rothko but considering how *this* viewer may bring art back into the world of their present, even as they necessarily engage with each artwork as a document of art history up to the time of its making, as a document of its own time, and as a work whose meaning is provisional in the present. I am suggesting a multiple, simultaneous, hybrid viewing that is art historical, even as it may prioritize the viewer's physical, intellectual, and emotional encounter with the work; and a viewing that necessitates examining the history, construction, and currency of the viewer's own interiority as it is activated through that encounter (this is the complex methodology of critique).

Rather than a Dadaist call to abandon museums (which is where my reasoning might otherwise take me), I'm advocating a different engagement. Mary Louise Pratt has described contact zones as "social spaces where cultures meet, clash and grapple with each other, often in contexts of highly asymmetrical relations of power, such as colonialism, slavery, or their aftermaths as they are lived out in the world today."[20] Museums, where culture(s) are collectively but differentially inhaled and inhabited, are cultural contact zones in the aftermath of colonialism and slavery.

Rather than institutional critique of museum structures, I'm disputing art's colonizing truth claims. Not to abandon museums, not to burn them down, but to revalue and repurpose their knowledge to other means. I've written earlier of art's excess, and here, through Rothko, I am drawing attention to the particular excess that is the now occupied world cultures that form the foundation of modernist and contemporary artworks.[21] This is the excess that conventional narratives of art history and bureaucracy forget, so that faulty memory is already conditioned to the minimal, essential artwork that can only be experienced "within." The "tragic" that Rothko refers to is not (in Guy Debord's sense) the spectacular downfall and loss of the primal past to which we seek reconnection but the ongoing present erasure of multiplicity, including the marginalization of those cultures that are the present incarnations of those mourned pasts. This is a forgetting and a colonization, in which we participate as modernists, as orientalists, and as neoprimitives.

Abstraction, as emotional, spiritual, and ideological landscape/territory—disembodied in a conventional sense but nevertheless haunted—is similarly implicated as a methodology of forgetting. Rothko is but one oeuvre in this cultural industry. It is instructive, but for a different study, to consider abstraction *as* embodied, *as* haunted by the disembodied and erased, as ravaged territory, considerations that would exact new demands for remembering and for adequately responsive languages. Artists such as Norman Lewis, Emily Kame Kngwarreye, Sam Gilliam, Frank Bowling, Charles Hossein Zenderoudi, Arpita Singh, Howardena Pindell, Linda Besemer, Susan Silton, and Anoka Faruqee come to mind, as well as the aforementioned Alma Thomas, and Ahmed Jabar Shareef (via Aaron Hughes), as differently demanding interlocutors of Rothko, and whose "abstract" works are variously embodied through intersecting

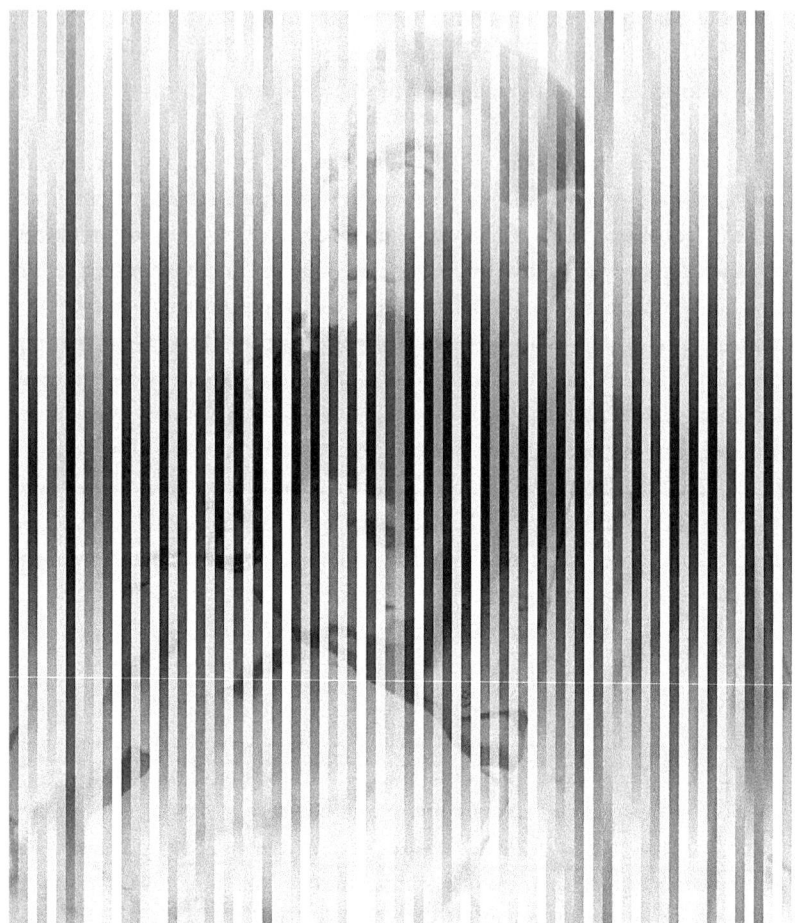

Fig. After.3 • Susan Silton, *On the Beach*, from *The Day, the Earth* series, 2007. Chromogenic prints, 72×65 in. Courtesy of the artist.

genealogies of *not* forgetting.[22] With Susan Silton, I'm thinking in particular of her plays on modernist stripes. In *The Day, the Earth* series (2007), stills from Cold War–era science fiction films underpin and hover over, within, and through hallucinatory stripes, dislocating where visual space is occurring, and similar to how I've discussed floaters. Here (or there), it is not only vision that floats and stings (to use Muhammad Ali's phrase) within and outside the body, it is culture, and social anxiety.

These interlocutors point to larger issues. What would be the effects of social art histories of multiple modernisms networking mobile cartographies of global culture? Imagine if the Museum of Modern Art (MoMA), New York, rehung its *entire* collection to reflect global "Modern Art," rather than a meager seven works, each accompanied by the wall label: "This work is by an artist from a nation whose citizens are being denied entry into the United States, according to a presidential executive order issued on Jan. 27, 2017. This is one of several such artworks from the Museum's collection installed throughout the fifth-floor galleries to affirm the ideals of welcome and freedom as vital to this Museum as they are to the United States."[23] Laudable as this "protest" was, it remains an unrepresentative, token gesture, especially given that five of the artists are Iranian-born. What if "ideals of welcome and freedom" *were* enacted by the museum? What would the art world look like, and how would it operate without the dominating narrative and real estate of white suprematism? How would art histories be understood, how would art be taught, and thought? How would artworks be experienced without a singular trajectory of greatness? Could we understand Rothko through contemporaneous Arab modernisms, say (rather than Arab modernisms being read as derivative of Euro American modernism)? What kinds of viewers would we become?

Given some of these questions, how might we rethink, or revalue, Rothko's five-point manifesto for the contemporary world?

1. *To us, art is an adventure into an unknown world, which can be explored only by those willing to take the risks.* Rather than the neocolonial cult of exploration, can art be rethought in how it acts in a shared, multiply occupied (and conflict-riven) world rather than an "unknown" one?

2. *This world of the imagination is fancy-free and violently opposed to common sense.* What are the imperatives to consider imagination, fancy-freedoms, and common sense as collective, culturally inflected and purposeful, that is, implicated in the world, rather than the unconstrained, "ethically free" escapes of individuals?

3. *It is our function as artists to make the spectator see the world our way— not his way.* How do multiple narratives of "seeing the world" intersect to produce "seeing across" and "seeing together" rather than producing dominant oversight and overseers?

4. *We favor the simple expression of the complex thought. We are for the large shape because it has the impact of the unequivocal. We wish to reassert the picture plane. We are for flat forms because they destroy illusion and reveal truth.* The inverses of these claims are equally valid; but it is more productive to refute simplistic binaries, as well as the notion of revealed,

singular truths. The assertion of the picture plane and flatness no longer carry the same formal and ideological weight as they once did within Euro American modernism, and the only truth they revealed was that the canvas is flat.

5. *It is a widely accepted notion among painters that it does not matter what you paint as long as it is well painted. This is the essence of academicism. There is no such thing as good painting about nothing. We assert that the subject is crucial and only that subject matter is valid which is tragic and timeless. That is why we profess spiritual kinship with primitive and archaic art.* Like "common sense" (point number 2), we can doubt "wide acceptance" as a principal guide, bring into question "good" anything (quality), and complicate oppositions between form and content, content and nothingness. Declarations of "kinship" with the "other" remain within colonial and anthropological models unless the "other" has the same rights, access, privileges, and "freedoms" of expression and criticism. Without equality, an imagined kinship becomes kingship.

It might be useful at this point to consider another "definition" of art, this time from the photographer Sarah Charlesworth, partly as a counterpoint to the male observations listed earlier within the glossary: art is not defined by the medium it employs but rather by the questions that it asks, by the propositions that it makes regarding its own nature as well as the nature of its world.[24]

I want to bring to someone like Rothko, and, by extension, to Euro American modernism, to art history, to art as experienced in the present, to art as currently taught, different sets of questions and propositions than the ones those histories and pedagogies routinely ask and make about their own nature and the nature of the world that they contribute in forming.

I'm not calling for replacing old forms and languages with new ones, which would be another method of forgetting. I *am* pushing toward seeing and remembering actively, and thinking, feeling, and speaking (about art) as decolonizing practices that unmake and remake the shared ideological culture in which we all now participate and to which we are all subject. My aspiration is ultimately toward "the possibility of undoing and unsettling—not *replacing or occupying*—Western conceptions of what it means to be human."[25] While still optimistic of art's role in "what it means to be human," my account is a negotiated refusal: negotiated, since it claims the right to knowledge, pleasure, and experience (in this instance, of Rothko, of late Euro American modernism), and a refusal of assimilation's active forgetting.

Notes

INTRODUCTION. A FOOT IN THE DOOR

1. *Merriam-Webster*, "Vex," a: to bring trouble, distress, or agitation to; b: to bring physical distress to; c: to irritate or annoy by petty provocations. https://www.merriam-webster.com/dictionary/vex.

2. Note the anachronism of the title "bachelor."

3. My use of "white" and "whiteness" point toward institutionalized, racialized inclusions, which have been legislated, enculturated, aestheticized, naturalized, normalized, and rendered invisible so as to mask their grounding in economics and categories of nonwhite, exploitable labor.

4. These kinds of alternative, underground, self-run spaces have never disappeared, as artists continue to seek some degree of independence and control over their own creative lives while negotiating poverty and societal neglect. Such spaces came back to (media and local government) attention following the fire of the Ghost Ship warehouse in Oakland in 2016, in which thirty-six people died. This particularly affected the Bay Area's creative music and artistic networks, as many of those who died were linked to the area's schools and nonprofit spaces.

5. My first job was as a supermarket shelf filler. I was fired after a week, deemed by the manager to be "too stupid" to work there, given my predilection to stock shelves by color and pattern (it didn't occur to me to document my arrangements as "art").

6. See the online interview, "FiPA Arts, Hardial Rai (British South Asian Theatre Memories)," March 25, 2014. British South Asian Theatre Memories Oral History Project is supported by Heritage Lottery Fund, SOAS University of London, APAF, Thurrock Council, Contact Theatre and Avaes Mohammad. https://www.youtube.com/watch?v=PGVwrN8CDxE.

7. Gallery notice, installed by Hounslow City Council in place of the removed art-work. "Indigenous" here referred to white English.

8. One of the main organizers was Stewart Home. The exhibition consisted of twenty-seven participants all exhibiting under the single name Karen Eliot. From an exhibition flyer: "Karen Eliot is a name that refers to an individual human being who can be anyone. The name is fixed, the people using it aren't. . . . The purpose of many different magazines and people using the same name is to create a situation for which no one in particular is responsible and to practically examine western philosophical notions of identity, individuality, originality, value and truth." Other exhibitions included *Against the Clause* at Community Copyart in 1988; *Copyart Goes South* at Bedford Hill Gallery; *Photocopyart* at Shaw Theatre; and *Copyart at the Cockpit* at Cockpit Gallery, all in 1987.

9. Cofounded with Bhajan Hunjan, Shaheen Merali, Symrath Patti, and Shanti Thomas.

10. In the United States, even in the present, in a marketing fantasy of integration, one is still more likely to find students of color in art schools' advertising than in their actual programs.

11. I use "marginalized" in the sense of societal gerrymandering, whereby individuals and groups are deliberately displaced from history, power, decision making, and agency.

12. This is a much bigger subject than can be addressed here. Some historicizing of BAM is currently being done by scholars and research groups such as Black Artists and Modernism, http://www.blackartistsmodernism.co.uk/. See also *The Place Is Here*, *Nottingham Contemporary*, curated by Nick Aikens and Sam Thorne, with Nicola Guy, February 4, 2017–April 30, 2017.

13. This was achieved primarily through the efforts of Shaheen Merali, and included the two of us, with Keith Piper, Sonia Boyce, and Ptika Ntuli. It was also where I met other American artists, including Yong Soon Min, later to become my partner and artistic collaborator.

14. Formed by a core group of artists, including Ken Chu, Bing Lee, and Margo Machida.

15. Useful references include Eddie Chambers, *Black Artists in British Art: A History Since the 1950s*; Alexandra Chang, *Envisioning Diaspora*; and Margo Machida, *Unsettled Visions: Contemporary Asian American Artists and the Social Imaginary*.

16. I was invited to teach the class by the then chair Sue Canning.

17. See, for example, Dennis Cooper, "Too Cool for School," *Spin Magazine*, July 1997, 86–94.

18. "To be human is to engage in relationships with others, and with the world. It is to experience that world as an objective reality, independent of oneself, capable of being known. . . . But man's separateness from and openness to the world distinguishes him as a being of *relationships*. Men, unlike animals, are not only *in* the world, but *with* the world." Paulo Freire, *Education for Critical Consciousness* (London: Bloomsbury Academic, 2013), 3; emphases in original.

19. Raymond Williams, *Keywords: A Vocabulary of Culture and Society* (New York: Oxford University Press, 2015).

20. The role of the teacher is increasingly scrutinized, politicized, and monetized in ways that severely challenge any notion of academic freedom, and already constrain how teachers feel that they can speak and act.

21. The TRC was based on an idea of "restorative justice," as opposed to the more commonly implemented model of "retributive justice."

22. Whether or not these manifestations become explicit is generally linked to moments of crisis. That they manifest and can be mobilized so immediately is evidence that they do not disappear but remain latent until called upon.

23. Édouard Glissant, *Poetics of Relation* (Ann Arbor: University of Michigan Press, 1997).

24. See, for example, Derek Alderman and Arnold Modlin, "(In)Visibility of the Enslaved Within Online Plantation Tourism Marketing: A Textual Analysis of North Carolina Websites," in *Journal of Travel and Tourism Marketing* 25 (2008): 3–4.

25. The title of a Henri Matisse painting from 1904.

26. To use Matisse's description, "What I dream of is an art of balance, of purity and serenity, devoid of troubling or depressing subject matter, an art that could be for every mental worker, for the businessman as well as the man of letters, for example, a soothing, calming influence on the mind, something like a good armchair which provides relaxation from physical fatigue." Henri Matisse, "Notes of a Painter," [1908], translated by Jack Flam, in *Matisse on Art*, Revised Edition (Berkeley: University of California Press, 1995).

27. Peter Schjeldahl, "Finding Solace in Henri Matisse's Nice," *New Yorker*, July 18, 2016, written following the Nice, France, attack by Mohamed Lahouaiej-Bouhlel, who drove a lorry into crowds celebrating Bastille Day on July 14, 2016.

28. Hilton Kramer, "Reflections on Matisse," *New Criterion*, Vol. 11 (November 1992): 7.

29. At the risk of omitting others, one can add to this list Alison Saar, Faith Ringgold, Hank Willis Thomas, Lorraine O'Grady, Lyle Ashton Harris, Martin Puryear, Noah Purifoy, Roshini Kempadoo, and Senga Nengudi.

CHAPTER 1. HOW *ART* CAN BE THOUGHT

1. See "Art," the *Merriam-Webster* online dictionary, http://www.merriam-webster .com/dictionary/art.

2. I'm being facetious, but this is not so far-fetched in other arguments. See, for example, Alva Noe, *Strange Tools: Art and Human Nature* (New York: Hill and Wang, 2015). Noe links breastfeeding and art as "organized" and "organizing activities" (his terms).

3. Albert Boime, *Art in an Age of Revolution, 1750–1800* (Chicago, IL: University of Chicago Press, 1987), xxi.

4. Aimé Cesaire quoted in Katherine McKittrick, ed., *Sylvia Wynter: On Being Human as a Praxis* (Durham, NC: Duke University Press, 2015).

5. Kobena Mercer, *Travel and See: Black Diaspora Art Practices since the 1980s* (Durham, NC: Duke University Press, 2016), xv.

6. Ferdinand de Saussure, *Course in General Linguistics* (1916) (New York: Columbia University Press, 2011).

7. These two exhibitions have already been examined and debated by other writers, and need no further comment from me here. See, for example, Thomas McEvilley et al., *Making Art Global*, part 2, *Magiciens de la Terre, 1989* (London: Afterall Books, 2013).

8. *Affecting Presence and the Pursuit of Delicious Experiences*, curated by Paul Davis, Curator of Collections, Menil Collection, July 17–November 8, 2015. See https://www.menil.org/exhibitions/229-affecting-presence-and-the-pursuit-of-delicious-experiences.

CHAPTER 2. ENTRY POINTS

1. Whether artists are born or nurtured remains a vexing question for art education, and one I address below.

2. I use all of these terms not as biological or intrinsic conditions but as socially produced formations. As Jennifer González notes, "Race is not a property; it is a relation of public encounter." González, "The Face and the Public: Race, Secrecy, and Digital Art Practice," *Camera Obscura* 24, no. 1 (2009): 56.

3. Various websites, such as artfacts.net, compile artist rankings, based on "a points system, which indicate the amount of attention each particular artist has received from art institutions."

4. Deborah Solomon, "How to Succeed in Art," *New York Times*, June 27, 1999, accessed August 29, 2014, http://www.nytimes.com/1999/06/27/magazine/how-to-succeed-in-art.html.

5. See off ramp gallery, Jane Chafin's Blog. MFA: Is It Necessary?—The Debate, July 12, 2011. http://janechafinsofframpgalleryblog.blogspot.com/2011/07/mfa-is-it-necessary-debate.html.

6. Jerry Saltz, "Generation Blank, The beautiful, cerebral, ultimately content-free creations of art's well-schooled young lions," *New York Magazine*, June 19, 2011. http://nymag.com/news/intelligencer/venice-biennale-2011—6/.

7. See, for example, Henri Neuendorf, "It's Official, 80% of the Artists in NYC's Top Galleries Are White," June 2, 2017, https://news.artnet.com/art-world/new-york-galleries-study-979049; for the full data, see http://www.havenforthedispossessed.org/, both accessed July 8, 2017.

8. One may apply, for example, Lisa Lowe's arguments to a specifically art (historical) and especially modernist context: "This economy [of affirmation and forgetting] civilizes and develops freedoms for 'man' in modern Europe and North America, while relegating others to geographical and temporal spaces that are constituted as backward, uncivilized, and unfree. Liberal forms of political economy, culture, government, and history propose a narrative of freedom overcoming enslavement that at once denies colonial slavery, erases the seizure of lands from native peoples, displaces migrations and connections across continents, and internalizes these processes in a national struggle of history and consciousness. The social inequalities of our time are a legacy of these processes through which 'the human' is 'freed' by liberal forms, while other subjects, practices,

and geographies are placed at a distance from 'the human.'" Lisa Lowe, *The Intimacies of Four Continents* (Durham, NC: Duke University Press, 2015), 3.

9. Linda Nochlin, "Why Have There Been No Great Women Artists?," *Women, Art, and Power and Other Essays* (Berkeley, CA: Westview Press, 1988).

10. Nochlin, "Why Have There Been No Great Women Artists?," 150.

11. Nochlin, "Why Have There Been No Great Women Artists?," 152.

12. My use of "art world" is to deliberately invoke its masking intentions.

13. Historical and contemporary examples of "separate but equal": Native American reservations; "Jim Crow" laws; the underdevelopment of poor neighborhoods; the unequal resourcing of "public" schools; lack of universal health care, and on and on.

14. Homi Bhabha, *Location of Culture* (London: Routledge, 2004), 2.

15. See Sara Ahmed, *On Being Included: Racism, and Diversity in Institutional Life* (Durham, NC: Duke University Press, 2012), for a close reading of how "diversity work" is both done and undone. See also *The Decade Show: Frameworks of Identity in the 1980s*, the New Museum, the Museum of Contemporary Hispanic Art, the Studio Museum, New York, May 12–August 19, 1990.

16. "Affirmative action" policies were first instituted under John F. Kennedy in 1961, and required that government employers "not discriminate against any employee or applicant for employment because of race, creed, color, or national origin." In 1965, under President Lyndon B. Johnson, affirmative action was extended to women.

17. I've been told by peers, for example, in the friendliest possible way, that the only reason I've been "given" what should be "their" teaching jobs was because I'm a "minority."

18. Robert Hughes, *Culture of Complaint: The Fraying of America* (New York: Oxford University Press, 2006).

19. Jarrett Earnest, "Dave Hickey (Part Two): In Conversation," *AQ, San Francisco Arts Quarterly* (*sfaq*) 2, no. 1 (2015): 12. Such a blatant example by Hickey of his own self-victimization and what he stands for as a "regular guy" remains unquestioned by the interviewer, a gay man who probably should have known better but who instead agrees with Hickey's assessment of art schools and mfa programs.

20. Judith Butler, "An Account of Oneself," in *Giving an Account of Oneself* (New York: Fordham University Press, 2005), 4.

21. It may also be the aspiration to join another group, through adopting *its* markers and values.

22. My reference is to Audre Lorde's essay "The Master's Tools Will Never Dismantle the Master's House," in *Sister Outsider: Essays and Speeches* (Watsonville, CA: Crossing Press, 1984).

23. bell hooks, *Teaching to Transgress: Education as the Practice of Freedom* (New York: Routledge), 4.

24. Steven Henry Madoff, ed., *Art School (Propositions for the 21st Century)* (Cambridge, MA: MIT Press, 2009), 46–47.

25. First performed in 1970 at the Oakland Museum, then held on a weekly basis at Marioni's own Museum of Conceptual Art (moca), San Francisco. Interestingly enough, the work is posited as an art school, with bartenders getting a "graduate degree" after tending bar three times.

26. Sasha Mann, "Q&A with Artist Tom Marioni," Hammer Museum, October 29, 2010, accessed August 14, 2014, http://hammer.ucla.edu/blog/2010/10/qa-with-artist-tom-marioni/.

27. In Madoff, *Art School*; for example, out of thirty-eight individually named contributors to the book, twenty-nine are male; twenty-eight are Euro American; and most are based in New York. These figures might reflect about as diverse as it gets, keeping in mind that this is within an attempt at a "radical" rethinking of art education.

28. The list of educator names is from Madoff, *Art School*.

29. Consider the political consequences of beer conviviality: in regard to the US presidential election of 2004, a Zogby/Williams poll asked, "Which presidential candidate would you rather have a beer with?" Fifty-seven percent of respondents preferred to have a beer with George W. Bush than with John Kerry, marking Bush's "likability" as a necessary requirement for a potential president.

30. The university Board of Trustees voted to block Salaita's appointment to a tenured position in the American Indian Studies program. In her open letter to the University of Illinois at Urbana-Champaign campus, explaining the board's actions, Chancellor Wise uses the terms "diversity" and "difference" six times, and "civility" three times. See John K. Wilson, "Chancellor Phyllis Wise Explains the Firing of Steven Salaita," August 22, 2014, http://academeblog.org/2014/08/22/chancellor-phyllis-wise-explains-the-firing-of-steven-salaita/. The case continued to take many turns, with Wise herself being subsequently fired by the board and denied her $500,000 bonus.

31. Freire, *Education for Critical Consciousness*, 4.

32. My references to Duchamp's *Fountain* are made with the caveat that this foundational moment of conceptual art might be predicated upon a deceit, a theft, and an erasure of a female artist. Questions have been raised that *Fountain* was actually the work of Elsa von Freytag-Loringhoven. If this is the case, and some evidence exists to support it, then *Fountain* is less of a subversive, conceptual gesture from the often-mentioned hyperintellect and wit of Duchamp, and more of a subversive, conceptual, *feminist* gesture from the radical intellect and biting (castrating?) wit of Freytag-Loringhoven.

33. See, for example, Charles A. Wright, Jr., "The Mythology of Difference: Vulgar Identity Politics at the Whitney Biennial, (1993)" in Zoya Kocur, Simon Leung, editors, *Theory in Contemporary Art since 1985*, 2nd edition (Malden, MA: Wiley-Blackwell, 2012), 263–79.

34. Paul Gilroy, *Postcolonial Melancholia* (New York: Columbia University Press, 2005), 72.

35. Ernesto Pujol, "On the Ground: Practical Observations for Regenerating Art Education," in Madoff, *Art School*, 4.

36. "The idea of freedom of agency itself is existentially impoverished. We must use that idea when we are casting our votes because the vote is an arithmetical reduction of the notion and everybody has one vote. Therefore, except for voting, we must exceedingly carefully consider this impoverished notion of freedom of choice and freedom of agency. To say you can join any institution and that way you are an agent, I think it's a very knavish or foolish thing to say. Agency is institutionally validated action and, there-

fore, it is necessary to develop the criticism of institutions that offer validation, and this is the role of the intellectual." Nazish Brohi, "Herald Exclusive: In Conversation with Gayatri Spivak," December 23, 2014, accessed January 12, 2018, http://www.dawn.com /news/1152482/herald-exclusive-in-conversation-with-gayatri-spivak.

37. I invoke Barthes as a figure fully absorbed into academia.

38. Roland Barthes, *Roland Barthes by Roland Barthes* (New York: Hill and Wang, 1975), 63.

39. Barthes, *Roland Barthes*, 63.

40. Barthes, *Roland Barthes*, 69.

41. I'm using "politically correct" here in the sense of "political convenience," of not drawing adverse political attention to one's self.

42. Even though technology also changes our relationship to and understanding of what constitutes a body, and how fixed, variable, and adaptable it might be.

43. The University of San Francisco advertising tagline is "Change the World from Here." A variation is provided by the Harvard Graduate School of Education's slogan: "Impact the World."

44. Gayatri Chakravorty Spivak, *An Aesthetic Education in the Era of Globalization* (Cambridge, MA: Harvard University Press, 2013).

CHAPTER 3. HOW ART CAN BE TAUGHT

1. Some readers will recall the lyrics of "War," (1970) the Edwin Starr song: "(War, what is it good for?) Absolutely nothing."

2. For the students' letter to the dean on May 28, 2015, outlining their reasons, see "Letter to USC from the Roski MFA Class of 2015," 16 July, 2015, http://mfanomfa .tumblr.com

3. *Wall Street Journal* online, May 16, 2015, accessed May 16, 2015, http://www.wsj .com/articles/dr-dre-and-jimmy-iovines-school-for-innovation-1415238722.

4. USC Jimmy Iovine and Andre Young, "Academy, Arts, Technology and the Business of Innovation: The Academy Experience," http://iovine-young.usc.edu/program /index.html.

5. Edward Said, *Representations of the Intellectual: The 1993 Reith Lectures* (New York: Vintage Books, 1994), 11.

6. Said, *Representations of the Intellectual*, xi.

7. Roland Barthes, *Camera Lucida: Reflections on Photography* (New York: Hill and Wang, 1981), 28.

8. Gayatri Chakravorty Spivak, "Terror: A Speech after 9-11," *Boundary 2: An International Journal of Literature and Culture* 31, no. 2 (2004): 81.

9. Beuys was by all accounts highly charismatic, energizing, and utterly generous to his students but also brutal in his criticism of their work, and espoused political ideas that were, in Benjamin Buchloh's words, "simple-minded Utopian drivel lacking elementary political and educational practicality." Benjamin Buchloh, *"Beuys: The Twilight of the Idols,"* in *Joseph Beuys: Mapping the Legacy,* ed. Gene Ray (New York: D. A. P., 2001). Quoted in Jan Verwoert, *Class Action*, Frieze online, September 2, 2006, accessed August 18, 2014, http://www.frieze.com/issue/article/class_action/.

10. James Elkins, *Why Art Cannot Be Taught* (Urbana and Chicago: University of Illinois Press, 2001).

11. Édouard Glissant, *Poetics of Relation* (Ann Arbor: University of Michigan Press, 1997), 139.

12. The student will likely accept the teacher's judgments only if the teacher is liked and respected; if this is not the case, the student might become more entrenched in their own views or even pursue the opposite of what they've been told is good, or keep doing what they've been told is bad. Another possibility is that the student will only seek out, like, and listen to the teachers who tell her that her work is good. Teachers are generally aware of these possibilities and may deliberately court popularity or antagonism.

13. The people who conduct the labor of maintaining rather than inventing— these being the future professions of the vast majority of art students—are those of whom I suspect James Elkins is speaking when he writes about "average people" and "mediocrity."

14. I'm using "focus" here very loosely to include different aspects of sensory input, emotional attachment, interpretation and analysis, imagination, and so on (all of which are bodily activities that might come under a general category of thinking).

15. Said, *Representations of the Intellectual*, 20.

CHAPTER 4. CRITIQUE AS RADICAL PROTOTYPE

1. The phrase "radical prototype" in this chapter's title is from Allan Kaprow's description of his "Happenings" as instigations of/for performance art. See, for example, Judith Rodenbeck, *Radical Prototypes: Allan Kaprow and the Invention of Happenings* (Cambridge, MA: MIT Press, 2014).

2. Michel Foucault (quoting Louis Althusser, "For Marx" [London, Allen Lane / New York, Pantheon, 1969], 168), *Archeology of Knowledge* (New York: Vintage Books, 1982), 5.

3. Édouard Glissant, *Poetics of Relation* (Ann Arbor: University of Michigan Press, 1997), 11.

4. I'm referring to "field" as used within anthropology, but also as articulated by Rosalind Krauss in her pivotal essay, "Sculpture in the Expanded Field," *October* 8 (spring 1979): 30–44.

5. This desire for "just getting along" is commonly encountered from students. Highly humanistic, it might also harbor a refusal to acknowledge difference—not of visual markers of race and gender but of political difference of viewpoint and positioning that might compete with, contradict, or oppose their own.

6. By "ownership" I mean who gets to define and enforce *their* arguments, *their* meaning.

7. This is also the ideal of democracy in action.

8. Critique space is protected only in the sense that *some* restrictions are removed on what participants say, because what they say can be examined dispassionately rather than simply reacted against with the likelihood of escalation.

9. The democratic ideal is that latent violence is defused through structural and procedural channels of voting, freedom of speech and assembly, equality under the law, and so on.

10. Informal conversation with Mary Kelly at the Whitney Independent Study Program, New York, 1993. I also want to note Kelly's profound influence upon my understanding and practice of critique.

11. James Elkins, *Why Art Cannot Be Taught* (Urbana and Chicago: University of Illinois Press, 2001), 114.

12. This "coming into being" means that an artwork can never be fully relegated to the past of "being finished"; neither can it be fully known.

13. James Elkins, *Art Critiques: A Guide*, 2nd ed. (Washington, DC: New Academia, 2012).

14. See Rita Felski, *The Limits of Critique* (Chicago, IL: University of Chicago Press, 2015).

15. These extracts are taken from Allan deSouza, "Graduate Critique Seminar," unpublished syllabus, University of California, Berkeley, fall 2013.

CHAPTER 5. HOW ART CAN BE SPOKEN

1. Rosi Braidotti, *Nomadic Theory: The Portable Rosi Braidotti* (New York: Columbia University Press, 2011), 271.

2. René Descartes (1596–1650), in *Passions of the Soul* and *The Description of the Human Body*, proposes the body as machine-like, "activated" by the mind or soul situated in the pineal gland. The gendering play is that of the mind/reason as male, the body/feeling as female.

3. Howard Singerman, "Excellence and Pluralism," *Emergences* 12, no. 1 (2002): 9.

4. Guy Debord, "Thesis 1," in *Society of the Spectacle*, trans. Donald Nicholson-Smith, 9th ed. (New York: Zone Books, 2006), 12.

5. Joanne B. Waugh, "Analytic Aesthetics and Feminist Aesthetics: Neither/Nor?" in *Feminism and Tradition in Aesthetics*, ed. P. G. Brand and C. Korsmeyer (University Park: Penn State University Press, 1995), 399.

6. One might compare and contrast the UK-based Black Arts movement (circa 1980–89).

7. Brendan Wattenberg, "The Pleasure of the Image: A Conversation with Isaac Julien," April 29, 2016, accessed January 15, 2017, https://aperture.org/blog/pleasure-image -conversation-isaac-julien/interview.

8. See, for example, Hannes Grassegger and Mikael Korgerus, "The Data That Turned the World Upside Down," January 28, 2017. https://motherboard.vice.com/en_us /article/how-our-likes-helped-trump-win.

9. I emphasize the taking back to point toward the initial "appropriation" (though it's rarely called that) from colonized countries and colonized peoples by European modernists such as Gauguin, Modigliani, Picasso, Matisse, and so on.

10. Antonio Gramsci, *Prison Notebooks*, quoted in Edward Said, *Representations of the Intellectual: The 1993 Reith Lectures* (New York: Vintage Books, 1994), 19.

11. Ben Davis, *9.5 Theses on Art and Class* (Chicago, IL: Haymarket Books, 2013), 63.

12. Arthur Danto, "The Artworld," *Journal of Philosophy* 61, no. 19 (October 15, 1964): 580.

13. George Dickie, *Aesthetics, An Introduction* (Indianapolis, IN: Pegasus Books, 1971), 101.

14. "Nor would these things be artworks without the theories and histories of the Artworld. . . . Whatever is the artistically relevant predicate in virtue of which they gain their entry, the rest of the Artworld becomes that much the richer in having the opposite predicate available and applicable to its members." Danto, "Artworld," 585.

15. Pamela Lee, *Forgetting the Art World* (Cambridge, MA: MIT Press, 2012).

16. See, for example, the populist journalism of Sarah Thornton.

17. Allan Sekula, in Nato Thompson et al., "Debating Occupy," *Art in America*, vol. 100, issue 6 (June/July 2012): 103.

18. "Constructed situations" is Sehgal's term.

19. Sehgal's work does indeed sell at high-end prices, through witnessed oral contracts (again, no material product), and in limited editions of the right to (re)production and display.

20. Nick Paumgarten, "Dealer's Hand," *New Yorker*, December 2, 2013, accessed February 26, 2016, http://www.newyorker.com/magazine/2013/12/02/dealers-handp, 47.

21. I don't know of any artists who set out to do this. If anything, artists pursue the work's logic, or become so familiar with the work that they fail to realize how shocking it might be to new viewers.

22. A critic confessed to me their disappointment that an exhibition, *The Matter Within: New Contemporary Art of India*, 2011, at the Yerba Buena Center for the Arts in San Francisco, was "not Indian enough."

23. Mary Louise Pratt, "Arts of the Contact Zone," *Profession* (1991): 35.

24. Paulo Freire, *Pedagogy of the Oppressed* (London: Bloomsbury Academic, 2012), 47.

25. "Free time" is always bought time, whether paid for by oneself, by one's parents, by one's privileges, scholarships, loans, and so on.

26. See, for example, 2014 Isla Vista killings, https://en.wikipedia.org/wiki/2014_Isla _Vista_killings; and Caitlin Dewey, "Inside the 'manosphere' that inspired Santa Barbara shooter Elliot Rodger," *Washington Post*, May 27, 2014, accessed December 28, 2017, https:// www.washingtonpost.com/news/the-intersect/wp/2014/05/27/inside-the-manosphere -that-inspired-santa-barbara-shooter-elliot-rodger/?utm_term=.de09792e4b96.

27. This "aestheticization" of suffering is endemic to photography, which many commentators, including Sontag, find highly problematic.

28. Susan Sontag, "The Heroism of Vision," in *On Photography*, 3rd ed. (New York: Farrar, Strauss and Giroux, 1978), 85.

29. Herbert Marcuse, "The Affirmative Character of Culture," quoted in Andreas Huyssen, "The Cultural Politics of Pop," in *Modern Art and Society: An Anthology of Social and Multicultural Readings*, ed. Maurice Berger (New York: Harper Collins, 1994), 257.

30. There is sufficient documentation and discourse about the concurrent Great German Art Exhibition and the Degenerate Art Exhibition in 1937 that I need not comment further on them.

31. Dave Hickey, *The Invisible Dragon, Essays on Beauty* (Chicago, IL: University of Chicago Press, [1993] 2009), 69.

32. I'm thinking of the outlaw mythos of the chopped Harley Davidson "Captain America" bike ridden by Peter Fonda in the film *Easy Rider* (1969, directed by Dennis Hopper), and "Little Bastard," the Porsche 550 Spyder in which James Dean died in 1955.

33. While heterosexual pornography functions more as mass-media spectacle "in private," it contributes to public space as a shared heterosexist fantasy of female objectification and availability.

34. For example, the depiction of postsurgery scars, and the injecting of testosterone.

35. *E pluribus unum* was adopted in 1782 but was replaced in 1956 by an act of Congress with the official motto "In God we trust." The implication is that since 1956, God is the real head of state.

36. One doesn't really hear of "rightist" or procapitalist artists describing themselves as "political." These artists are more likely to invoke the ostensibly apolitical terminology of "tradition," "truth," "nature," "human values," and "authenticity."

37. Rosi Braidotti's phrases; Braidotti, *Nomadic Theory*, 32.

38. Jerry Saltz, "Saltz on the Trouble with Mega-Galleries," Vulture.com, October 13, 2013, accessed September 20, 2015, http://www.vulture.com/2013/10/trouble-with-mega-art-galleries.html.

39. Press release for *Christian Maychack*, Gregory Lind Gallery, San Francisco, April 2015.

40. Press release for *Jeppe Hein: Distance*, LIFE *International Space for Emerging Arts*, Saint-Nazaire, France, June 2015.

41. Press release for *John Chiara*, Haines Gallery, San Francisco, February 2015.

42. These two terms have been used by fellow artists on public panels to refute my criticism of what I considered outmoded ideas.

43. Roland Barthes, *Roland Barthes by Roland Barthes*, trans. Richard Howard (New York: Hill and Wang, [1975] 1977), 47.

44. To borrow Anthony Downey's phrase. Anthony Downey, "Critical Imperatives," *Wasafiri, International Contemporary Writing,* 21, no. 1 (2006): 48.

45. Michael Hardt and Antonio Negri, *Empire* (Cambridge, MA: Harvard University Press, 2000). Quoted in Downey, "Critical Imperatives," 41.

46. Walter Kaufmann, trans., "On Truth and Lie in an Extra—Moral Sense," in *The Portable Nietzsche* (New York: Penguin, 1994), 46.

47. See for example, the exhibition *The Global Contemporary: Art Worlds after 1989*, at the ZKM Center for Art and Media, Karlsruhe, Germany, and *The Global Contemporary and the Rise of New Art Worlds*, ed. Hans Belting et al. (Cambridge, MA: MIT Press, 2013).

48. As one example of various "ice" works, see Liberate Tate, *Floe Piece*, 2012, https://vimeo.com/channels/360124/35078978.

49. Geoffrey James, *Daily Promises That Create Motivation*, Inc.com, December 31, 2012. accessed July 8, 2013, https://www.inc.com/geoffrey-james/daily-promises-that-create-motivation.html.

50. Richard Florida, *The Rise of the Creative Class—Revisited* (New York: Basic Books, 2014).

51. Each of these cases has its own complexities, which cannot be examined in any detail here. Similar questions and protests are occurring across the arts, in music, cinema, theater, literature, and poetry.

52. I first heard the phrase, "democracy of images," used by Laura Owens in relation to her own work. Laura Owens, Winifred Johnson Clive Foundation Distinguished Visiting Painting Fellow, untitled seminar, San Francisco Art Institute, February 24, 2009.

53. *William Eggleston: Democratic Camera, Photographs and Video, 1961–2008*, organized by the Whitney Museum of American Art, New York, in association with Haus der Kunst, Munich, November 7, 2008 through January 25, 2009.

54. Roland Barthes, *Camera Lucida: Reflections on Photography* (New York: Hill and Wang, 1982), 35.

55. Deleuze and Guattari's term. Gilles Deleuze and Félix Guattari, *Anti-Oedipus: Capitalism and Schizophrenia* (New York, Penguin, [1977] 2009).

56. I'm deliberately invoking this binary as typically moralistic categorizations of women (within art history).

57. Sontag, "Melancholy Objects," in *On Photography*, 57.

58. Compare Donald Trump's epithet, "shithole countries." See for example, Ed O'Keefe and Anne Gearan, "Trump, condemned for 'shithole' countries remark, denies comment but acknowledges 'tough' language," *The Washington Post*, January 13, 2018. https://www.washingtonpost.com/politics/trump-acknowledges-tough-language-but -appears-to-deny-shithole-remark/2018/01/12/c7131dae-f796-11e7-beb6-c8d48830c54d _story.html?utm_term=.doc06d098138.

59. This requires a much longer discussion. I am grateful, however, to Michael Mascuch for his research and insights into the American depiction of the Vietnam War.

60. C. G. Jung, "The Concept of the Collective Unconscious," in *The Archetypes and The Collective Unconscious*, part 1, vol. 9 of *The Collected Works of C. G. Jung* (Princeton, NJ: Princeton University Press, 1981).

61. Frantz Fanon, *Black Skin, White Masks* (New York: Grove Press, 1952), 188, 145.

62. Michael Jackson, "The Way You Make Me Feel," on *Bad* (Epic Records, 1987).

63. Nina Felshin, "A Photo Exhibit about Israel and the West Bank that Chooses Sides," *Hyperallergic*, May 13, 2016, http://hyperallergic.com/298529/a-photo-exhibition -about-israel-and-the-west-bank-that-chooses-sides/?ref=featured. See also Arthur Lubow, "For 12 Photographers, an Anxious Gaze on Israel and the West Bank," *New York Times*, February 11, 2016, http://www.nytimes.com/2016/02/14/arts/design/for -12-photographers-an-anxious-gaze-on-israel-and-the-west-bank.html?_r=0. See also Roberta Smith, "Capturing Human Moments amid Chaos in Israel and the West Bank," *New York Times*, February 18, 2016, https://www.nytimes.com/2016/02/19/arts/design /capturing-human-moments-amid-chaos-in-israel-and-the-west-bank.html.

64. Susan Sontag, *Regarding the Pain of Others* (New York: Picador, 2004).

65. Sister Corita Kent, "Ten Rules for Students, Teachers and Life," in *Learning By Heart: Teachings to Free the Creative Spirit*, 2nd ed. (New York: Allworth Press, 2008). The "Rules" are commonly but mistakenly attributed to John Cage, who contributed only Rule 10.

66. Kendall Buster and Paula Crawford, *The Critique Handbook: The Art Student's Sourcebook and Survival Guide* (Upper Saddle River, NJ: Prentice Hall Press, 2010).

67. James Elkins, *Why Art Cannot Be Taught* (Urbana and Chicago: University of Illinois Press, 2001), 78.

68. See, for example, *The Encyclopedic Palace*, curated by Massimiliano Gioni at the Venice Biennale in 2013. Centered on the paintings of Carl Jung, a major premise was that "true" creativity happens in social isolation. Similarly, *Vive Arte Viva*, curated by Christine Macel at the Biennale in 2017, celebrated magic and shamanism as "extrasocial" creativity.

69. Sara Ahmed, *The Cultural Politics of Emotion* (Edinburgh, UK: Edinburgh University Press, 2004), 6.

70. Eve Kosofsky Sedgwick, *Touching Feeling: Affect, Pedagogy, Performativity* (Durham, NC: Duke University Press, 2003), 64–65.

71. *Merriam-Webster* online defines "feminism" as: "1: the theory of the political, economic, and social equality of the sexes," and "2: organized activity on behalf of women's rights and interests." At the time of copy editing this book (January 2018), I can note the resurgence of "organized activity on behalf of women's rights and interests," such as in the #MeToo movement, https://metoomvmt.org.

72. See Ana-Cecilia Alvarez, "Bend It Like Benglis," *New Inquiry*, October 20, 2014; and Richard Meyer, "Lynda Benglis," *Artforum*, November 2004, for close readings of the context and aftermath of Benglis's ad.

73. Michael Wolf, *Tokyo Compression* (Berlin: Peperoni Books, 2010).

74. Marc Garanger, *Femmes algériennes 1960* (Biarritz [Pyrénées-Atlantiques]: Atlantica, 1960).

75. I use the phrase "biologically argued" to suggest that these too are social constructions, argued through medicalized, psychologized, and ultimately legal evidence.

76. Judith Butler, *Gender Trouble: Feminism and the Subversion of Identity* (New York: Routledge, 1990), 2.

77. I have to admit, however, that an exhibition titled *Masculine Painting* with only women artists sounds like a worthy inquiry.

78. Butler, *Gender Trouble*, 5.

79. Evident in his dogged reworking of themes and scenes. A revelation for me was the New York Metropolitan Museum of Art's exhibition *Matisse: In Search of True Painting*, December 4, 2012–March 17, 2013. In foregrounding Matisse's repainting and overpainting within thematic series, the exhibition emphasized the persistent labor in his investigative and methodical practice. Matisse's report card would say "works hard" rather than "great" (my own report card might say "can juggle contradictory values").

80. In psychological tests, "gut reactions" have been shown to be typically wrong, even to the point of being endangering reactions. This is not to dismiss that the body reacts and responds, nor that intelligence and sentience are literally embodied. How we get from that physicality to visual language and tactile form is a cultural, historicized process that can be investigated beyond biology. See, for example, Paul Bloom, *How Pleasure Works: The New Science of Why We Like What We Like* (New York: Norton, 2010).

81. Also shown in the Whitney Biennial in 1993, as a ground zero for the works produced by artists.

82. I include conceptual art here as a cross-disciplinary, postmedium-based practice that nevertheless develops its own authenticities.

83. Even though Kawara died in 2014, the *Today* series seems to continue toward infinity in a continuing present.

84. "All I want anyone to get out of my painting, and all I ever get out of them, is the fact that you can see the whole idea without any confusion. . . . What you see is what you see." Frank Stella, "Questions to Stella and Judd," interview by Bruce Glaser, edited by Lucy R. Lippard, *ArtNews* 65 (September 1966): 55–61.

85. In what might be the first *printed* use of the phrase, Carol Hanisch writes, "One of the first things we discover in these groups is that personal problems are political problems. There are no personal solutions at this time. There is only collective action for a collective solution." Carol Hanisch, "Some Thoughts in Response to Dottie [Zellner]'s Thoughts on a Women's Liberation Movement." Originally presented to the Women's Caucus of the Southern Conference Educational Fund, 1969. Later printed as "The Personal Is Political, in *Notes from the Second Year: Women's Liberation: Major Writings of the Radical Feminists*, ed. Shulamith Firestone and Anne Koedt (New York: Radical Feminism, 1970).

86. Press release of *Don't You Know Who I Am? Art after Identity Politics*, curated by Anders Kreuger and Nav Haq, Museum of Contemporary Art Antwerp, Belgium, June 13 through September 14, 2015.

87. See, for example, Kimberlé Crenshaw, *On Intersectionality: Essential Writings* (New York: New Press, 2016).

88. See Roland Barthes, "The Death of the Author," in *Image-Music-Text* (New York: Hill and Wang, 1977), 142–48.

89. Donald Judd, "Specific Objects," *Arts Yearbook* 8 (1965): 74–82. Reprinted in *Art in Theory, 1900–2000*, ed. Charles Harrison and Paul Wood (Malden, MA: Blackwell Publishing, 2005), 827.

90. Clement Greenberg, "Avant-Garde and Kitsch," *Partisan Review* 6, no. 5 (1939): 39.

91. Greenberg, "Avant-Garde and Kitsch," 45.

92. The term 3Ds originated in Japan.

93. Consider, for example, the three-year strikes proposed by Gustave Metzger (1977–80) and Stewart Home (1990–93). For an insightful and recent analysis, see Nick Mirzoeff, "The Power of Protest One Year After the #J20 Art Strike," *Hyperallergic*, January 19, 2018, https://hyperallergic.com/422416/the-power-of-protest-one-year-after-the-j20-art-strike/.

94. Claire Bishop, *Artificial Hells, Participatory Art, and the Politics of Spectatorship* (London: Verso, 2012), 277.

95. Laura Mulvey, *Visual and Other Pleasures* (New York: Palgrave MacMillan, 2009).

96. See, for example, the #MeToo Movement, https://metoomvmt.org.

97. W. E. B. Du Bois, *The Souls of Black Folk* (Greenwich, CT: Fawcett Publications, 1961); Fanon, *Black Skin, White Masks*. See also Frances Beal, "Black Women's Manifesto; Double Jeopardy: To Be Black and Female," in *Sisterhood Is Powerful*, ed. Robin Morgan (New York: Vintage Books, 1970).

98. The poster's additional text reads, "Less than 5 % of the artists in the Modern Art sections are women, but 85 % of the nudes are female."

99. Marshall McLuhan, *Understanding Media: The Extensions of Man* (Cambridge, MA: MIT Press, [1964] 1994).

100. I confess that I relish the thought of students debating these timelines with their art professors.

101. Fredric Jameson, "The Cultural Logic of Late Capitalism," in *Postmodernism or the Cultural Logic of Late Capitalism* (Durham, NC: Duke University Press, 1991).

102. Albert Boime, "*Manet's Un Bar aux Folies-Bergère as an Allegory of Nostalgia*," in *Zeitschrift Für Kunstgeschichte*, No. 2 (1993): 235.

103. Ahmed, *Cultural Politics of Emotion*, 47.

104. I'm making a dubious separation between intellect and emotion, used here to suggest different priorities given by viewers to *describe* their experiences.

105. Sontag, *On Photography*, 15.

106. Sontag, *On Photography*, 15.

107. Abigail Solomon-Godeau, "Going Native: Paul Gauguin and the Invention of Primitivist Modernism," in *Art in America* 77 (July 1989): 118–29.

108. Drawing upon Oswald de Andrade's Manifesto Antropófago (Cannibal Manifesto) of 1928, the Brazilian Tropicália movement of the 1960s and 1970s proposed *anthropophagia* as a "cannibalizing" process ingesting European and indigenous cultures to produce a hybrid, national modernism.

109. J. L. Austin, *How to Do Things with Words* (Cambridge, MA: Harvard University Press, 1975).

110. Judith Butler, *Bodies That Matter: On the Discursive Limits of "Sex"* (New York: Routledge, 1993), xii.

111. David Zwirner Gallery, New York. February 15 to March 17, 2007.

112. Peter Schjeldahl, "Of Ourselves and of Our Origins: Subjects of Art," *Frieze Magazine* 137 (March 1, 2011). https://frieze.com/article/ourselves-and-our-origins-subjects-art.

113. This is not so far-fetched; Consider Marina Abramović's remake of her and Ulay's performance *Work Relation* (1978) as an Adidas commercial "reimagined through the lens of the 2014 FIFA World Cup."

114. Julien Benda, *The Treason of the Intellectuals*, trans. Richard Aldington (New York: Norton, [1928] 1969), 43, quoted in Said, *Representations of the Intellectual*, 6.

115. See Serge Guilbaut, *How New York Stole the Idea of Modern Art* (Chicago, IL: University of Chicago Press, 1983). See also Frances Stonor Saunders, "Modern Art Was CIA Weapon," *Independent*, Sunday October 22, 1995.

116. David Levi Strauss, "Photography and Belief," in *Between the Eyes: Essays on Photography and Politics* (New York: Aperture, 2005), 77.

117. Debord, *Society of the Spectacle*, 12.

118. Pierre Bourdieu, "Structures, *Habitus*, Practices," in *The Logic of Practice*, trans. Richard Nice (Stanford, CA: Stanford University Press, 1990), 53.

119. Sara Ahmed, *Living a Feminist Life* (Durham, NC: Duke University Press, 2017), 86.

120. See Wassily Kandinsky, *Concerning the Spiritual in Art* (Mineola, NY: Dover Publications, 1977).

121. The full quote from Karl Marx is: "Religion is the sigh of the oppressed creature, the heart of a heartless world, and the soul of soulless conditions. It is the opium of the people." *Camille Pissaro: Letters to His Son Lucien*, ed. John Rewald (New York: Kessinger Publishing, [1943] 2007), quoted in Solomon-Godeau, "Going Native," 78.

122. I'm using "autoethnography" here in the sense that James Clifford advocates: "Though it portrays other selves as culturally constituted, it also fashions an identity authorized to represent, to interpret, even to believe—but always with some irony—the truths of discrepant worlds." James Clifford, *Predicament of Culture: Twentieth-Century Ethnography, Literature, and Art* (Cambridge, MA: Harvard University Press, 1988), 95.

123. Hal Foster, *The Anti-Aesthetic, Essays on Postmodern Culture* (New York: New Press, 1998), xi.

124. Michael Fried, "Art and Objecthood," in *Art and Objecthood: Essays and Reviews* (Chicago, IL: University of Chicago Press, 2011), 155.

125. Edmund Husserl, quoted in Max Horkheimer, "Traditional and Critical Theory," in *Critical Theory: Selected Essays* (New York: Continuum, 2002), 190.

126. One might compare, for example, the dramatically diverging but concurrent beliefs in evolution and "intelligent design" (ID). The former is a working theory, since it is able to account for all available facts and observed phenomena. New discoveries, for example, in epigenetics, further underscore evolutionary theory and allow it to adapt rather than be detracted or debunked. In contrast, "ID" is based on the unexamined premise that only intelligence can produce what its adherents call "complex and specified information" (one would have to begin by examining what is meant by "intelligence," which is a social construct rather than a scientifically neutral one). A further footnote: according to Freud, the id is a "striving to bring about the satisfaction of the instinctual needs," motivating immediate gratification regardless of reality. Sigmund Freud, *New Introductory Lectures on Psychoanalysis*, standard ed. (New York: W. W. Norton, 1933), 105–6.

127. Horkheimer, *Critical Theory*, 207.

128. Danto, "Artworld," 572.

129. Danto, "Artworld," 581.

130. Art restoration, which risks the loss of the ruin's aura, is a refusal of decay.

131. Space is delineated so as to designate it as a boundaried place, even if that "place" is now only the rectangular framing of the photograph itself.

132. Karen Archey, "Timeliness," *MAP Magazine*, no. 25, reproduced in *Time, Documents of Contemporary Art*, ed. Amelia Groom (Cambridge, MA: Whitechapel Gallery, MIT Press, 2013), 126.

133. There are still holdouts, however, from individuals to entire photography departments.

134. Holland Cotter, "700-Hour Silent Opera Reaches Finale at MoMA," *New York Times*, May 30, 2010.

135. Joe Wilson, in an interview with Fox News host, Chris Wallace, following his apology to President Obama: "I believe in the truth. What I heard was not true." Interview transcript, "Fox: Rep. Joe Wilson Talks 'You Lie!' and Health Care," *Washington Post*, September 13, 2009, accessed February 7, 2016, http://www.washingtonpost.com

/wp-dyn/content/article/2009/09/13/AR2009091301559.html. For contextualizing Wilson's outburst in relation to Southern/Confederate race politics, see also Maureen Dowd, "Boy, *Oh, Boy*," *New York Times*, September 12, 2009, http://www.nytimes.com /2009/09/13/opinion/13dowd.html?_r=0. Also see Maureeen Dowd, "Rapping Joe's Knuckles," *New York Times*, September 15, 2009, http://www.nytimes.com/2009/09/16 /opinion/16dowd.html.

136. See the artwork of Aimé Ntakiyica as counter to the Euro everyman.

137. See Michel Foucault, *This Is Not a Pipe* (University of California Press, 1983).

138. The term "unconscious mind" was coined by the philosopher Friedrich Schelling (1775–1854) and introduced into English by his contemporary, the poet Samuel Taylor Coleridge (1772–1834). It seems fitting that the idea of an unconscious is indebted to a philosopher and a poet.

139. Richard Dyer, "The Matter of Whiteness," in *White* (London: Routledge, 1997), 3.

140. Dyer, "Matter of Whiteness," 2.

141. Édouard Glissant, in Manthia Diawara, "Conversation with Édouard Glissant aboard the Queen Mary II (2009)," *Nka: Journal of Contemporary African Art*, November 28, 2011.

142. Paul Gilroy, *Postcolonial Melancholia* (New York: Columbia University Press, 2005), 36.

143. Said, *Representations of the Intellectual*, 11.

144. Throughout this book, I have similarly used the first-person plural "we" to variously suggest readers, students, artists, art viewers, US Americans, citizens, and humans.

145. Peter Schjeldahl discussing Rembrandt's painting *The Night Watch* (1642) in "New Amsterdam, the Art World column," *New Yorker*, April 22, 2013, 110.

146. Gilroy, *Postcolonial Melancholia*, 32.

147. For a closer analysis of some of these briefly mentioned points, see, for example, Anthony Downey, "Zones of Indistinction: Giorgio Agamben's 'Bare Life' and the Politics of Aesthetics," in *Third Text* 23, no. 2 (March 2009): 109–25.

148. Nandita Sharma, "Strategic Anti-Essentialism: Decolonizing Decolonization," in *Sylvia Wynter: On Being Human as Praxis*, ed. Katherine McKittrick (Durham, NC: Duke University Press, 2015), 166.

149. Arlene Croce, "Discussing the Undiscussable," *New Yorker*, December 26, 1994 / January 2, 1995.

150. A review by a critic who had actually seen the work describes it variously as "major and often startling[ly] new," a "true work of art, both sensitive and original," a "tightly disciplined form," and "an amazing blend of simplicity and sophistication." Anna Kisselgoff, "Dance Review; Bill T. Jones's Lyrical Look at Survivors," *New York Times*, December 2, 1994, http://www.nytimes.com/1994/12/02/arts/dance-review-bill -t-jones-s-lyrical-look-at-survivors.html.

151. Croce, for example, in more recent years, appears to maintain her stance of a once-pure art form being polluted by social and political "issues." Another dance critic revisits Croce's arguments: "For dance purists, brought up on the abstract traditions of Balanchine and Merce Cunningham, the answer is simple: dance should remain unpolluted by politics. . . . Croce rarely speaks publicly these days, but did break her silence in

a faxed statement tome: 'Choreographers mix dance with politics because it is the only way to get attention. And get grants too, probably. The importance of a work is equated with the nobility of the sentiment it expresses. I've stopped attending dance attractions because the last thing I want to see is dancers wasting their time on some high-minded godawful piece of choreography. I don't want to be told about Iraq or Bush or Katrina by someone younger and dumber than I am.'" John O'Mahoney, "Baghdad Ballet," *Guardian*, September 28, 2006, http://www.theguardian.com/stage/2006/sep/28 /dance.iraq.

152. "Curious unity" is Michel Foucault's term. Michel Foucault, "What Is an Author?" in *Language, Counter-Memory, Practice: Selected Essays and Interviews* (New York: Cornell University Press, 1980).

AFTERWORDS. *HOW, NOW*, ROTHKO?

1. *Mark Rothko: A Retrospective*, the Museum of Fine Arts, Houston, September 20, 2015–January 24, 2016.

2. "Western discoverers: explorers, merchants, conquerors, ethnologists—those men of intelligence, faith, and law." Édouard Glissant, *Poetics of Relation* (Ann Arbor: University of Michigan Press, 1997), 25.

3. John Graham, *System and Dialectics of Art* (New York: Delphic Studios), 1937. Reproduced in *Mark Rothko: A Retrospective* (New York: Solomon R. Guggenheim Foundation, 1978), 15.

4. Achille Mbembe, *Critique of Black Reason* (Durham, NC: Duke University Press, 2017), 42.

5. Letter dated June 7, 1943, published June 13, 1943. These sections are reproduced in *Mark Rothko: A Retrospective*, 39.

6. I realize that this sounds like "intelligent design."

7. I'm thinking of the murder in 2014 of Eric Garner, and his dying refrain of "I can't breathe."

8. For clarification of the term "respite" in contrast to Matisse's "escape," see Aruna D'Souza, "Alma Thomas," review, *4 Columns*, accessed September 23, 2016, http:// 4columns.org/d-souza-aruna/alma-thomas.

9. *Untitled*, 1957, cat. no. 40, in *Mark Rothko: An Essential Reader*, ed. Alison de Lima Greene (Houston, TX: Museum of Fine Arts, Houston, 2015), 88.

10. Harold Rosenberg, "The American Action Painter," in *The Tradition of the New* (Boston, MA: Da Capo Press, [1959] 1994), 23–39.

11. My reference is to Freud's psychosexual development of the "anal stage." Sigmund Freud, On Sexuality: *Three Essays on the Theory of Sexuality and Other Works* (New York: Penguin, 1991).

12. Without overfeeding the metaphor, there is much to consider in relation to digestive systems; when does food become part of the body? When does "waste" stop being one's body?

13. If only for the applicability of its title to Rothko, see Jack Halberstam, "White Men Behaving Sadly," February 22, 2017, https://bullybloggers.wordpress.com/2017/02 /22/white-men-behaving-sadly-by-jack-halberstam/.

14. My personal inquiry into artistic representations of smoking would account for the multiply gendered, racialized seductions, intimacies, (dis)identifications, and violences of "harems," "opium dens," and bar scenes, the various modernist self-portraits with pipes and cigarettes from Magritte to Félix Vallotton's *La Blanche et la Noire* (1913), as well as Marlene Dietrich, Frida Kahlo, Jean Genet's *Un chant d'amour* (1950), Philip Guston, Richard Prince, and Sarah Lucas.

15. Consider, for example, "The colonized is elevated above his jungle status in proportion to his adoption of the mother country's cultural standards." Frantz Fanon, *Black Skin, White Masks* (New York: Grove Press, 1952), 18.

16. Adrienne Edwards, "Blackness in Abstraction," in *Art in America*, Vol. 103, Issue 1, January 2015, 64.

17. The etymology of the term "bureaucracy" refers to rule of the desk or office; in the present we might think of the rule of the desktop, which infiltrates all aspects of our lives as never before.

18. Max Fisher, "Stephen K. Bannon's CPAC Comments, Annotated and Explained," *New York Times*, February 24, 2017, accessed December 22, 2017, https://www.nytimes .com/2017/02/24/us/politics/stephen-bannon-cpac-speech.html.

19. Aaron Hughes, AHMED: *A Selection of Ahmed Jabar Shareef's Photographs,* video, May 25, 2006, http://www.aarhughes.org/#item=ahmed.

20. Mary Louise Pratt, "Arts of the Contact Zone," *Profession,* (1991): 33–40.

21. This "occupation" entails not only the syphoning of culture but also the containment and erasure of occupied peoples from being active cultural agents within the present.

22. Thanks to the art historian Jackie Francis for returning Norman Lewis to my attention and sparking this line of thought. Regarding Arpita Singh, I'm thinking particularly of her previously unexhibited works from the 1970s that were shown in her solo exhibition *Tying Down Time*, at Talwar Gallery, New York, May 6–August 11, 2017.

23. Jason Farago, "MoMA Protests Trump Entry Ban by Rehanging Work by Artists from Muslim Nations," *New York Times*, February 3, 2017, https://www .nytimes.com/2017/02/03/arts/design/moma-protests-trump-entry-ban-with-work -by-artists-from-muslim-nations.html?_r=0. See also Shiva Balaghi, "MoMA's Travel Ban Protest Exposes a Legacy of Closeted Modernism," *Hyperallergic*, March 15, 2017, http://hyperallergic.com/365397/momas-travel-ban-protest-exposes-a-legacy-of-closeted -modernism/. This is a tightly researched article that investigates the consequences of some of my questions.

24. Sarah Charlesworth, "Postmodernism and Photography," panel paper for the Society for Photographic Education, reproduced in Leslie Dick, "Intentional Accidents: Reflections on Sarah Charlesworth's Stills," *X_TRA Contemporary Art Quarterly* 18, no. 3 (spring 2016): 5.

25. Katherine McKittrick, *Sylvia Wynter: On Being Human as Praxis* (Durham, NC: Duke University Press, 2015), 2.

Bibliography

Agamben, Giorgio. *Homo Sacer: Sovereign Power and Bare Life*. Stanford, CA: Stanford University Press, 1998.

Ahmed, Sara. *The Cultural Politics of Emotion*. Edinburgh, UK: Edinburgh University Press, 2004.

———. *Living a Feminist Life*. Durham, NC: Duke University Press, 2017.

———. *On Being Included, Racism, and Diversity in Institutional Life*. Durham, NC: Duke University Press, 2012.

Appadurai, Arun. *Fear of Small Numbers: An Essay on the Geography of Anger*. Durham, NC: Duke University Press, 2006.

Appiah, Kwame Anthony. *Cosmopolitanism: Ethics in a World of Strangers*. New York: W. W. Norton, 2006.

Austin, J. L. *How to Do Things with Words*. Cambridge, MA: Harvard University Press, 1975.

Balaghi, Shiva. "MoMA's Travel Ban Protest Exposes a Legacy of Closeted Modernism." *Hyperallergic*, March 15, 2017.

Barthes, Roland. *Camera Lucida: Reflections on Photography*. New York: Hill and Wang, 1981.

———. *Image-Music-Text*. New York: Hill and Wang, 1977.

———. *Roland Barthes by Roland Barthes*. Translated by Richard Howard. New York: Hill and Wang, [1975] 1977.

Beal, Frances. "Black Women's Manifesto; Double Jeopardy: To Be Black and Female." In *Sisterhood Is Powerful*, edited by Robin Morgan, 340–53. New York: Random House, 1970.

Bennett, Tony, Lawrence Grossberg, and Meaghan Morris, eds. *New Keywords: A Revised Vocabulary of Culture and Society*. Malden, MA: Blackwell, 2005.

Berger, Maurice, ed. *Modern Art and Society: An Anthology of Social and Multicultural Readings*. New York: Harper Collins Press, 1994.

Bhabha, Homi. *Location of Culture*. New York: Routledge, 2004.

Bishop, Claire. *Artificial Hells, Participatory Art, and the Politics of Spectatorship*. London: Verso, 2012.

Bloom, Paul. *How Pleasure Works: The New Science of Why We Like What We Like*. New York: W. W. Norton, 2010.

Boime, Albert. *Art in an Age of Revolution, 1750–1800*. Vol. 1. Chicago, IL: University of Chicago Press, 1987.

———. "Manet's Un Bar aux Folies-Bergère as an Allegory of Nostalgia." In *Zeitschrift Für Kunstgeschichte*, No. 2 (1993): 234–48.

Bourdieu, Pierre. *The Logic of Practice*. Translated by Richard Nice. Stanford, CA: Stanford University Press, 1990.

Braidotti, Rosi. *Nomadic Theory: The Portable Rosi Braidotti*. New York: Columbia University Press, 2011.

Buster, Kendall, and Paula Crawford. *The Critique Handbook: The Art Student's Sourcebook and Survival Guide*. Upper Saddle River, NJ: Prentice Hall, 2010.

Butler, Judith. *Bodies That Matter: On the Discursive Limits of "Sex."* New York: Routledge, 1993.

———. *Gender Trouble: Feminism and the Subversion of Identity*. New York: Routledge, 2015.

———. *Giving an Account of Oneself*. New York: Fordham University Press, 2005.

———. "What Is Critique? An Essay on Foucault's Virtue." In *The Political*. Edited by David Ingram, 212–28. London: Basil Blackwell, 2002.

Carroll, Noel, ed. *Theories of Art Today*. Madison: University of Wisconsin Press, 2000.

Chambers, Eddie. *Black Artists in British Art: A History Since the 1950s*. New York: I. B. Taurus, 2014.

Chang, Alexandra. *Envisioning Diaspora: Asian American Visual Arts Collectives, from Godzilla, Godzookie, to the Barnstormers*. Beijing: Timezone 8 Editions, 2009.

Clifford, James. *The Predicament of Culture: Twentieth-Century Ethnography, Literature, and Art*. Cambridge, MA: Harvard University Press, 1988.

Cotter, Holland. "700-Hour Silent Opera Reaches Finale at MoMA." *New York Times*, May 30, 2010.

Crenshaw, Kimberlé. *On Intersectionality: Essential Writings*. New York: New Press, 2016.

Danto, Arthur. "The Artworld." *Journal of Philosophy* 61, no. 19 (October 15, 1964): 571–84.

———. *What Art Is*. New Haven, CT: Yale University Press, 2013.

Davis, Ben. *9.5 Theses on Art and Class*. Chicago, IL: Haymarket Books, 2013.

Debord, Guy. *Society of the Spectacle*. 9th ed. Translated by Donald Nicholson-Smith. New York: Zone Books, 2006.

Deleuze, Gilles, and Félix Guattari. *Anti-Oedipus: Capitalism and Schizophrenia*. New York: Penguin, [1977] 2009.

de Saussure, Ferdinand. *Course in General Linguistics*. Translated by Wade Baskin. New York: Columbia University Press, [1916] 2011.

Diawara, Manthia. "Conversation with Édouard Glissant aboard the Queen Mary II." *Nka: Journal of Contemporary African Art*, November 28, 2011.

Dick, Leslie. "Intentional Accidents: Reflections on Sarah Charlesworth's Stills." *X_TRA Contemporary Art Quarterly* 18, no. 3 (spring 2016): 4–31.

Dickie, George. *Aesthetics, An Introduction*. Indianapolis, IN: Pegasus Books, 1971.

Downey, Anthony. "An Ethics of Engagement: Collaborative Art Practices and the Return of the Ethnographer." *Third Text* 23, no. 5 (2009): 593–603.

Drucker, Johanna. *Sweet Dreams: Contemporary Art and Complicity*. Chicago, IL: University of Chicago Press, 2006.

D'Souza, Aruna. "Alma Thomas." *4 Columns*, September 23, 2016, http://4columns.org/d-souza-aruna/alma-thomas.

Du Bois, W. E. B. *The Souls of Black Folk*. Greenwich, CT: Fawcett Publications, 1961.

Dyer, Richard. *White*. London: Routledge, 1997.

Edwards, Adrienne. "Blackness in Abstraction." *Art in America*, January 2015. Vol. 103, Issue 1, 62–69.

Elkins, James. *Art Critiques: A Guide*. 2nd ed. Washington, DC: New Academia, 2012.

———. *Why Art Cannot Be Taught*. Urbana and Chicago: University of Illinois Press, 2001.

Fanon, Frantz. *Black Skin, White Masks*. New York: Grove Press, 1952.

Farago, James. "MoMA Protests Trump Entry Ban by Rehanging Work by Artists from Muslim Nations." *New York Times*, February 3, 2017.

Felski, Rita. *The Limits of Critique*. Chicago, IL: University of Chicago Press, 2015.

Firestone, Shulamith, ed. *Notes from the Second Year: Women's Liberation: Major Writings of the Radical Feminists*. New York: Radical Feminism, 1970.

Florida, Richard. *The Rise of the Creative Class—Revisited*. New York: Basic Books, 2014.

Foster, Hal, ed. *The Anti-Aesthetic: Essays on Postmodern Culture*. New York: New Press, 1998.

Foucault, Michel. *The Archeology of Knowledge*. New York: Vintage Books, 1982.

———. *Language, Counter-Memory, Practice: Selected Essays and Interviews*. New York: Cornell University Press, 1980.

———. *This Is Not a Pipe*. 25th ed. Berkeley: University of California Press, 1983.

Freire, Paulo. *Education for Critical Consciousness*. London: Bloomsbury Academic, 2013.

———. *Pedagogy of the Oppressed*. London: Bloomsbury Academic, 2012.

Freud, Sigmund. *New Introductory Lectures on Psychoanalysis*. Standard ed. New York: W. W. Norton, 1933.

Fried, Michael. *Art and Objecthood: Essays and Reviews*. Chicago, IL: University of Chicago Press, 2011.

Fulford, Jason, and Gregory Halpern, eds. *The Photographer's Playbook: 307 Assignments and Ideas*. New York: Aperture Foundation, 2014.

Garanger, Marc. *Femmes algériennes 1960*. Biarritz (Pyrénées-Atlantiques): Atlantica, 1960.

Gilroy, Paul. *Postcolonial Melancholia*. New York: Columbia University Press, 2005.

Glissant, Édouard. *Poetics of Relation*. Ann Arbor: University of Michigan Press, 1997.

González, Jennifer. "The Face and the Public: Race, Secrecy, and Digital Art Practice." *Camera Obscura* 24, no. 1 (2009): 56.

Graham, John. *Systems and Dialects of Art*. New York: Delphic Studios, 1937.

Greenberg, Clement. *Art and Culture: Critical Essays*. Boston: Beacon Press, 1961.

Gregg, Melissa, and Gregory J. Seigworth, eds. *The Affect Theory Reader*. Durham, NC: Duke University Press, 2010.

Guilbault, Serge. *How New York Stole the Idea of Modern Art*. Chicago, IL: University of Chicago Press, 1983.

Halberstam, Jack. "White Men Behaving Sadly." Bully Bloggers. February 22, 2017. https://bullybloggers.wordpress.com/.

Hardt, Michael, and Antonio Negri. *Empire*. Cambridge, MA: Harvard University Press, 2000.

———. *Multitude*. New York: Penguin, 2004.

Harris, Jonathan, ed. *Globalization and Contemporary Art*. Malden, MA: Wiley-Blackwell, 2011.

Harrison, Charles, and Paul Wood, eds. *Art in Theory: 1900–2000*. Malden, MA: Blackwell, 2005.

Hickey, Dave. *The Invisible Dragon: Essays on Beauty*. Chicago, IL: University of Chicago Press, [1993] 2009.

hooks, bell. *Teaching to Transgress: Education as the Practice of Freedom*. New York: Routledge, 1994.

Horkheimer, Max. *Critical Theory: Selected Essays*. New York: Continuum, 2002.

Hughes, Robert. *Culture of Complaint: The Fraying of America*. New York: Oxford University Press, 1993.

Jameson, Fredric. *Postmodernism or the Cultural Logic of Late Capitalism*. Durham, NC: Duke University Press, 1991.

Jones, Kellie. *EyeMinded: Living and Writing Contemporary Art*. Durham, NC: Duke University Press, 2011.

Joselit, David. *After Art*. Princeton, NJ: Princeton University Press, 2013.

Jung, Carl G. "The Concept of the Collective Unconscious." In *The Archetypes and The Collective Unconscious*. Part 1, vol. 9 of *The Collected Works of C. G. Jung*. Princeton, NJ: Princeton University Press, 1981.

Kandinsky, Wassily. *Concerning the Spiritual in Art*. Mineola, NY: Dover Publications, 1977.

Kaufmann, Walter, trans. *The Portable Nietzsche*. New York: Penguin, 1994.

Kent, Corita, and Jan Steward. *Learning By Heart: Teachings to Free the Creative Spirit*. 2nd ed. New York: Allworth Press, 2008.

Krauss, Rosalind. *The Originality of the Avant-Garde and Other Modernists Myths*. Cambridge, MA: MIT Press, 1986.

Lee, Pamela. *Forgetting the Art World*. Cambridge, MA: MIT Press, 2012.

Lorde, Audre. *Sister Outsider: Essays and Speeches*. Watsonville, CA: Crossing Press, 1984.

Lowe, Lisa. *The Intimacies of Four Continents*. Durham, NC: Duke University Press, 2015.

Machida, Margo. *Unsettled Visions: Contemporary Asian American Artists and the Social Imaginary*. Durham, NC: Duke University Press, 2009.

Madoff, Steven Henry, ed. *Art School (Propositions for the 21st Century)*. Cambridge, MA: MIT Press, 2009.

Mann, Sasha. "Q&A with Artist Tom Marioni." Hammer Museum. October 29, 2010, https://hammer.ucla.edu/blog/2010/10/qa-with-artist-tom-marioni/.

Mbembe, Achille. *Critique of Black Reason.* Durham, NC: Duke University Press, 2017.

McEvilley, Thomas, et al. *Making Art Global.* Part 2, *Magiciens de la Terre, 1989.* London: Afterall Books, 2013.

McKittrick, Katherine, ed. *Sylvia Wynter: On Being Human as a Praxis.* Durham, NC: Duke University Press, 2015.

McLuhan, Marshall. *Understanding Media: The Extensions of Man.* Cambridge, MA: MIT Press, [1964] 1994.

Mercer, Kobena, ed. *Exiles, Diasporas, and Strangers.* Cambridge, MA: MIT Press, 2008.

———. *Travel and See: Black Diaspora Art Practices since the 1980s.* Durham, NC: Duke University Press, 2016.

Mignolo, Walter D., and Arturo Escobar, eds. *Globalization and the Decolonial Option.* London: Routledge, 2013.

Mirzoeff, Nick, "The Power of Protest One Year after the #J20 Art Strike." *Hyperallergic,* January 19, 2018.

Mulvey, Laura. *Visual and Other Pleasures.* New York: Palgrave MacMillan, 2009.

Nelson, Robert S., and Richard Shiff, eds. *Critical Terms for Art History.* Chicago, IL: University of Chicago Press, 2003.

Nochlin, Linda. *Women, Art, and Power and Other Essays.* Berkeley, CA: Westview Press, 1988.

Noe, Alva. *Strange Tools: Art and Human Nature.* New York: Hill and Wang, 2015.

Pratt, Mary Louise. "Arts of the Contact Zone." *Profession* (1991): 33–40.

Rancière, Jacques. *The Ignorant Schoolmaster: Five Lessons on Intellectual Emancipation.* Translated by Kristen Ross. Stanford, CA: Stanford University Press, 1991.

———. "Notes on the Photographic Image." *Radical Philosophy* 156 (July 2009): 8–15.

Rodenbeck, Judith. *Radical Prototypes: Allan Kaprow and the Invention of Happenings.* Cambridge, MA: MIT Press, 2014.

Rosenberg, Harold. *The Tradition of the New.* Boston, MA: Da Capo Press, [1959] 1994.

Said, Edward. *Culture and Imperialism.* New York: Vintage Books, 1994.

———. *Representations of the Intellectual: The 1993 Reith Lectures.* New York: Vintage Books, 1994.

Saunders, Frances Stonor. "Modern Art was a CIA Weapon." *Independent,* October 22, 1995.

Sedgwick, Eve Kosofsky. *Touching Feeling: Affect, Pedagogy, Performativity.* Durham, NC: Duke University Press, 2003.

Singerman, Howard. "Excellence and Pluralism." *Emergences* 12, no. 1 (2002): 71–89.

Smith, M. K. "What Is Pedagogy?" *Encyclopaedia of Informal Education.* 2012. Accessed January 15, 2017. http://infed.org/mobi/what-is-pedagogy/.

Sontag, Susan. *On Photography.* 3rd ed. New York: Farrar, Strauss and Giroux, 1978.

———. *Regarding the Pain of Others.* New York: Picador, 2004.

Spivak, Gayatri Chakravorty. *An Aesthetic Education in the Era of Globalization.* Cambridge, MA: Harvard University Press, 2013.

———. *Death of a Discipline.* New York: Columbia University Press, 2005.

———. "Terror: A Speech after 9–11." *Boundary 2: An International Journal of Literature and Culture* 31, no. 2 (2004): 81–111.

Strauss, David Levi. *Between the Eyes: Essays on Photography and Politics*. New York: Aperture, 2012.

Wadhwa, Anita. *Restorative Justice in Urban Schools: Disrupting the School-to-Prison Pipeline*. New York: Routledge, 2015.

Waugh, Joanne B. "Analytic Aesthetics and Feminist Aesthetics: Neither/Nor?" In *Feminism and Tradition in Aesthetics*, edited by P. G. Brand and C. Korsmeyer, 399–415. University Park: Penn State University Press, 1995.

Williams, Raymond. *Keywords: A Vocabulary of Culture and Society*. New York: Oxford University Press, 2015.

Wolf, Michael. *Tokyo Compression*. Berlin: Peperoni Books, 2010.

Wright, Jr., Charles A. "The Mythology of Difference: Vulgar Identity Politics at the Whitney Biennial, (1993)." In *Theory in Contemporary Art since 1985*, 2nd edition, edited by Z. Kocur and S. Leung, 263–79. Malden, MA: Wiley-Blackwell, 2012.

Index

aboutness, 86–87, 187

Abramović, Marina, 248, 297n113

abstract expressionism, 93, 135, 193, 226

abstract/ion, 87–89; aboutness and, 86; art participation and, 275; authenticity and, 88, 89; forgetting and, 279–80; within genres, 88; innovative, 88; narrative and, 209; as nonrepresentational, 87; as reality, 88; representation and, 228–30; as social filter, 265; technology and, 88; truth and, 252. *See also* representation

Abwiyeti, Wanyi, 31

academic, 15, 89–92; elitism of, 91; original-ity and, 213; politics of, 11. *See also* art education; intellect

activism: aesthetic, 15–16, 222; artivism as, 11, 185, 220; on discrimination, 6; environ-mental, 209; on immigration, 6; political, 99, 104, 126; remembering in, 17; trans, 171; worker, 123

Adams, Ansel, 210, 245

Adorno, Theodor, 23, 240

advertising, 35–36; art as, 129–30; by art schools, 284n10; audience, 108, 196; auton-omy and, 111; capitalism and, 123; language of, 53. *See also* art market; branding

aesthetics, 12, 92–95, 98, 227, 236–38, 240; activism and, 15; Aristotelian poetics in, 217; art theory and, 240; beauty in, 92, 93, 95, 115–19; Black, 94; coalitions, 94–95; emotionally descriptive language of, 94; everyday and, 158; fascist, 225; feminist, 94; gendered, 93; intention and, 98; interiority/exteriority in, 92; masculine, 94; nature and, 211; racialized, 93; of reparation, 94–95; representation, 116; of status quo, 158, 217, 221; taste and, 236–38; traditional, 94

affect, 95–97; democracy and, 144; emotions and, 156; geopolitics and, 96; mass regulation of by media, 96–97; originality and, 212. *See also* emotions; feelings

affecting presence, 32, 96

affective economy, use of term, 272–73

affirmative action, 41, 163, 287n16

affirmative sabotage, use of term, 56

agency, 97–98; aesthetic, 32, 98; creativity and, 138, 202; discourse and, 97; freedom of, 288–89n36; individual and collective, 97; intervention and, 97–98

agenda, 97, 98, 119

forgetting and, 282; refusals and, 49–50; universalism and, 257

attachments/detachments, 157, 179

audience, 108–9, 262

Austin, J. L., 217

authentic/ity, 25, 109–11; abstraction and, 88, 89; capitalism and, 124; culture and, 141; documentary, 153; honesty in, 109–11, 175–76; marginalization and, 110; originality and, 109. *See also* truth

authority: artistic, 188–89, 190, 225; of discourse, 152; of intuition, 187; judgments on art quality, 81, 221; of past, 112, 266; populism and, 39; professional, 27; self-affirming, 38; self-perpetuating, 81; subjectivity and, 231; subversion of, 98–99; of viewers, 261

autoethnography, 111, 234

autonomy, 27, 53, 111–12; abstraction and, 88; beauty and, 116; of creativity, 138

avant-garde, 90, 111, 193

Avant-Garde and Kitsch (Greenberg), 193

Bachelor of Fine Arts (BFA), 2, 3, 58. *See also* art education

bad/good art, 38, 81, 112–15. *See also* quality

Baldessari, John, 45–46, 121, 194, 266

b/anality, 158, 247, 271–72

Bandung Conference, 202

Bannon, Steve, 275

Bar at the Folies-Bergère, A (Manet), 203

Barthes, Roland, 52, 59, 129, 144, 210, 238, 244

Baudelaire, Charles, 232

beauty: in aesthetics, 92, 93, 95, 115–19; art as, 22, 240; as elevating, 19; forgetting and, 19; standards of, 118, 197; truth and, 116, 225–26

Benda, Julien, 225

Benglis, Lynda, 164–65

Benjamin, Walter, 187, 212, 227, 240

betrayal, 260

Beuys, Joseph, 45, 61, 102

Bhabha, Homi, 3, 40

biennales, 58–59, 109, 134

Bishop, Claire, 195

Black art/artists, 19, 47, 113, 257, 284n12

Black Arts Movement (BAM), 6, 94, 284n12

Black British artists, 7

Black Lives Matter, 216, 270

Black nationalism, 94

Blackness, 47, 182

Black Panther Party (BPP), 111

Black Phoenix (journal), 6

blockbuster exhibitions, 108

Boal, Augusto, 68, 216

body and desire, 119–20

body politic, 119–21, 167–68

bohemians, 107, 138–39

Boime, Albert, 24, 203

boring, 121–22, 194

Bourdieu, Pierre, 230–31

bourgeois: art industries and, 97; bohemians and, 138; conformity in, 90; decomposition of, 52; shock value and, 232

Bourriaud, Nicholas, 24

Bradford, Mark, 269

Braidotti, Rosi, 89

branding, 107, 111, 122, 152, 255. *See also* advertising

Breeze Rustling through Flowers (Thomas), 269

Brooks, David, 138

Buchloh, Benjamin, 289n9

Buddhism, 233–34, 270

bureaucracy, 47–48, 260, 276, 279, 301n17

Butler, Judith, 1, 42, 68, 77, 168, 170, 171–72, 217

Cage, John, 190, 199

camp, 194. *See also* kitsch

capitalism, 47, 122–28, 194, 202–3, 205, 227, 230–31; abstraction and, 89; affect and, 96; galleries and, 127–28; global, 27, 40, 203, 231, 256–57; realism in, 130; victimhood and, 261. *See also* cultural capital; labor

Cartesianism, 91

Cartier-Bresson, Henri, 214, 244

cartography, 25–26, 89, 209, 280–81

Celmins, Vija, 252

Cesaire, Aimé, 25

Cézanne, Paul, 48, 203

Chafin, Jane, 36–37, 37–38

challenges, 128, 235–36

Chang, Shu Lea, 7

chaos, 128–29

Charlesworth, Sarah, 282

chauvinism, 143

Chávez-Delgado, Matt Smith, 215

Chicago, Judy, 238

citizenship, 168, 218

civility, 46–47, 116, 236

civil rights, 47, 80, 151, 223, 270

Clifford, James, 298n122

Cold War, 226, 280

Cole, Thomas, 210

Coleridge, Samuel Taylor, 299n138

collage, 22, 27, *146,* 237, 256

collectivity, 211, 213

collegiality, 10, 46

colonialism: agency under, 50; appropriation under, 140–41, 275–76, 291n9; control of history through, 17; on empty land, 118; forgetting and, 279; global terror of, 135; modernism/postmodernism and, 205; on native tradition, 246; as parasitic culture, 231; slavery and, 7, 17, 19, 101, 202, 230, 260, 279; as tasteful, 173; use of term, 16. *See also* decolonization; postcolonialism

commodity culture, 148, 221

common sense, 35, 43–44, 53, 129, 131, 158, 222, 268, 281, 282. *See also* political correctness (PC)

communication, 129–31, 201. *See also* message; propaganda

communism, 4, 134

Community Copyart, 4

concept/ual, 131–33, 135, 142, 176–77, 262, 288n32, 296n82

confabulation, 185

connoisseurs, 43, 117, 236

conservatism, 90, 158

consumerism, 88, 138

contemporary art, 21, 131, 134–35; abstraction and, 87; beauty and, 118; commerce in, 107, 262; critique of, 79; education and, 89, 247; excesses of, 279; expansiveness of, 25–26; Indian, 7; narrative and, 209; now-ness in, 37; originality and, 212; as

relational, 111–12; role of dreams, 155–56; situationists and, 185; suffering and, 103; usable objects in, 148. *See also* modern/modernism

context/ual, 29, 43, 53, 69, 136–37; abstraction and, 87–88; ambiguity and, 98; engagement and, 150, 166, 220; nature and, 210; prioritization and, 96; social context, 238, 279; truth and, 251

copying, 100. *See also* appropriation

Corot, Camille, 23

Cotter, Holland, 248

Courbet, Gustave, 48

Cox, Renée, 237

Craig-Martin, Michael, 45–46

creative/creativity, 37, 90, 101, 137–39; agency and, 202; autonomy of, 138; vs. culture, 247; design and, 148; extrasocial, 295n68; individualism and, 202; refusals and, 52. *See also* artists; talent

critique, 107; allegories for, 80; authenticity and, 110; bad, 77–81; common forms of, 68–69; conflict irresolution and, 74–77; difference and, 76–77; discrimination and, 76; doubt and, 81–83; as embodied experience, 120; genealogies, 67–68; graduate course description, 83–84; institutional, 27, 98, 279; interiority and, 77; interrogation and, 30; knowledge and, 70–71; language of, 73–74, 80; marginalization and, 82; medium-specific, 78–79; methodologies, 5, 68–71, 73, 78, 279; modernism and, 80; pedagogy and, 67; professionalism and, 78; as radical prototype, 12, 67–84; space of, 290n8; as therapy, 79–80; training, 71–73; venue and, 72

Croce, Arlene, 259, 260, 299–300n151

cryptomnesia, 185

cultural capital, 44, 46, 101–2, 122, 125–27

cultural practices, 24, 25, 86, 109, 186

culture: appropriation of, 100, 141; art as, 147; burden of representation in, 161; commodity, 148, 221; vs. creativity, 247; dominance in, 38; empathy and, 208; English, 5; as hierarchical system of values, 141; identity and, 139–41, 177–80; performance and, 217; politicized, 222; practices, 24, 25, 86, 109, 186; subjectivity and, 230; syphoning of, 301n21; truth and, 251; Western, 100. *See also* appropriation; identity; popular culture

curation, 6, 7, 32, 33, 51, 83, 105, 128, 171, 217

Dadaism, 53, 158, 239, 279
Dali, Salvador, 141, 267
dance, 25–26, 299–300n151, 299n150
Danto, Arthur C., 24, 104, 204, 241
dark/ness, 68, 142
Darwin, Charles, 187, 202
Davis, Ben, 104
Davis, Paige, 204
Day, the Earth, The (Silton), *280*
Debord, Guy, 94, 230, 279
decolonization: language and, 13, 20, 54; pedagogy and, 12, 13, 16; practices of, 100, 282; through art/political work, 20; use of term, 16
deconstruction, 36, 38, 275
decontamination, 116
decorate/defecate (Ramos), *18*
decoration/decorative, 142–43
Degas, Edgar, 23, 25
degenerate art, 117, 151
dehumanization, 47, 101
democracy/democratic: abstraction and, 88; appropriation and, 100, 145; artistic, 143–45; culture and, 141; derivation and, 145; ideal of, 290n9; of images, 294n52; political correctness in, 223; pro-, 134; sub-jectivity and, 230; unconscious and, 254
demographics, 10, 101–2, 125, 137, 182–83
derivation/derivative, 100, 145–47, 152, 159–60, 184, 247, 281. *See also* appropriation
Derrida, Jacques, 177
Descartes, René, 291n2
design, 147–48
design-y, use of term, 148
desire: body and, 119–20; male gaze and, 148–51; political correctness and, 223
deSouza, Allan: biographical information, 1–12; *Polar Sky, xii*

destruction, 52, 53, 226, 256
detachments/attachments, 157, 179
determinism, 187, 212
Dickie, George, 24, 104
didactic/ism, 15–16, 30, 151–52; ambiguity and, 98–99; beauty and, 118; boredom and, 121; experiential, 91; pedagogy and, 14; politics and, 221
difference: adaptive, contemporary, 52–53; assimilation and, 47–48, 257; critique and, 76–77; individualism and, 47; politi-cal, 290n5; refusals and, 54
difficult art, 91
digital imagery, 88, 94
discourse, 152–53; agency and, 97; art as, 27–29, 104; in artworld, 104; foundations, 13, 171; identity politics and, 181; object-hood in, 87; proposals and, 27–28; truth and, 251
discrimination, 8–9, 183; in art institutions, 1, 8–9; critique and, 76; equality and, 40–42; pedagogy against, 11, 13; quality and, 43; reverse, 41; self-perpetuating cultures of, 10. *See also* racism
dishonesty, 175–76
diversity, 12; in art education, 8–11, 44–45; equality and, 40–42; work, 41
documentary, 153–55
dogma, 98, 180, 206, 250; language and, 52, 54, 56; truth and, 251
dream, 155–56, 270. *See also* unconscious
Du Bois, W. E. B., 196
Duchamp, Marcel, 23, 48, 87, 93, 288n32
Dyer, Richard, 256–57

Earth Paintings (Thomas), 269
economy: affective, 272–73; market, 94, 109
education. *See* art education
Eggleston, William, 144–45
Eisenhower, Dwight, 124
Elbow Room exhibition, 6
Elkins, James, 12, 64, 79, 80, 159, 290n13
embodied subjects, 14–15
emotions, 97, 156–57, 272–73, 297n104. *See also* feelings; specific emotions
endurance. *See* time

Marcuse, Herbert, 116, 240

marginalization, 6, 119, 142, 145–46, 223, 279; authenticity and, 110; critique and, 82; identity and, 250

Marioni, Tom, 45

market economy, 94, 109. *See also* art market

marketing. *See* advertising

Marshall, Kerry James, 142

Martinez, Daniel Joseph, 49–50, 275

Marx, Karl, 202, 227, 233, 298n121

Marxism, 97, 125, 193, 240

masculinity, 24–25, 39, 90, 165–66, 170, 203, 250, 273

Master of Fine Arts (MFA), 12, 36, 56, 57–59, 59–60, 159. *See also* art education

Matisse, Henri, 18–19, 172–73, 267, 295n79

Mbembe, Achille, 268

McCollum, Allan, 263

McLuhan, Marshall, 199

Medalla, David, 6

mediocrity, 41, 114, 197–98, 290n13

meditation, 198–99

medium and message, 199, 201

megagalleries, 107, 127–28

melancholia, 19, 210, 270

memory: in activism, 17; emotions and, 273; forgetting and, 19–20; history and, 199–201; inspiration and, 185; modernism and, 19; sensory, 72, 199–200, 201; short-term, 200. *See also* remembering

Meninas, Las (Velázquez), 203

Mercer, Kobena, 6, 25

message: ambiguity of, 98; concepts, 131; meaning of, 131; medium and, 199, 201; of political art, 99. *See also* communication

metaphors, 70, 151, 223, 225, 271. *See also* allegories; analogies

Metropolitan Museum of Art (New York), 31–32, 53

Metzger, Gustave, 296n93

Meurent, Victorine, 168

MFA. *See* Master of Fine Arts (MFA)

mimesis, 27, 87, 111, 228, 252

Min, Yong Soon, 7

minorities, 16, 38, 178

misogyny, 4, 115–16

(Modern) Formations III (Kim), *253*

modern/modernism, 201–6; activism, 17; appropriation and, 291n9; critiques and, 80; Euro American, 40, 95, 198, 231, 279, 281–82; European, 145, 202, 206, 212; forgetting and, 18–19; genius and, 203; hybrid, national, 297n108; in social art history, 280–81; text and, 238; unconscious and, 254. *See also* contemporary art; postmodernism

MoMA. *See* Museum of Modern Art (MoMA)

Mondrian, Piet, 267

mood, 117, 206–7. *See also* emotions; feelings

moved, 207–9, 240–41. *See also* emotions; feelings

movements, 32

multicultural art, 38, 259

Mulvey, Laura, 195–96

Munch, Edvard, 132

Museum of Conceptual Art (MOCA), 287n25

Museum of Modern Art (MoMA), 31–32, 281

museums: as cultural contact zones, 279; demographics in, 102; as establishment power, 97–98; as healing space, 19; objects in, 261

Museum Tags (Martinez), *50*

mystery, 24, 38–39, 178

mythologies of art, 29, 97, 205

Nakadate, Laurel, 165, 166

narcissism, 10, 119, 181

narrative, 52–53, 153, 209

nationalism, 42, 105, 173, 176, 179, 183, 258; Black, 94

nature/natural, 209–11; forgetting and, 17; instinct and, 211; in landscape, 17, 210; mediated, 24; through temperament, 23

Nauman, Bruce, 251–52, 262

Nazis, 61, 117, 177, 198

Negri, Antonio, 130

neutrality, 32, 35, 88

Newkirk, Kori, 269

newness, 22, 67, 130, 135, 137

Nochlin, Linda, 39

noncollegiality, 10, 46
normalization, 16, 182
notoriety, 108–9, 114, 172

Obama, Barack, 250–51, 298–99n135
Ofili, Chris, 237
Olympia (Manet), 168, 203
On the Beach (Silton), *280*
optimism, 282
original/ity, 37, 100, 109, 211–13
orthodoxy, 78, 223
ostracism, 8, 10, 89–90, 184
Other, the, 68
outside/outsiders, 51, 78, 107, 176, 258.
   See also inside/insiders
Owens, Laura, 294n52

Paladino, Shari, 48
Panchayat, 4–5
Papastergiadis, Nikos, 24
Paris Salons, 48, 51
parody, 22, 164, 212, 252, 262
parole, 30–31, 32–33, 97, 214. *See also*
   langue
participatory art, 220, 266
particularity, 252, 256, 275
pastiche, 109, 135, 159, 160, 212, 256
patriarchy, 16, 163–64, 185, 232
Paul, Saint, 185
PC. *See* political correctness (PC)
pedagogy, 11–16, 20, 44, 216; as art, 216;
   critique in, 12, 67; decolonization and,
   12, 13; defined, 14; against discriminatory practices, 11, 13; embodied subjects
   and, 14–15; expressionist need for, 159;
   function of, 175; gender equality and, 163;
   methods of, 45; modernism and, 206;
   outdated, 54; subjugation and, 14; turn
   toward, 212; as utopian, 13
performance, 213–17; agency and, 98; culture
   and, 140; gender and, 170; as intervention,
   216; painting as, 271; of radicalness, 90;
   sculpture as, 214, 216; as self-expression,
   161; text as, 238; time and, 244, 246.
   See also theatrical
pessimism, 154

photography: beauty in, 116; critique of, 78;
   as drawing/painting with light, 214, 278;
   gaze and, 169–70; notable, 144; space in,
   298n131; time and, 244–46
Picasso, Pablo, 146, 197–98, 267, 272
Pissarro, Camille, 48, 233
plagiarism, 4, 23, 109, 185, 211. *See also*
   forgeries
plain-speak, 53–54, 73, 211
Plato, 186, 227, 271
poetics and politics, 217–18
poiesis, 217
Polar Sky (deSouza), *xii*
polemical, 13–14, 64, 173
political correctness (PC), 42, 129, 138, 180,
   222–23. *See also* common sense
political/politics: of academia, 11, 91; of
   aesthetics, 92, 93; agenda, 97, 98, 119; as
   all encompassing, 219; art/artivism and,
   6, 11, 12, 15, 35, 99, 122, 185, 209, 218–22,
   260, 293n36; British racial, 5; cultural, 219;
   difference in, 290n5; effects, 19, 220–21;
   efficacy, 212, 219; history as, 174; idealism
   and, 20; labor, 103–4; mood, 207; poetics
   and, 217–18; propaganda, 225–26; propaganda and, 218; as situational, 221; subversion, 31. *See also* body politic; geopolitics;
   identity politics
Pollock, Jackson, 214, 215, 270
Pompidou Center, 31–32
Pop art, 93, 193, 204
popular culture, 73, 85, 91, 105, 108, 193
populism, 38–39, 53, 142, 175, 217, 221, 257
pornography, 164, 293n33
postcolonialism, 27, 70, 83, 120, 202, 205, 275.
   See also colonialism
postmodernism, 49, 100, 201–6, 238
poststructuralism, 70, 255. *See also*
   structuralism
practice of art, 12, 223–24
Pratt, Mary Louise, 111, 279
preconceptions, 40–41, 81–82, 224
presumptions, 10, 23, 100, 109, 147, 219
primitive art/primitivism, 159; neo-, 214, 267
Primitivism in Twentieth-Century Art (exhibition), 31–32

process: art as, 28–29, 224–25; representation and, 229. *See also* journey; practice; work

professionalism: critique and, 78; design and, 147; discipline and, 173; industries/institutions and, 105; in practice, 224

projections, 99, 169

propaganda, 30, 129–31, 218, 225–26

psychoanalysis, 9, 70, 79, 83, 155, 254, 273–74, 298n126

psychographics, 96, 144

psychopaths, 184

Pujol, Ernesto, 49

quality, 12, 38–39, 112–15, 226–27; discrimination and, 43; idealized, 42–43; as truth, 225–26

queerness, 47, 121, 163

racialized art, 11, 55, 283n3, 301n14; critique of, 167; double consciousness in, 154; exclusions in, 182; in generalized experience, 93; subjects of, 82, 226

racial profiling, 120, 167

racism, 4, 5, 6, 9–10, 19, 82–83, 101, 223. *See also* discrimination; white suprematism

radicalness: of critique, 67–84; performance of, 90; subversion and, 235

Ramos, Sofie, 18

readymades, 22, 27, 87, 108, 109

realism, 130, 153, 226. *See also* surrealism

reality: abstraction as, 88; art as reimagining, 24; representation and, 227–28; rules of, 184; utopian, 24. *See also* truth

realness, 110, 228

Reflecting Woman at Bar (Davis), *204*

refusalon, 47, 49–53, 275

Rembrandt van Rijn, 258

remembering: active, 282; colonization and, 17, 19; as episodic, 200; vs. forgetting, 205; through representations, 227. *See also* forgetting; memory

representation, 19, 227, 228–30. *See also* abstraction

Ricoeur, Paul, 82

Riefenstahl, Leni, 225

Rodger, Elliot, 115

Rose, Barbara, 36, 37–38

Rosenberg, Harold, 270, 271

Rosler, Martha, 214

Rothko, Mark, 13, 87, 180, 215, 217, 229, 240, 247, 265–82; brand recognition of, 152; early works, 266–67; manifesto of, 268, 281–82; melancholia of, 270; modernism of works, 205, 265; responses to paintings of, 198, 266, 270–78; on tragic, 279

Saar, Betye, 19

sabotage, 56, 123, 216

Said, Edward, 59, 65, 257–58

Salaita, Steven, 46

Salgado, Sebastião, 116

Saltz, Jerry, 37–38

Saussure, Ferdinand de, 30

Schelling, Friedrich, 299n138

Schjeldahl, Peter, 18, 224, 258

Schneemann, Carolee, 237

Scream, The (Munch), 132

sculpture: as performance, 214, 216; social, 102

Sedgwick, Eve Kosofsky, 162

Sehgal, Tino, 106, 216, 261–62

Sekula, Allan, 106

self: alterity and, 231; emotions and, 273; expression through, 159; identity and, 179; originality and, 211; performance and, 217; subjectivity of, 124, 230–32. *See also* identity

self-consciousness, 188, 203, 238, 271

self-doubt, 82–83

self-expression, 5, 159–60

Self-Portrait with Whip (Mapplethorpe), 237

seminal, use of term, 232

semiotics, 30–31, 214. *See also* linguistics

Semiotics of the Kitchen (Rosler), 214

Serra, Richard, 215

Serrano, Andres, 237

Sex Objects (Green), *165*

Shareef, Ahmed Jabar, 278, 279

Sharma, Nandita, 259

Sherman, Cindy, 245

Ship (Wilson), *277*